D1594756

José de Bustamante and Central American Independence

José de Bustamante and Central American Independence

Colonial Administration in an Age of Imperial Crisis

Timothy Hawkins

THE UNIVERSITY OF ALABAMA PRESS

Tuscaloosa

I could not have written this book without the assistance of scores of friends, family, and colleagues—too many, unfortunately, to name here—who have been more than gracious with their time, ideas, critiques, and support over the past decade. Thank you. For special service to the cause, I would like to acknowledge the mentorship of Ralph Lee Woodward and the patience of Margaret Hurdlik. Despite so much help, I must take complete responsibility for any errors of fact and interpretation found within.

This book is dedicated to my grandmother, Estelle Murzyn.

T.H.

Copyright © 2004
The University of Alabama Press
Tuscaloosa, Alabama 35487-0380
All rights reserved
Manufactured in the United States of America
Typeface: Minion

∞

The paper on which this book is printed meets the minimum requirements of American National Standard for Information Science–Permanence of Paper for Printed Library Materials, ANSI Z39.48–1984.

Library of Congress Cataloging-in-Publication Data

Hawkins, Timothy, 1967–
José de Bustamante and Central American independence : colonial administration in an age of imperial crisis / Timothy Hawkins.
p. cm.
Includes bibliographical references and index.
ISBN 0-8173-1427-X (cloth : alk. paper) 1. Bustamante y Guerra, José de, 1759–1825.
2. Guatemala. Audiencia—History—19th century. 3. Central America—History—19th century. 4. Government, Resistance to—Central America—History—19th century.
5. Self-determination, National—Central America—History. I. Title.
F1437.H39 2004
972.81′04′092—dc22

2004006608

Contents

Introduction

José de Bustamante and the
Historiography of Central American Independence

In contrast to the extensive scholarship devoted to the independence of most of Latin America, the bibliography of Central American independence has always been small.[1] The primary reason for such neglect is that the Kingdom of Guatemala experienced a rather subdued separation from Spain in comparison with that of other colonies. As a consequence, historians of the period have long struggled with the problematic task of writing a history of independence without a struggle for independence. Ultimately, this conundrum has prevented the historiography from moving beyond the tradition of *historia oficial* handed down by nineteenth-century national historians. In the absence of a more viable paradigm to explain the distinctive path taken by Central America, research into the period has not kept pace with that of other areas of the former Spanish empire.

For most national historians of the nineteenth century, the Latin American independence period offered an unparalleled opportunity to address the birth of their respective nations from the perspective of a dramatic, turbulent, and heroic transformation from colony to nation-state. In Mexico, chroniclers such as Fray Servando Teresa de Mier and Carlos María Bustamante created founding fathers out of Miguel Hidalgo and José María Morelos. In South America, the liberators, José de San Martín, Simón Bolívar, and Bernardo O'Higgins, became central figures in the independence histories of Benjamín Vicuña MacKenna,

Miguel Luís Amunátegui, Bartolomé Mitre, and others. Through these works, legendary events such as the *Grito de Dolores,* San Martín's march across the Andes, and Bolívar's *Campaña Admirable* were fixed in the national consciousness and demonstrated the power of national and popular unity. More than simply histories of the transition from colony to nation, these accounts of independence were instrumental in the promotion, projection, and development of a sense of national identity among the populations of Mexico and the South American republics.

Almost alone among the former Spanish colonies, however, Central America did not experience a sustained or widespread independence movement in the period 1810–1821. Instead, it watched quietly as the rest of the empire was torn apart by rebellions, revolutions, and the military confrontation between royalist and patriot armies. No independence leader of more than provincial significance surfaced at the time. And separation from Spain, when it finally came, was achieved peacefully but haphazardly within the framework of the 1821 *Plan de Iguala,* with the isthmus joining the Mexican Empire of Agustín de Iturbide before setting out on its own. By 1840, the nation that had been the consequence, if not the goal, of independence had divided into five barely viable pieces.

Not surprisingly, this history created problems for those interested in writing and interpreting the independence of Central America according to the standard set by Mexican and South American historians. Lacking liberators, a violent struggle, clear examples of public unity in support of independence, and a unified nation, Central American historians made do with what they had, piecing together an interpretive framework for independence out of failed or aborted uprisings, conspiracies, the deeds of the patriotic *ayuntamiento* (municipal council) of Guatemala City, and various martyred or repressed revolutionaries. Deprived of a central hero, these historians instead created an archvillain, arguing that the passivity of the Kingdom of Guatemala during the 1810s was the consequence of the brutal, oppressive administration of Captain General José de Bustamante y Guerra (1811–1818). At once the inhibitor and precipitator of independence, Bustamante became the personification of Spanish absolutism, supervising a "reign of terror" that stifled dissent and crushed overt opposition to Spain during this decade.

At the same time, however, his policies were seen as hardening the sentiment for independence among Central Americans, thereby leading to the great movement for liberation that overwhelmed a more pliable captain general in 1821.

First elaborated by Alejandro Marure in the 1830s, this characterization quickly pervaded the Central American Liberal historiography of the nineteenth century. Incorporated into the *historia patria* of writers such as Rafael Aguirre Cinta and Agustín Gómez Carrillo, it entered the school systems and became part of the established, official explanation of the regional independence experience. Revitalized by Ramón Salazar early in the twentieth century, the negative view of Bustamante has managed to infuse both native and foreign views of Central American independence to the present.

Considering the progress made over the past decades toward a greater understanding of the independence movements in other parts of the Spanish empire, the long-term dependence among historians of Central America upon a historically suspect interpretation of independence is all the more striking. This paradigm was created and developed to fill the need for a national history in Central America. It was based upon certain assumptions about the nature of the Latin American struggle for independence that do not necessarily fit the Central American experience. As a result, it has tended to distort both the role of Bustamante and the sentiment for independence in the kingdom in order to conform better to the standard model.

To a great extent all accounts of Central American independence have been shaped by the first, Alejandro Marure's *Bosquejo histórico de las revoluciones de Centroamérica desde 1811 hasta 1834*. Originally published in 1837 following a commission from the Guatemalan chief-of-state, Mariano Gálvez, the *Bosquejo histórico* was expected to serve as part of the national history of the Central American Federation and as a means to bind the young nation together by recounting the shared, patriotic struggle for independence. Yet, it was also the product of a scholar whose father was Mateo Antonio Marure, a prominent intellectual, republican, and victim of the Bustamante regime. These two factors, Liberal nationalism and family tragedy, led Marure to paint a vivid picture of the Bustamante decade as one characterized by a titanic struggle between the forces of fanaticism and superstition, led by the captain general, and those of liberty, symbolized by Marure's martyred father and other Central American patriots.

The central theme of this monumental work is the inevitable victory of the Liberal cause in Spanish America. According to Marure, this movement, a product of the American and French Revolutions, took hold in the Spanish empire following the French invasion of Spain and allowed Americans to proclaim "the same principles against the Metropolis that it [Spain] had utilized against [Napoleon]."[2] Yet, while these events precipitated revolts throughout most of the empire by 1810, "the Kingdom of Guatemala remained peaceful and submissive instead of becoming angry over the deceptions of the Metropolis."[3] Into this scene stepped Bustamante, and, in one of the most widely reproduced and influential passages in Central American historiography, Marure wrote:

> This Spaniard had recently demonstrated his zeal against the pro-independence movement at his posting in Montevideo and was one of the most suitable peninsulars to delay the emancipation of the Guatemalans. Hard, inflexible, suspicious, absolutist, vigilant, and reserved, his method of governing was in perfect harmony with his character. He reinvigorated the measures which he found established to contain insurrection and adopted newer and stricter ones; he systematized the persecutions and denunciations and had a special knack for choosing his agents and spies; he constantly disobeyed the moderate provisions which the Metropolis at times would decree in favor of the disloyal and took charge of their cases in the most arbitrary manner.[4]

Despite such oppression, the sentiment for independence survived in the kingdom and sparked a series of haphazard uprisings in San Salvador and Nicaragua at the end of 1811. Marure described these early revolts as premature, poorly planned, and incomplete: "honorable for their instigators, but unlucky for the nation."[5] San Salvador, León, Granada, and the Belén conspiracy of 1813 launched a new generation of republican activists and martyrs, but little else. For Marure, the uprisings served only to increase the despotism of the colonial administration, which prevented Central America from achieving its rightful independence until Bustamante was recalled in 1818.

During the long Conservative domination of the region that followed the collapse of the Federation in 1838, Central Americans did not develop an alternative historiographical tradition to compete with that of Marure. Thus, with the return of the Liberals by 1871, Guatemalan historians either simply picked up where Marure left off—a prime example being Lorenzo Montúfar's *Reseña histórica de Centro-América*—or, when dealing with the preindependence decade, summarized and enlarged upon his conclusions. With the *Reforma* government's growing emphasis on public education and historia patria, the image of Bustamante as detailed in the *Bosquejo histórico* began to reach a wide audience.

Much as this second generation of Liberals tempered the fervent idealism of Marure's progressive age with a strong belief in the benefits of order, their negative impression of Bustamante was likewise qualified by acknowledgment of his particular gifts of command. One of the leaders of the Liberal Reforma, Miguel García Granados, described this period in his memoirs:

> Ever since 1811 . . . there had been efforts and movements in favor of independence in San Salvador as well as Nicaragua, and perhaps these would have grown if not for the vigor, prudence, and skill of Captain General Bustamante, who had arrived at this time to take command in Guatemala. This governor was endowed with the qualities that, in a country that by the nature of its government should be ruled despotically, constitute the gift of command. Without being cruel, he knew how to inspire not only respect but also terror, and his vigilance was admirable. He knew, then, to cut off danger at its roots, and during the entire time his administration lasted, he maintained Guatemala at peace and bound to Spain.[6]

While García Granados emphasized the relative calm of the Bustamante years, implying that the great push for independence occurred only between 1818 and 1821, the official view of the independence period was more expansive. Other writers, notably the historians Agustín Gómez Carrillo and Rafael Aguirre Cinta, in a number of patriotic, classroom-oriented works, took great pains to link the Kingdom of Guatemala to the great revolutionary movements of the early 1810s while reasserting Bustamante's role as the "Great Inhibitor of Independence."

Taking his cue from Marure, Gómez Carrillo declared in his *Estudio histórico sobre la América Central* that "[t]he desire for independence penetrated the Kingdom of Guatemala, the same as in Mexico, Colombia, and Peru, and was helped by the political emancipation of the United States as well as the prestige of the principles which the French Revolution proclaimed to the world."[7] From his perspective, the Spanish imperial crisis of 1808 made separation from the metropolis a real possibility, and the natural consequences in the Americas were the 1810 Hidalgo revolt, the creation of revolutionary juntas in South America, and the Central American uprisings of 1811:

> In 1811 Marshal González Saravia left his command . . . with General Bustamante y Guerra to take his place; but although the terror which this latest official instilled with his conduct was expected to intimidate the friends of liberty, such aspirations did not languish; rather, they became more noticeable and spread in all directions, with the struggles undertaken in Mexico and South America by the illustrious patriots Hidalgo and Morelos, San Martín, and so many other legendary heroes of the grand Hispano-American epic contributing to this.[8]

For Gómez Carrillo, the fight with Bustamante created a number of Central American heroes deserving of a place alongside the great emancipators of Spanish America: Manuel José Arce, José Matías Delgado, José Francisco Córdova, and José Francisco Barrundia, among others. In the years to follow they would all receive their just biographical attention from Central American historians as the pantheon of the *próceres* of independence began to fill.[9]

Along with the various promoters of independence from across the kingdom, the great moments in the Central American struggle against Spanish oppression received increased attention in the national histories of the late nineteenth century. Up to this point, El Salvador and Nicaragua could claim a monopoly on overt opposition to the crown. However, in his *Lecciones de historia general de Guatemala, desde los tiempos primitivos hasta nuestros dias, arregladas para uso de las escuelas primarias y secondarias de esta republica,* Rafael Aguirre Cinta argued in favor of a kingdomwide movement of emancipation that included not only the uprisings of San Salvador, León, and Granada but those of Guatemala as well.

As in previous works, Aguirre Cinta emphasized the revolutionary links between Spanish America, the United States, and France. According to him, this movement finally reached Central America on 14 March 1811, the date Bustamante took office, and precipitated a "muffled storm [that] began to agitate the kingdom: the ideas of liberty were propagated secretly, and the seeds of independence began to grow."[10] In an almost complete paraphrase of Marure, Aguirre Cinta continued: "There was none better than Bustamante to delay the emancipation of Guatemala. Inflexible and suspicious, absolutist, vigilant, and reserved, he dictated as many measures as he thought necessary to contain the movements of insurrection; he encouraged denunciations, promoted espionage, took charge of the cases of treason, and, under any pretext, ordered imprisonments or exiles."[11] In the face of this oppression, however, "superior souls, courageous during the misfortune of their country, and lofty spirits, who scorned danger, forged the first conspiracies that leaned towards the absolute independence of the kingdom."[12]

According to Aguirre Cinta, the uprising at San Salvador led directly to the Belén conspiracy of December 1813 in Guatemala City. Whereas Marure had dismissed it as an event "famous because the supporters of Spain accorded it too grave a character and an importance which it really did not have,"[13] by the end of the century this failed coup had become a fundamental part of the *historia patria* of Guatemala, serving as proof of Guatemala's contribution to the independence movements on the isthmus. Ultimately, despite this difference of opinion, Aguirre Cinta concludes with Marure that "these attempts, all in vain at the time, served to embolden the spirits and give strength to the liberal ideals which were being squeezed by the circle of iron imposed by the terrifying regime of Bustamante."[14]

By the end of the nineteenth century, a consensus had been reached in Central America regarding the essential nature of its struggle for independence. Drawing inspiration from the work of Marure, the established, official interpretation of the period described this process as an isthmus-wide movement with various manifestations throughout the kingdom, as an heir to the great liberal democratic revolutions of the United States and France, and as a full-fledged cousin to the Mexican and South American independence struggles. Captain General Bustamante appeared as the primary deterrent to the early achievement of independence, with his repressive policies providing both a sense of unity of persecution among the Central American patriots and a crucible in which the subsequent, successful drive could be forged. As the twentieth century unfolded, this interpretation, as yet unchallenged, would develop in two ways. As exemplified by Antonio Batres Jáuregui's *La America Central ante la historia*, Bustamante scarcely deserved attention, becoming either the anonymous, tyrannical captain general or the only slightly more defined stereotype, "the one-eared Bustamante" aligned against the Central American patriots, those "sons of the *pueblo* who distinguished themselves most while braving removals from office, tortures, and even death."[15]

However, the greatest influence on modern independence historiography, as well as the most potent vehicle for the Bustamante myth, has proven to be Ramón Salazar's 1928 study, *Historia de veintiún años*. Significant for the detail with which the two decades prior to independence are described, this work reinvigorated the Marure tradition through a systematic execration of Bustamante's role as governor. For Salazar, Bustamante's arrival was a "fatal moment" for Central America that led directly to the outbreak of rebellion:

> Bustamante had been governing scarcely eight months and there already reigned in the country a muffled displeasure with him. Absolutist from birth, a sailor and soldier by occupation, a despot on board a ship as well as on land, with an imposing figure and a haughty character, he was disgusted that pro-independence creoles were making the town council into a type of forum where not only the future of the colony was being discussed but also that of the entire Monarchy.[16]

This intense anticreole sentiment on the part of the governor, Salazar argues, turned progressive, liberal, and loyal Americans and their institutions against Spain, a reaction that spawned the subsequent creole uprisings in San Salvador, Nicaragua, and Guatemala. What could have been a "Regime of Liberty" under the enlightened Constitution of 1812

became "The Terror," as Bustamante began cracking down on open political discourse: "The letter of the Constitution was a ridiculous false-
hood for Bustamante. A man totally without law more than one guided
by his whims, he had his hand on the throat of the *patria,* hoping to
strangle it upon its first breath and kill off any signs of life."[17]

With the *Historia de veintiún años,* the image of Bustamante as the
ogre of independence reached its most perfect manifestation. In much
the same manner that the words and perspective of Marure could be
traced across the nineteenth century, Salazar became the dean of
twentieth-century independence historiography in Central America. As
it turned out, the most fervent promoter of his interpretation emerged
very quickly. With the work of J. Antonio Villacorta Calderón, the Bustamante myth became even more firmly entrenched in the historical
identity of Guatemala.

Villacorta, in his *Historia de la Capitanía General de Guatemala,* explained the independence struggle as a long conflict between the allies of the municipal council of Guatemala City and the "arbitrary and
despotic" Spanish officials represented by the captain general. Thus he
stated, "The highly patriotic conduct of the Guatemalan Ayuntamiento
between 1809 and 1810 was known and commented upon throughout
the rest of the kingdom, which was governed by intendants who, in imi-
tation of the extreme position of the captain general, saw reasons for
mistrust everywhere and persecuted those who showed the smallest
signs of discontent."[18] With this statement, Villacorta aimed to preempt
the claims of San Salvador and Nicaragua to be the progenitors of Central American independence. With the ayuntamiento promoting the
sentiment of liberty as early as 1809, and with the "evil influence" of
Bustamante ensuring that in the capital "persecutions were the order of
the day" from 1811 forward, Guatemala could now honorably claim an
important, precipitating role in the liberation movement and still explain away its subsequent inactivity.[19]

In this context, Villacorta argued that 1813 was a "year of proof for
Guatemala." With the Salvadoran and Nicaraguan uprisings suppressed,
numerous patriots in prison, and Bustamante prepared to "make use of
all his power," leading Guatemalan creoles began to plan a revolution in
the Belén convent.[20] Placing this conspiracy on the level of the revolutionary developments in San Salvador and Nicaragua, Villacorta made

Belén the culmination of the first phase of the independence movement in the kingdom, with the result that "[t]he iron hand of Governor Bustamante weighed unbearably upon the creoles of the Captaincy General of Guatemala: he had weakened the subversive movements of San Salvador, Nicaragua, and Guatemala, he had the leading authors of those first buds of liberty in the prison at court, and his followers entertained themselves with the extremely cruel treatment he gave to the convicted."[21]

For both Salazar and Villacorta, Bustamante was guilty of three overarching crimes: creating, or at least promoting, intense animosity between creoles and Spaniards; suppressing Guatemala's best chance for a continued relationship with Spain, the Constitution of 1812; and developing the framework of repression that kept the various expressions of creole discontent from becoming successful revolutions.[22] Marure's implication, assumed but never overtly presented by either historian, that this repression guaranteed a more powerful anti-Spanish sentiment following Bustamante's departure in 1818, would be explored in a number of influential works written at midcentury, including Sofonías Salvatierra's *Contribución a la historia de Centroamérica* and Arturo Valdés Oliva's *Caminos y luchas por la independencia*.

To a great degree, the Salvatierra study reworked the ground already prepared by Marure and Salazar, presenting Bustamante as a heavyhanded, implacable tyrant who smothered Central America's early bid for independence. The uprisings of 1811, 1813, and 1814 receive intense treatment, as do the rounds of persecutions, deportations, confiscations, torture, and imprisonment that followed. For Salvatierra, however, there was no question that these persecutions "produced as a necessary reaction the absolute conviction, which had long been forming, that the kingdom's government should pass into the hands of the creoles. And the extent of this awareness reached such a level that one cry was enough to make the weapons of conquest fall from the royalist hands that held them on the fifteenth of September 1821."[23] In other words, Salvatierra argued that the counterinsurgency policies favored by the Bustamante regime actually helped in the propagation and consolidation of independence sentiment by precipitating a strong reaction among otherwise hesitant patriots. Valdés Oliva would take this position one step further.

Like his predecessors, Valdés Oliva viewed Bustamante as "despotic, cruel, vengeful, and deceitful," arguing that the Spaniard was chosen specially by his superiors for command in America because of these qualities.[24] He explained:

> When writing about the independence of Central America it is of inter-
> est to make an account of the principal motives for such a great event. As
> a result, we will describe with broad strokes the administrations of the
> last three captains general, and, with somewhat more references and de-
> tails, perhaps, that of Bustamante y Guerra, due to three very special cir-
> cumstances: because he appears in our times with unique characteristics
> and made himself quite notorious with his harshness . . . [;] because the
> seven years of Bustamante's regime was the period of the greatest politi-
> cal unrest in Spain and America; and because there is not the least danger
> in affirming that, due in part to these events but more to the drastic
> measures of the captain general, this age was for the Kingdom of Guate-
> mala the period of gestation of the new nation, with his repression serv-
> ing as the impulse for its birth.[25]

Valdés Oliva supports this assertion with a recitation of the well-established pattern of events: Central America, along with the rest of the empire, awoke to the "splendid sunrise of liberty" by 1808 and began to put an end to the interminable "days of oppression"; some areas had early successes, while in others, most notably Mexico and the Kingdom of Guatemala, "the patriots were sacrificed in the armed struggle without the unvarying rhythm of revolution being detained"; the repression of the Bustamante regime increased as provincial uprisings occurred, though its greatest focus was on the capital, Guatemala City; and, while he could have searched for some accommodation through the Cádiz constitution, instead Bustamante's "irritability increased and he put a lot of effort into ridiculing the law."[26] In the end, this process led to the sustained period of abuses against the people of Central America that "compelled the patriots to accelerate their plans to free the colony from Spain. Nothing the king did to alleviate the conditions of the kingdom's towns in the days ahead succeeded in altering the conduct of those who longed for liberty as the only solution for the people. The dictatorship of Bustamante was a powerful factor in this."[27]

The Bustamante myth, created by Marure and developed over more than a century by a long list of the most influential historians of Central

America as an integral part of the regional independence epic, remained essentially unchallenged until the 1960s. By that time, however, more systematic historical methodology, the waning of the Liberal tradition among politicians and intellectuals, and the first signs of interest in the period from foreign scholars, produced significant alterations to the established paradigm. The preliminary revision was led by the Salvadoran historian Rodolfo Barón Castro in his 1961 biographical essay *José Matías Delgado y el movimiento insurgente de 1811*.

While focusing on the role of Delgado in the first significant Central American uprising of the independence period, Barón Castro also addressed squarely the difficult situation facing the Spanish authorities at the time. According to him, the split between leading creoles and the crown took place before the arrival of Bustamante, with unscrupulous Spanish officials like the soon-to-be-deposed Salvadoran intendant José Gutiérrez and institutions such as the *Tribunal de Fidelidad,* established under Bustamante's predecessor, serving as the leading causes of discontent. Noting that opinions on the captain general depended on one's point of view, Barón Castro felt that the time had come for a less passionate perspective. His Bustamante, in contrast to previous portraits, was "a studious and learned man, a proven patriot, and an effective officer," who was tough, determined, but not inclined to violence.[28] "[H]e understood," wrote Barón Castro, "that his strictest obligation was to maintain the territory under his command free from unrest. . . . It is logical that the patriots tried in every manner possible to limit his authority and agitate against the measures he took. This was the most basic dialectic of the struggle. But they found it very difficult to incite him to actions not in accordance with clemency or even less with honor."[29] In dramatic contrast to earlier studies, Barón Castro painted Bustamante as a skillful and successful politician, whose role as governor of the Kingdom of Guatemala naturally conflicted with many of the positions taken by the creole autonomists and patriots, but who never ruled tyrannically in preserving order. Instead of looking back on the period secure in the certainty of independence and the unanimity of popular sentiment for it, Barón Castro established 1811 as the first of many years in which Central Americans would be divided over their visions of the future.

Hubert H. Bancroft had provided the first significant history of Central America for an English-speaking audience in the 1880s, yet his research on the period of independence proved little more than a paraphrase of Marure and remained unchallenged for more than seventy years.[30] As with Barón Castro's work, the first English-language revisionist account of independence was made in a biography of one of the period's central figures. Unencumbered by the weight of the Liberal legacy, Louis Bumgartner's 1963 study *José del Valle of Central America* dramatically altered the historical image of José de Bustamante.

Drawing on substantial primary research, Bumgartner sketched an outline of the independence period and Bustamante's actions that tended to reinforce the conclusions of Barón Castro. Thus, Bumgartner found that the creole/peninsular rivalry and the climate of suspicion so often blamed on the hard-line policies of Bustamante were consequences of an inevitable conflict over governing philosophies that began in 1808 with the collapse of the Spanish monarchy.[31] Upon arriving in the colony in 1811, the year following the outbreak of armed insurrection in Mexico and South America, Bustamante was faced with the reality that accommodating the creole desire for autonomy would appear treasonous to Spain, while preserving the status of Central America in the empire would provoke cries of tyranny. Described as a "steadfast royal servant," the captain general demonstrated his loyalty to the crown by refusing all attempts to share his authority with the creoles, though his early policies could fairly be described as moderate in light of the context. In fact, reversing the argument of Salazar and Villacorta, Bumgartner argued that the Guatemala City ayuntamiento deliberately provoked Bustamante and set out to make him appear arbitrary and tyrannical in order to further the autonomist (though not the independence) position.[32] With the return of absolutism in 1814, Bustamante personified an empire that was divided against itself; however, according to Bumgartner, this did not detract from his strength as a governor or his skill in keeping the peace during the seven critical years of his administration. In the end, Bumgartner concluded, Bustamante's tenure had little effect on the path taken by Central America toward independence.

If Rodolfo Barón Castro and Louis Bumgartner indirectly paved the way for the modern reevaluation of the Bustamante myth with their studies of José Matías Delgado and José del Valle, in 1971 the Guatemalan historian Clemente Marroquín Rojas made a frontal assault, with his

Historia de Guatemala, on the fundamental assumption about Central America's role in the Spanish American struggle for independence that had been nurtured by nationalist historians since the 1830s:

> We have noted that Guatemala did not suffer destructive revolutionary shocks. The war was devastating in Mexico, New Granada, Venezuela, Chile, in all the Spanish dependencies; however, our Captaincy General registered only two rebellions by small groups and two conspiracies with no lasting consequences. Governor Bustamante is criticized for his firmness and active vigilance, but considering the situation that surrounded the Kingdom this is unfair. All leaders should behave like Bustamante, with the exception of those who conspire against the authority in whose service they govern, as Gainza would do, and in the end Iturbide as well.[33]

Having reduced the colony's contribution to regional liberation from Spain to two insignificant uprisings and a pair of failed plots, Marroquín Rojas continued his revision of the Bustamante image by turning to the details of those signs of discontent: "Bustamante y Guerra is accused of initiating a period of abuses and arbitrary acts, both in the Kingdom's capital and the provincial centers, a tyranny that gave rise to the preliminary uprisings for emancipation. Nevertheless, the coup in San Salvador, which did not result from independence aspirations or from the supposed tyranny of the governor, demonstrates that this individual was not as fierce and terrible as he is made out to be."[34]

As evidence for this perspective, Marroquín Rojas cited certain facts about the handling of the rebellions that had been either ignored or manipulated by earlier historians. He saw the 1811 Salvadoran uprising as primarily directed against the unpopular Intendant Gutiérrez (a not uncommon expression of discontent at the time), with Bustamante still enjoying somewhat of a honeymoon in his relations with the colonial elite. In fact, following news from San Salvador, Bustamante went to the ayuntamiento of Guatemala City for advice, ultimately choosing two of its members to mediate a peace and replace the deposed intendant, an act that "refutes all that literature which paints Bustamante y Guerra as a terrible governor." Similarly, in Nicaragua, Bustamante confirmed the León protestors' candidate for intendant, thereby proving that he did not act "like the ogre that historians have asserted, but rather as an able politician." Offering similar support for Bustamante as regards the Granada uprising, the constitutional question, and relations with the Guatemalan ayuntamiento, Marroquín Rojas concluded by dismissing previous accounts of this period as "patriotic, inspiring, but not historical."[35]

Regarding the larger issue of Central American sentiment for independence during the Bustamante years, Marroquín Rojas argued that the traditional fealty of the Kingdom of Guatemala was scarcely disturbed by the minirevolts of 1811–1813 and that very little effort was needed from Bustamante to restore the region to peace and tranquility by 1814. From this perspective, Bustamante was neither the suppressor nor the instigator of independence. Instead of taking part in a liberation movement forged by repression, Central America followed the path toward emancipation only as a consequence of the imperial chaos resulting from the Riego revolt in 1820.[36]

While the position taken by Marroquín Rojas did not precipitate a full-scale reappraisal of the historia patria of Central America, his work was followed in 1986 by the most thorough revision to date of the independence period and, consequently, the Bustamante myth. In *Centroamérica, de la colonia al estado nacional (1800–1840)*, Julio Cesar Pinto Soria investigated the social climate of the period and argued that far from being engaged in liberation struggles, the Guatemalan creoles themselves were responsible for suppressing the drive for independence in the kingdom. Fearing social unrest and the possible loss of status following emancipation, the conservative elite actively allied itself with the imperial hierarchy: "This class fear pushed the wealthy creole to look for protection and common interests with the acting authorities in order to block the impetus of popular unrest, an attitude which would make itself felt in all the provinces, but which would stand out in Guatemala where Bustamante found his most effective support in his struggle against the uprisings between 1811 and 1814."[37]

By implication, the image of Bustamante drawn for a century by Central American historians—Pinto Soria named Marure and Salazar as the primary examples—served as a means to hide this collaboration. While Bustamante was clearly an energetic opponent of independence, one who "distinguished himself during his term in office through dictatorial measures," he should never have been blamed for the lack of success of the Central American revolutionary movements, a failure that for Pinto Soria was entirely home grown.[38] Like Marroquín Rojas, Pinto Soria creates a new, though somewhat less benign, image of Bustamante that emphasizes the captain general's fierce loyalty to Spain, his absolutist nature, and his repressive measures, but also the weakness of his position without extensive creole support.

In 1976 R. L. Woodward published his survey *Central America: A Nation Divided,* a work that reflected and helped precipitate an upswing in interest in Central America among U.S. scholars. In his short review of the late colonial period Woodward took the position that independence sentiment was negligible on the isthmus and, therefore, easily controlled by the colonial administration. The creole elite—essentially the merchant oligarchy headed by the House of Aycinena—fought Bustamante and his allies over political and economic power within the context of empire, resulting in the unprecedented formation of political parties but not in independence. Instead, the break with Spain came about as a consequence of events that postdated the replacement of Bustamante in 1818. "A man of singular dedication to duty and unswerving in his loyalty to the Crown as well as to the principles of authority and absolutism," Woodward's Bustamante displayed none of the terrifying qualities that had long made him the ogre of Central American independence historiography.[39]

Expanding on this new perspective in *Government and Society in Central America, 1680–1840,* Miles Wortman presented the captain general as a victim of his times, struggling to do his duty in the face of forces over which he had no control. Instead of the instigator of the *terror bustamantino* he was "an archetypal Bourbon bureaucrat, honest and determined to fulfill his role in maintaining centralist, royal authority at a time when the center was giving out. . . . Bustamante is an example of a public figure, trapped by historical circumstances, who is considered a fool at best, a tyrant at worst, despite his efficiency and abilities."[40] In this context, none of Bustamante's actions would have appeared benign to the liberal creole elite who regularly competed with him for control over a colony destabilized by an economic depression and the proximity of bloody revolutions. To explain Bustamante's reluctance to share power with the local assemblies, Wortman noted that the consequence of such action in Argentina and Venezuela was outright independence and that "a fine line existed between political maneuvering within the empire and revolutionary movements."[41] Fearing such a fate for Central America, Bustamante cracked down on any sign of challenge to the status quo, including liberal legislation from Spain. His measures, however, did not prove a major factor in disturbing the kingdom's relationship with Spain. Ultimately, argued Wortman, it was the utter collapse of the Spanish state and the corresponding disintegration of its authority to govern in the Americas that compelled Central Americans to choose independence in 1821.

Though challenged in recent years, the use of the Bustamante myth as an analytical framework for independence has continued to appeal to some historians. In 1978, Mario Rodríguez revitalized it in his persuasive account of the creole response to Spanish constitutional reforms, *The Cádiz Experiment in Central America, 1808–1826*. Arguing from the American perspective, Rodríguez stressed the creole infatuation with autonomy as a viable response to the region's problems and, therefore, an alternative to independence. While such a solution seemed possible in 1811, according to Rodríguez, Bustamante's overt constitutionalism and moderation during his first year in power was transformed by the Granada uprising into a deep distrust of creole motives and, ultimately, into the repression known as the *terror bustamantino*.[42] Following this "metamorphosis," Bustamante allied with the institutions of colonial domination—that is, the Church and the military—to prevent Spanish liberal reform from succeeding in the colony, a campaign that helped precipitate independence by "exacerbat[ing] the divisions between Spaniard and Creole" and providing Americans with the necessary psychological alienation from Spain.[43] In this account, the conflict reached its peak in 1813 as Bustamante's obstruction of the works of the progressive Guatemalan ayuntamiento and his deliberate efforts to delay constitutionally mandated elections, among many other arbitrary acts, culminated in the aborted Belén conspiracy, a symbol of Central American frustration with the empire and with their sick, inflexible, vengeful governor.[44]

At present, the Central American independence historiography remains divided over the two positions championed by Pinto Soria and Rodríguez, while in the context of historia patria neither perspective could be expected to draw much support. The tradition established by Marure, with its reliance on a strong, kingdomwide, long-term pro-independence sentiment, a *terror bustamantino,* and, as a result of this repression, an inevitable emancipation, has played an effective role in the consolidation of national identities in Central America, providing heroes, enemies, founding fathers, and examples of popular unity in the face of oppression. Much of this framework falls apart without Bustamante as the focal point of anti-Spanish sentiment, however, leaving Central America to face the prospect of an accidental founding, with little internal support for independence and, perhaps, not a little opposition to it.

The most recent works by two of Central America's most distinguished scholars exemplify this challenge to construct a new independence paradigm and place Bustamante in the correct historical context. In Carlos Meléndez Chaverri's 1993 *La independencia de Centroamérica,* Bustamante personifies the despotism of the crown: he was an inflexible defender of Spanish interests who saw disloyalty everywhere and who believed that instilling fear of authority was the only solution to unrest.[45] Stressing the development of a national consciousness in Central America that paralleled the revolutionary wars in Mexico and South America and served as the basis for independence on the isthmus, Meléndez states: "What degree of responsibility falls to Bustamante in the step toward the declaration of Central American independence taken shortly after his departure? We do not know for certain; however it is undeniable that his conduct contributed to the formation of a consciousness amenable to independence, even in more moderate sectors, which, lacking this preliminary experience, might have adopted less extreme positions."[46] Still, Meléndez goes on to acknowledge that independence would have been impossible if Mexico had remained Spanish in 1821. A speculative history of independence that focuses heavily on the intellectual atmosphere among the educated elites, this work follows Villacorta and Rodríguez in assuming the worst of Bustamante and reinforcing the importance of the struggle between the absolutist captain general and the liberal ayuntamiento.

In contrast, Héctor Pérez Brignoli draws upon the influence of Pinto Soria and Marroquín Rojas in the third volume of the *Historia General de Centroamérica,* also published in 1993, entitled *De la ilustración al liberalismo (1750–1870).* Here, Pérez Brignoli writes of the alliance between the creole oligarchy and the Spanish state. Fearing unrest among the lower classes, the elites provided Bustamante with valuable assistance in preserving order, especially through the religious and military corporations. The challenges to this balance, highlighted by the Marure school as signs of independence sentiment, were in fact examples of the Aycinena faction's devotion to free trade and their disaffection with the protectionist leanings of the colonial bloc at a time when the state was at its weakest.[47] Pérez Brignoli makes no explicit pronouncement on the role of Bustamante as governor at this time; in essence, the captain general did what any Spanish official was expected to do and therefore deserves no special attention. The few revolts that did occur were essentially the product of disenfranchised urban groups locked out of this arrangement. With the empire all but lifeless by 1821, the creoles then eased Central America out from under Spanish control and into the protection of Mexico. Independence became the last solution for the merchant and landowning elites who desired only to maintain their own status.[48]

Clearly, little room for compromise exists between these two competing accounts of Central American independence. What appears necessary at this point is a different approach to the period. Although the Liberal historiographical tradition has been refined in the 150 years between Marure and Meléndez, it nevertheless continues to view the Central American experience in the context of the larger Hispano-American struggle for independence. But the history of Latin American independence has consistently downplayed one fundamental aspect of the story. Lost in the emphasis on the causes of revolution, the revolutionary leaders and their supporters, and the often painful efforts to establish and preserve independent states is the equally fundamental effort by colonial officials and royalist partisans to maintain the integrity of the Spanish empire in the face of disinterest and apathy, as well as political and social unrest.

The study to follow has been conceived as the first modern comprehensive account of the Bustamante administration and will attempt to answer the long-standing questions raised about Central American independence through a new perspective. The fact that the Kingdom of Guatemala was one of the few regions of the Spanish empire that did not experience a sustained, armed independence movement in the period 1810–1821 provides an unparalleled opportunity to interpret this period within the context of the preservation of empire rather than the struggle for independence, to explore the methods utilized by imperial officials to maintain order there, and to address the degree and nature of support for Spanish rule in the colony. This perspective, intrinsic to a more complete understanding of modern Central America and to the study of independence throughout Latin America, will also have a great impact on the continued historiographical viability of the Bustamante myth.

This study of the Bustamante regime will focus on a number of fundamental questions dealing with Spanish colonial administration during the waning years of the empire. How did Spain expect its colonial governors to react to the threat of insurrection? How was colonial governance affected by the political crisis in Spain during the Napoleonic invasion (1808–1814) and the shift from absolutism to constitutionalism to absolutism on the part of the loyalist governments? To what extent did his counterparts and colleagues inspire Bustamante's policies? How effective was the mechanism designed to confront threats to colonial stability? Was the colonial bureaucracy united? How did it relate to local groups—both loyalists and subversives?

Inspired in part by Hugh Hamill's and Brian Hamnett's studies on counterinsurgency in New Spain, as well as the findings of Timothy Anna, Jorge Domínguez, and Michael Costeloe on the administrative challenges resulting from the breakdown of the empire, this work argues that Bustamante constructed a successful counterinsurgency state based on a framework set during the previous administration and guidelines provided by the viceregal authorities in neighboring Mexico.[49] Yet unlike New Spain under viceroys Venegas and Calleja, the Kingdom of Guatemala under Bustamante managed to avoid some of the more extreme elements of the royalist reaction to rebellion.[50] Far from being an instrument of official terror, his counterinsurgency system included both conciliatory and repressive measures and stopped well short of a complete militarization of society. His policies were neither arbitrary nor brutal, nor did they produce significant popular opposition. Nevertheless, they proved to be particularly divisive and controversial within the highest levels of colonial society. Ultimately, this limited counterinsurgency state helped preserve the Kingdom of Guatemala for the crown, but at the same time it led to Bustamante's downfall and eventual vilification by powerful Guatemalan elites.

The questions concerning the Central American attitude toward independence are equally important yet perhaps more speculative. To what extent did the revolutionary virus that swept other parts of the empire infect the isthmus? Were certain segments of society more susceptible than others? How did creole/peninsular rivalry affect the colony? What role did the creole elite play in preserving order or fomenting unrest? What actually caused the sporadic revolts in the Kingdom of Guatemala? Little is known about variations in independence sentiment between regions and social groups or about the fundamental nature of the revolts that did occur; investigations into the Central American militias have yet to be undertaken; and the work that has begun elsewhere on the Church and independence can only be partially advanced here.[51]

Yet, a step back from traditional historiography and the claims of historia patria seems to indicate that the vast majority of the population was decidedly conservative in its attitude toward the revolutionary and liberation movements sweeping Europe and Spanish America at the time. Certain groups, such as the creole elite, played an active role in restoring order following potentially incendiary uprisings. In contrast, it was the inaction of other social groups, particularly the indigenous communities, that proved fundamental to the survival of Spanish rule considering the contemporaneous events in New Spain. Most of the unrest that did develop was sparked by local concerns and sustained only by the uncertainties of the time. Once the imperial crisis passed in 1814, the kingdom returned to its traditional quiescent state. Those who did advocate a more radical future for the colony, certain educated creoles and ladinos who made up a small part of the minority groups to which they belonged, simply could not mobilize any widespread popular support for their positions until 1821 at the earliest.

By emphasizing the difficult times in which Bustamante governed, the orders he had to preserve loyalty and tranquility in the colony, his limited political options, and the confusion of attitudes toward independence on the part of the local population, a new portrait of the captain general will emerge. Instead of a servant of despotism and an early practitioner of institutional terror, the captain general was a product of the progressive Bourbon monarchy. He was raised and educated in a climate of enlightened absolutism, an environment that profoundly shaped both his character and his administrative outlook. While his worldview increasingly clashed with that of the Guatemalan creoles, he remained faithful to it and the concept of empire throughout his career.

This focus on the preservation of empire should also have significant implications for the history of the other Spanish American liberation movements. Nowhere in the Americas, except perhaps in the Río de la Plata, was a complete break with Spain made during the 1810s. The struggle for independence suffered many reverses and potential failures in Chile, New Granada, Mexico, and Venezuela, with Peru expressing almost no enthusiasm for the cause and Cuba preserving its colonial status until 1898. In its hesitant, haphazard, and drawn-out response to revolution, then, Central America exhibited characteristics common to the region as a whole as the imperial crisis unfolded after 1808. Before the history of Latin America during this period can be understood, the equivocal attitude toward independence illustrated by Central America under Bustamante must first be fully investigated.

1

The Creation of
a Spanish Colonial Official

José de Bustamante's life and career spanned what was arguably the most significant six decades in Hispanic history since the first half of the sixteenth century, the momentous era that saw both the political unification of Spain and the consolidation of its vast overseas empire. It was his misfortune, however, to witness the unraveling of almost all that had been achieved during that earlier period. Born in the northern province of Asturias on 1 April 1759, Bustamante was a child of the Spanish Enlightenment who experienced firsthand the impact on Spain of the political, social, and economic reforms that began with the arrival of the first Bourbon king in 1700. The short-term effects of these reforms on the Spanish empire were profound, and Bustamante grew up in an ostensibly prosperous and influential state. By the time of his death on 10 March 1825, however, Spain was a shadow of its former self, having suffered through decades of improvident leadership, foreign invasion, a devastating civil war, and the loss of most of its American colonies.

Bustamante was no disinterested observer of these events. During his fifty years of service to the crown as a naval officer and colonial official, he played an important role both in the rejuvenation of Spain's political, imperial, and military fortunes and in its dramatic collapse. Beginning in 1770, he rose through the ranks of the Spanish navy in the years of its greatest influence and distinguished himself as a combat officer. As second-in-command of the Malaspina expedition that traversed the Pacific between 1789 and 1794, he helped promote the practical expression of the Spanish scientific Enlightenment. As governor of Montevideo from 1796 to 1804, he became in many respects the quintessential Bourbon-era colonial official. And from 1811 to 1818, he brought this diverse experience to the Kingdom of Guatemala where, as governor and captain general, he emerged as a central figure in the crown's desperate efforts to preserve the loyalty of its American subjects following the 1808 Napoleonic invasion of Spain. Returning to Spain in 1819, an embittered Bustamante watched helplessly from a series of senior administrative posts as the empire crumbled.

In many significant ways, José de Bustamante embodied late eighteenth-century Spanish attitudes toward class, politics, and the role of the individual within the established social order. In a society that placed a high premium on *limpieza de sangre* (purity of blood) and regarded a lineage of Old Christian forebears as a principal determinant of rank, he was particularly proud and protective of his ancestry and his status as an *hidalgo*. *Hidalguía*, which defined the essential quality of nobility, was held by much of the population of Spain's northern coast, comprising the modern-day provinces of Galicia, Asturias, Cantabria, and Vizcaya, although such a pedigree did not necessarily carry with it wealth or power. An especially high percentage of impoverished hidalgos lived in the Cantabrian highlands around Santander in the district known as La Montaña. They survived by farming small plots of land and working in small-scale commerce or the shipbuilding industry, which was the region's primary contribution to the Spanish economy. During the eighteenth century, thousands, in fact, left for better opportunities in the Spanish American colonies, where commercial and social success beckoned. This movement became the most important peninsular migration to the Americas since the conquest.[1]

Bustamante's early life in Asturias, however, was somewhat different from the typical experience of the north-coast petty hidalgo.[2] He was born José Joaquín Antonio de Bustamante Guerra de la Vega Rueda Cobo Estrada Zorlado, the second son of Joaquín Antonio de Bustamante Rueda and Clara Guerra de la Vega, residents of the small *montañés* town of Ontaneda, a stop along the road connecting Santander with Burgos. The Bustamantes were a well-established regional family who traced their lineage back to a ninth-century forebear named Rod-

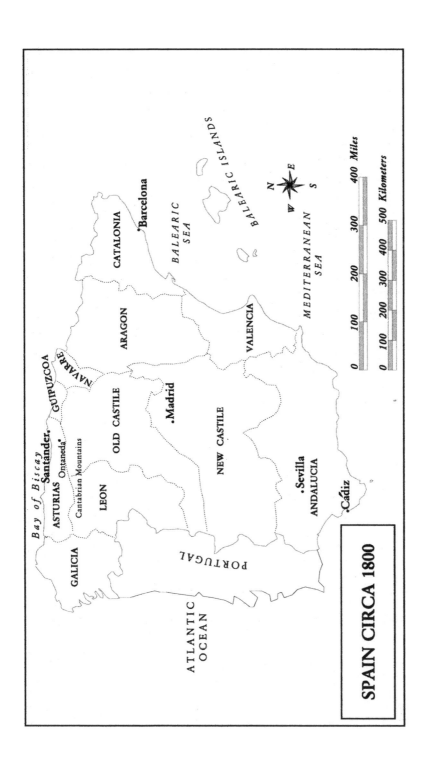

SPAIN CIRCA 1800

rigo, the founder of their *hidalguía*, as well as their ancestral seats of Quijas, Bustamante, and Cadalso. The descendants of Rodrigo who took the *apellido* Bustamante became heirs to a number of *señoríos* (landed estates) in the northern provinces of Santander, Palencia, and Burgos. José de Bustamante, himself, was a member of the fourth line of the House of Alceda, a branch of the family tree that had settled in the province of Santander. This line sent many of its members to Chile and Mexico over the course of the eighteenth century, but Bustamante's immediate kin remained tied to Alceda and Ontaneda.[3] Although never achieving the level of the titled aristocracy, the family consistently demonstrated its rank through an appropriate dedication to civil and military service, an Old Christian ancestry, a dependence on the king's purse, and the returns from its estates for income.[4]

Charles III inherited the throne of Spain scarcely four months after Bustamante's birth and held it until his death in 1788. As a result, the kingdom of Bustamante's youth and early adulthood was the Spain of enlightened absolutism and reform-minded governance. For three decades the country experienced relative prosperity during which the crown attempted to reverse 150 years of political, social, and economic stagnation through a series of administrative, military, ecclesiastical, and economic initiatives. Many of these measures focused upon the American colonies, where they succeeded in stimulating colonial trade, mining, and industry; centralizing imperial bureaucracy and taxation; and reorganizing imperial defenses. Often these achievements came at the expense of American interests, thereby fostering an element of colonial frustration with Spanish rule in the years before the independence movements. The short-term impact in Spain, however, was positive, with tax revenues and commercial activity within the empire reaching all-time highs.[5]

The reformist mentality encouraged by the crown was pragmatic and conservative in nature, with an emphasis on revitalizing the established order instead of rejecting a failed system. Rather than entrusting the governance of the state to the traditional aristocracy, Charles cultivated a new group of lesser nobility known as the *manteistas*, who were devoted supporters of the monarchy and who imposed on Spain and the empire an absolutist bureaucratic model that contrasted sharply with the pre-Bourbon system of governance and its reliance on compromise and consensus.[6] These men drew on the lessons of the Enlightenment for inspiration and were devoted to practical knowledge as a means to draw the Spanish empire into the modern age. But they also knew where to draw the line. As the historian John Lynch says of José Monino, conde de Floridablanca, one of the best examples of the new breed of Bourbon bureaucrat, this type of Spaniard was "aware of the world, ready to learn, but quick to react."[7] During the last half of the eighteenth century, a new generation of colonial officials, among whom José de Bustamante would figure prominently, brought this reformed political perspective to the Americas.

With its treasury full of revenue extracted from a revived imperial system, the crown proceeded to spend great amounts to increase the strength of the Spanish military. While both branches benefited from such attention, the revival of the navy during the late eighteenth century was profound and should be considered one of the great achievements of the Bourbon state.[8] Naval power was essential in order to compete on the international stage with Britain and to defend Spain's valuable colonies against foreign depredations, not to mention simply to communicate and trade with them. The navy protected shipping lanes and ports, guarded against illegal commerce and piracy, escorted American treasure fleets, and transported Spanish armies across oceans during the incessant colonial wars of the period. Most significantly, the navy was often the only visible symbol of Spanish sovereignty in a vast and vague sphere of influence that stretched from Europe in the west to the Philippines in the east and from Tierra del Fuego in the south to California in the north.

However, military expansion proved valuable to Spain in other ways as well. In many respects, the Spanish navy also benefited from the Spanish Enlightenment. The crown utilized the new navy as a tool for the scientific, political, social, and economic development of the empire, financing a number of explorations whose primary goals were designed to improve the state's understanding of its resources and to promote useful knowledge. The most talented naval officers of the period displayed impressive scientific and intellectual credentials. They trained in an environment that encouraged observation, experimentation, and activism, in addition to the traditional military attributes of patriotism, duty, and loyalty.

Naval reform had begun in earnest during the reign of Ferdinand VI (1746–1759) and was directed by the leading political figure of the time, the Marquis de la Ensenada. By the early 1700s, the old decentralized naval system, which relied on a small number of autonomous armadas deployed in strategic zones, had completely collapsed.[9] As late as 1751, Spain could muster only eighteen ships-of-the-line and fifteen lesser vessels in defense of the empire (this is to be compared with the 100 ships-of-the-line and 180 frigates outfitted for service by England at the same time).[10] Unable to begin serious commercial reform in such an environment, Ensenada, who began his political career as secretary of the Admiralty, called for immediate spending to raise the size of the navy to one hundred vessels, of which half were to be ships-of-the-line, arguing that "without a navy the Spanish monarchy cannot be respected."[11]

Ensenada's fall from power in 1754 and the death of Ferdinand VI five years later did not alter this philosophy. To meet the high goals set by his predecessor, Charles III revived the shipbuilding industry in its traditional centers of Santander, Cádiz, El Ferrol, and Cartagena, and by 1770 Spain could boast a navy of fifty-one ships-of-the-line, twenty-two frigates, and twenty-nine other vessels, numbers which made it the second-largest maritime force in the world.[12] Spending continued through the War of American Independence, Spain's one successful venture against Britain, and into the 1790s when the navy reached its peak of influence. The naval program proved so successful, in fact, that by 1798 Spain could outfit 76 ships-of-the-line, 51 frigates, and 184 lesser ships.[13] However, the Napoleonic wars dealt a fatal blow to this rebuilding effort, with the Battle of Trafalgar in 1805 marking the collapse of the Spanish navy as an effective fighting force.

Like many other members of the minor Spanish nobility, the Bustamante family had a long history of military service, viewing it as both a natural career choice for their class and one of the few that promised an escape from provincial obscurity. In 1770 the eleven-year-old José was sent across the peninsula to Cádiz, where he was enrolled in the *Escuela de Guardiamarinas,* the principal training school for those intending a naval career. The education he received there, which translated into a distinguished military and administrative career, proved to be the dominant influence on his worldview. Fortunately for him, he entered the

Marina española at perhaps the pinnacle of its institutional development and prestige.

Much as the basic infrastructure of the navy was transformed in the mid-eighteenth century, the naval academy at Cádiz that Bustamante entered in 1770 also benefited from the new priorities of the crown. Its revitalization was directed by Jorge Juan, a naval officer and scientist who, along with Antonio de Ulloa, had led a famous naval expedition to the Indies in the 1730s that, in part, helped convince the crown of the need for drastic imperial reform. Juan redirected the academy curriculum along enlightened and scientific lines, with a special emphasis on new techniques of astronomical observation and navigation, and he added an entire section of "higher studies" to complement the basic curriculum.[14] Here the technological and strategic military innovations that had been developed in northern Europe earlier in the century entered Spain. Within a matter of years, the academy had trained many officers, including Bustamante, who performed feats of navigation, exploration, and military strategy that made Spain a serious rival of England at the time. As John Lynch notes, Spain finally "acquired a professional officer corps, recruited and trained for the job rather than taken from the merchant navy or privateers."[15]

Bustamante's career upon graduating from the *Escuela de Guardiamarinas* in 1774 illustrates the important role of the navy within the imperial system of Charles III; the young officer was taken to all corners of the world in pursuit of Spain's military, commercial, political, and scientific interests.[16] As an *alférez de fragata* (second ensign), the lowest ranking shipboard officer, Bustamante first saw combat in 1774 on an expedition sent to relieve the Spanish stronghold of Melilla, on the Moroccan coast. His next service on troop transports to Havana and Puerto Rico brought him to the Americas for the first time. On the return voyage, Bustamante's squadron was escorting a treasure ship through the Bahamas when it ran aground; his skills helped free it, and he received commendations from the commanding officer as well as a promotion to *alférez de navío* (first ensign) for his services.

During a subsequent tour at sea that took him as far as Manila, Bustamante attained the rank of *teniente de fragata* (second lieutenant). By 1779 Spain was at war with Britain, and on the return voyage from Manila his ship came under attack by two English corsairs. In a battle that lasted three hours, Bustamante was gravely wounded. His ship was captured and taken to Ireland, where he spent some months in captivity. Upon his return to Spain in 1780 he was cleared by a naval tribunal of any wrongdoing in the incident and quickly received a new position as *teniente de navío* (first lieutenant) on board the ship-of-the-line *Triunfante*. In this role, Bustamante participated in the Spanish siege of Gibraltar of 1781–1782 and in a major engagement against an English fleet near the Straits on 20 October 1782, during which his ship received severe damage.

Following the end of the war in 1783, Bustamante was transferred to the *Septentrion* and given an important position as *oficial de ordenes de la escuadra* in a flotilla of four warships, which successfully escorted thirty-three million pesos back to Spain from Mexico. This service won Bustamante the rank of *capitán de fragata* (commander) on 15 November 1784, less than one month after he had continued a family tradition by becoming a *caballero* (knight) in the Order of Santiago.[17] In 1788, following a four-year hiatus from active duty, he emerged as second-in-command of the *San Sebastián,* one of six warships under the command of José de Córdoba that toured the Mediterranean for the purpose of upgrading and improving naval designs and practices. Thus, by the age of thirty José de Bustamante had already carved out a successful and promising career in the Spanish navy.

At some point during his military service, Bustamante became acquainted with another young, talented, and adventurous officer, Alejandro Malaspina.[18] A son of the Italian marqués de Morillo, Malaspina began his service in the Spanish navy in 1774, studied at the *Escuela de Guardiamarinas,* and followed a career path that closely paralleled Bustamante's, with the significant exception that by 1786 the Italian had already sailed around the world in command of the warship *Astrea.* Fiercely driven, and perhaps influenced by the famous precedent of the Juan and Ulloa expedition, Malaspina followed up his circumnavigation with plans for a more ambitious project: a voyage around the world that would combine geographic exploration and scientific discovery with a thorough investigation of the political, social, and commercial status of the Spanish colonies. A man perfectly in tune with the inquisitive spirit of the times, Malaspina found in Bustamante a like-minded compatriot with the requisite determination and navigational skills to help him carry out his plans. Thus, on 10 September 1788, the two *capitanes de fragata* made an official proposal to Charles III's Ministry of the Navy requesting two ships, funds, and other support necessary to outfit such an expedition.

The crown proved more than willing to sponsor the project. In fact, from its perspective there was much to be gained. From a purely patriotic standpoint, Spain had a national interest in competing with England and France for the glory associated during the Age of Enlightenment with the promotion of human knowledge, a scientific and geographic challenge that the travels of Cook and La Pérouse helped initiate in recent decades.[19] The Malaspina expedition also offered the opportunity to challenge growing English and Russian influence in unexploited Spanish territory along the Pacific coast of North America, to reconfirm Spanish claims in Asian and Atlantic waters, and to investigate other security concerns of the empire.[20] The fundamental goal of the voyage was to clarify the boundaries of Spanish influence through more precise cartographic measurements and displays of the flag. The reformist crown, however, also expected Malaspina and Bustamante to improve exploitation of colonial resources with intensive scientific investigations of floral, faunal, and mineral resources in the empire, to chart the best commercial routes, to investigate the conditions of ports and coastal defenses, and to report back on political and social conditions in the Americas.[21] In this manner Spain expected to reap the benefits of a three-decade policy of naval reform that allowed such an expedition to be successfully imagined, outfitted, and led.

The two officers each received a brand-new ship to command, with the expedition leader Malaspina in the *Descubierta* and Bustamante as captain of the *Atrevida*. Each traveled with a crew of one hundred, which included sailors, naturalists, botanists, surgeons, painters, and cartographers. The voyage was expected to encircle the globe and to last three years from the departure date of 30 July 1789. Instead, it took five years for the expedition to return to Spain, following alterations in the planned route that led the captains to return to the Americas from Asia. The reach of the expedition was, in fact, tremendous. Between 1789 and

1791, the ships visited every Spanish American colony except Venezuela, sailing around Tierra del Fuego from Montevideo and then up the Pacific coast of the American continents to Acapulco.[22]

With orders from Spain to investigate the mythical Straits of Anian at 60 degrees north latitude, where Ferrer Maldonado had claimed in 1588 to have discovered the Northwest Passage, Bustamante, a newly appointed *capitán de navío* (post captain), sailed on from New Spain toward Alaska.[23] In December 1791, the ships began the Pacific crossing to the Philippines, which they reached two months later. Bustamante then sailed alone to Macao and the Chinese coast, before rejoining Malaspina for a detour that took them past New Guinea and Australia to New Zealand. From there the ships traversed the South Pacific and arrived at Callao, Peru, on 31 July 1793. One year later, on 21 September 1794, the *Descubierta* and *Atrevida* sailed into the Spanish port of Cádiz laden with goods, specimens, samples, observations, and drawings taken from four continents. The captains received a tremendous reception at the court of Charles IV, and within a year both were promoted to *brigadier general* (commodore) for their services. When asked to report on their findings, however, Malaspina and Bustamante quickly discovered that they had returned to a country (and a continent) markedly different from the one they had left in 1789.

Both Alejandro Malaspina and José de Bustamante were products of the Enlightenment, in the sense that each believed in progress through the application of human reason. Having matured when they did and within such a rarified social environment, neither found the idea of revolutionary change at all appealing. Among the European powers, Spain, in particular, lacked a strong tradition of political and social radicalism. To the greatest degree possible in his adopted country, however, Malaspina was a reformer, and opinions that did not cause him any trouble in 1788, while Charles III still reigned in Spain and Louis XVI in France, became liabilities in 1795. In the interim, the Bourbon monarchy in France had fallen, war had swept over Europe, Spanish armies had been defeated by those of the French Republic, and the new king, Charles IV, had allowed a young and inexperienced favorite named Manuel Godoy to assume the reins of power. The energetic, activist state of Charles III had given way to one that would be in almost permanent crisis until its collapse in 1808.

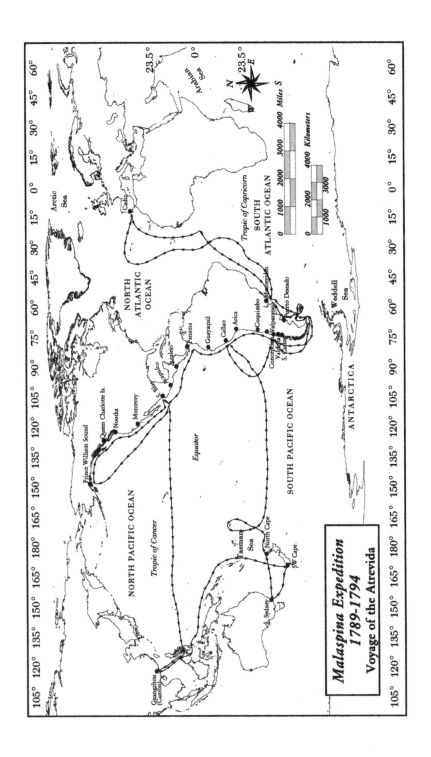

Malaspina Expedition
1789-1794
Voyage of the Atrevida

Prior to the departure of the expedition in 1789, Malaspina had written a detailed essay on the relationship between Spain and its colonies. In part a justification for the voyage he was about to make, his *Axiomas políticos sobre la América* argued that the empire itself was the cause of Spain's decline and proposed a drastic reorganization of the colonial order along the lines of the modern British Commonwealth if the colonies were to be kept.[24] Malaspina believed that Spain could never know enough about the New World to administer it effectively. From his perspective, the crown continued to govern the Indies as a conquest, treating its inhabitants, both Indians and creoles, as less than full citizens, at a time when many Americans desired more equity in the relationship. He, therefore, argued that Spanish America should receive political autonomy and be allowed to set its own commercial policy. Tithes, tributes, commercial monopolies, and other outdated examples of Spanish imperialism should also go in the interest of forging a new relationship—one based on shared tradition, language, religion, and culture—that would give Spain the benefits of empire without the problems.[25] Malaspina clearly hoped that his expedition would provide him with the standing and evidence he needed to convince the crown to revise its colonial policies.

Similar views became an important part of the imperial reform movement that later emerged under the auspices of the liberal Constitution of 1812. However, while the absolutist state survived, the views received little favorable attention. If anything, the Bourbons were great proponents of aggressive centralization as a means of imperial reform and renewal, though in 1795 few people were thinking about reform at all, with retrenchment and consolidation the only viable political options following a disastrous defeat by the French Republic. Nevertheless, upon his return to Spain, Alejandro Malaspina became embroiled in the political scene. Perhaps gambling on his newly won stature as a hero in the midst of failure, he presented himself as a reformer, a pacifist concerning France, and an opponent of Godoy. In the fall of 1795, Malaspina was implicated in a plot to overthrow the favorite and brought up on charges of sedition before the Council of State. Convicted on 27 November, he was stripped of all his titles and honors and imprisoned in La Coruña, where he languished before finally being freed in 1803. He returned to Italy and died there in 1810.[26]

The fate of Alejandro Malaspina highlights the development of an intellectual cleavage among the generation of Spaniards who matured under Charles III and emerged under Charles IV to hold positions of power during the imperial crisis of 1808–1826. Malaspina personified the group of enlightened reformers who broke with the crown during the ascendancy of Godoy, subsequently became known as liberals, and ultimately championed colonial autonomy and *comercio libre* in debates over the Constitution of 1812 during the Spanish American wars of independence. Yet, despite the dramatic changes in Spanish fortunes between the reigns of Charles III and his son, many in this Enlightenment generation continued to hold fast to the Bourbon ideal of absolutism, centralization, and conservative (though still proactive) reform. Malaspina's compatriot, José de Bustamante, soon proved himself an unparalleled representative of that perspective.

A proven leader, talented, resourceful, and energetic, Commodore Bustamante was a valuable asset to the crown in 1796. At the age of thirty-seven, he had already spent two-thirds of his life in active defense of the empire, traveling widely and absorbing the mentality of enlightened absolutism through a reenergized navy that considered itself a symbol of the unity of the Hispanic world.[27] Whereas Malaspina saw his career collapse in a misguided attempt to play politics, the pragmatic Asturian steered clear of any such entanglements and, instead, turned the expedition to his advantage. Drawing on his military training and extensive travel in the empire, Bustamante presented the crown with a detailed report on how to secure the commercial and defense needs of the American colonies in the midst of the European hostilities, a study that found favor with Godoy.[28]

Although the Bourbon state made a habit of appointing military men to political commands in the Americas, Bustamante's experience overseas by this time made him an especially attractive candidate for a colonial position. In fact, security concerns in the New World that resulted from the wars of the French Revolution made a military background almost a prerequisite for colonial administration. On 18 August 1796, Manuel Godoy, soon to be named Prince of the Peace, signed the Treaty of San Ildefonso with France, an offensive alliance that compelled Spain to put its army and navy at the disposal of its revolutionary ally. This action was followed less than two months later by a declaration of war against Britain.[29] Considering the vast naval resources of England and its long tradition of attacks on Spanish possessions in the New World, the Spanish American colonies needed appropriate leadership. Accordingly, on 13 September 1796, Bustamante was appointed *gobernador militar y político* of the strategic port and province of Montevideo and *comandante general* of its naval station on the Río de la Plata.

Governor Bustamante reached Montevideo on 11 February 1797 and immediately took control of a vibrant and fast-growing region of some forty thousand inhabitants uncomfortably situated between the powerful viceregal capital of Buenos Aires and the Portuguese territory of Brazil.[30] Commanding the eastern shore of the mouth of the La Plata estuary, the land that later became the nation of Uruguay had only recently been settled by Spain as a bulwark against Portuguese expansion. It developed as a frontier outpost, with *estancias* (ranches) devoted to cattle production fueling the growth of the interior and with contraband commercial operations rife along the coast and in the provincial capital of Montevideo, a city of fifteen thousand little more than sixty years old. As a result of these peculiar origins, conflicts over trade with Buenos Aires and over borders with Brazil characterized much of the eighteenth-century history of the *Banda Oriental.*

The population of Montevideo received Bustamante well, in part because he replaced Antonio Olaguer, the previous governor, whose relationship with the city ayuntamiento had sunk so low that the municipality had lobbied the crown for his removal. As the primary representative institution of the *estancieros* and merchants who dominated the social and economic life of the colony, the town council of Montevideo played an important consultative role in the administration of the province. However, Bustamante, as the king's representative in the Banda Oriental, wielded broad authority in his jurisdiction.[31] He presided over the ayuntamiento of Montevideo and, technically, needed no local input to govern.

Bustamante, nevertheless, made an active effort to administer the region in concert with the needs of the population, as he saw them. In fact, his administration was remarkably progressive. Within a month of his arrival he sent the viceroy of the Río de la Plata an extensive diagnosis of the province's problems and his strategy for the defense and commer-

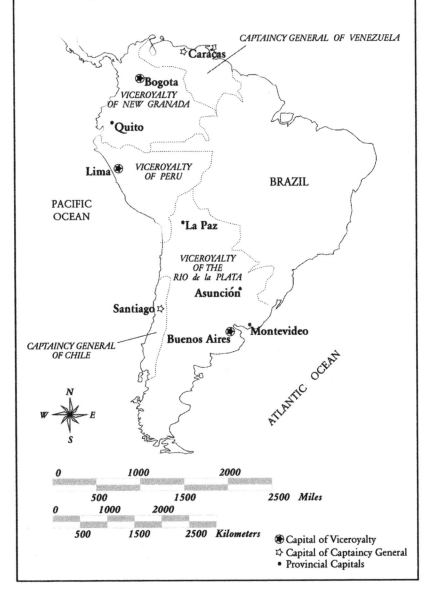

SPANISH SOUTH AMERICA CIRCA 1800

CAPTAINCY GENERAL OF VENEZUELA

☆ Caracas

⊕ Bogota

VICEROYALTY
OF NEW GRANADA

• Quito

Lima ⊕

VICEROYALTY
OF PERU

BRAZIL

PACIFIC
OCEAN

• La Paz

VICEROYALTY
OF THE
RIO de la PLATA

Asunción •

Santiago ☆

CAPTAINCY GENERAL
OF CHILE

Buenos Aires ⊕   • Montevideo

ATLANTIC OCEAN

N
W   E
S

| 0 | 1000 | | 2000 | |
| 500 | | 1500 | | 2500 Miles |

| 0 | 1000 | 2000 | |
| 500 | 1500 | 2500 Kilometers | |

⊕ Capital of Viceroyalty
☆ Capital of Captaincy General
• Provincial Capitals

cial stimulation of the port of Montevideo.[32] Three weeks later, the governor called a town meeting to solicit local ideas for developing the colony. He emphasized the need for orderliness (*buena policía*) and sanitation and then convinced the public to accept a one-*real* tax per household to pay for civic improvements. Working with the ayuntamiento, he managed to push through a livestock tax that raised forty thousand pesos for church construction, restoration of the Casa de Cabildo, road and bridge development, and other infrastructure projects. Other taxes brought in money for potable water and public washing facilities (*lavaderos*), much-needed reforms that did a great deal to improve the health and living conditions in the city. In addition, under Bustamante's watch, frontier territory in the northeast was incorporated into the province and the native Chorrúas Indians were brought under Spanish control.[33]

The knowledge Bustamante acquired during his naval career and his travels throughout the empire was then put to use in the economic and military development of the port of Montevideo. In the best Enlightenment manner, he translated his experiences and observations into action, proposing the construction of the city's first commercial wharf and promoting increased commercial activity between towns along the coast and the river system. By 1802, Montevideo's maritime traffic had expanded to servicing nearly two hundred ships per year. To secure this new commercial center, Bustamante worked at improving provincial defenses: he commanded a small fleet of warships for coastal watch and one permanent company of artillery stationed in Montevideo; he also maintained a volunteer battalion of infantry militia, a cavalry regiment, and a frontier guard, totaling some two thousand men in all.[34] While not overwhelming, these forces helped to keep the region intact in the midst of war with Britain and Portugal. During a difficult period for Spain and most of the empire, in fact, the Banda Oriental appeared to flourish. According to the Uruguayan historian Francisco Bauza, much of the credit for this dramatic progress was due to the enlightened administration of José de Bustamante, who "proved himself to be always hardworking, active, and upstanding in the observance of his obligations."[35]

While Bustamante's sense of duty made him sensitive to the role that the Spanish administration could play in the development of its colonial possessions, and while he did not refrain from enlisting the local population in these efforts, he remained firmly convinced of the need to preserve and promote the supreme authority of the crown in all its manifestations vis-à-vis challenges from local individuals or corporations. An incident with the Montevideo ayuntamiento in 1799, which foreshadowed similar conflicts in Guatemala, highlights this aspect of his political persona. During one of the frequent ceremonial functions associated with his position, Bustamante refused to allow the councilmen to enter the governor's palace with their staffs of office in hand.[36] This attitude on the part of Bustamante, though perhaps unwise, was not arbitrary. Throughout his career he presented himself as a faithful defender of Spanish sovereignty, and a great deal of this defense concerned the symbols and ceremonies that distinguished the king's representative in the Americas from other officials. The ayuntamiento naturally refused to give up its symbols of authority and filed a complaint with the viceroy. Rebuffed by Buenos Aires and following a similar ceremonial disturbance in 1800, the town council again petitioned for redress, but without success.

Overall, relations between the population of the Banda Oriental and their governor remained cordial throughout his administration, as Bustamante would recall with pride in an open letter that he sent to the Montevideo council in 1811 upon taking command in Guatemala.[37] By his own account his subjects even petitioned the crown to extend his service beyond the traditional five-year term, a proposal that was initially accepted but later undone due to "one of the palace intrigues that lead to the ruin of empires."[38] While Bustamante may have owed his governorship to his loyalty to Manuel Godoy in the midst of the palace intrigues of 1795, by the first years of the new century he had begun to temper his sense of duty to the unpopular favorite of the crown in response to what he considered an abdication of Spain's sovereignty through entangling alliances with revolutionary France. So much of Bustamante's character was based on his conception of the value of being a *puro Español* and so many of his actions "inflexible in upholding the dignity of this name," that when a group of French ships attempted to enter the port of Montevideo without acknowledging the Spanish authorities there, Bustamante compelled them to "show respect to a nation accustomed to imposing it."[39] Such impertinence, combined with a running feud between Bustamante and the viceroy and *Consulado de*

Comercio of Buenos Aires, hurt his reputation at court and seems to have contributed to his recall in the summer of 1803.[40]

After seven successful years as governor, Bustamante left Montevideo on 9 August 1804 in command of a small flotilla of four frigates: the *Medea,* the *Fama,* the *Mercedes,* and the *Clara.*[41] The ships had originated in Peru and were returning to Spain with treasure, other nonmilitary supplies, and a number of civilian passengers; no special precautions had been taken to protect them since European hostilities had ceased with the 1802 Peace of Amiens. However, on 5 October four English warships overtook the Spanish frigates within sight of the Iberian peninsula. At this point, the English Commodore Graham Moore communicated his orders to capture the treasure ships and return them to England. Completely unprepared for a fight and severely outgunned, Bustamante ordered his ships to open fire on the English, who responded with a barrage that sank the *Mercedes* and severely damaged the *Medea.* Having suffered the loss of one ship with 249 casualties and the disabling of another, Bustamante surrendered the remainder of the flotilla, which was then escorted to England.

Comfortably detained in London, Bustamante and the Spanish ambassador immediately lodged a formal protest over the confiscation of the five million pesos carried by the flotilla. They then obtained audiences with leading members of the British Admiralty and government in an effort to secure the return of the portion of the treasure that was private or had been set aside to pay the salaries of the officers and sailors. The incident proved unpopular in public opinion after its disclosure in the media, and the crown agreed to return 239,000 British pounds. After a number of months in detention, Bustamante and the other passengers of the flotilla were finally repatriated. Once in Spain, he asked that the navy conduct an immediate court martial to review his conduct in the incident. On 29 December 1805, a *junta de generales* praised Bustamante's defense of Spanish honor and cleared him of any personal wrongdoing in the loss of the ships. A royal order dated 10 January 1806 then established his fitness for all types of command, and Bustamante took a place on the *Junta de Fortificación y Defensa de Indias* in July 1807.[42]

Less than a year after assuming this post, Bustamante witnessed the collapse of the Spain he had known from birth. By 1807 Spanish politics had become fatally divided between the backers of Manuel Godoy, which group for all intents and purposes included only the king and queen, and the backers of the heir to the throne, Ferdinand, who had the support of much of the population. After years of scandal, war, and economic depression, the crown itself, in the person of Charles IV, had become tarnished, a situation compounded by the fact that Charles had recently allowed his ally, Napoleon, to occupy Spain in an effort to subjugate Portugal. In April 1808 the palace animosities came to a head with a popular uprising at Aranjuez directed against Godoy that ultimately caused Charles IV to abdicate the throne in favor of his son. In the midst of this political turmoil, Napoleon ordered the competing Bourbons to meet with him in France. On 2 May, news reached Madrid from Bayonne that both Ferdinand and Charles had surrendered their rights to the Spanish crown to Napoleon, who then bestowed it upon his brother, Joseph. The capital immediately rose in revolt against its French occupiers. Opposition to the French then spread rapidly across the peninsula, thereby sparking the Spanish war for independence.[43]

As a high-ranking naval officer, former colonial official, and nobleman, José de Bustamante was approached in July 1808 by José de Mazarredo, the newly appointed *afrancesado* Minister of the Navy, and asked to swear obedience to the new king, José I. He responded by declining the honor and resigning his position in government and the navy. Describing the events of this summer to a friend in Lima in a letter that was published in the *Minerva Peruana*, Bustamante wrote:

> I cannot explain to you what my spirit has suffered due to the atrocious conduct of the French and the terrible oppression in which they have kept us here for four months: suffice it to say that the intrusive king tried to force the leading classes, including the generals, to swear an oath of loyalty to him and to the new constitution which he presented: and although I was the first to renounce my military office, the ministers Urquijo and Mazarredo were not content with this; instead, the supposed king allowed them to try and force me into it as if I were a nobody. Together, over the space of two hours, these same two assaulted me with tricks, seductions, and threats, in the hopes of overcoming my inflexibility until the point was reached where I told them that even with a knife at my throat I would never swear allegiance to a king who had

reached the throne after so many iniquities, nor to a constitution that would reduce Spain to slavery and misery: upon which I was forced to escape on foot in order to pick up a mount some distance from this city so as to avoid the obligatory measures imposed by the French, leaving my family exposed and in an obvious state of grief, forced to follow me however they can. But the French are going to pay for all this and the nation will triumph gloriously.[44]

In the safety of Andalusia, Bustamante offered his services to the *Junta Central*, the recently established loyalist government charged with defending the sovereignty and patrimony of the deposed King Ferdinand VII.

Although the Junta Central had consolidated itself throughout Spain by 1809 as the legitimate authority representing the crown, the collapse of the monarchy opened up a Pandora's box of constitutional issues regarding the relationship between the metropolis and its colonies in the absence of the sovereign. In this political vacuum unrest and dissent flourished, with many in the Americas arguing for a new imperial order based on local autonomy. In fact, as word of the dissolution of the Spanish monarchy arrived in the colonies, the authority of Spanish administrators there began to be challenged. Initial efforts to establish American-dominated juntas in Mexico City, Upper Peru, Quito, and Buenos Aires failed, although these setbacks did not quell the appeal of autonomy for an increasing number of disaffected creoles. The crown, therefore, was obligated to act quickly to ensure the loyalty of its American possessions to Spain and to preserve them intact.

More than anything else, the preservation of empire called for effective and creative governance on the part of the colonial officials, for in the coming months no one could predict how much support Spain itself would be able to offer. In José de Bustamante, the Junta Central had a proven administrator with years of experience in the Americas and a long record of service and loyalty to the crown, and it moved quickly to find a place for him to serve. In October 1809, Bustamante was named president of the Audiencia of Charcas (Upper Peru), but he was then reposted to the Audiencia of Cuzco (Peru) following news of the death of the incumbent, Francisco Muñoz.

This decision, however, was also quickly reversed. In April 1810, upon the dissolution of the Junta Central and its replacement by the Council of Regency, Bustamante found himself appointed captain general, governor, and president of the Kingdom of Guatemala, a command with a more significant military role than the previous positions in a territory of great strategic importance to Spain. By this point, revolutionary uprisings had begun to engulf the Río de la Plata and Venezuela. These revolts threatened to end Spanish rule in the Americas permanently, and the loyalist Spanish government, which had been mobilized to recover Spain itself, was now forced to defend and reconquer its overseas possessions as well. Bustamante, with his proven record of success in Montevideo, was a logical choice for such delicate operations. Finding passage across the Atlantic on board an English warship, the recently promoted *teniente general* (vice admiral) immediately departed for his new administrative position. Confident in his governing capabilities and prepared to "excuse no fatigue or sacrifice" in procuring "the general happiness and prosperity of that beautiful country," he landed in the fall of 1810 on a continent that would soon explode in revolution against all he represented.[45]

2

The Kingdom of Guatemala on the Eve of Independence

The Kingdom of Guatemala circa 1800 was no longer the depressed and isolated frontier settlement that Murdo MacLeod describes in his magisterial study *Spanish Central America: A Socioeconomic History, 1520–1720*.[1] Nor had Central America yet irrevocably slipped into the destructive pattern of internecine conflicts, political fragmentation, and fragile export-oriented monoculture that would dominate the subsequent two centuries and reconfirm the region's status as a backwater. Instead, the colony to which José de Bustamante was posted as captain general proved to be one of the great (if short-lived) success stories of the Bourbon reforms of the eighteenth century.[2] Starting about 1750 the Kingdom of Guatemala experienced an economic boom resulting from the cultivation of indigo (*añil*) and the relaxation of restrictive Spanish trade laws, factors that contributed to the incorporation of Central America into the developing Atlantic commercial economy. During this period, Central America became a valuable part of the Spanish empire, at times remitting yearly revenues to Spain in excess of 350,000 pesos.[3] Energized by growing contacts with the outside world and influenced by Enlightenment thought, a powerful network of Guatemala-based creoles began to consolidate into a social and economic oligarchy with kingdomwide influence. Finally, the Bourbon administrative reforms, the most important of which was the establishment of intendancies during the 1780s, spurred provincial political, economic, and institutional development as well. By the first decade of the nineteenth century the colonial administrative unit known as the Audiencia of Guatemala, with a total population exceeding one million, ranked second to Mexico in terms of demographic size.[4]

This half century of economic expansion, political consolidation, and social transformations, in many respects a golden age for the Kingdom of Guatemala, started to show signs of breakdown as the nineteenth century began, in large part because of the reemergence of European hostilities following the French Revolution and their impact on international commerce. Contemporaries remained optimistic that further reforms would restore the region to prosperity. By this time, however, imperial officials were more concerned with the preservation of the colony in the face of the threat to Spanish America following the French takeover of Spain than with economic revitalization measures. The crown could not ignore the strategic importance of Central America: it served as the bulwark of Spanish authority in the lower Caribbean; it dominated the weak southern flank of Mexico; it offered direct access into South America through the Panamanian isthmus; and it was in direct confrontation with English settlements in Belize and the Mosquito Coast. Therefore, when José de Bustamante, as the new president, governor, and captain general of the kingdom, came to office he was compelled to emphasize the military aspect of his authority to a much greater degree than had his predecessors. As an institution, the captaincy general *was* a military designation. While military duties may have been de-emphasized at times in relation to the other powers of the king's senior representative on the isthmus, the reverse was true by the first decade of the nineteenth century. Unfortunately for Spain, the new imperial perspective, which subordinated social and economic reform policies and civil justice to defense concerns, appeared misplaced to a relatively loyal population facing an economic depression and served as the root cause of much of the opposition that Bustamante would face over the course of his term in office.

In an era in which governments struggled continuously to surmount the immense challenges of space and time, when round-trip communication with Spain took months and the transit of internal correspondence was measured in weeks, the ability of colonial governors to ensure domestic tranquility depended heavily upon the stability and viability

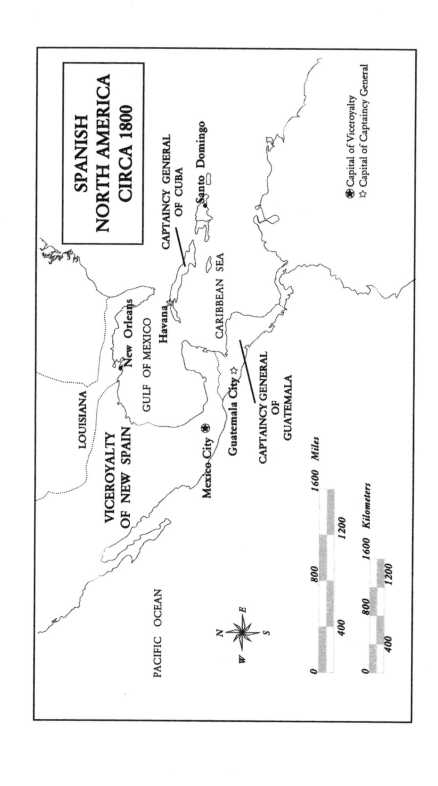

SPANISH
NORTH AMERICA
CIRCA 1800

VICEROYALTY
OF NEW SPAIN

LOUISIANA

PACIFIC OCEAN

GULF OF MEXICO

New Orleans

Havana

CAPTAINCY GENERAL
OF CUBA

Santo Domingo

CARIBBEAN SEA

Mexico City

Guatemala City

CAPTAINCY GENERAL
OF
GUATEMALA

⊕ Capital of Viceroyalty
☆ Capital of Captaincy General

N
E
S
W

0   400   800   1200   1600 Miles

0   400   800   1200   1600 Kilometers

of the administrative infrastructure. Prior to the arrival of Bustamante in 1811, Spain had had three hundred years of experience governing Central America, a heritage that left both positive and negative imprints on the colony. On the one hand, the legitimacy of the Spanish crown to govern was deeply rooted among all segments of the population, and its institutions were both recognized and familiar. On the other hand, years of stagnation and isolation helped breed a climate of mistrust and corruption among relatively autonomous imperial officials, a situation that often complicated relations between the bureaucracy and the local population, as well as among the bureaucrats themselves, and that the crown attempted to rectify with its political reforms of the 1780s. What follows is an outline of the Spanish administrative infrastructure in Central America on the eve of the arrival of Bustamante—the machinery of government with which he, for better or worse, attempted to preserve the colony for Ferdinand VII.

At the close of the Spanish period, the colonial administrative unit known variously as the Kingdom, the Audiencia, or the Captaincy General of Guatemala stretched from the western border of the modern Mexican state of Chiapas to the frontier between Costa Rica and Panama. With its capital located at Guatemala City, the kingdom was divided into fifteen provinces: the *intendencias* of Ciudad Real (Chiapas), Comayagua (Honduras), León (Nicaragua), and San Salvador (El Salvador); the *alcaldías mayores* of Totonicapán, Sololá, Sacatepéquez, Chimaltenango, Verapaz, Sonsonate, Escuintla, and Suchitepéquez; the *corregimientos* of Quetzaltenango and Chiquimula; and the *gobernación* of Costa Rica. Each province had its own administrative official who, like the captain general, was appointed by the crown. The provinces were in turn subdivided into smaller jurisdictions known as *partidos* or *subdelegaciones,* each with its own junior administrator chosen by the captain general. At the base of the Spanish administrative pyramid were the local magistrates (*jueces*) and the ayuntamientos, the town councils for both the *república de indios* and the *república de españoles* that were dominated by local elites.[5]

As a consequence of Bourbon efforts to improve the administration of the Spanish American empire, the Kingdom of Guatemala witnessed some significant political reforms between 1780 and 1810. The drive toward "centralization of power and modernization of government institutions" that characterized late eighteenth-century Spain in particular had an impact on political boundaries and their respective colonial offices.[6] As in all parts of the empire, imperial officials in Guatemala, from the captain general and the *oidores* (judges) of the audiencia down to the *alcaldes mayores* and *corregidores*, were entrusted, with varying degrees of autonomy, with authority over four areas of administration: *gobierno*, which concerned general supervision of political affairs, church issues, internal security, and commerce; *justicia*, or civil and criminal law; *hacienda*, which concerned taxes, rents, and remittances to the royal treasury; and *guerra*, which covered defense and military matters.[7] Whereas Habsburg practice had been characterized by bureaucratic decentralization and the fusion and confusion of authority over these duties among officials and institutions, the goal of the Bourbon crown was to make Spanish imperial administration more rational, with direct lines of communication between overseas officials and Spain and a clearer delineation of powers within the American bureaucracy. The consequences of this policy for Central America at the close of the colonial period were significant.

The Kingdom of Guatemala was technically part of the larger viceroyalty of New Spain, though distance from Mexico City, poor communications, and a tradition of direct contact with Spain helped keep the region effectively autonomous throughout the colonial period. The chief imperial official in the kingdom was the captain general, whose powers were augmented by his role as governor of the colony, president of the audiencia, and *superintendente subdelegado de la Real Hacienda*. As C. H. Haring states, the captain general "exercised supreme authority within his jurisdiction as the direct representative of the sovereign," though the wide-ranging powers of an eighteenth-century governor took many decades to develop.[8]

In the sixteenth century this official was known primarily as the governor general or president-governor (*presidente gobernador*). In his role as governor, he exercised civil and political power and could "issue ordinances of local application, subject to ultimate royal approval."[9] He had the power to appoint most of the second tier of the colonial bureaucracy, and he held the local *patronato* with respect to church administration. His status in the colony was augmented by his position as president of the audiencia, which allowed for the supervision of the leading legislative and judicial institution in Guatemala, the only significant rival to the authority of the governor. Appointment to the specific position of captain general, which was not standard policy before 1609, made this official the chief military figure in the colony as well, with command over the standing army and militias.[10] It is testimony to the growing emphasis on the military role of the colonial governors over the course of the eighteenth century that the latter title came to define the office above all others. Finally, in the eighteenth century, the creation of the office of *superintendente subdelegado de la Real Hacienda* gave the captain general/governor greater control over the royal revenue. He was assisted in his duties by a number of personal advisors, secretaries (*escribanos*), legal counsels (*asesores*), and other crown bureaucrats. For his services, the governor was paid a salary of ten thousand pesos per year.[11]

Despite these extensive powers, the governor or captain general also faced considerable limitations on his authority. The crown appointed the highest officials in the colonial bureaucracy, including the intendants, alcaldes mayores, and corregidores, after receiving nominations from the governor. These bureaucrats assiduously protected their positions and could appeal unfavorable rulings by their superiors directly to the Council of the Indies. In addition, in the administration of the kingdom the captain general was bound by centuries of legal precedent, "the voluminous legislation of a paternalistic monarchy" that reserved the right to direct colonial affairs from Spain. The most significant challenge to the authority of the governor, however, was found in Guatemala City itself, where the audiencia sat.[12]

Of the four areas of imperial administration, the audiencia served primarily as an instrument of *justicia*, though its authority was felt across the length and breadth of colonial life.[13] As a court, it served as the highest appeals tribunal in the colony, hearing civil and criminal cases from the provincial or local *jueces de primera instancia*, the alcaldes mayores, corregidores, and the *alcaldes ordinarios*, as well as cases from the corporate judicial system that involved, for example, the trade and merchant guilds (*consulados*). The audiencia was the court of first instance for criminal cases that occurred in and around Guatemala City, and it also took precedence in cases concerning the imperial bureaucracy or treasury. While the captain general served as president of the tribunal, he held no vote in cases involving *justicia*.

The most important executive role of the audiencia came in the context of the *real acuerdo,* a regular meeting of the court and president during which issues concerning the political and economic state of the kingdom were deliberated.[14] Here the members of the audiencia served as a consultative council to the governor and had the opportunity to affect state policy and administration through the issuance of *bandos* (ordinances) of local application, subject, as always, to final approval from Spain. Interpretation and enforcement of the innumerable decrees and laws coming from Madrid was another fundamental duty of the audiencia. And, in addition to their work on the tribunal, individual oidores could also be found serving on other administrative *juntas* (committees), such as that of the *Real Hacienda.*[15] Finally, during the period following the death of a governor or in his absence, the audiencia served as the supreme executive, thereby underscoring its place at the heart of the imperial bureaucracy.

The audiencia of Guatemala in 1810 had space for five oidores, one of whom served as *regente* (regent) and presided over the tribunal in the absence of the president. Because of deaths, transfers, and inevitable delays in nomination, the tribunal often was not at full strength. In addition to the judges, the audiencia employed two *fiscales* (crown attorneys), one for civil cases and the other for criminal, and a number of professional lawyers, secretaries, and clerks. A seat on the audiencia was one of the most highly prized positions in the Spanish bureaucracy, for the judges were appointed by the crown and had no fixed term of office. Salaries ranged from sixty-six hundred pesos for the regent to thirty-three hundred for an oidor.[16] While both creoles and peninsulars were eligible for this high office, by the end of the colonial period the crown had come to rely almost exclusively on peninsular appointments.

In 1802 Captain General Antonio González Saravia complained to Spain that "there was a faction completely opposed to the government, because it wanted to assume power, make all official decisions, and achieve in this manner its goals."[17] This opposition group apparently included some members of the audiencia who disagreed with the commercial policies promoted by the governor. In fact, competition and conflicts over power and privilege regularly strained relations between audiencias and governors over the course of the colonial period, resulting in an environment in which "a recalcitrant or hostile audiencia might make an infinite amount of trouble for its presiding officer, and at times effectively clog the wheels of royal government."[18] These rivalries tended to be compounded as a result of the tendency of the Bourbon crown to choose its overseas governors from the ranks of the military, thereby almost ensuring a cultural clash between the officers and oidores. And, by 1810, the imperial crisis allowed the captain general to expand his authority vis-à-vis the other colonial officials in Guatemala, though not without engendering some degree of resentment on the part of the bureaucracy.[19]

At the provincial level, the arrival in Central America of the intendancy system in the mid-1780s was the most dramatic example of the political centralization policies of the Bourbon crown. These reforms carved out four semiautonomous provincial units in the kingdom, each of which was to be administered by an intendant, appointed by Spain, with far-reaching financial, judicial, and military powers. Designed to stimulate local economies, streamline imperial bureaucracy, and bring to an end the local corruption endemic to the system of corregidores and alcaldes mayores, intendancy reform had an impact on the region best described as equivocal. Provincial self-awareness increased with the political reform. Local economies, however, showed few sustained signs of rejuvenation, and intendants often did little to distinguish themselves from their predecessors.

Like the governor of the kingdom, an intendant was the supreme authority in his district.[20] The intendants had power over provincial taxation, tribute, and the treasury and administered the king's rents. In judicial matters they served as appellate judges for civil and criminal cases adjudicated in the first instance by the local alcaldes ordinarios. They also controlled the provincial militias. Entrusted with carrying out laws and decrees made in Madrid and Guatemala City, these officials also had the right to appeal decisions directly to the king. On a daily basis, their primary responsibilities were geared toward promoting "progress" in the Enlightenment sense. This meant preserving order, stimulating commerce, industry, and education, increasing royal revenue, improving transportation infrastructure, and ridding local government institutions, that is, the ayuntamientos, of their Habsburg-induced stagnation. In these matters, intendants found assistance from *tenientes letrados,* officials specializing in judicial concerns, and *subdelegados,* subordinates who were put in charge of specific subdivisions of the intendancy known as *partidos*. As with oidores, intendants could be either creole or peninsular, though the trend was clearly in favor of Spanish-born officials. As with governors, the crown tended to appoint military men to these posts.[21]

Despite the intendancy reforms, corregimientos and alcaldías mayores still existed in the kingdom, particularly in Guatemala itself, which was not made into an intendancy because it was the seat of the colonial government. Serving "at the economic, social, and political intersection of Spanish and Indian Central America," the officials of these jurisdictions, which tended to be much smaller in size though not necessarily in population than the intendancies, administered justice (primarily as a court of second instance for cases appealed from municipal judges); presided over municipal councils; enforced superior decrees; managed tribute collection, local commerce, and labor policies; and coordinated provincial security issues.[22] Like the intendants, these provincial officials were subordinate only to the governor and audiencia in the kingdom.

Unlike the other provinces, Costa Rica was not administered by an intendant, an alcalde mayor, or a corregidor. Technically under the jurisdiction of the intendancy of Nicaragua, it retained some autonomy as a gobernación, a status all parts of the colony held during the sixteenth century but that survived only in Costa Rica by 1810. As such, the sparsely populated, frontier province had its own gobernador, whose powers approximated those of the officials mentioned above, but whose military duties predominated.[23]

With respect to the preservation of Spanish rule in Central America, the importance of these officials cannot be overstated. It was through these intendants, alcaldes mayores, corregidores, and governors that the captain general in Guatemala City in fact administered the kingdom. Given the geography of Central America, transportation and communication within the colony at the close of the colonial period were extremely time consuming, thereby ensuring that most decisions in the countryside were made without prior review from the imperial officials in the capital. In addition, a provincial official could make use of his relative isolation to block or delay decrees from his immediate superiors, whether for personal gain or in the interests of his region. Nevertheless, for the most part—and particularly with respect to matters of security and defense—they tended to reflect and enforce the will of the captain general and king without resistance. Captain General Bustamante was forced to rely heavily on these officials for information about the colony. He depended on their ability to maintain the tranquility of their jurisdictions, to notify him promptly in case of threats to the public welfare, and to carry out his orders on a wide range of matters. Not surprisingly, his success or failure as governor was closely tied to the smooth functioning of the Spanish bureaucracy in general and to these provincial officials in particular.

By 1810, although a serious effort had been made over the past thirty years to revitalize colonial bureaucracy from the provincial level on up, what was perhaps the most overt change during this time had appeared within the bounds of municipal government. As the only significant political institution dominated by Americans, ayuntamientos or *cabildos* rode the wave of economic expansion and creole self-awareness that characterized the late eighteenth century toward a position at the center of colonial affairs that was scarcely imaginable fifty years earlier. Among the fifteen *ayuntamientos de españoles* that existed in the Kingdom of Guatemala at the turn of the century, a growing interest in self-governance and a willingness to challenge the imperial system began to emerge. Spurred by the monarchical crisis of 1808, many, in fact, attempted to expand their powers by arguing that they were the true representatives of the people, a position that infuriated crown representatives such as Bustamante.

Ayuntamientos were made up of *regidores* (councilmen) and *alcaldes ordinarios* (magistrates), plus a number of lesser officers such as *síndico* (counsel), *alguacil mayor* (constable), *alférez mayor* (royal standard-bearer), *fiel ejecutor* (inspector of weights and measures), and *escribano* (notary).[24] The size of the council depended upon the size of the municipality; all had two alcaldes, though tiny San Pedro Sula operated with two regidores while Guatemala City had twelve.[25] Most councilmen purchased their seats or inherited them, though when necessary the council could appoint a regidor on a temporary basis. This practice tended to leave council seats in the hands of the local creole elite, primarily indigo merchants and *hacendados,* who monopolized municipal government to serve their own interests.[26]

Such tenacity is understandable considering the powers of the institution. At the local level, the influence of the ayuntamiento was profound, encompassing both the urban area under its jurisdiction and the surrounding villages and countryside. It was responsible for land and labor distribution, tribute, building permits, commercial supervision, infrastructure maintenance, and roads; it provided for a police force and jail and could raise militias; it oversaw medical and educational facilities and regulated merchants; it held authority over civic festivals; and, in order to pay for these services, it had the power to tax, though most municipal revenue came from rents, fines, duties, and the sale of offices and licenses.[27] Finally, alcaldes ordinarios, who were elected by the regidores to one-year terms, were magistrates with original jurisdiction over civil and criminal cases. Long underrepresented in colonial administration, the creoles, therefore, used their predominant position on the ayuntamientos to exercise political power in the kingdom.

By the time of Bustamante's arrival in Central America, the ayuntamiento of Guatemala City had become much more than a municipal corporation whose duties were limited to city services and local justice. It now assumed for itself the role of spokesman and representative of all Guatemalans, as well as mentor and advisor to the provincial town councils. If the captain general had his network of bureaucrats throughout the kingdom relaying information back to the capital about the state of the provinces, the Guatemala City ayuntamiento was equally well informed about local conditions, keeping up a wide network of correspondence with the regional municipalities. When the relationship between the colonies and Spain was rewritten after 1810, this ayuntamiento lost no time in improving its position at the expense of the colonial bureaucracy.

Not to be ignored in a summary of colonial bureaucratic institutions in the Spanish empire is the Catholic Church. Four bishoprics served the needs of the kingdom at this time: the archdiocese at Guatemala City, which encompassed 424 parish churches and served some 500,000 faithful, and the bishoprics of León (88 parishes), Ciudad Real (102 parishes), and Comayagua (145 parishes), which together served the rest of the colony.[28] In many respects, the huge bureaucracies administered by the Church, with its vast network of religious scattered throughout Central America, were more fundamental than the colonial state and its officers in preserving the integrity of the kingdom. As Miles Wortman noted,

"While the secular authorities created the framework, the church integrated and unified the colony through religion and its vast fiscal power. It insured the loyalty of the colony to the empire through proselytizing hispanic-catholicism. Where the state lacked soldiers to stem uprisings, the church was present."[29]

Although the Bourbon crown, concerned about this potential threat to the authority of the state, had great success during the last decades of the eighteenth century in attacking the resources of the Church and thereby increasingly limiting its role in society to spiritual matters, in 1810 the Guatemalan Church remained a fundamental institution of colonial life. There were invariably more clerics in the kingdom than state officials, they tended to have greater reach than the colonial bureaucracy, which as a rule remained in hispanicized urban environments, and, as parish priests in indigenous towns, they came to wield great influence, often by administering community and *cofradía* funds and serving as influential conservative advocates for tradition and restraint. In addition, traditional church control over education, health, charity, and welfare matters had not been completely eroded by the ecclesiastic reforms of the crown, to the frustration of municipal authorities.[30] As Captain General Bustamante quickly discovered, control over the Church and its bureaucracy was a great asset in the hands of imperial officials charged with maintaining the tranquility of the colony. In Archbishop Ramón Casaus y Torres, who also arrived in Guatemala in 1811, Bustamante found an ally who proved more than willing to put the resources of the church into the hands of the state.

Apart from the church and the state, Bustamante was expected to rely upon the kingdom's military defenses as a major instrument of imperial control. As seen in chapter one, the administrative reforms of the Bourbon crown found a productive outlet in the military, where great efforts were made to bring the Spanish armed forces up to par with those of the other European powers in an effort to defend Spain's valuable colonies. While all parts of the empire experienced some military reform in the eighteenth century, the Kingdom of Guatemala did not witness the same degree of militarization as that experienced by other colonies.[31] At the end of the Spanish period, the kingdom was defended by a small line of Caribbean forts running from Petén Itzá and San Felipe del Golfo Dulce in Guatemala, to San Fernando de Omoa, Trujillo, and the Inmaculada Concepción at the mouth of the Río Tinto in Honduras, to the fort at the mouth of the Río San Juan in Nicaragua, plus minor fortifications on offshore islands. Poorly manned and in a constant state of disrepair, these defenses were little more than symbols of Spanish sovereignty in a region whose climate and endemic diseases proved to be a sufficient disincentive to foreign invasion or settlement. Following the Treaty of San Ildefonso (1796) with France, which resulted in the eruption of hostilities between Spain and England, the crown ordered the *subinspector de tropas* in Guatemala, Roque Abarca, to see to the organization of a *regimiento fijo de infantería* for the fortifications along the Mosquito Coast. By 1802, scarcely a battalion of regular soldiers was ready to join the small numbers of artillery units stationed there. After this point the crown looked to companies of newly settled black troops to guard the Caribbean coast.[32]

In the interior, the colonial government relied first upon a few hundred Spanish regulars, organized in companies of artillery, cavalry, and infantry, who were scattered among the larger settlements, including Guatemala City, León, San Salvador, and Granada.[33] With very few professional Spanish soldiers to go around, the crown had agreed in the late eighteenth century to the creation of battalions of *Milicias disciplinadas* as a supplemental force. Provided with the military *fuero* (legal privileges) as an inducement to join, many native Guatemalans, both creole and mestizo, became officers and soldiers in these units. Each battalion had space for some 767 men, but few managed to operate at full strength. Nevertheless, at the time of the arrival of Bustamante the number of active militia regiments in the kingdom was impressive: two operated in San Salvador, while Comayagua, Tegucigalpa, León, Nueva Segovia, Quetzaltenango, Cartago, and Guatemala City each had one. Full regiments were stationed at Santa Ana, Granada, and Chiquimula, and the smaller towns of Olancho, Yoro, Verapaz, Ciudad Real, Nicoya, San Pedro Sula, Trujillo, and El Realejo each had a varying number of militia companies at hand. While it is impossible to ascertain the exact number of troops operating in the Kingdom of Guatemala in 1810, considering the deployments listed above it is safe to estimate that Bustamante had at least ten thousand men at his disposal during his tenure in office.[34]

As has been noted, the Kingdom of Guatemala was one of the most populous colonies in Spanish America by 1810. With respect to the cultural and racial makeup of its population, it was also one of the most complex. Of the 1.2 million people living in Central America at this time, approximately one-half could be found in Guatemala itself. The province of San Salvador held some 250,000 inhabitants, while 186,000 lived in Nicaragua, 135,000 in Honduras, 100,000 in Chiapas, and 63,000 in Costa Rica. Guatemala City was the largest urban center with some 25,000 inhabitants, followed by San Salvador at 12,000 and Quetzaltenango at 11,000. The other major cities, Granada, León, Comayagua, Ciudad Real, and Cartago, did not exceed 9000.[35] The majority of Central Americans, some sixty-five percent of the kingdomwide population, were native Americans. Most of the indigenous communities, however, were concentrated in the highlands of Chiapas, Guatemala, and El Salvador. *Ladinos* (the local term for hispanicized Indians and mestizos) made up approximately thirty-one percent of the total population and were the majority in the provinces of San Salvador, Honduras, Nicaragua, and Costa Rica. Creoles, those Americans of direct Spanish descent, and a few immigrant *peninsulares* made up most of the remaining four percent of the inhabitants, with small communities of Africans along the Caribbean coast rounding out the colonial population.[36]

Although a distinct minority in the kingdom, creoles and peninsulars monopolized social, economic, and political power, creating a tight-knit oligarchy based on kinship and common interests that survived mostly intact through the end of the colonial period. By 1800, however, fault lines had begun to develop within the elite over a number of issues, a conflict only made worse during the 1808–1814 captivity of the king when political representation in the empire became a primary topic of debate. Peninsular Spaniards traditionally occupied the highest offices of church and state in the colony, while American Spaniards found positions in the second-tier bureaucracy and at the municipal level. Creoles were the leading merchants and landowners, however, as well as the greatest beneficiaries of the economic expansion of the late eighteenth century. Efforts to translate this economic strength into some degree of autonomous political power invariably caused tension among the elites and created a growing sentiment within creole circles that "scheming and calculating royal officials [were] threatening their economic and political positions with bothersome and misguided laws."[37] Of course, peninsular officials responded to this position in a standard way—by emphasizing the weight of numbers. As Bustamante explained in 1812, of the 740 posts in the colonial bureaucracy, 700 were controlled by the creole elite.[38]

The aristocratic character of the Guatemalan elite was confirmed in 1780 when the most powerful merchant in the kingdom, Juan Fermín de Aycinena, purchased the title of marquis, thereby becoming the only titled nobleman in Central America.[39] A peninsular by birth, Aycinena married well upon his arrival in what is now Antigua Guatemala and proceeded to use his business savvy and family connections to build an enormous commercial empire that stretched the length and breadth of the kingdom. This unchallenged financial position allowed Aycinena access to the imperial hierarchy undreamed of by earlier generations of elites, and the inroads he made became the foundation for later creole challenges to the Spanish system. He befriended governors and used his wealth to cultivate ties with lower levels of the imperial bureaucracy, providing loans and securities to a number of provincial officials in return for advantageous access to local markets and commodities. In addition, Aycinena worked to solidify the position of his family in the kingdom through marriage with the colonial elite. The success of this marital policy expressed itself most strikingly in *cabildo* records. Between 1770 and 1821 five intermarried families dominated the ayuntamiento of Guatemala City: Aycinena, Asturias, Batres, Barrutia, and Pavón. By the end of the colonial period, other names such as Arrivillaga, Nájera, Coronado, Gálvez, Montúfar, Palomo, and Manrique would be included among the network of interrelated elites known collectively and derisively as the Family.[40] Monopolizing the local offices of church and state around Guatemala City, not to mention the various commercial corporations and guilds, the Aycinena-led Family became a formidable force in colonial life, as well as a potential threat to the peninsular hierarchy and older provincial elites through its growing political power and control over much of the kingdom's resources.

A significant characteristic of the Central American creole elite at this time was its enthusiastic reception of Enlightenment culture and thought, an ideological (and generational) shift that began to take place during the 1790s. As the only institution of higher learning in the colony, the University of San Carlos in Guatemala City helped to propel this movement. Progressive faculty such as Fr. José Antonio Liendo y Goicoechea, Dr. José Felipe Flores, Dr. Narciso Esparragosa y Gallardo, Dr. Antonio Carbonel, and Dr. Matías de Córdova taught the latest in science, philosophy, economics, and law to the kingdom's best and brightest.[41] In 1794 the *Sociedad Económica de Amigos del País* was established to promote the practical application of the Enlightenment creed of "reason and progress" in the economy, government, commerce, transportation, education, and the arts. By 1800, the Guatemalan *Sociedad* was one of the more active in the Spanish world, with 149 members spread throughout the kingdom.[42]

Through the University of San Carlos, the *Sociedad Económica*, and publications such as the *Gaceta de Guatemala,* which helped the colony stay up to date on the latest European trends and fashions, the creole elite became fluent in the language of the times and fervent advocates of reform. After the fall of the monarchy in 1808, however, imperial officials were compelled to restrict intellectual and political freedoms "in the name of patriotism and security."[43] Such measures, of course, only served to complicate relations between the creole elites and their peninsular overlords, for in many cases during the imperial crisis the enduring Enlightenment mentality among creoles expressed itself as support for free trade, political autonomy, equality for Americans within the empire, and the Constitution of 1812.

The presence of such sentiments among the creole elite, however, did not alter the intrinsically conservative nature of the colonial oligarchy, for reform was most often self-servingly promoted by the Aycinena Family as a way to come out ahead in its long-running competition with the imperial hierarchy over power and privilege. The Aycinenas did not speak for those peninsular and creole merchants who operated outside the sphere of influence of the Family, who dominated the Consulado de Comercio (the merchant guild), and who gave great support to the besieged crown. Nor were the provincial elites, who deeply resented the stranglehold on commerce maintained by capital merchants, always represented by the powerful voices on the Guatemala City ayuntamiento. Instead of a monolith, the colonial oligarchy was an upper class comprising a wide range of interest groups: the imperial bureaucracy, the Church, the Guatemala City aristocracy, non-Family peninsular and creole elites in the capital, and the provincial elites. Even these groups were often divided against themselves when generational or regional attitudes are taken into consideration. Over the course of the independence period, the perspectives, ideologies, and alliances of these elite segments regularly shifted, though one sentiment kept them united until 1821: a common desire to preserve their status in relation to the ladino and indigenous majorities.[44]

As R. L. Woodward has noted, the "most significant change in the eighteenth century was the growth and emergence of the ladino sector."[45] By 1810 this large segment of Central American society began to make itself felt in direct proportion to its numbers, primarily as an incipient urban middle class, though lack of class consciousness was one major obstacle to such a designation. In the larger cities and towns across the kingdom, ladinos were the majority of inhabitants. Some were upwardly mobile professionals and merchants, educated and acculturated according to the terms set by the creole elite. Many others made a living as tradesmen and skilled laborers, or they subsisted as the mass of unskilled, undereducated, and urban poor, which concerned the upper classes because of its size and potentially violent subculture. In the countryside, ladinos could be found as indigo producers, commercial farmers, farmhands, and subsistence farmers. Over the course of the late colonial period, the Spanish bureaucracy was inclined to support and develop ladino society, thereby creating a large and economically viable middle sector in the hope that it would serve as a bulwark of support for Spain and an ally against the pretensions of the creole aristocracy.[46] Although most of the explicit independence sentiment in the colony came from ladino professionals, who often mobilized the urban "rabble" to pressure the colonial government, the repeated failure of these plots underscores the fact that the vast majority of the ladino population in the Kingdom of Guatemala remained loyal to Spain up to 1821.

Indigenous Central America in 1810 was a self-contained, fragmented, rural culture.[47] Concentrated in the western part of the kingdom, these descendants of the Maya had little contact with the hispanicized colony, except as a source of tribute, a producer of food, and a provider of labor. Drawing on memories of the 1780–1783 Tupac Amaru revolution in Peru, slave revolts in Haiti, and the more recent race wars in Mexico, most elites viewed the Indian population as a potentially destabilizing and destructive element should the kingdom be convulsed by a civil war over the legitimacy of Spanish rule. Despite this concern, the indigenous communities in Central America remained at peace during the entire Bustamante administration.

Apart from the general social makeup of the colony and its political administration, the third major factor that affected the efforts of Bustamante beginning in 1811 to preserve the Kingdom of Guatemala for Spain was the shape of its economy. The development of a viable export commodity for the first time in the history of the colony precipitated dramatic economic transformations over the course of the eighteenth century. Between 1765 and 1795, Guatemala was the world's leading producer of indigo, a development that helped shift commercial networks from traditional Pacific routes to the Caribbean, accelerated the region's move toward capitalism and a free labor market, built the foundations for Guatemala City merchant hegemony over provincial producers, and fostered political centralization as a means to improve the collection of commercial taxes.[48] After 1795, competition from other parts of the Spanish empire (most notably Venezuela) and certain British possessions, a decline in the quality of indigo produced in Central America, a series of terrible locust plagues between 1802 and 1805, and the commercial disruption caused by the wars of the French Revolution resulted in a rapid collapse of the indigo-led prosperity. Thus, when the Spanish monarchy fell in 1808, the imperial officers in Guatemala found themselves confronted by a political crisis that only complicated the existing economic one. While both reflected poorly on Spanish administration, economic concerns appear to have caused the majority of the disturbances in the region during the independence period and, ultimately, hindered the colonial government in its response to unrest.[49]

Of course, the majority of the population in the colony did not materially benefit from the indigo boom. Most were peasants and subsistence farmers and remained well outside the orbit of the Atlantic commercial market. The wealth that was produced flowed primarily to the small network of merchants in the capital, among which the House of Aycinena was the largest. With their strategic location at the heart of the colony, their control over its commercial hub, and their monopoly over sources of capital, the Guatemalan merchants were able to set prices for a wide assortment of products, including Salvadoran indigo, Honduran silver, and Nicaraguan livestock. To defend their position, individual producers of the dyestuff established in 1782 an Indigo Growers Society, while all segments of provincial society appealed to the crown for protection from the Guatemalan middlemen.[50] Little, in fact, was forthcoming, with the position of the merchants only improving after the 1793 establishment of the Consulado de Comercio.[51] Part of a long Spanish tradition of monopoly with respect to commerce, the Consulado was a natural development for Central American merchants who wanted increased commercial autonomy in an age of trade liberalization. Officially, its role was to "administer mercantile justice, supervise commercial activity, and aid in developing the colonial economy."[52] While the crown hoped that it would promote general prosperity, the tribunal became yet another instrument of control for the Guatemalan oligarchy, exerting a great deal of influence over official commercial policy across the kingdom.

Initially, the Consulado served as a bastion of power for the Aycinena Family, though by 1810 this elite faction had shifted the bulk of its attention to the Guatemala City ayuntamiento. By this time, the corporation was dominated by "peninsulars and creoles whose economic interests were closely aligned with the Cádiz merchant houses," in other words, the traditionalists who would become important opponents of the economic liberalization and free trade policies promoted by the Family.[53] Along with small-scale manufacturers and artisans, the Consulado came to form part of an anti-contraband, anti-Aycinena alliance that Bustamante attempted to cultivate and that tended to exacerbate the divisions between peninsular and creole elites.

Neither the Consulado nor its more progressive counterpart, the *Sociedad Económica,* which was dissolved by order of the crown between 1800 and 1810, managed to find a solution to the economic challenges that confronted the Kingdom of Guatemala after 1797 and that lasted until independence in 1821. Between 1790 and 1797 the kingdom experienced its highest trade levels ever, with indigo production remaining the centerpiece of the colonial economy. The outbreak of war with Great Britain in 1798, however, led to the blockade of Spanish harbors and an immediate collapse in the indigo market. At the same time, a series of poor harvests and locust infestations contributed to a decline in the Nicaraguan and Honduran cattle industry, as well as in Nicaraguan cacao production. After a short eighteenth-century revival, Honduran silver mining was again in full recession. As a consequence of war short-ages, local textile producers were hit hard by dramatic increases in con-traband trade, an activity that the Family hoped to monopolize and that Captain General González did little to discourage.[54]

Spain itself proved to be an obstacle to economic recovery in Central America. Between 1804 and 1808, the kingdom was forced to send more than one million pesos to the cash-starved Spanish crown as part of the *Consolidación de vales reales*. Taxes increased to pay for war expendi-tures. And, from 1808 to 1810, the depressed but loyal colony sent another million pesos to Spain in the form of *donativos* (donations) to help sup-port the loyalist government in its fight against the French.[55]

The decade-long free fall from economic prosperity to severe depres-sion took a heavy toll on the imperial bureaucracy. By the early 1800s the kingdom could no longer support itself, with expenses outpacing in-come by over fifty percent per year.[56] The colonial administration de-pended on four primary sources for its revenue: the state's share of the church tithe; returns on the government monopolies over tobacco and spirits (*aguardiente*); Indian tribute; and taxes on commerce (*alcabala*) and trade (*almojarifazgo*).[57] Income from the latter source predominated during the boom years but became less and less reliable after 1800. In-come from the tithe was never significant. And, in 1810, the Junta Cen-tral abolished the tribute. After 1812, in fact, profits from the tobacco monopoly became "the foundation of the fiscal system," accounting for more than fifty percent of state revenue between 1815 and 1819.[58] Unfor-tunately, this did not prove to be a sufficient resource for an increasingly empty treasury. Thus, upon taking office in 1811 as governor and captain general of the Kingdom of Guatemala, José de Bustamante was forced to meet real and perceived challenges to the sovereignty of Spain with very few financial means at his disposal, with a divided and disgruntled elite, and without the security of a unified command.

3

The Imperial Crisis and Colonial Defense, 1798–1811

After two and a half centuries of relative isolation, the Kingdom of Guatemala spent the second half of the eighteenth century transforming itself into a model colony of the newly energized Spanish empire. Within a generation of the start of the indigo boom in the 1760s, Central America had a viable commercial link to the Atlantic economy that brought wealth to the colonial elite and expectations for more significant economic development. On the political level, Guatemala found itself governed by a reformist monarchy that seemed intent on institutionalizing the latest in administrative philosophy. Culturally, the isthmian elite now had access to the great body of Enlightenment science, technology, and literature produced during the century and began to put it to practical use. Even a catastrophic series of earthquakes that hit the region in 1773 and destroyed the great capital city of Santiago de Guatemala (now Antigua Guatemala) appeared to many not as an obstacle to progress but rather as an opportunity to build a modern capital that might symbolize the dawning of a new age.

Though profound, such rapid transitions did not appear to destabilize the well-entrenched Central American society. Peninsular and creole elites continued their domination of local political, economic, and social institutions, at times competing with but most often sustaining each other. No self-conscious urban middle class existed to challenge this symbiotic relationship, and rural groups, both Indian and ladino, remained particularly insulated from the new ideas of the time. Thus, the Kingdom of Guatemala approached the last decade of the eighteenth century more prosperous and tranquil than at any time in its history.

Nevertheless, neither this recent experience with precipitous economic and political change nor the underlying stability of Central American society prepared the colony for the first decade of the nineteenth century. This period began with the collapse of the indigo market, thereby threatening the region's economic stability, and ended with the collapse of the Spanish monarchy, resulting in a more serious challenge to Guatemala's political order. In very short order, the kingdom was forced into a prolonged state of emergency that would severely tax the resources, infrastructure, and imagination of the imperial bureaucracy charged with its administration.

The crisis that hit the Kingdom of Guatemala at the turn of the century resulted in large part from the dislocations that developed in the Western world as a consequence of the wars of the French Revolution. This epic struggle pitted a society that had rejected the institutions and values of the Old Regime against the defenders of the established order, including Spain. Instead of the much more familiar wars over commerce, colonial hegemony, dynastic issues, or religion, the Atlantic world for the first time faced a predominantly ideological conflict.

More than most inhabitants of the Atlantic world during the wars of the French Revolution, the subjects of the Spanish monarchy had strong reasons to fear the goals and designs of revolutionary and imperial France. Defeated almost immediately after entering the war against the French Republic in 1793, Spain spent the next twenty-five years struggling to overcome the devastating consequences. First, a ruinous alliance with its former enemy resulted in a crippling British blockade of Spanish ports that cut communications and trade between Madrid and its American possessions for more than four years. To pay the war reparations demanded by France, Spain then risked the ire of its American subjects by initiating in 1802 the massive confiscation of church wealth known as the *Consolidación de vales reales*. One year later, Charles IV returned the colony of Louisiana to France. And in 1805 the Spanish navy was annihilated while fighting alongside the French at the Battle of Trafalgar. Unfortunately, this decade of repeated disasters and failed leadership was only a prelude to the events of 1808 when Napoleon decided to overthrow the Spanish Bourbons. As the Spanish population rose up against the French occupation in a brutal six-year war of liberation, the political bonds that held together the Spanish empire began to unravel. By the 1810s the political, social, and economic crises that had reverberated across Spain and its American possessions over the previous two decades brought the Spanish empire to the verge of extinction.

Considering the fate of Spain as both an enemy and ally of France, anti-French sentiment was an early, ubiquitous, and enduring development in the Hispanic world during this period. As with twentieth-century communism, many believed the revolutionary French capable of spreading anarchy, rebellion, and atheism like a disease among otherwise healthy, contented populations. In the uncertain environment created by the imperial crisis, Spanish colonial officials were forced to confront the distinct possibility of revolutionary activity emerging on their side of the Atlantic among French expatriates and those Spanish subjects who were considered *afrancesados* (Francophiles).

This anti-French sentiment, in particular, had a significant impact on the Kingdom of Guatemala, where it often bordered on hysteria. Within the colonial bureaucracy, Francophobia played an important role in the development of a counterinsurgency policy for the kingdom in the absence of an active insurgency, for it was assumed that Central America would at some point be a target of subversives. In fact, the notorious passivity of Central America during the Latin American wars of independence can be linked in part to the decision of its governors to confront with force the perceived threat to the kingdom after 1808 from French and *afrancesado* provocateurs, agents, and spies. The French menace eventually became a convenient way to maintain political and military control over the colony in the midst of the larger Latin American upheavals.

The first suggestion that the Kingdom of Guatemala faced a challenge from French revolutionaries and their allies came on 21 October 1794, when Captain General José Domás y Valle issued a report to the *Junta Superior* of the colony. The governor expressed his concern over news of disturbances in Mexico City that had been traced to "the depraved designs by which some Frenchmen and others addicted to their ideas have intended to incite the inhabitants and natives to rebel-

lion by following the example of France."[1] With positive evidence of
the contamination of New Spain by the revolutionary virus, Domás y
Valle decided to implement preventive measures to quarantine the Kingdom of Guatemala. His primary response was to order a mounted company of the *Regimiento de Dragones Provinciales* to patrol the streets
of Guatemala City. The captain general then created a new ten-man
guard to watch over his residence and the *sala de armas* (armory) in the
capital, "so as to prevent their being surprised" during an uprising.[2]
While these actions were restrained when compared with the counterinsurgency policies imposed by his immediate successors, Domás y
Valle's reaction set an important administrative precedent. For the next
twenty years, the governors of Guatemala recognized "French" influence, whether from foreign agents or *afrancesado* natives, as the most
serious threat to the stability of the kingdom and Mexico as the most
likely conduit for subversives and revolutionary sentiment. At the same
time, the colonial administration turned away from the civil bureaucracy and judiciary in favor of the military as its most powerful weapon
against real and potential unrest.

Domestic concerns—in particular, the impact of the collapse of the
international indigo market on the kingdom's economy—dominated
the colonial administration until the "sad and unfortunate news" of the
events at Bayonne arrived in Guatemala City from Mexico at midday
on 13 August 1808.[3] In a top-secret communique to Captain General
Antonio González Saravia, Viceroy José de Iturrigaray of New Spain en-
closed the latest newspaper reports of the historic meeting between Napoleon and the Spanish Bourbons in which Charles IV and his son
Ferdinand VII renounced the Spanish throne in favor of the French emperor. With the capital in a state of nervous anticipation, González ordered all the leading officials in the colony, both civil and ecclesiastical,
to meet in a *junta general* the following day to discuss the news. Early
the next morning in the royal palace the secretary of the Guatemala
City ayuntamiento read the documents to the assembled audience. Following a brief statement from González the junta examined the material and came to the unanimous conclusion that the acts of abdication
would not be recognized in the Kingdom of Guatemala.[4]

With the news of the collapse of the monarchy also came reports
of the beginning of organized resistance to the French occupation of

Spain. Captain General González, therefore, quickly launched a defensive strategy for Guatemala. The governor ordered the closing of Central American ports to French ships and tightened departure and arrival documentation and registration for all vessels. On 5 September, González published the declaration of war against Napoleon made in June by the Spanish loyalists and confiscated French-owned property in the colony. On the sixteenth, concerned about a decline in his military capacity, he wrote to the ayuntamiento and proposed the enlistment of single men and widowers without children into the *Batallón de milicias* of the capital. Three days later, the first *donativo patriótico* (patriotic donation) was established to allow loyal citizens the opportunity to aid the Spanish resistance.[5] Having received an anonymous denunciation, the Spanish administration also began investigating its first case of subversion, that of a creole accused of inciting Guatemalans to take advantage of the crisis and rise up against their Spanish oppressors.[6]

On the surface, the Central American population appeared fervently loyal to Ferdinand and the imperial bureaucracy in the months after news of the abdications broke. On 17 October, in fact, a huge celebration took place in Guatemala City to coincide with the publicization of the donativo. By the end of the year, the colonial authorities published a proclamation entitled *Guatemala por Fernando VII*, which the ayuntamiento had prepared in recognition of the completion of a monument to the king.[7] This close cooperation between Spanish officials and creoles did not last long, however. Events soon compelled the colonial authorities in Guatemala to increase their sensitivity to issues of patriotism, loyalty, and the threat of foreign subversion, a move that forced them to see their American subjects as potential enemies rather than as allies.

Although the conflict was limited to Iberia, the Spanish War for Independence (more famous in Napoleonic history as the Peninsular War) was as much a challenge to the continued existence of the Spanish empire as it was to the survival of the Spanish nation. In light of the French occupation of Madrid, Spanish loyalists formed provincial governing juntas in the first weeks after the *Dos de Mayo* uprising. These soon coalesced into a Junta Central, based in Seville, which provided the nation a viable level of organized resistance. Though the Junta's authority was accepted with little opposition in Spain, establishing its legitimacy at the

imperial level proved a more elusive achievement. As word of the dissolution of the Bourbon monarchy reached the American colonies, the
right to rule of the crown-appointed administrators there began to be
challenged from a number of directions. In the absence of Ferdinand,
supporters of the Seville Junta competed with advocates of the *rey intruso,* Napoleon's brother Joseph, who reigned as José I. Others promoted the claims of Ferdinand's sister Carlota, who had escaped Europe
with her husband, the prince regent of Portugal, and resided in Río de
Janeiro. Most ominously, some colonials attempted to establish American-
dominated juntas in Mexico City, Upper Peru, Quito, and Buenos Aires.
All these latter efforts failed, but they represented a significant and growing interest in political autonomy on the part of discontented creoles.[8]

No such movement emerged in the Kingdom of Guatemala in 1808,
but the González administration was clearly forewarned. According to
the journalist and poet Simón Beragaño y Villegas, some in the crowd at
an October rally mixed in "death to the *chapetones* (Spaniards)" with
the "*vivas*" to Ferdinand VII. Rumors concerning the replacement of
the captain general raced through the capital, and one regidor of the
Guatemala City ayuntamiento, José María Peinado, was quoted as having stated that the Guatemalans should have elected a junta of their own
following the news from Bayonne.[9] Imperial officials could not ignore
the growing political self-awareness among Central Americans, but it
had not reached the point where such sentiment actually posed a threat
to the colony. For the moment, González remained in control of the
Kingdom of Guatemala, and on 20 January 1809 he confirmed the kingdom's recognition of the Junta Central as the legitimate authority for
the empire during the absence of Ferdinand.[10]

Despite the unqualified signs of support, including the remittance of
more than one million pesos in donations to loyalist forces in Spain over
the course of 1809, which Central Americans provided their captive
king and his lawful representatives, the administration of Antonio González quickly became preoccupied with external and internal subversion.[11] This obsession, described by Louis Bumgartner as the "tricolor
scare," would have a profound influence on the relationship between the
colonial government and its subjects in the difficult years to come.[12]
With Spain nearly overrun by French armies and evidence of colonial
discontent emerging in Mexico and South America, the survival of the

empire was clearly in doubt. And the nature of the reports from imperial officials now arriving in the colony led the authorities in Guatemala
City to expect the worst.

Apprehension that France might have active designs on Spain's overseas empire had been growing in the colonies since Napoleon came to
power, and the events in Bayonne seemed to confirm the worst fears
of loyal Spanish subjects. It appears, however, that Napoleon, himself,
hoped that the change in dynasty in Spain would not alter the relationship between the American colonies and their metropolis.[13] A unified
Spanish monarchy open to French commerce served the interests of the
emperor better than a difficult and costly campaign to bring the colonies under direct French control. While numerous letters from Napoleon
in the spring and summer of 1808 indicate that he was prepared to send
substantial military forces, supplies, and funds to the Americas to prevent the English from conquering the colonies, other records show that
he had already sent more than thirty agents to the region to persuade
locals to accept Joseph Bonaparte as their new king.[14]

By the following year, however, Napoleon had become convinced
that his brother would never be recognized as king of Spain by Spanish
America.[15] This realization forced the emperor to transform his American agenda, for his primary concerns remained expanding French trade
in the region and preventing England from acquiring new colonies there.
Thus, on 12 December 1809, Napoleon declared that France would support the independence of Spain's American colonies. It was the emper-
or's hope that this statement, which came as a shock to the Bonapartist
court in Madrid, would win over creoles and encourage them to seek
French protection as they fought both the English and the Spanish for
their liberty. At the same time, it would secure Joseph Bonaparte's position in Spain, itself, by eliminating the colonial financial support that
Napoleon believed kept the Spanish resistance on the peninsula alive. To
carry out the emperor's orders, the French government once again decided to send agents and provocateurs to the Americas. This time, however, they were instructed to persuade creoles that the abdication of the
Spanish Bourbons made independence a legitimate act, that Napoleon
would support them with troops and military supplies if necessary, and
that France wanted nothing more than their friendship.[16]

These machinations did not go unobserved by the loyalist government in Spain. On 14 April 1809, the Spanish Junta Central published a *Real Orden sobre el modo de proceder contra extranjeros y naturales del país que sean sospechosos de fidelidad* (royal order on the means of proceeding against foreigners and natives whose loyalty is suspect). This decree ordered colonial governors to reinstate a particular ordinance contained in the Laws of the Indies (*ley* 9, *título* 27, *libro* 9) that prohibited dealings with foreigners. The Junta then declared that anyone who was not a supporter of Ferdinand should be sent to Spain and that imperial officials should proceed against them "with all the prudence and activity demanded by measures so important to the tranquility, security, and good-governance of the population."[17] Within ten days of the arrival of the decree in Guatemala City on 21 July, González sent copies to all intendants, alcaldes mayores, corregidores, *comandantes,* judicial magistrates, and church leaders in the kingdom and asked them to notify him immediately of anything that might relate to this "grave and delicate matter."[18]

Even before the *Real Orden* was received in Guatemala, reports of subversive activity had reached the captain general. In May the administration brought charges of treason (*infidencia*) against Agustín Vilches, a Guatemala City barber. According to the trial testimony, Vilches was accused of spreading rumors that the French had conquered Spain, had disbanded the Junta Central, and were about to take over the Americas. Convinced that "within two months Mexico and Guatemala will be French," Vilches then argued that the *chapetones* should be sent home.[19] Because of the barber's reputation as an oracle among the urban lower class, the colonial government was concerned that his "political blasphemes" would prove "harmful to the tranquility of this loyal populace." Accordingly, he was tried and convicted of subversion by the audiencia and sentenced to imprisonment in Spain.[20] Two months later the alcalde mayor of Totonicapán passed along to the governor an appeal from the intendant of Oaxaca for the arrest of a man named Andrés, who was suspected of being "addicted to the French."[21]

While the political opinions of subjects such as Vilches and Andrés might not seem significant enough to mobilize the security apparatus of the Kingdom of Guatemala, the authorities found it difficult to separate these cases from other, more ominous developments. On 18 September the audiencia received a denunciation of the behavior of one of the regidores of the Nicaraguan town of Rivas, José Antonio Bustos, who was accused of acts of disloyalty and pro-French sentiment. According to the report written by Luís de Aguilar, on 30 April 1809, the entire town had turned out in a grand and solemn ceremony to swear an oath to the king. As a regidor, *alférez mayor,* and the man chosen to give the oath, Bustos was one of the principal figures in the celebrations, and a parade of townspeople stopped at his house to escort him to the plaza. Along the way, the happy crowd held aloft a portrait of the king and chanted "Long Live Fernando Septimo, Long Live Our King," but Bustos apparently said nothing. At the end of the ceremony, Bustos scandalized the crowd by returning home alone. The following day a Mass of thanksgiving was scheduled, and Bustos initially declined to participate, relenting only in the face of severe criticism. At the church, he refused a seat next to the *alcalde primero* and left immediately after the conclusion of the service. Later, as a procession passed his residence, Bustos appeared at his door looking very grave, all of which prompted Aguilar to exclaim, "Who, upon observing such scandalous deeds and in the midst of such a critical time as the present when traitors to the Crown have openly declared themselves, would not believe that Bustos is one of them—has he shown signs of being anything else? If the French were to appear suddenly at our doorstep we are convinced that he would immediately go over to them."[22]

Aguilar then proceeded to denounce Bustos as a law-breaking and corrupt *tavernero,* the owner of five taverns who had taken advantage of his political office to subvert laws against the clandestine production and trade in *aguardiente.* Now this self-serving official was bringing scandal down on the town's civil and religious ceremonies, causing Aguilar to exclaim, "These actions, sir! What else can they be but those of a Napoleonist!" In the charged atmosphere of post-Bayonne Central America, Aguilar recognized the inordinate attention colonial officials had placed on loyalty and used the "French scare" to discredit his enemy. Whether or not the claim was made in good faith, others soon found this tactic to be an effective but dangerous political weapon.

In fact, the ayuntamiento of Ciudad Real used similar accusations to justify the forced removal from office of José Mariano Valero, the interim intendant of Chiapas, who was imprisoned and charged with infidencia in the fall of 1809.[23] In its report to the captain general, the municipal corporation made a detailed defense of what was in effect a provincial *golpe de estado*. According to the council, when news of the fall of the monarchy reached Chiapas, Valero "had the nerve to declare that it was all the same whether Juan or Pedro governed, that is, Napoleon or Ferdinand." In the months that followed, Valero did not show any distress at the fate of the king, and the ayuntamiento became convinced that he recognized the Napoleonic usurpation of the Spanish crown. Valero seemed to confirm this by boasting of his fluency in French, teaching it to his children, and claiming French descent. In fact, the councilmen recorded with horror that the intendant admonished those who referred to Napoleon without the respect due a reigning monarch, as if one could be "respectful of the man who stole our king." In debates, he maintained that the emperor was a figure of Biblical significance, and he followed the progress of French conquests across a map of Europe, always contrasting the great size of Napoleon's empire with "the smallness of Spain." As if that were not enough, Valero supposedly declared that Ferdinand would bring back despotism if restored to the throne.

According to the regidores, this behavior brought such "terror and consternation" to the hearts of the people that even a French emissary would be unable to do more damage. When wild celebrations had broken out in Ciudad Real following reports of the Spanish victory at Bailén (22 July 1808), the intendant "managed to interrupt the festivities and cut off the exclamations of loyalty." He then ordered the bust of Ferdinand, which had been paraded around town by the celebrants, to be returned to his home. By October, seditious verses lampooning the intendant were found throughout the town.[24] To the ayuntamiento these verses not only reflected Valero's unpopularity among the residents of the provincial capital but also the degree to which his presence might become a destabilizing force. As intendant of Chiapas, Valero was the supreme representative of the crown in a province "full of Indians who treated him as a king . . . with the result that in the event of an invasion by our Enemies via any of the surrounding areas we would be lost, because in the same way that a magnet is drawn to steel, those people would be drawn to their passionate Valero."[25] And so, with the full support of the leading citizens of the province, the ayuntamiento unilaterally deposed the intendant on 21 September 1809.

Naturally, Valero saw this matter in a much different light, in which the charge of "*infidencia a la Monarquía Española y adhesion a la Dominacion Francesa*" was simply a cover for the illegal actions of his political enemies. Upon hearing of the imprisonment of the intendant, the audiencia ordered Valero transferred to Guatemala City for trial. The case of the deposed governor, not surprisingly, proved a difficult one for the colonial government. Valero, a peninsular from Granada, had arrived in Chiapas in 1798 as *teniente letrado* for the province and, apparently, had immediately begun to use his position to improve his financial situation. In addition to the charge of infidencia, in fact, Valero was accused of abuse of office. According to the audiencia, which met to discuss this situation on 15 November, the first crime was sufficient grounds for his removal, following the recent royal order on subversion. However, the second, under normal circumstances, was something that should be reserved for an end-of-term *residencia* (administrative review).[26] Since the ayuntamiento of Ciudad Real did not wait for the crown to remove Valero but instead took the law into its own hands, the council had set a dangerous precedent. Perhaps concerned about the implications of a ruling at this time, the González administration left the matter unresolved. The case then degenerated into a furious letter-writing campaign of recriminations and accusations between the ayuntamiento, the former intendant, and their respective supporters that lasted until independence.[27]

By the end of 1809, the captain general and his subordinates did not need the private citizens of Nicaragua or Chiapas to confirm for them the threat that French subversion held to public order. Early in November, González received a warning from the Junta Central that the government of José I had definite plans to promote "the uprising of the Americas" by keeping the Council of the Indies together and confusing Americans with "newspapers full of falsehoods and other seditious reports." The Junta then closed this message with an admonition to its officials that "the security of these dominions, the complete conservation of the Monarchy, and the health of the Patria demand that no measures be ignored that might dispel the intrigues and tricks which the Tyrant relies on to destroy [our] harmony."[28]

At this point, the official representative of the Junta Central in the United States, Luís de Onís, began to send a series of warnings to Spanish authorities in the Caribbean about the existence of a large group of Napoleonic agents based in New Orleans.[29] Onís warned that 150 French officials were known to be in southern Louisiana waiting for orders to disperse across Spanish America. Others had apparently gone to Hispaniola, where they received support and protection from the Haitian government. Onís also gave official weight to rumors about a well-armed French fleet supposedly patrolling the Caribbean. These reports caused the captain general of Cuba to put the defenses of Havana on alert and to send out searches for the phantom flotilla. The captain general of Venezuela, with a more detailed account of the sighting of a French squadron of fourteen warships near the island of Trinidad, actually mobilized his coastal forces in January 1810 to prepare "to resist the invasion that might occur on those shores."[30] Such warnings proved groundless, however, for French ships only operated in the Caribbean during this period as corsairs. They attacked shipping and threatened coastal settlements but ultimately had their greatest impact in heightening the tension and insecurity sweeping across Spanish America.[31]

By the end of 1809 official circles in Guatemala City had begun to exhibit signs of this anxiety, despite the fact that the fall of the Spanish monarchy had been greeted with defiance by the population of Central America. Campaigns for patriotic donations to aid the peninsular war effort took in a surprising amount of money for such a cash-poor and economically depressed community. In addition, creole political and commercial institutions worked alongside the colonial administration to preserve at least a facade of tranquility and a business-as-usual manner as the heart of the empire struggled against the full weight of the French invasion.

Nevertheless, constant warnings from Spain and imperial officials about French subversive operations in the region, rumors of Napoleonic agents in the countryside and ships in the Caribbean, and signs of political disturbances in the kingdom and across the empire were impossible to ignore for long. While Guatemala was peaceful at the moment, the captain general believed that this situation could change overnight. When the first reports of the abdication of the Bourbons reached Spanish America in 1808, creoles in Mexico and South America had agitated for increased political participation in the empire. The ensuing political unrest in Mexico caused the peninsular elites there to overthrow the viceroy, a *golpe* that only served to heighten tensions in the viceregal capital. No one knew how long the crisis in Spain would last or whether the loyalists could hold out against the heretofore invincible Napoleon.[32] Communications with the metropolis were difficult, news was unreliable, and it came from a dizzying array of sources. To make matters worse, a severe outbreak of yellow fever along the Caribbean coast of Guatemala and Honduras that began in 1809 resulted in the closing of the port of Trujillo, a major entrepot for the region.[33] And, of course, the economic crisis continued unabated, with the European wars and blockades effectively shutting down international commerce.

The new year brought no relief to the situation faced by González and the colonial administration in the Kingdom of Guatemala. Instead, 1810 witnessed a series of events that helped the imperial crisis spread like wildfire across Spanish America. French advances in Spain resulted in the dissolution of the Junta Central by the end of January, the evacuation of the loyalist forces to Cádiz, and the establishment of a five-member administrative Council of Regency. With its legitimacy under question, the council's first act was the calling of a national Cortes, an assembly of elected representatives from around the empire that would meet in Spain and draw up a constitution.

Instead of easing concerns about the state of Spanish resistance, reports of these disconcerting events provided the excuse for revolutionary forces in Caracas, Buenos Aires, Chile, and New Granada to begin independence movements. While Central America remained quiet in the face of the deteriorating loyalist position in Spain and the new uprisings in the colonies, the government in Guatemala City was not lulled into a false sense of security. Taking its cue from measures recently applied in Mexico and Peru, the captaincy general began to construct a comprehensive security apparatus designed to preserve Spanish authority in Central America and repulse any internal or external threat to the colony. Though in part initiated and supported by the creole oligarchy, the administration's new attention to defense and increased inflexibility with respect to subversion quickly became points of contention between the two governing groups. While little dissension was discernible on the surface, this year proved to be a major turning point in the relationship between creole and peninsular elites in Central America.

If the colonial government recognized the potential for political catastrophe in the wake of the Napoleonic invasion of Spain, Central American elites saw nothing but opportunity. The native-born community in the colony was dominated by a small, well-organized, well-placed network of families centered in and around Guatemala City and headed by the House of Aycinena. They were the leading merchants, landowners, and clerics on the isthmus and wielded significant local power as officeholders in the capital's ayuntamiento and consulado. Although these creoles possessed few of the high offices in the Spanish administration, their economic clout, their interlocking kinship ties, and their monopoly over local political institutions and the lower rungs of the colonial bureaucracy made them a significant counterweight to the peninsular community in Guatemala. Yet, fiercely protective of their status at the top of the social and economic hierarchy, the creole elites were careful to preserve a close relationship with the Spanish officials in the colony. While there is evidence to show that a so-called creole consciousness had developed here and that the rivalry between creoles and peninsulars that was such a large part of the late colonial experience across the empire also existed in Central America, by 1808 these sentiments could not outweigh the strong desire on the part of the oligarchy to maintain the status quo.[34] True revolutionary sentiment, however rare, proved to be almost the exclusive domain of the secondary elites in the colony, the junior creole and ladino professionals and clergy who had much less stake in the colonial system and were more open to liberal political viewpoints.

Conflicts emerged between these two elite groups after 1808 because the status quo came to mean different things for the Guatemalan oligarchy and the peninsular administration. The creoles, above all, wanted security, both for their position in society and for their property. For three hundred years Spain had protected them from the indigenous and ladino masses, but the political chaos on the peninsula had proven to be a threat to the stability of the colonial system. Fearing the extension of political anarchy to the colonies, the Guatemalan oligarchy found many opportunities to demonstrate its loyalty to Spain and the empire between 1808 and 1810.[35] It quickly became clear, however, that the structure of colonial government was changing as a result of the Napoleonic invasion, and creoles could sense that some of these changes might bring more of the security they desired. The establishment of the Junta

Central in 1808 and its invitation to Americans on 22 January 1809 to elect representatives to the new government offered colonials their first real chance to participate in imperial politics.[36] More important, this January statement by the Junta declared that henceforth America was to be considered an equal part of the Spanish monarchy and seemed to indicate that traditional colonial divisions between peninsular and creole should be abolished.

However, the fall of the monarchy and the threat from France made Captain General González and the peninsular community fiercely protective of the structure of Bourbon colonial administration. With revolution in the air, any attempt to modify the traditional system was considered inherently subversive. The relationship between the Spanish bureaucrats and the creole elite was close, but it was not quite equal, for the delicate balance of power between the two groups that helped keep the colony free from revolution was predicated in part upon the assumption (at least in the minds of the peninsulars) that the creole community would defer to Spanish officials on general issues of colonial governance and security. The decrees from the Junta Central in 1809 threatened to give creoles sufficient leverage to demand some kind of power-sharing arrangement and, perhaps, autonomy.[37] To an administration operating in the absence of the king, in the midst of war, and besieged by constant threats of subversion, the growing political pretensions of the creole community could not have been welcome. Now, the creoles had no compunction about complaining to Spain, as the Guatemala City ayuntamiento did in January 1809, about the "chiefs, prelates, and magistrates" who were sent to the colonies "persuaded that to maintain and conserve Spanish America it was necessary to rule with an iron rod."[38] The new system, as Alcalde Peinado declared to Deputy-elect Manuel José Pavón in March 1810, could finally free Guatemalans from "the evils that the distance of the Throne and its lack of the necessary information about the kingdom's local political situation have caused over the course of 284 long years."[39]

In 1810 the leading creole political institution in the Kingdom of Guatemala, the ayuntamiento of Guatemala City, began to take advantage of the imperial crisis to expand its jurisdiction into areas of imperial defense, internal security, and international commerce.[40] By this point it had become the de facto mouthpiece for the creole community across the isthmus in dealings with the colonial government, maintaining a vast correspondence with other municipal councils that allowed it to funnel news and opinions to the provinces and gauge the political sentiment in these areas. Not surprisingly, at this time the major concern of the capital and provincial elites proved to be the kingdom's lack of adequate defenses in the face of the French scare.[41]

After debating the potential threats to the kingdom, the ayuntamiento came to the conclusion on 13 February 1810 that it would ask the colonial authorities to purchase some thirty to forty thousand muskets from the British colony of Jamaica and request that the urban militia units be expanded.[42] Although most councilmen were convinced that Guatemala was in sufficient danger to merit such measures, one regidor, José de Isasi, made a passionate argument that the appeal for arms and troops was in fact superfluous and potentially dangerous. Isasi declared that the French could never pose a serious threat to the colony: the French had no plans to distract themselves from their European adventures and had no Caribbean fleet or base upon which to mount such an operation; even if they did, they would never get past the English navy, and if they managed to land on the isthmus, the geography and climate would decimate their advance. Thus, the purchase of these weapons would only remove valuable funds from the treasury that could be used instead for more substantial and beneficial projects. Most important, Isasi believed that this military build-up would threaten the tranquility of the colony by needlessly alarming the population and, perhaps, initiating uproars that could not be controlled. Finally, the regidor stated that if the rumors of French emissaries and internal subversion were true, then the colonial government should be left to make the necessary security arrangements.[43] Unpersuaded, the ayuntamiento charged the Marquis of Aycinena with making the majority representation known to the captain general.

González responded favorably to the council's petition, telling Aycinena that he would have his military advisor and commander of the Royal Artillery Corps, Colonel José Méndez, report on the state of the kingdom's defenses during an upcoming *junta de guerra* (council of war). On 23 March, three days before the meeting was to take place, Alcalde Peinado told the ayuntamiento that he had acquired an English gazette that reported an alliance between France and the United States.

The newspaper indicated that one consequence of the agreement would be the formation of naval squadrons whose duty was to patrol the Atlantic and cut off all communications between Spain and its colonies. Peinado interpreted this report as a potential prelude to a French invasion and, therefore, vindication for the council's recent petition.[44]

On 26 March, Captain General González, Colonel Méndez, Ramón Anguiano (intendant of Comayagua), José de Aycinena (colonel of the Guatemala City militia battalion), Tadeo Piñol (colonel of the Guatemala City dragoons), and Captain of Engineers Juan Bautista Jáuregui met to discuss the state of the kingdom's defense, the lack of armaments, and the needs of the military units and fortifications.[45] The first order of business was to read the royal order of 28 February 1795 authorizing captains general "in extraordinary situations to work as circumstances may demand, according to the principles of war, in whatever manner your zeal and military expertise might suggest to you." Then, the council read the ayuntamiento petition regarding the purchase of additional arms from Jamaica, which the regidores justified by the "need in the kingdom for functional weapons to sustain its sworn loyalty against any foreign invasion and especially in the unpleasant event of general misfortune on the Peninsula." At this point González reviewed the various failed pleas for military supplies made by his administration to Spain and other parts of the empire during the previous six years. New Spain, he noted, could not help because that colony also faced a severe shortage of arms. Then the junta heard Méndez's report on the scarcity of armaments among the artillery, infantry, and cavalry units in the kingdom. With this sobering information at hand, the council members resolved to direct a petition to the viceroy of Peru asking for any available light artillery and shot. Convinced that the colony could not rely solely on outside aid, the junta resolved to stimulate weapons production in Central America itself by initiating an apprentice program in the region's armories. Finally, the decision was made to send another request to Spain by the first mail, elaborating the desperate need in the colony for muskets, pistols, and swords. There seemed to be little doubt in the minds of these seasoned military officers that the Kingdom of Guatemala would be hard pressed to defend itself in the event of any external threat or internal unrest.

Two weeks later, on 9 April, the junta met again, with Méndez offici-
ating in place of the ailing González.[46] It was decided to send details of
the resolutions made in March to the royal consulado, along with more
detailed information about the state of the kingdom's weaponry. Méndez reported that the colony had some 7350 muskets in good condition
and 1791 that needed some repair. The council agreed that a request
should be made to the crown for ten thousand more muskets and bayo-
nets, two thousand swords or sabres, and two thousand pistols, but
it also recognized that Spain would probably be unable to supply its
colony with the needed arms and that the United States might be the
only source for such a large weapons shipment. A calculation was made
as to the potential cost—some 150,000 pesos—and the junta members
took this opportunity to dissolve the council and refer the matter to
the royal treasury.[47] On 16 April González approved these decisions and
the matter passed to the *Real Tribunal y Audiencia de la Contaduría de
Cuentas.*

To the dismay of all involved, the tribunal reported in early May that
the treasury held only 31,121 pesos and suggested another donativo patriótico to cover the rest of the expense. The defense situation seemed
so dire that the royal treasurer called for an emergency meeting between
senior figures from the administration, the audiencia, the treasury, the
ayuntamiento, the consulado, and the Church, as well as the administrator of the *alcabala,* the director of the tobacco monopoly, Deputy
Pavón, and other influential members of the community. He hoped that
the colonial oligarchy would come together at this time of crisis and decide how to raise the money, "whether by a general subscription in the
manner of a donativo, or through a loan to be floated on the funds in
the royal treasury, or finally if it would be more convenient to provide
some kind of tax exemption and raise the money through commercial
negotiations."[48]

The opportunity for the peninsular administration and the creole
oligarchy in Guatemala City to unify behind the cause of colonial defense passed. Instead, what resulted from this crisis were two reports,
one from the ayuntamiento and a response from the consulado, which
demonstrated the degree to which the interests of the two communities
had diverged since 1808. The creole-dominated council saw this situa-

tion as an opportunity to push for commercial liberalization, arguing that free trade—which the well-financed and well-connected House of Aycinena could be expected to dominate—would sufficiently stimulate the kingdom's economy to satisfy the increased defense needs. Of course, the Spanish empire remained closed to foreign commerce at this time, and the Spanish merchants on the consulado did not want to give up their monopoly. Instead, they argued that a more limited purchase of arms could be achieved through taxation of church wealth and that the rest could be made by Guatemalan industries.[49] In the end the governing elites could not come to an agreement over the funding problem, the essential military supplies never reached the isthmus, and the administration became even more concerned about the kingdom's exposure to foreign invasion.

Early in April the Guatemala City ayuntamiento received a letter from its counterpart in the Nicaraguan city of Granada.[50] The *Granadinos* informed the Guatemalan regidores that a regiment of soldiers stationed in that city had orders to return to Guatemala, thereby leaving the province exposed to an enemy invasion. They petitioned the Guatemalans to intercede with the captain general and ask him to suspend this transfer or to replace the troops with an armed militia unit. The ayuntamiento went to Méndez, who replied that the troop movement was necessary and could not be changed. Despite this setback, over the course of the next few months provincial ayuntamientos from Rivas, Nicaragua, to Quetzaltenango, Guatemala, continued to send details of their security needs to the Guatemala City regidores, thanking them for the representations already made to the colonial authorities and asking them, "as the principal organ for the assertion of our requests," to continue to press for improved defenses, more armaments, and an increased militia presence in the countryside.[51]

The sense of urgency emanating from this provincial correspondence was due to the fact that by late spring 1810 the French scare had reached its highest level in the Kingdom of Guatemala as news of the imminent collapse of Spanish resistance on the peninsula merged with reports of more French subversion in the region and the outbreak of revolution in other American colonies. On 22 April González issued to his provincial officials and military commanders the most comprehensive orders to date regarding the measures to be taken against French agents:

I have now received detailed warnings that the Machiavellian French Government has dispatched various emissaries throughout our Americas to spread proclamations and letters falsely assumed to be from our King Ferdinand VII, that some of these vile messengers have arrived in the United States from where they will be sent to other parts of our most loyal possessions, and that among these destinations is the Gulf of Honduras, where they are insane enough to believe that they will be able to disseminate their venom and encounter allies among the faithful inhabitants of the most loyal, religious, and peaceful kingdom on earth. . . . Assuming that the enemy, as audacious as he is astute, will increase his snares, for our part we must redouble our vigilance and zeal in capturing and punishing him, in the unanticipated event that some emissaries manage to enter this happy land.[52]

The captain general then listed eight new regulations whose effective purpose was to seal Central America off from the outside world. Except in special humanitarian circumstances, no foreigner would be allowed into the kingdom for any purpose and no foreign ships or passengers would be allowed to have any contact with land. Contact between captains and port authorities was now limited to inquiries into cargo, with any communications and papers to be sent directly to Guatemala City. Regarding ships from Spain and the empire, officials were to scrutinize passports, passenger lists, and ship licenses and were not to allow anyone to disembark without permission from the commander of the port. Any captain suspected of disloyalty was to be arrested immediately. In addition, "since the emissaries can arrive in the guise of sailors, servants, officers, or in other disguises, the greatest vigilance will be taken with every stranger without distinction: their actions, conversations, friendships, connections upon disembarking, and where they stay must all be observed." Locals who housed these strangers had to report daily to the military commanders and justices with information about their conduct and opinions on public matters, on pain of treason. The travelers, themselves, were expected to show their passports and papers upon demand, to have vouchers for their character, and to state the purpose of their trip to the satisfaction of local authorities. Hoping to preclude the potential for abuse of these new regulations, González added a final order, charging his officials to be cautious, prudent, and sensitive when dealing with "good subjects" but to remain vigilant in the face of such a "malignant enemy."

Within a few weeks, the captain general decided that even these strict regulations were not sufficient. On 15 May, he ordered all foreign residents and travelers who had been in the kingdom less than two years to report immediately to the nearest judge or official with their passport, work accreditation, witness testimony to their character, and anything that would assure the judge of their loyalty. Any nonnative who did not comply would be arrested and held liable for his own defense. Each jurisdiction was expected to make a list of the names of these individuals and send a copy to Guatemala City. Public and private innkeepers who provided shelter to foreigners were to notify authorities within two hours of their arrival and have the strangers present themselves within six hours. A particular concern for the colonial government was that the emissaries might travel disguised as muleteers. Thus, local judges were told to examine everyone of this particular occupation. Anyone who denounced one of these spies or emissaries would be eligible for a minimum reward of five hundred pesos, while those with knowledge of subversive activity who did not come forward would be punished without compassion as accomplices to treason.[53]

The captain general announced these new measures because he had begun to receive the names of suspected French emissaries, seemingly reliable evidence of subversion that caused him to redouble his warnings to his provincial authorities. By the end of the month, colonial officials throughout the kingdom were on the lookout for Estanislao Oropera, Ciriaco Betolaza, Fermín Esparragosa, and Juan Chagaray, *afrancesado* Spaniards who, according to official reports, had been recruited by Napoleon to incite rebellion in the provinces. González also warned his subordinates that other agents had arrived in Havana and were ready to infiltrate Central America. His information was so detailed that he could assert with confidence that one emissary would remain on the island of Jamaica to collect news and information about the kingdom from coastal *contrabandistas*.[54]

Coming from the highest levels of imperial administration, the reports that González received in May 1810 about French-sponsored espionage created a siege mentality among colonial officials. In addition to the list of emissaries supposedly en route to Guatemala, the government soon received evidence from Spain that ten more were on their way to Mexico, while six were headed to Lima and three to New Granada. According to this intelligence the United States was the most popular base of operations: the agents Juan Arévalo and Estanislao Morales apparently directed much of the espionage from New Orleans, but others were reported in Charleston and Baltimore. A man named Mateo Cervantes worked out of California, and more were believed to be in Jamaica, Curacao, Caracas, and Barlovento.[55]

In the face of these threats, the captain general expected his intendants, alcaldes mayores, and corregidores to act quickly to take the necessary precautions and alert their respective populations. By 28 May, Prudencio de Cózar, the alcalde mayor of Totonicapán, had his own version of González's ordinances drafted, printed, and prepared for distribution among local justices and ayuntamientos. The first three orders read:

1. No stranger, whether from this kingdom or from Europe, will be permitted to settle in any town while remaining unknown; in this there will be no tolerance or deference given, even if the stranger is dressed as a priest or is a women, either white or colored.

2. At the moment that a stranger arrives, a careful investigation will be made as to his name, his hometown, his occupation, and whether or not he has a passport or documents that vouch for his character; then, this information will be sent to me as quickly as possible by the local judges who will continue to pay careful attention to the actions of the stranger, the people with whom he deals, and whether he says anything that might demonstrate his ties to the French.

3. If he actually demonstrates his attachment to them and says anything against our Government, he is to be arrested immediately, securely detained, and sent to this capital by the same officials who captured him; in addition, everything in his possession, without exception, must also be turned over, with the most careful attention given to his papers.[56]

Cózar ended his proclamation by mentioning both the reward for information and the punishment for silence.

Such measures proved to be more than empty gestures. From the town of Huimanguillo, on the border between Tabasco and Chiapas, Juan Urgell, the local magistrate and a lieutenant in the militia, informed his superiors about a worrisome case of subversion. According to his report, a well-known member of the community, Bernardo Camacho, tried to secure a temporary passport for one Manuel Flores, who was posing as an inhabitant of a nearby town. With Camacho vouching for his character, Flores received the passport and used it to travel to Ocuapán, where he was heard speaking out against the loyalist government in Spain and in favor of Napoleon. On 20 April 1810, Urgell received an official denunciation against Flores that made him believe he was dealing with a French spy. The official immediately set off in pursuit of the suspect, whom he captured four days later. Searching the suspect's belongings, Urgell discovered

> two little relic bags with cords that allow them to hang them around the neck: when they were opened, four strips of paper were found in one, five in the other, along with a note, six codes for writing, codes for numbers, the French names Francisco Carriere, Simon Face, Juan Moreau, Juan Francisco Sarie, Sena, Mexharie, and a diary with a bunch of numbers, names of subjects, streets, and house numbers, apparently from Madrid. In addition we found a multitude of papers from lawsuits the suspect has had in the Capital and in Campeche, from which we discovered that his name is really Juan Francisco O'Horan de Argüello.[57]

In the alcaldía mayor of Verapaz, the González regulations were exercised against three travelers from Campeche suspected of being French emissaries. On 29 May the acting alcalde mayor, Angel Valenzuela, reported that he had stopped and interrogated three men "dressed as *Campechanos*."[58] Two were Spaniards, Ramón Colmenero and Pedro Sánchez, while the third, Pedro Mongiste, was from the Yucatecan province of Mérida. All were merchants who had lived a number of years in Veracruz and had set off from Campeche to do business in the Yucatán and the Petén. While in custody in Salamá, the men apparently convinced Valenzuela of their loyalty. In his report to the captain general, the alcalde mayor asked that the men be released and wrote that "they have demonstrated in their conversations a great love for King, Religion, and Country, detesting and abhorring the perfidious ideas of the most cruel and abominable monster in nature, Bonaparte."[59]

Reports of subversion were not limited to the provinces, however. On 26 May, the alcalde primero of Guatemala City, Cayetano Pavón, informed the captaincy general of an incident that had recently been brought to his attention. In this case, a servant named Andrés Minera described a conversation he had with a coworker, Francisca Rodríguez, who confided in him that she was very worried about what was being said about the French. She then told him that a sugar vendor had overheard two people in a tavern discussing the situation, one of whom declared that "Napoleon's law is better than our own."[60] In the end, a bearded and well-dressed man who met the description of one of these characters and who looked French was arrested.

Even the Church was affected by this climate of fear and insecurity. Church officials told their priests to publicize the descriptions of possible spies, along with the rewards offered, to their parishioners at weekly mass. The faithful were warned to turn over, on pain of excommunication, any information, papers, or documents they might have "that incites, induces, or seeks to influence our separation from the Monarchy, the sovereignty represented by the Cortes, or the governing authorities."[61] The church hierarchy expected its priests to impress upon the population the dangers that confronted the kingdom, the Catholic religion, and Spanish culture, as well as the horrible consequences of rebellion. To prevent these evils, all were told to scrutinize closely anyone who seemed foreign or different, so as to discover "if they are spies, emissaries from Bonaparte, or his followers."[62]

In these desperate times the captain general was forced to implement new and untried measures to preserve order. On 19 May, González ordered the establishment of urban militias throughout the kingdom.[63] Ayuntamientos and local justices assumed responsibility for registering all able-bodied men between the ages of fifteen and forty-five and for giving commissions to the most distinguished members of the community. González emphasized that the draft should be viewed as a patriotic duty, not as a hardship, and that local councils and churches should work together to promote it. The members of the Guatemala City ayuntamiento wasted no time in making the necessary inquiries and passing out commissions, most of which went to the regidores themselves. As the proclamation ordered, the city was divided into six jurisdictions (*quarteles*), corresponding to parish lines, then subdivided again into twelve neighborhoods (*barrios*), to which were assigned two militia officers. With the help of the parish churches, the officers registered the male inhabitants of the barrios according to age, marital status, racial status, and whether or not the men could serve in the cavalry. After a year of work, the ayuntamiento had a list of 3277 men ready to be called up at a moment's notice.

The problem, however, with this heightened state of security was that it threatened to foster the growth of hysteria. On 22 May, the captain general attempted to preempt this concern in a public manifesto that dealt with the state of Spanish resistance, the role of America in the war, the designs of Napoleon on the colony, and the defenses of Central America. González told his subjects that Guatemala had little to fear from the French. From his perspective, invasion was all but impossible because of the unhealthy conditions of the coast and the proximity of British military posts. An armed advance through the mountainous terrain of the colony was also unfeasible, especially with the poor condition of the roads, "conditions which at other times we have justly lamented, but which now are reasons to be secure and confident, for their conjuncture is not found anywhere else." Even if an attempt were made, the captain general declared, "all of the most effective means of vigilance and precaution have been taken, others are being taken at this very moment, and still more will be taken as conditions warrant. The garrisons at the northern ports are well provided with good artillery. The militia forces along the coast are as good as veterans, as a result of the continuous details they are made to work. The regular troops, and any others that can be brought together, will be trained under my eyes or on my orders."[64]

Meant to ease public fears, this proclamation came at another unfortunate time for the colonial administration. On the very same day it was issued, notices arrived in Guatemala about French victories in Andalusía, the collapse of the Junta Central, the creation of the Council of Regency, and the withdrawal of loyalist forces to the island-city of Cádiz. With Spain effectively conquered and the Junta dissolved, the question of legitimacy again reared its head in the Spanish colonies. Although the Kingdom of Guatemala showed no signs of unrest, colonial officials could not assume that even more political uncertainty would be absorbed without the propriety of continued Spanish rule being called into question. And, of course, they could have no idea as to the impact of this news on other, more volatile parts of the American empire.

With these concerns undoubtedly on his mind, González ordered an immediate swearing of loyalty to the Council of Regency.[65] Then, two days later, the captain general issued a proclamation informing the colony of his decision to set up a *Tribunal de Fidelidad* (Tribunal of Loyalty) to administer the 15 May regulations, take denunciations, and direct prosecutions of cases of subversion. The new council was composed of three senior Spanish officials: Colonel José Méndez, commander of the Royal Artillery Corps; Joaquín Bernardo de Campuzano, *oidor decano* of the audiencia; and Joaquín Ibáñez, *auditor de guerra*. Convinced of the authenticity of the warnings of "infamous emissaries being sent to these provinces," González explained that

> [t]he most pernicious scheme that the execrable usurper and his satellites have used around the world is that of sowing discord in communities, inciting terror and mistrust in government, and spreading rumors of imagined or false events. No such evil or prejudicial influence has been experienced so far in this tranquil and well-behaved country; but if by any chance it is felt, the Tribunal of Loyalty will watch for it, prosecute it, and punish it with sagacious energy, considering as suspects of *infidencia* all impure disturbers of the peace.[66]

The captain general expected the tribunal to investigate and prosecute all cases of subversion falling under the jurisdiction of the 15 May edict. Along with these responsibilities came extensive authority over local police, judges, and military commanders. Denunciations to the tribunal were kept secret, and prosecutions could now be directed against those who did nothing more than suggest "differences or divisions between European Spaniards and American Spaniards."[67] Although the tribunal was by no means the prelude to the creation of a police state in Guatemala, its existence demonstrated the concern among senior officials that continued Spanish rule could not be taken for granted but had to be actively buttressed with institutional supports. It was also the first attempt by Spanish officials, though by no means the last, "to circumvent creole-administered courts in cases of suspected treason."[68]

The *Tribunal de Fidelidad* was not González's personal inspiration, however. Instead, the captain general brought to Guatemala an institution that originated in Spain in 1808 as the *Tribunal de Vigilancia* and that reached the American colonies in September 1809 when Archbishop/ Viceroy Francisco Lizana y Beaumont of New Spain established the *Junta de Seguridad y Buen Orden*.[69] All three were created with the general goal of rooting out subversion, uncovering evidence of French intervention, and protecting the legitimate governments against insurrection. Concerned that he not be charged with making unilateral and experimental policy decisions, González ordered his ministers to adhere to the regulations and jurisdictional precedents laid out by the Spanish and Mexican models.

The establishment of the *Tribunal de Fidelidad* in Guatemala marked another important step in the evolution of the relationship between the peninsular administration and the creole community. Over the course of its year of existence, the Guatemalan tribunal investigated just over thirty cases of potential subversion in the colony. Most of these dealt with reports of treasonous conversations or opinions (*conversaciones inquietas* and *seductivas, palabras sediciosas*), false passports or incorrect travel documentation, and anonymous graffiti or broadsheets favoring the French.[70] It was not overly aggressive in its activities; even the historian Ramón Salazar admitted that the tribunal acted in a very circumspect, careful, and deliberate manner.[71] But it had an impact nonetheless. As Brian Hamnett has noted with respect to the Mexican junta, these institutions invariably caused the line between political differences and treason to blur.[72] As the cases of Intendant Valero and others demonstrated, the government could not ignore or minimize common complaints against officials when accusations of disloyalty were added. Many more innocuous statements of opinion, disputable comments, and rumors also assumed heavier significance in this climate, especially when reported anonymously and in the context of personal vendettas.[73]

Most important, however, the existence of the *Tribunal de Fidelidad* precipitated the first real rupture between the colonial administration and the Guatemala City ayuntamiento during the imperial crisis. Throughout the month of May, the creole oligarchy remained overtly supportive of the new security measures. Concern over French subversion had caused the ayuntamiento to advocate a major purchase of arms and the creation of urban militias, and it proved to be a vigorous transmitter of provincial insecurities regarding the kingdom's defense. When González's antiemissary regulations came out, the regidores took it upon themselves to transmit the information to provincial municipalities and to encourage innkeepers to pay close attention to travelers.[74] And the ayuntamiento wasted no time in making the militia draft a reality once the captain general signed off on the idea. The lack of action regarding the purchase of arms caused some frustration among creoles during this time, as did the consulado's rejection of their free trade plans, but such sentiment did not appear to affect their patriotic zeal when the government needed their support.

The fall of the Junta Central, however, clearly shook the creole oligarchy. The news reached the ayuntamiento on 22 May by way of Colonel Méndez, but without direct and indisputable confirmation of the events in Spain the council appeared uncertain of its position and decided to take no action.[75] The following day, the captain general remitted to the regidores the official act installing the Council of Regency, along with the council's decree calling for the convocation of a general and extraordinary Cortes comprised of delegates elected from around the empire. And, two days later, González ordered the kingdom to swear loyalty to the new supreme government in Spain. Although the issue was debated repeatedly in council meetings during the two weeks that followed, the ayuntamiento refrained from voting on the oath of allegiance until 8 June, in spite of the efforts of some peninsular regidores to force the issue. During this time, the regidores read reports from Spain on the fall of Andalusía and popular uprisings in Seville and argued over earlier decrees from the Junta Central. In the end, the ayuntamiento voted to recognize the new government, but only by a plurality. Raising the sensitive issue of the "rights of Guatemala" in the imperial context, four dissenting creoles argued that the Junta Central allowed for American representation while the Council of Regency was a five-person executive. Although the establishment of a Cortes appeared to offer some American participation in imperial governance, these regidores declared that Guatemala should wait before making a commitment.[76]

That the Guatemalan ayuntamiento believed it had the authority to vote on the recognition of the supreme government, with four leading councilmen actually declaring their opposition to the motion, illustrates the degree to which the institution had begun to consider itself the legitimate institutional repository of American rights on the isthmus and, as such, an equal partner with imperial officers within the Spanish colonial administration. Fully aware of the weakness of the imperial system, the Guatemalan ayuntamiento came out of the crisis of May 1810 determined to spearhead a movement toward greater creole influence over isthmian governance. In the months to come, this more confrontational perspective played itself out in the council's supervision of the election of a Guatemalan representative to the imperial Cortes and the drafting of a detailed set of instructions for this delegate to take to Spain. But first, the Guatemalan regidores decided to attack the *Tribunal de Fidelidad* as a prime example of a colonial system that heretofore had given Americans no voice but that seemed unable to survive now without their support.

On 19 June, the ayuntamiento received a report from its síndico (legal counsel), Francisco Arrivillaga, that alleged strong public dissatisfaction with the composition of the tribunal. Arrivillaga recommended that a deputation be sent to the captain general asking him to change its representation to include Americans, "so as to avoid all factional spirit that is so harmful to society."[77] According to the creole elite, "although this Tribunal has as its principal objective the investigation of any Emissaries of the Tyrant who may reach this kingdom, all of whom are Europeans according to the list, it is nevertheless composed of three Europeans, a fact which . . . can't help but prove sensitive to Americans."[78] Moreover, the basic need for such a body in an ostensibly loyal colony appeared to reflect the Spanish administration's lack of confidence in its subjects. Thus, the council could not help but notice that although the kingdom "has been faithful and constant in its loyalty, a political inquisition of Europeans was still necessary which, by instilling terror among the population, practiced repression to the fullest extent of its obligations."[79]

Two alcaldes ordinarios took this argument to González, and on 10 July they reported back to the council. According to their statements, the captain general received them ungraciously, considered their petition impertinent, and declared that he would fill the tribunal with Americans when it was convenient for him. In light of this response, the ayuntamiento decided to send an official complaint to Spain.[80] The local elite did not end the pressure on González, however. Creole regidores repeated the council's position in a letter to the captain general at the end of July. Here, they asked explicitly that the number of judges on the tribunal be increased "to five, or seven, and that half of these be creoles."[81] They also explained that Colonel Méndez, although an honorable man, was simply not an acceptable choice as one of the members, considering his French wife. Using a strategy that would be perfected in the years to come, the letter then attacked the legality of the tribunal on a number of fronts: first, as a usurpation by the governor of the sovereign power to create new, permanent, and ordinary institutions; second, as an illegitimate use of administrative advisors as a court of justice; third, as an unlawful bypassing of the normal judicial system; and fourth, as a wrongful utilization of an institution created in Mexico under potentially different circumstances. In a veiled threat, the authors concluded that if the American position were not taken into consideration, the kingdom would be more open to the divisions that could lead to its destruction.

By this time, however, the ayuntamiento had begun to refocus its attention on the election of a deputy to represent the kingdom in the upcoming Cortes. On 24 July, in a process similar to that followed earlier in the year in the selection of a representative to the Junta Central, the name of Dr. Antonio de Larrazábal, a cleric and scholar from the University of San Carlos and a member of a leading creole family, was picked from a jar containing the names of seven candidates of the oligarchy. The Cortes to which Larrazábal was elected had been charged by the Council of Regency with writing a constitution for the Spanish empire, and this gave the creole elites the hope that they could now have a direct impact on the formation of a new governing philosophy based on equal political and social rights for Americans, free trade, and some degree of colonial autonomy. As a consequence, the ayuntamiento determined to provide a set of instructions for Larrazábal to take to Spain detailing the positions he would be expected to support. On 17 August, Regidores Peinado, Aycinena, and Antonio de Juarros received the commission to prepare the work, although Peinado did the majority of the writing. By the end of October, the *Instrucciones para la constitución fundamental de la monarquía española y su gobierno* were ready for Larrazábal who, unfortunately, did not arrive in Spain until August 1811, far too late to play a role in the promulgation of the constitution. Copies of the *Instrucciones,* however, were sent to all the other ayuntamientos in Central America, where they played a major role in consolidating creole sentiment and confirming the predominance of the Guatemalan council in creole affairs across the country.

As a formal representation of the political and economic beliefs of the Guatemalan elite in the last decade of the colonial period, the *Instrucciones* is a remarkable document.[82] The work provides a picture of a creole community dedicated to the concept of a constitutional monarchy, one that could preserve the oligarchy's own aristocratic sense of entitlement while, at the same time, allowing for reform of the traditional absolutist character of the peninsular-led regime. The *Instrucciones* reflects the mentality of a well-educated, Enlightenment-oriented group of individuals, familiar with the arguments of Smith, Montesquieu, and Rousseau, and aware of the republican sentiments that precipitated the American and French Revolutions. The creoles hoped to expand commercial opportunities on the isthmus via free trade, to exploit underutilized resources, and to stimulate productive capacity through scientific means. These men wanted access to high imperial office; they expressed "liberal" sentiments before the term came into general use, telling Larrazábal to press for constitutional guarantees of property, free speech, and other individual rights; they promoted the concept of a republic of laws; and they expected a significant decentralization of power under the new regime.[83] Over the course of the next decade, the Guatemalan oligarchy continued to believe that these goals could best be met within a reformed imperial structure. Therefore, they refrained from seeking independence and, at times, actively worked to suppress revolutionary outbreaks. Nevertheless, their political and economic perspective as expressed in the *Instrucciones* caused frequent clashes with the colonial government on the isthmus, which could not help but see imperial reform as the first step toward imperial disintegration.

By the end of the summer, in fact, the kingdom had begun to receive unsettling news from South America about the revolutionary movements that had swept Venezuela and New Granada in the months following the collapse of the Junta Central. On 4 September, the ayuntamiento of Granada passed to its Guatemalan counterparts printed material it had received that detailed the acts of the ayuntamiento of Cartagena de Indias in the days following the overthrow of the Spanish governor, Francisco Montes, and the establishment of an independent junta. González considered this information subversive and ordered the Guatemalan regidores to surrender it. Then he proceeded to prohibit all communication and commerce with the rebellious city and colony. With four dissenting peninsular votes, the ayuntamiento refused to turn over the material from Cartagena and decided, instead, to send another representation to the Council of Regency protesting the suspension of contact with New Granada as prejudicial to the well being of Guatemala.[84]

González was furious with this unprecedented act of disobedience. In a letter to the Council of State on 10 September, he declared that the recent news from South America had led him to believe that the ayuntamiento, "composed now of more Americans than Europeans," would foreswear its belated recognition of the newly formed Council of Regency: "[T]hey have seen their own ideas followed and to a certain degree realized in Cartagena de Indias; and this fact, which they have savored, has instilled in them new strength for claims and desires common throughout America."[85] This insubordination, if not implicit blackmail, continued, he wrote, in the efforts of leading creoles to persuade him to support free trade. In an attempt to punish the municipal council, the captain general then asked the crown to appoint a corregidor for the capital, a request that the regidores vigorously protested and that was never implemented.[86]

During this time of internal conflict between the creole and peninsular elites, the external threat to the colony did not disappear. In early September the colonial administration had to deal with another warning from the Council of Regency about Napoleonic emissaries. The crown expected this latest group of spies to enter Spanish America in disguise through the Mexican province of Texas and proceed from there to other parts of the empire. The Council of Regency was so concerned about this particular threat that it decided to give its colonial governors the power to execute anyone suspected of being a French spy or emissary without additional authorization. On 10 September, the captain general put this decree into effect in the kingdom.[87]

Only five days later, far to the north in the Mexican town of Dolores, the Hidalgo revolt began, an event that permanently altered the political environment in Central America. This uprising, which originated as a small creole conspiracy, was designed, ironically, to free the colony from French-dominated Spain. However, it quickly became a mass-based military insurrection with the potential to overturn the political and social structure of New Spain. Thus, by the end of 1810 the Spanish authorities in Guatemala faced a raging civil and race war in a highly influential neighboring colony that threatened to spill across the border with little warning.

To the south, Captain General González surveyed another open rebellion against Spain that put at risk the fragile tranquility of the isthmus. On 2 January 1811, the ayuntamiento of Guatemala City received a letter from the municipal authorities in Panama City. The Panamanians had an invitation in hand to send representatives to the new *Junta Suprema* in Santa Fe de Bogotá that had just declared the independence of the Viceroyalty of New Granada. Still faithful to Spain, Panama refused the proposal and instead sought support from Guatemala. The Guatemalan regidores thanked the Panamanians, assuring them that they could always count on "the immutable loyalty of this kingdom for our King Fernando VII."[88] Still, for colonial officials, this talk did not hide the fact that Central America was now surrounded by colonies in revolt.

On the surface, the Kingdom of Guatemala at the end of 1810 exhibited a remarkable degree of stability and loyalty, considering the political upheavals of the previous two years, the hysteria produced by the French scare, and the revolutionary movements convulsing other parts of the Spanish empire. As González noted in January 1811:

Although the Kingdom . . . is connected at one end with South America and at the other end with New Spain, and to the south and north has frequent contact by sea with the countries affected by the vertigo of political innovations; and although these provinces do not lack the causes of agitation which are common throughout America, relative to location and circumstances; despite all of this, I continue to have the incomparable satisfaction of maintaining good order, harmony among a diverse group of inhabitants, and the most perfect submission to legitimate authority.[89]

To forestall insurrection within the colony, the Spanish colonial officials had been careful to balance conciliation with the more repressive measures taken to combat subversion. Nevertheless, at this time the primary force behind the preservation of order was the Central American creole elite. Notwithstanding the increasingly frequent political and economic conflicts between the creole and peninsular communities, the Guatemalan oligarchy never wavered in its fidelity to Ferdinand VII and a reformed imperial system. Part of the reason for this was practical: living among a large indigenous population compelled them to preserve a close relationship with the colonial officials of the crown, lest a lower-class revolt erupt that necessitated military suppression. But there was also a strong sense that the creole community would benefit the most from the move toward a liberal, limited, and constitutional monarchy and that this trend should be supported as much as possible.

The collapse of the monarchy had a great impact on this segment of the population. A great gap existed between being subjects of an actual sitting monarch, fully in control of his legitimate sovereign power, and declaring loyalty to a symbol, and the creole community hoped to exploit this space. As soon as the ayuntamiento chose a deputy to represent the kingdom in the Junta Central early in 1810, the oligarchy became a more confident, politically active force for change, a transformation most apparent in the *Instrucciones*. On 3 November 1810, in words that would never have been used if Ferdinand VII were actually on the throne, the ayuntamiento wrote the Council of Regency to ask that the Cortes, which had just gone into session, be precluded from work on the constitution until Guatemala's delegate arrived: "But if the Cortes finds itself compelled to pass fundamental laws, to make reforms, to set up any other establishment, or, most particularly, to agree to or provide for any other form of government than that national one established during the absence of Fernando VII, Guatemala is formally opposed to anything being created without its express agreement, a right to which it is entitled."[90] Near the end of December, when the news arrived in Guatemala City of the installation of the Cortes, the ayuntamiento congregated to swear an oath of loyalty to the new supreme government. While the sentiments were genuine, the council proceeded to qualify its deed by referring explicitly to the 3 November letter, an act that hinted the creoles expected imperial politics to be more attuned to their needs and desires in exchange for their continued support. One month later, the ayuntamiento made a point of citing in the *Actas Capitulares* the Cortes decree declaring "the absolute equality under the law that America should enjoy with Spain as two integral and essential parts of the entire monarchy."[91]

In this confused and ever-shifting political environment, the ayuntamiento felt entitled to expand its jurisdiction from liquor licenses, agricultural policy, food distribution, and other local commercial and political issues into intercolonial relations. On 29 January 1811, Regidor Peinado made a presentation concerning the unrest in Mexico. He declared that the insurrection in New Spain could very well have a negative impact on the rest of the population of Middle America and that it was the duty of every good citizen to seek an end to such a grave threat to the nation and any of its parts. As a result, he urged the council to ask the captain general to offer "his good offices and mediation to the viceroy of Mexico in order to ascertain what the insurgents are seeking, and to see if it would be possible to organize a Congress of Deputies from around the kingdom and come to a settlement which would calm the dangerously excited spirits."[92] González, apparently, refused to make the necessary overtures.

By the beginning of 1811, the ayuntamiento had begun to address and arbitrate issues of internal discontent as well. Loyalty to Ferdinand did not necessarily preclude the inevitable frustration with certain colonial officials. However, in these troubled times, traditionally benign confrontations between a community and its governor carried potentially dangerous sparks. Legitimate petitions against the government looked like incitement to unrest. Unavoidable institutional delays appeared to be signs of prejudice or stalling. Provincial ayuntamientos complained to the Guatemala City council, while provincial governors appealed to the Spanish administration, a development that exacerbated the creole/peninsular split and usually left both sides unsatisfied and embittered. On 27 January 1811, the ayuntamiento of Sonsonate sent a follow-up letter to the Guatemalan council bemoaning the lack of action taken by González in its case against the "arbitrary and despotic" alcalde mayor of the province. Desperate for the removal of this official, the Sonsonate elders declared that his continued presence threatened the tranquility of the community. Then, in a statement that illuminated the greatest threat to continued Spanish rule on the isthmus, the ayuntamiento asked rhetorically: "In the present circumstances in which our brothers shed their blood in Spain to defend their liberty, can we live in tranquility under a tyranny that debases us?"[93] By the end of the year, in fact, such exasperation with the actions of peninsular officials in San Salvador and Nicaragua led to the outbreak of the first revolts in Central America.

In February, however, the most important thing on the minds of the Spanish administration and the creole elite was the imminent arrival of a new captain general. José de Bustamante had landed in Mexico the previous summer, from where he initiated contact with the ayuntamiento of Guatemala City, declaring his hope "that your light and knowledge will guide me in the success of my plans, which are directed only towards the happiness and general prosperity of that beautiful country, and the expansion and embellishment of its dignified capital."[94] He did not actually set out for Central America until the end of the year and did not reach Guatemala itself until March 1811.

The Kingdom of Guatemala on the eve of Bustamante's arrival was a colony at peace, outwardly calm but tense and insecure about the future. It was loyal to Spain, despite the sharp downturn in its political and economic fortunes since 1800, but it also did not lack the conditions that caused uprisings in other parts of the empire. In many respects, the faith the population exhibited in Spanish leadership amounted to a fear of innovation and a desire for stability and tradition in uncertain times. Both these revolutionary and conservative attitudes are illustrated in a unique request made by the ayuntamiento of Granada to their Guatemalan counterparts on 22 February. The regidores explained that they were convinced the tranquility that the kingdom had maintained to that point in the midst of such widespread unrest was due in large part to the faith the people had in Captain General González. The Nicaraguans argued that the governor had acquired such vast knowledge about the region during his time in office that it would be dangerous to let him leave. In the present circumstances, a new governor, lacking the requisite experience, would invariably breed discontent and insecurity, which other colonies had used as an excuse to break from Spain. Thus, the council proposed that the ayuntamientos of the kingdom confer with the captain general about the possibility that he remain in office, in effect staging a *golpe de estado* against the incoming governor.[95]

The Guatemala City ayuntamiento received the proposal early in March and responded immediately. Reports of the new captain general had long since reached Guatemala, causing no lack of concern among the creole elite. During the ten years of the comparatively relaxed administration of González, the Aycinena oligarchy had built up a powerful political base in the capital's ayuntamiento that complemented their domination of the region's commercial activities. In addition to their roles as merchants and indigo producers, the Aycinenas were also the dominant importers of contraband into the kingdom, a practice that González tolerated and that proved to be quite lucrative. At Montevideo, however, Bustamante had proven himself to be a fervent opponent of both illicit trade and creole political pretensions, positions that could have caused the Guatemalans to give serious consideration to the Granadan argument.

Instead, the ayuntamiento decided to use this opportunity to reconfirm its faith in Spain and the imperial system, implicitly rejecting a path toward independence that they would revisit a decade later. Regidor José de Aycinena wrote back stating that the request arrived a bit late for serious consideration and that it should have been made when González's transfer was first announced. At that stage, such a proposal

> would not have been illegal, as it is now, in addition to potentially being the origin of great disturbances and fatal consequences: this Ayuntamiento has positive reports of the character, motivation, and other good qualities of His Excellency José de Bustamante, who, in addition, has a thorough political and moral understanding: since he is already in the kingdom, and lacking any motive whatsoever to doubt the legitimacy of his appointment, or of his skill in governance, this Ayuntamiento does not find any reason to ask the Crown for his suspension: and, finally, since such an idea, and others that follow naturally, might result in certain enmities which could tarnish the noble and reputable loyalty of this kingdom, this Cabildo relies upon the prudence and notoriously good situation of the individuals on your illustrious corporation to keep the spirits of the faithful inhabitants of your province within the limits of submission and respect for the authorities, for the public happiness results from such harmony.[96]

Expecting the best, the Guatemalans then awaited the arrival of their new governor.

For the Spanish administration in the Kingdom of Guatemala, the period between the fall of the monarchy and the beginning of Bustamante's tenure as captain general produced four disturbing realizations. First, the defensive capabilities of the colony were limited and might not be sufficient to ward off a potential foreign invasion. Second, the isthmus could not remain unaffected for long by the revolutionary movements in South America and New Spain. Third, economic and political conditions in the provinces were difficult to assess or treat and threatened to spark serious disturbances. Fourth, the creole elite, though still loyal, had carved out a larger political role for itself in the midst of the imperial crisis, and its sustained pressure for greater reforms would inevitably bring it into direct competition with the colonial bureaucracy.

In response, the González administration developed a number of measures designed to control insurrection in the region and suppress signs of dissent. Through his antiemissary regulations, González strengthened and clarified the chain of command between the capital and local magistrates, cultivated an atmosphere of suspicion, and fleshed out threats to public order. He initiated the first significant assessment and mobilization of the kingdom's military resources and promoted the creation of urban militias. His *Tribunal de Fidelidad* represented the greatest step toward an interventionist regime, if not a police state, heretofore seen in Central America. And, his government made every effort to resist the encroachment on its political and economic jurisdiction by the Guatemalan ayuntamiento. In the years to come, Captain General Bustamante drew on this unequivocal administrative precedent as he developed an even more systematic policy of counterinsurgency to preserve Spanish rule on the isthmus.

4

The Preservation of Empire, 1811

Vice Admiral José de Bustamante y Guerra, named by the government of Ferdinand VII to the office of governor and captain general of the Kingdom of Guatemala and president of the royal audiencia, arrived in Guatemala City on 14 March 1811 to assume command of a colony at peace and firm in its loyalty to Spain. The welcome he received from the local population reflected no animosity toward this latest in a long line of Spanish governors, nor did it hint at the turmoil then enveloping the Spanish world. Instead, the residents of the capital rallied that day hopeful that peace and stability would soon return to the empire.

For more than a month, the ayuntamiento of the capital had planned the reception of the new governor, making preparations that illustrated the council's desire to be recognized as an equal among the senior colonial institutions. Responsibility for the festivities was delegated to José de Aycinena and José María Peinado, who estimated the expenses at fifteen hundred pesos, funds that the regidores thought could come from excise taxes but that they hoped the audiencia would cover. In the weeks that followed, the two institutions argued over the cost of the celebrations. Finally, the audiencia authorized a nineteen-hundred-peso budget. In the meantime, the municipal council arranged the details of the official welcome reception, including a lavish buffet and two orchestras, and worked feverishly to put the capital in a celebratory state, decorating the parade route and calling on citizens to adorn their homes and as many of the adjacent streets as possible.[1]

The ayuntamiento then turned its attention to the incoming governor. On 22 February Regidor Francisco Pacheco left the capital as the head of an advance team to meet Bustamante on the road. At Chimaltenango, Pacheco greeted Bustamante on behalf of the ayuntamiento and asked for his support in a minor dispute with the audiencia over the means of transportation to be used on the day of his arrival. The regidores had planned to receive the governor-elect on horseback, while the oidores wanted to use carriages. Bustamante agreed to the ayuntamiento plan.[2]

The formal services for the reception of the new governor began on 13 March in Mixco, a town just outside Guatemala City. Here Bustamante received delegations from the *cabildo ecclesiástico,* the ayuntamiento, and other corporate groups.[3] He spent the night there and was conducted to the capital the following morning in a carriage drawn by six mules. The first stop was at the south end of the city in a specially prepared house next to the Church of the Calvary. There, Bustamante was introduced to the ayuntamiento and many of the leading individuals in the kingdom. On behalf of the municipal council, Peinado gave a welcome speech and presented the distinguished guests and corporate bodies, which included Captain General González, the College of Lawyers, various prelates, and university figures. Then, on horseback, Bustamante paraded through the streets of Guatemala City with Alcalde Moreno, Regidor Palomo, and González, who conducted him to the Convent of Santa Clara, where the audiencia had assembled. From there the procession proceeded to the cathedral, where the governor-elect received the *cabildo ecclesiástico* and where the main welcoming ceremony, including a Te Deum, was held.

Immediately following this event, the kingdom's senior civil and religious officials crossed the Plaza Mayor to the royal palace. Surrounded by the audiencia in the Hall of the Real Acuerdo, "on his knees with one hand on the Cross and the other on the Bible," Bustamante took his oath of office, swearing his allegiance to the Catholic faith, espousing his loyalty to the Spanish nation as represented by the Cortes, administered by the Council of Regency, and symbolized by King Ferdinand VII, and pledging to obey, defend, execute, and enforce all the decrees, laws, and orders that might emanate from these sovereign bodies.[4] Now in full possession of his official powers, Captain General Bustamante emerged from the royal palace to receive from the military units and their officers, the ayuntamiento, and the community at large their protestations of loyalty and oaths of allegiance to him. The rest of the day was given over to celebration.

The welcome given to Bustamante was to all appearances an appropriate and enthusiastic one, and the captain general seemed to enter into his new duties full of confidence in the future. On 24 March, Bustamante prepared an open letter to the ayuntamientos on the isthmus, expressing his desire to promote the kingdom as an "integral part of the great Spanish family" and adding that "we should all hope that the happy age of a prosperous monarchy and all of its parts, established on indestructible foundations, is close at hand."[5] With this first proclamation, Bustamante declared his intention to be an activist administrator, a positive force in the development of Central America. Acknowledging that decrees from Madrid or Guatemala City would be shaped by local conditions, needs, and interests, he admitted that he would be unable to govern effectively without a comprehensive understanding of the state of the kingdom. As a result, he asked the ayuntamientos to send him detailed reports on the political, economic, and social conditions of the various provinces and municipalities. They were to pay particular attention to "agriculture, industry, and commerce, mining or other things that might contribute to the region's wealth, provincial policing and the administration of justice, and anything in general which might contribute to the respective affluence or poverty of a community." In a private letter to the Guatemalan ayuntamiento also dated 24 March, in which he thanked the regidores for their warm welcome and asked for the support of their experience and wisdom, Bustamante declared his "sincere desire to govern this kingdom under the principles of justice and public welfare, which I have been credited with in other positions."[6]

Two days later Bustamante paid a visit to the ayuntamiento. There he again expressed his gratitude for the displays of respect and esteem shown him by the population and reiterated his desire to govern successfully and to contribute to the general welfare of the kingdom. In response, Peinado declared the council's "satisfaction over the arrival of

[Bustamante] and expectations that our homeland will achieve prosperity and well-being under his administration and influence."[7] The captain general left the regidores with copies of his 24 March circular, reassured that his governing philosophy had met a receptive audience.

Yet, as a conscientious colonial official, Bustamante felt the need to reinforce his first statement to the kingdom with a more detailed document that outlined his plans for the future, his duties as he saw them, and his expectations for his new subjects. He wanted the population of Central America to see him as a man of action, not just of words, to understand his perspective on the most important issues of the day, and to recognize both his genuine desire for cooperation as well as the limits to his flexibility. Thus, on 13 April, Bustamante issued a fifteen-page address "to all the authorities and inhabitants of the kingdom under his command" that painted a remarkably candid portrait of a faithful public servant who defined his duties and worldview in a manner that some in his audience had begun to question.

As in his circular of 24 March, Bustamante first reaffirmed his "desire, which I have called fervent, to promote and execute the welfare of this kingdom to the fullest extent of my powers." To prove his qualifications as an administrator, he offered a brief account of his background, beginning with the famous Malaspina expedition that allowed him to develop his powers of observation and reasoning through direct experiences with the world. Bustamante placed particular emphasis on his service in Montevideo, which taught him about "the complicated offices of America" and gave him his first opportunity to confront the French, while his dramatic rejection of the *afrancesado* supporters of José I demonstrated his "fidelity and patriotism." Bustamante presented himself as a self-made man, with little taste for books or extravagant theories, who learned through example and comparison. In his professional capacity he considered himself to be a supremely responsible officer, devoted to the concept of duty, and proud of his status as a "pure Spaniard." Without mincing words the governor explained that he realized early on that "the art of command is learned through its true principle, which is the art of obedience." In his military-trained mind, society could not function without an administrative structure with a clear chain of command that stressed respect for superiors and a sense of responsibility on the part of all citizens.[8]

As Spanish America navigated the imperial crisis, Bustamante felt the need to instruct his subjects on the concept of patriotism and its obligations. Having offered his own career as a model of selfless public service in which duty and obedience played a major role, the new captain general proceeded to deliver a stinging critique of incipient creole consciousness—the growing propensity on the part of creoles to identify themselves as Americans and to define their needs and goals as distinct from those of their peninsular cousins. In his view, just as the *afrancesados* in Spain followed personal, selfish interest when welcoming Napoleon into Spain, so did Spanish Americans err who used the weakness of the crown to break free from legitimate authority. Instead, Bustamante held fast to an imperial ideal that emphasized common tradition and a shared destiny, thereby demonstrating the ideological gulf that would contribute to years of misunderstanding, distrust, and hostility between some Guatemalans and their governor. Still, until subsequent events sharpened these differences and provided justification for repressive measures, Bustamante remained optimistic that his vision of an all-inclusive empire could be preserved. To that end, he explained:

> The masses confuse the words *patria* and *país,* patriotism and citizenship. The country where one is born, where one develops reason, where one's soul forms its most permanent impressions, deserves and inspires affection. But how distinct is the wide, true love for the *Patria,* which includes all of the peoples united by the same social bonds, all those under one Religion, one King, one Law, one culture, one will and one character which distinguishes us from all others! For Spaniards *Patria* is every place on earth populated by our ancestors, inhabited by their worthy descendents, governed and defended by their laws. . . . For the good Spaniard there is no distinction between kingdoms, nor between the provinces which comprise the vast extent of the Monarchy: the good Spaniard loves the State, which is the indivisible collection of all; he loves equally every one of its parts, from whose welfare results the well-being of all.[9]

With this in mind, Bustamante expected all responsible patriots to recognize the dangers confronting the *patria* at the time and to work tirelessly to restore the monarchy. From his perspective, any effort to take advantage of the weakness of the state to advance personal or regional interests was tantamount to treason.

As Bustamante saw it, his duties and obligations were relatively straightforward: "To preserve these provinces in total peace, tranquility, and calm; to endeavor that they be raised and ennobled; to provide for the rule of justice, reward and punishment, the good treatment of the natives, and their conservation and defense." He planned to govern as in Montevideo, according to rational, methodical designs, with administrative mechanisms sensitive to new methods and principles of reform. Bustamante also declared his support for the political reorganization being effected by the delegates to the Cortes, "whose installation I yearned for, I worked for, and I incited with all my heart when timidity, ambition, and political errors raised obstacles to this sacred anchor of our hopes." In his mind, the 24 March circular demonstrated his good faith and willingness to cooperate with the reform process.[10]

Although he recognized that he had not yet acquired extensive knowledge of Guatemalan affairs in the month he had spent in office, Bustamante offered some general observations he had made to that point regarding isthmian development. His primary concern was that Central America was too sparsely populated to see economic progress. As a result, the colony could not sustain the types of projects that created wealth, thereby leaving most people idle and impoverished. The governor promised to end unemployment by strengthening artisan guilds and promoting the textile industry. He also expected the revitalized *Real Consulado* and *Sociedad Económica* to do their patriotic duty and find new ways to employ the population. As a complement to these proposals, Bustamante came out vehemently against contraband trade, asserting that its practice interfered with "the great good in fostering and promoting domestic industry, saintly industry, which by focusing on objects of solid utility diffuses among all groups of the state the principle of life that constitutes its vigor and strength."[11] Those who practiced it, in his opinion, were public enemies, unpatriotic, and a threat to the economic welfare of the kingdom. Therefore he pledged to support the laws against contraband with all the powers at his disposal, a statement that must have worried the House of Aycinena. Turning his attention to mining, Bustamante stated that he had asked for advice while in Mexico about ways to revitalize this industry. In his mind the problems that had slowed output stemmed from a lack of capital, poor technology, difficult locations, and a poor work force. Friends in Peru and New Spain were supposed to provide him with more suggestions for improvement, but the revolutionary movements had delayed these reports.[12]

At this point, the governor turned his attention to the uprisings in New Spain, that "fatal spectacle, horror of humanity, eternal shame of its ungracious and depraved instigators!"[13] For Bustamante the revolutionary movements were particularly horrible, for they occurred on heretofore peaceful, civilized, and law-abiding lands. He reiterated his happiness at being in Guatemala, a place where loyalty and patriotism were so clearly valued:

> What a pleasant contrast Guatemala offers to the sad images of other areas, agitated by insane discord. I congratulate myself for having come to a country where loyalty walks alongside prudence, and patriotism, which in other parts is the hypocrisy of separatists, alongside rational subordination, which is the guardian angel of communities. Thus, according to one author's expression, while the vultures tear themselves apart, there are also silkworms whose silent and peaceful work is enjoyed by subsequent generations.[14]

Ultimately, Bustamante recognized that it was his obligation to preserve the calm that distinguished Guatemala from most of the other Spanish colonies with all the means at his disposal. In a statement that can be interpreted as his a priori defense of the imposition of repressive measures after the sustained outbreak of insurrection in early 1812, the captain general declared:

> In order to maintain such a fortunate state of harmonious tranquility no effort will be too arduous for me, nor will there be any prudent measures that I will not adopt from those which caution may suggest to me. Experience has shown me that insignificant causes can, during turbulent times, produce the most lamentable results: how political opinions can lead one astray and the contagious influence of such mistakes; how the Tyrant [Napoleon] has calculated and calculates according to these er-

rors, and how he uses them to incite and advance by creeping methods, as immoral as they are subtle. But experience has also shown me that the continuous recollection of the justice of our cause and of its fundamental principles, incessant vigilance, and energy and rectitude in command are walls of bronze against which the perverse arts of . . . Machiavellianism shatter, along with all public and secret enemies, and those who, unaware, do their bidding or contribute to their detestable goals.[15]

There was no doubt in his mind that the unrest in Spanish America resulted from a "horrendous system of universal subversion" directed by the tyrant Napoleon. As an official of the Spanish crown it was his duty to resist it to the end, to "die for the Patria and for its saintly laws; but to die while completing the arduous responsibilities of my position as completely as I understand them." These duties "suggest to me that so long as this kingdom enjoys its enviable tranquility, I should procure for it the wealth that it justly deserves . . . that which the Supreme Government of the Nation paternally desires for it, and that which it should expect from a good governor in the present circumstances."[16] Significantly, Bustamante saw his duties and actions as governor linked to the continued stability of the kingdom and the obedience of the population. So long as the status quo remained, Bustamante would be able to work in a cooperative, constructive, and flexible manner toward the greater welfare of the Kingdom of Guatemala. His first duty, however, was to the crown and empire. The entire decree, with its constant referrals to patriotism, was meant to encourage fidelity to Spain, but it also served as a subtle warning that the new administration would tolerate no signs of dissension from the established order.

The spring of 1811 was distinguished by three events that appeared to belie the precariousness of the Spanish position in Central America and even offered hope for reconciliation between Americans and peninsulars. On 2 May the *Gaceta de Guatemala* published reports on the defeat and capture of the principal leaders of the Mexican insurrection, including Hidalgo. In response, Bustamante ordered a Te Deum and a grand celebration that included all of the major colonial officials.[17] On 24 May the captain general, perhaps angling for creole support, reported to Spain that "the Tribunal of Loyalty set up by my predecessor has ceased its operations; the cases which were pending in it will pass with-

out delay to the criminal courts."[18] And, finally, the government received word a short time later from Archbishop-elect Father Ramón
Casaus y Torres, who was making his way to the kingdom from Mexico,
where he had been a leader in the clerical establishment's opposition to
Hidalgo. In a letter of introduction to his new congregation and the local authorities, Casaus praised the "enviable tranquility" of the kingdom and its "docile and pious Peoples."[19]

During these first two months in office, in fact, Bustamante felt free
enough to address issues that had little to do with subversion or colonial
defense. Concerned with the high rate of violence and homicide in the
capital, the governor proposed a reorganization of the system of *alcaldes
de barrio,* the establishment of a more streamlined judicial process, and
the lighting of the city streets, among other things. On 4 May he proposed to the ayuntamiento that land around the capital be cleared for
grazing to improve the movement of livestock from the provinces.[20] Despite occasional jurisdictional disputes between the ayuntamiento and
the colonial government, it appeared that the kingdom had resolved its
major sources of instability.

The Kingdom of Guatemala could not shut itself off from the outside world, however. For this reason neither the Spanish authorities nor
the creole oligarchy neglected the issue of security during this tranquil period. In a special session on 17 April the audiencia reviewed a decree from the Council of Regency that had been sent in December 1810.
In it the Council reiterated its warnings about French subversion and
made a special plea to religious leaders, from bishops to parish priests,
to use their special standing among the population to promote loyalty
to the crown and to confront the danger facing the empire with public and private prayer services.[21] With the French scare still very much
alive, the ayuntamiento proposed on 30 May that the kingdom's defenses
be augmented by the creation of a special urban militia composed of
Spanish volunteers. Bustamante responded positively to this suggestion and asked the council to send him a list of those willing to volunteer. He then made a recommendation of his own, arguing that the
capital needed a *cuerpo de serenos* (corps of night watchmen) to patrol
the streets and protect the population from crime and subversive behavior.[22] On 18 June, Bustamante declared his intention to increase government vigilance after receiving a warning from the viceroy of New Spain

about a new French agent who had recently arrived in New Orleans.[23] One week later, the ayuntamiento continued the focus on security by passing on to the captain general, as "a new proof of its loyalty and subordination to authorities," three copies of two papers printed with the mark of the *Junta Superior* of Cádiz, one of which included an article entitled "Critical observations on a conversation between a Frenchman and a citizen of the island of León regarding the rights of the Princess of Brazil to the eventual succession of the Spanish Throne." As the papers did not carry an official postmark or a letter of remittance, the ayuntamiento was suspicious enough of their origins to turn over the material to the colonial authorities.[24]

The issue of French subversion remained high on the agenda of the colonial government in Guatemala City throughout 1811. However, despite the constant attention of senior officers to this threat and the security infrastructure already established by Captain General González, the actual implementation of defense regulations depended heavily on the active participation of provincial officials. The direct authority of the colonial governor did not extend far beyond the outskirts of the capital, and when Bustamante issued kingdomwide decrees he could rarely confirm that his orders were ever fully carried out. The concept of a central power with the ability to enforce its laws and impose its will on the entire area under its jurisdiction or of a police state consisting of a complex web of bureaucracy with sensitive links between the government and the population was not a part of the late colonial experience of Central America. Difficult terrain, poor communications, entrenched local interests, and a small, overextended colonial bureaucracy all limited the effective power of the Spanish government in Guatemala City. The efforts of Captain General Bustamante to preserve order in the kingdom were made on the foundations of a tenuous administrative structure, which forced him to rely heavily on the abilities of his provincial officials and the assistance of the local population to achieve his goals.

A prime example of this relationship has been preserved in the detailed correspondence between Bustamante and Narciso Mallol, the alcalde mayor of Totonicapán y Huehuetenango. Mallol, who took control of this strategic province in the western highlands of Guatemala in April, was one of the more enthusiastic supporters of the new captain

general. Over the course of his first year in office, he served on the front
lines of the battle against subversion, since his jurisdiction fronted the
kingdom's borders with New Spain. However, the orders he received
from Guatemala City—and his efforts to implement them—would have
been familiar to all the intendants, alcaldes mayores, and corregidores
from Chiapas to Costa Rica.

Bustamante's circular of 13 April sparked the first letter from Mallol.
On 11 May he wrote to assure the new governor of the full support of his
province in the "fulfillment of your high obligations."[25] Initially this
meant little more than increasing agricultural output on Bustamante's
recommendation that extra food be grown to assist the population of
New Spain in their efforts to recover from the destruction of the Hidalgo insurrection and removing a local magistrate whose abuses of
his Indian charges had reached the ears of the captain general.[26] At the
end of June, however, the alcalde mayor received new warnings from
the capital of French emissaries who had reportedly entered the region
through Campeche, Tabasco, and other areas along the southern Gulf of
Mexico. Bustamante asked Mallol to alert all the local officials in his
province to step up the identification of strangers and travelers, especially those from the designated areas, while stressing the extreme gravity
of the situation and the need to confront suspicious activity with severity.[27]

Mallol responded on 4 July that he had sent the necessary orders to
his magistrates and judges "to impede the fatal ideas of the abominable
French government." He stated his concern, however, that "the good
laws establishing regulations that there be no doubt as to the legitimacy of the subjects traveling from one part to another are not being observed, [because of] circumstances and the general disinclination
to do so on the part of those who govern the towns."[28] Mallol viewed
Huehuetenango as particularly vulnerable to penetration by French
agents because of the short distance to the unprotected Gulf through
the protected waterways of the Lacandon forests. As a consequence, he
recommended to Bustamante that a special commissioner be appointed
to a new district (*partido*) of Chiantla, to be carved out of the area just
north of the town of Huehuetenango, and he went so far as to propose
a candidate, the Spaniard Joaquín Mont. Since "Chiantla is the point

through which those who travel from the indicated areas must pass," Mallol thought that it deserved special attention from the colonial authorities.[29] Bustamante agreed with the alcalde mayor, authorized him to make the changes, and stressed that Mont be given the "most strict assignment to watch over and guard against the introduction of any stranger or contraband."[30]

By early August Bustamante was able to send Mallol detailed descriptions of two "very suspicious" travelers who had entered the kingdom from New Spain. The first suspect was approximately forty years of age, "of regular size and build, full in the face, with an olive-skinned, grainy, and yellowish complexion, large black eyes, long, curly hair, and a full beard," while his younger partner was "tall and well built, white-skinned, with curly chestnut-brown hair that was cut in front, a round face, bluish eyes, and a regular beard."[31] According to the report, they also traveled on mules with special brands. With this information, the captain general expected his alcalde mayor to investigate each and every stranger passing through the province whose "character, baggage, conversation, or other motives might cause just suspicion" and encouraged him to make every inn and guest house aware of their obligation to check documents and register their guests with the proper authorities. To do so, Mallol had a number of copies of the travelers' description printed and distributed for use by local authorities and concerned citizens.[32]

One month later Bustamante alerted the provinces to another potential emissary. In a letter to Mallol dated 9 September, the captain general provided a detailed portrait of a spy identified only as Monsieur Greffe. This colorful character, reputed to be an officer in the French Imperial Guards, was making his second visit to Central America after having escaped from a local prison on an earlier occasion. In addition to the usual physical characteristics of the suspect, the official description noted that Greffe spoke Spanish with a perfect Andalusian accent and emphasized the fact that Greffe wore a small wig or toupee to hide the scars from various cranial wounds, a detail that Bustamante hoped would betray the emissary. Ending this particular dispatch, the captain general repeated his hopes that Mallol would use this information to "redouble his vigilance and encourage all the magistrates, ministers of justice, and

faithful inhabitants of his jurisdiction to redouble theirs as well . . . proceeding with the case with the activity and zeal which an assignment of
such gravity demands."[33]

Mallol did what he could and passed the warning and description
of Greffe to his subordinates as quickly as possible. On 21 September
Hermenegildo López, the *juez preventivo* of Nebaj, wrote to the alcalde
mayor that "in my time in office I have not seen any emissary come
through, but I will keep watch and pay careful attention to all the strangers that may come to these towns."[34] He ended his dispatch by complaining that someone or something (*algún demonio*) must have passed
through the area, for the Indians had begun to ignore him and disobey
his orders. Three days later, Nasario Argueta, the *juez preventivo* of San
Antonio Huista, a town deep in the Cuchumatán Mountains, reported
that he had explained to the Indians and ladinos under his jurisdiction about Monsieur Greffe and the need to be vigilant, though he knew
of no emissaries in the region.[35] In October, Mallol heard back from
his *juez preventivo* in San Pedro Solomá, Marcos Castañeda, who declared that

> in order to comply with this severe obligation I have repeatedly explained
> to all the judges of the towns under my jurisdiction in their own lan-
> guage the strict obligations that will be entrusted to them, and the severe
> penalties to which they will be subject if they allow any unknown person
> to travel over the unfrequented roads between their towns and the haci-
> enda of Chancob and Chiantla, and in particular the cited Mr. Greffe. . . .
> For my part I pledge, though it be detrimental to my life, not to allow
> anyone to pass without careful examination, even if he comes dressed as
> a priest, a soldier, or a mendicant, since simply by bypassing the *camino
> real* he makes himself highly suspicious.[36]

In this manner, Bustamante's warnings about French emissaries and
other subversive activity descended the administrative hierarchy and
reached deep into the Central American countryside. While the decrees
undoubtedly served to energize certain subordinate officials eager to
play a role in regional defense, their general effectiveness is harder to
gauge, for actual implementation depended upon the personal discretion of local authorities and the extent of cooperation offered by the

local population. One unintended consequence of such regular reports of subversion and foreign penetration, however, was a rising climate of fear and insecurity in the kingdom, which would contribute to the destabilization of a number of rural communities.

Civil authorities were not the only ones to whom the captain general appealed in the fight against French conspiracy. In September, Mallol received and distributed throughout his province a circular that Bustamante directed to members of the church establishment. In this bulletin the governor explained that new reports indicated Napoleonic spies had become accustomed to wearing clerical disguises, both secular and regular, in their efforts to penetrate the kingdom. In light of this development, he was compelled to prohibit travel without passport by anyone except the most well-known or high-ranking officials. He therefore expected the Church to assist him in this matter by having members of the clergy with compelling reasons to travel first report to the proper civil authorities for the requisite documentation.[37]

By the end of the year, concern over French subversion in Guatemala peaked again, with Bustamante sending out a new description of a suspected emissary to his provincial officials during the first week of November.[38] On 11 November, Mallol turned this latest warning from the capital into a general circular on the French threat and addressed it to "all the judges and magistrates, and all the loyal citizens and heads of families of my jurisdiction." The announcement informed the local population that another emissary threatened the province, provided a detailed description of the individual, offered a reward of five hundred pesos to anyone who discovered his whereabouts and a thousand pesos to the one who managed to apprehend him, and threatened severe punishments, including death, to anyone found guilty of hiding or aiding "such a public enemy."[39] The alcalde mayor then ordered that his decree be printed and distributed throughout the alcaldía mayor of Totonicapán y Huehuetenango and that *alcaldes pedaneos* make special rounds in order to deliver it to the community. For the benefit of the large indigenous population of the region, Mallol expected his Indian magistrates to translate the decree, to provide copies for those who could read, and to explain it to anyone who could not. Finally, Mallol decided to initiate security patrols in the town of Totonicapán to be undertaken by the *alcaldes pedaneos* and the regidores of the ayuntamiento. To the extent possible with his resources, Mallol attempted to sensitize his province to the French threat and provide a basic security apparatus to combat subversion. However, as he noted in a letter to Bustamante, "this alcaldía is composed of two *partidos* and 51 towns spread out over an area more than 60 leagues in longitude and 50 in latitude, which makes it indispensable to have at a minimum four avenues of communication for the distribution of orders, since with only two more than a month and a half can elapse before a response is received."[40] With provincial governors facing similar obstacles across the isthmus, the task of preserving the political and social stability of the colony proved to be a constant challenge for the administration in Guatemala City.

Aside from the persistent threat of French emissaries, the Kingdom of Guatemala experienced a number of seditious and subversive acts of varying levels of severity over the course of 1811. By the time of its dissolution in May the *Tribunal de Fidelidad* had registered eight new cases worthy of investigation to add to the twenty-five it had opened the previous year. These latest additions included the prosecution of Francisco Barberena "for having proffered expressions against religion and the state"; Antonio Campos for "suspicion of adherence to France"; José Gabriel Vela for pro-Napoleonic sentiments; José Francisco Córdoba, the secretary (*escribano*) of the ayuntamiento of Guatemala City, for discussing "seditious matters in a conversation"; and Pedro Barriere, the *teniente letrado* of San Salvador, for suspicion of infidencia.[41] The tribunal also received reports from officials in San Salvador concerning seditious material that had been distributed in the capital of the province, unrest fomented there by Father Miguel Delgado and others, and subversive pronouncements made by the Franciscan cleric Mariano Vargas. Over the course of the summer, the Spanish administration also leveled charges against Manuel Osorio for anti-European statements and Tomás Martín Torres for attempted revolt.[42] While nothing about these cases indicated that the Kingdom of Guatemala was on the verge of rebellion against the crown—in fact most of these defendants were either released for lack of evidence or received a pardon—their notoriety contributed to a growing sense of insecurity in the besieged colony.

Two specific examples from the first half of the year underscore the combustible nature of the charges swirling around Central America at this time. The first case, that of Encarnación Balladares, came to the attention of José Salvador, the intendant of Nicaragua, on 23 April, when Balladares, a soldier in the Eighth Infantry Battalion of the Militia of León, was arrested for making subversive statements. According to Salvador's report, Balladares was responsible for spreading rumors in the town of Chinandega that Guatemala City, San Salvador, and León had erupted in revolt, news that greatly disturbed the community. When questioned, the soldier admitted making the statements but declared that he meant no harm, for he got the information from a poster on the cathedral and believed that the news was well known in town. Salvador sent the details to Bustamante asking for advice on how to proceed, as the question of legal jurisdiction now had to be taken into consideration because Balladares was a soldier with the *fuero militar*. The captain general turned the matter over to his *auditor de guerra,* Joaquín Ibáñez. Arguing that "this crime is one which disturbs the public tranquility, and attacks the security of the Community, touching on infidencia and *lesa Majestad,*" Ibáñez recommended that the case be sent to the audiencia, which he believed had authority over such crimes, regardless of *fuero.*[43] The reasonable fear on the part of the Spanish administration was that rumors, lies, and misinformation could do as much damage to colonial security as an active insurgency. On 31 May the *oidor fiscal* (crown attorney) reported that he doubted Balladares's excuse, since he presented no witnesses to support the idea that such information was widely held to be true in the town, but decided, nevertheless, that Balladares qualified for a royal pardon and ordered him released.

The other case of sedition that received serious attention was that of Pedro Barriere, the *teniente letrado* and *asesor ordinario* of San Salvador, who was accused of the crime of infidencia by the intendant of the province, Antonio Gutiérrez Ulloa. Bustamante received the complaint on 2 June and immediately prepared a report for the audiencia. While no evidence of subversion against him could be substantiated, Barriere, a Spanish subject of French descent born on the island of Santo Domingo, had clearly run afoul of the provincial authorities of San Salvador. With Gutiérrez leading the charge, they decided to use his dangerous ancestry to declare him unfit for command, arguing that all of the warnings issued against the French made it impossible for the population to treat Barriere with the respect his office deserved or to accept his orders and suggestions. Bustamante found this argument persuasive, considering "the delicate circumstances of the present day and those that might occur unexpectedly" and the fact that the asesor had already applied for retirement, but he decided to take no action without the opinion of the audiencia.

On 26 July the oidor fiscal noted in response that the audiencia had been forced to deal with the antipathy between Gutiérrez and Barriere and the former's efforts to get rid of his asesor since March 1809. In the opinion of the judge, there was no reason to consider any of Barriere's actions subversive or even suspicious, and his accuser's behavior in the matter was not above reproach. Oidor González considered the details of Barriere's ancestry a nonissue, since Santo Domingo was under Spanish rule at his birth and he had repeatedly demonstrated his loyalty to the crown in the years that followed. As a result, he found no grounds for Barriere's removal from office as required by law; instead, the oidor fiscal believed that a great deal of harm would follow if such action were taken, for "if the People found it easy to influence the removal of officials, no one would be secure in the position he holds."[44] As an example, the oidor cited the fact that the priest Dr. José Matías Delgado and two other residents of San Salvador had recently petitioned the superior government for the removal of Intendant Gutiérrez himself, whom they accused of "suspicious" activity. The judge concluded by recommending that the intendant and the asesor come to some sort of arrangement to promote a more harmonious relationship between the two.

However, Bustamante had other plans. With the final decision of the audiencia not immediately forthcoming, despite the written opinion from González, and with reports of more complaints and disturbances in San Salvador, the captain general recalled Barriere on 22 August, noting that "the present circumstances and the peculiarities of the province of San Salvador" made such action necessary.[45] When it came down to a question of provincial stability, Bustamante simply determined that legalistic arguments and the regular administrative decision-making process were not flexible enough to maintain Spanish rule. On 6 November the audiencia was forced to accept this result.

During this period of relative stability on the isthmus, the Guatemala City ayuntamiento continued to press for political reform and increased American representation in the administration of the empire, as well as its own elevation within the hierarchy of colonial government. On

15 July Regidor Peinado brought to a council meeting a draft proposing that the Cortes Deputy Antonio de Larrazábal promote the establishment of *juntas provinciales* in the kingdom along the lines of those created in Spain.[46] One month later, following a discussion about the supply and price of meat, the ayuntamiento decided to solicit from the crown the honorific title of *excelencia* (excellency), a privileged rank that the captain general and the municipal councils of the other capitals of kingdoms held. The members justified their request by noting "the singular loyalty with which [the ayuntamiento] has conducted itself during such dangerous times as the present while the rest of the kingdoms in both Americas have experienced convulsions."[47] José de Aycinena received the commission to prepare the necessary documents, and the council sent its formal request off to Larrazábal on 11 October.

In the meantime, the ayuntamiento made a concerted effort to raise the level of political consciousness in the kingdom by taking upon itself the responsibility to print and distribute throughout the provinces copies of its 1810 *Instrucciones,* which had made a significant impression in Cádiz, and other news from the Cortes relating to American concerns as reported by Guatemala's interim deputies in Spain. At the end of September, the council sent to the printer the latest dispatch from the *diputados suplentes* (substitute deputies), material that included highly favorable reviews of the *Instrucciones* and "the proposals made in favor of these Americas by all its representatives, indicating that which has been conceded, refused, and referred."[48] However, concerned that such sensitive political information and decentralized lines of communication threatened the authority of the colonial government in the provinces, Bustamante suspended the printing process and confiscated the material in question. The ayuntamiento viewed this action as an attack on the new laws guaranteeing freedom of the press and in early October sent a deputation to discuss the matter with the captain general. Bustamante explained that he had no desire to impede press freedoms, but only wanted to know what was included in the publications, a right that he claimed as governor and that he had to exercise in the interim before the new censorship board (*tribunal censorio*) began its operations. Declaring that he now found no reason to stop the publications and was satisfied with the conduct of the ayuntamiento, Bustamante returned the material to the printer and allowed the process to continue.[49]

In fact, by the fall of 1811 Bustamante had ample reason to mistrust the motivations of the ayuntamiento and had begun to believe that a growing number of Central American creoles were giving serious consideration to the idea of political autonomy. However unintentionally, the status reports solicited by the governor in his 24 March and 13 April decrees to the provincial elite contributed to this trend. With direction from the Guatemala City ayuntamiento, the provincial councils coordinated their concerns and suggestions to Bustamante over the course of the summer.[50] The most comprehensive review of the state of the kingdom, however, came from the capital itself, and in October its principal author, José de Aycinena, had the entire thirty-six-page report printed and distributed across the isthmus at his own expense.[51] This document stands as a barometer of creole concerns and political sentiment in the summer of 1811.

On behalf of his colleagues Aycinena first felt compelled to stress the fact that the council had already addressed the political state of the kingdom in its *Instrucciones* and continued to investigate "the causes of its decadence, while considering the most viable means of improvement and perfection in all public sectors."[52] These many deliberations, in fact, had convinced the ayuntamiento that the solution to Guatemala's problems was simple: the establishment of a constitutional system of government for the empire. In an interesting counterpoint to Bustamante's position on the relationship between *patria* and *país*, which stressed supernational sentiments as a means of unifying the empire, Aycinena argued that a constitution was fundamental to the survival of such a heterogeneous polity, for it could incorporate "provincial particularities" into one great whole. Ominously, he then declared that "the constitution is so necessary that on it depends whether or not we have a patria."[53] The ayuntamiento report also applauded recent Cortes decisions establishing the principles of liberty, equality, and property as the foundations for the new constitution and emphasized the particular importance of equality as a basic right.

Belatedly, the council then turned its attention to the particular obstacles to development in Guatemala itself. Aycinena explained to Bustamante that two other reforms would result in a dramatic transformation of the kingdom's fortunes: the introduction of an educational infrastructure to modernize the *costumbres* (customs) of the lower classes, in particular the Indians, and the abolition of the state monopoly on *aguardiente,* the source of much of the state's income and, according to the creoles, a contributing factor in the poor productivity of the lower classes. The regidores then promised that they were disposed "to fight to the end against every kind of subversion, to excuse no fatigue in preserving unity and tranquil peace, to contribute in any way possible to the prosperity and betterment of this republic, and finally to defend the patria, though it be necessary to uproot ourselves from nature's bosom, from our children, and from everything else that we love in this world."[54]

Shortly after the Guatemalan report had been distributed around the colony, however, the ayuntamiento received a response from its counterpart in the town of Quetzaltenango. This reply demonstrated that an imperial constitution and a few social reforms administered by the colonial administration were not viewed as adequate by some provincial creoles. Instead, the Quetzaltenango regidores demanded "a Junta of Deputies from all the provinces based in the capital."[55] The Guatemala City council promised the Quetzaltecos that this was its ultimate goal too, an admission that underscored the deepening political division between the Spanish officials and the Central American creole elite.

The sentiments expressed by the Central American ayuntamientos in the summer of 1811 concerning constitutional reform and provincial autonomy, though in line with the perspective of much of the loyal creole population of Spanish America at the time, could only be viewed as a disconcerting trend by the governing authorities on the isthmus. This new political order promoted by Spanish Americans in 1811 and later expressed in the Constitution of 1812 promised creoles direct access to three new governing institutions: the Cortes in Spain; the regional juntas or assemblies known as the *diputaciones provinciales;* and the elected ayuntamientos constitucionales.[56] In contrast, the traditional imperial authorities (the viceroys, governors, audiencias, and lesser officials) found themselves threatened by a corresponding decrease in power. As if these changes were not destabilizing enough, reformists expected to implement them in the midst of rebellion, civil conflicts, and international wars. In an empirewide atmosphere of political insecurity, external threats and internal revolts, and questions concerning the stability and legitimacy of the Cádiz constitutional experiment, many colonial governments began to resist the growing pressures for American autonomy. By the end of 1811, as the growing political tension transformed itself into provincial revolts, the Bustamante administration felt compelled to promote a concentration of power in the hands of the captain general and a turn toward martial law.

In the midst of all the political maneuvering between creole and peninsular elites in the colony, the issue of internal security reappeared. On 6 October, the Guatemala City ayuntamiento received an urgent plea from its Panamanian counterpart that asked the Guatemalan regidores to convince Bustamante to send arms and money to Panama for the defense of the isthmus. In short supply of both, the captain general replied that the kingdom could only help out with food, powder, and shot.[57] One week later, Bustamante sent a reminder to the ayuntamiento that the establishment of urban militia companies, proposed by the municipal council on 31 May, had not been completed. The captain general was especially enthusiastic about this plan and lauded the "patriotic zeal" that conceived it and its promise to preserve the public tranquility as well as provide valuable military training to the population.[58] Emphasizing the patriotic duty of all true Spaniards, Bustamante pressured the ayuntamiento to proceed quickly with the nomination and election of captains, lieutenants, and lesser officers to the four companies being organized in the capital. By the first week in November the preparations were complete. At least with respect to colonial security issues, it appeared that the Spanish administration and the creole elite remained close partners, for the list of proposed officers included some of the most powerful names in the kingdom.[59]

The month of November opened with more disconcerting news about potential subversive activities in the kingdom. On the eighth Bustamante notified the ayuntamiento that his administration was tracking a suspected French emissary in the capital. The captain general urged the municipal alcaldes to be more vigilant in their rounds and the regidores to work to "tranquilize spirits and remove any malignancies that might originate from this public enemy or result from his arts and schemes."[60] Four days later he issued another bulletin on the subject to the council. This included the physical description that had also been distributed to provincial officials, though Bustamante feared that such public notices had caused the spy to alter his appearance. The captain general explained that any stranger without a passport and a reasonable account of his activities should be considered suspect and that the warnings should be distributed to all towns, haciendas, and farms and among all segments of the population. This reiteration of the administration's antisubversive policies was only a prelude to his real subject, however. Bustamante then added that anyone who disseminated rumors or information favoring the French or the Mexican insurgents, who spoke out against the colonial government and Cortes, who tried to incite hostility between Americans and Europeans, or who did anything to disturb or delude the innocent population of Guatemala would be considered a public enemy.[61] In this manner, the governor attempted to link disgruntled and potentially disloyal sentiment with international espionage and treason, thereby setting the stage for a crackdown on dissent of any form. The ayuntamiento responded that it had been as diligent as possible on the matter of subversion and would happily continue to perform its obligations as laid out in the decree.[62]

The reintroduction of the French emissary onto the Guatemalan political scene at the end of 1811 might have been a convenient way to distract creole attention from constitutional reforms and reinforce the role of the Spanish government as the guarantor of public security. In fact, few issues united the governing elites, both creole and peninsular, like the fear of unrest and subversion. This does not mean that Bustamante manipulated public opinion with a cunningly constructed fictitious enemy. He, like González, had enough evidence and precedent to conclude that the threat did exist and that precautions needed to be taken. In his report to the ayuntamiento, Bustamante cited even more royal warnings on the issue and noted that one of the emissaries had actually returned to France and published details of his travels through Guatemala.[63] Whether real or imagined, however, the French emissary was certainly a figure of strong symbolic importance in the Kingdom of Guatemala. When he made his appearance, as he did repeatedly between 1808 and 1812, he underscored the precariousness of the Spanish empire in the face of insidious enemies, both internal and external, that threatened to overturn the old order with dangerous new ideas.

As fate would have it, the first news of popular uprisings in San Salvador reached Guatemala City during the ayuntamiento deliberations over Bustamante's call for increased vigilance and improved security measures. Although the unrest arose with no clear advance warning, the events in San Salvador between 5 and 9 November illuminate the tense political and social climate that had developed in the Kingdom of Guatemala since 1808, with the actions of both the insurgents and the colonial government affected by a number of competing forces: liberal politics, local rivalries, provincial autonomous sentiment, creole/peninsular conflicts, the French scare, elite cooperation, and popular loyalty to Spain.

The Salvadoran rebellion that ended Bustamante's honeymoon in Central America was in part precipitated by concern in the Guatemalan Church over subversive priests. With the Hidalgo revolt in New Spain demonstrating the impact rebellious clergy could have on a restless population, the new archbishop, Ramón Casaus, arrived in Guatemala determined to prevent a similar movement from emerging there. In September, Casaus received a letter that had been sent from the Mexican viceroy to the prefect of the Convent of Belén in Guatemala City.[64] In it Viceroy Francisco Venegas made clear his concern that the regular orders, with their protected spaces, rights, communication, and costume, might offer cover for subversive activity and rebellious minds. He therefore asked the Guatemalan Church to extend the same vigilance, surveillance, and supervision to its clergy that the civil authorities gave to the general population as part of the fight against sedition. Because of the threat to the empire, the viceroy also emphasized that renegade priests were to be subject to civil punishments if they were found to be promoting insurrection. Taking the hint, Casaus began to make covert inquiries that led to reports that the Salvadoran priests Nicolás, Manuel, and Vicente Aguilar were conspiring to seize the arms and funds deposited in the *sala de armas* and *cajas reales* in the city of San Salvador in preparation for the complete overthrow of Spanish authority in the province.[65] By the end of October, Manuel was in a Guatemalan prison on suspicion of *infidencia* and a warrant had been issued for the arrest of his brother Nicolás.

This development, which combined an attack on a popular local family with the issue of Salvadoran civil and religious autonomy from authorities in Guatemala, seems to have been the crisis that segments of the Salvadoran elite were looking for to force their separatist agenda. On 4 November, a mob in San Salvador surrounded the house of the intendant, Antonio Gutiérrez Ulloa, and demanded the end of the persecutions of the Aguilar brothers. By the next day, they were calling for the removal of the intendant and all peninsular officials in the province. With leading creoles such as Dr. José Matías Delgado, Bernardo and Manuel José Arce, and Juan Manuel Rodríguez directing events, the population overran the offices of the colonial authorities, taking weapons and money and confining the peninsular officials. On the strength of this movement a new ayuntamiento was installed on the sixth to lend legitimacy to these acts. On the following day, the Salvadoran elite established a junta to govern the intendancy while at the same time declaring its continued loyalty to Ferdinand VII and the Cortes. Here was unambiguous evidence of creole proautonomy sentiment. The junta, defending its actions as a restoration of the natural rights of the community after three centuries of despotic Spanish rule, temporarily assumed the authority of the deposed intendant (before appointing José Mariano Batres to the post) and called on the rest of the province to unite behind it.[66]

In a reaction perhaps more indicative of majority political sentiment in the region than were the views expressed by the small revolutionary segment of the San Salvador elite, this appeal to join the revolt was met with near-unanimous opposition from the other major towns in the intendancy. On 9 November, deploring the disgraceful rebellion and "prepared to defend Law, Patria, Religion, and King," the ayuntamiento of San Miguel burned the Salvadoran proclamation in the town square and published a *proclama* of its own calling on the populace to remain loyal and calm.[67] Shortly thereafter, the town councils of Santa Ana, San Vicente, Sonsonate, and Zacatecoluca also registered their disapproval and offered to participate in the restoration of Spanish authority in the provincial capital. Without orders from Guatemala City, in fact, the alcalde primero of San Vicente set out toward San Salvador with more than 250 troops composed of dragoon and militia companies from San Vicente, San Miguel, Olancho, and Usulután.[68]

By 10 November details of the events in San Salvador reached the capital and caused a great commotion. Bustamante and the colonial administration received regular reports on events from Intendant Gutiérrez and the loyalist ayuntamientos, while the insurrection leaders attempted to turn Guatemalan popular sentiment in their favor with propaganda, signed "The Americans of San Salvador," that called for the overthrow of Spanish authorities.[69] The creole elite in Guatemala City, however, immediately came out in favor of the preservation of Spanish rule. With Bustamante's warnings about French subversion fresh in its mind, the ayuntamiento drafted a proclamation on 12 November to the kingdom designed to reinforce "peace, unity, and fidelity" with Spain.[70] Written by José de Aycinena, the *oficio* explicitly linked previous warnings from the crown about Napoleonic machinations to contemporaneous outbreaks of revolution in Mexico, Buenos Aires, New Granada, Quito, and Chile. Convinced that at least one "vile" emissary was operating in the kingdom, sowing sedition and discord, "with the perverse end that armed groups will form, battle, and consume each other in the process," the ayuntamiento expressed its complete confidence in the "patriotic zeal" and ceaseless vigilance demonstrated by Bustamante and its willingness to assist in efforts to conserve "in all its parts the inalterable tranquility of the kingdom." With the terrible example of the civil war at hand in neighboring Mexico, the Guatemalan elite decided in November 1811 that it had to promote a "love of order" and harmony between creoles and peninsulars as its official response to the Salvadoran uprisings.

If the response to this proclamation from the ayuntamiento of León is any indication, much of the kingdom's elite shared this conclusion.[71] Expressing its satisfaction with the Guatemalan ayuntamiento's patriotism in the face of such unrest, the Nicaraguan regidores declared that they were working hard to preserve the peace and maintain the subordination of the lower classes despite the "internal unease" produced by the events in San Salvador. Vigilantly pursuing "the preservation of good Government" and "the defense of the sacred cause," the Leonese elite came out against the divisiveness of creole/peninsular factionalization, concerned that the growing prejudice against peninsulars would express itself in violence from the *pueblo bajo* (lower class). Fearing such an outcome, the ayuntamiento made clear its confidence in the Bustamante administration's efforts to promote the general welfare of the kingdom.[72]

In his deliberations on the correct way to restore order to San Salvador, Bustamante was able to count on more than words of support from the Guatemalan ayuntamiento. In fact, the active cooperation between the colonial government and the municipal council in the restoration of order in San Salvador was a significant if ephemeral development, one that did not survive the spread of insurrection to other parts of the kingdom by 1812. On 15 November the ayuntamiento and captain general assembled in a special session devoted to finding a peaceful means of ending the challenge to Spanish rule. The regidores proposed sending a delegation to San Salvador to mediate the dispute and nominated Aycinena and Peinado as their representatives. Taking this idea one step further, Bustamante decided to make Aycinena the new intendant of the province, thereby disposing of the unpopular Gutiérrez and his illegitimate successor at one blow while imbuing their Guatemalan replacement with the weight of crown-sanctioned authority. Aycinena and Peinado departed the capital four days later charged with restoring order to the rebellious province and carrying the captain general's offer of a general pardon if the Salvadorans accepted the reimposition of crown rule.[73]

According to Bustamante, this moderate response to rebellion, a policy that he termed "prudent reconciliation" (*conciliación prudente*), developed out of his own personal preference for ending the dispute, the lack of adequate military resources to impose his will on the province, and the pressures of the Guatemalan elite to negotiate directly with the rebels.[74] He was disinclined to give the ayuntamiento credit for its assistance in the pacification, arguing that the municipal council had no right to participate in such issues but that it would have been imprudent to reject the Aycinena and Peinado delegation. Nevertheless, while accepting such aid, he negotiated directly with José Matías Delgado and Bernardo Arce in San Salvador and made preparations for a military invasion of the province should the policy of moderation fail.

Confusion over long-term goals, poor planning, a lack of support from the rest of the province, and the opportunity to negotiate with Guatemalan creoles instead of a royal army led the leaders of the revolt in San Salvador to seize the offer to submit peacefully to Intendant Aycinena. The Guatemalan delegation, which included civil and religious leaders, was welcomed into the city on 3 December and immediately recognized by the ayuntamiento. Two days later, Aycinena published the amnesty decree, noting that future unrest would be met with swift punishment.[75] In return, the intendant agreed to hear a series of

petitions of grievances that he promised to remit to the authorities in
Spain. But there was another reason the revolt ended on such a restrained
note. As the Salvadoran regidores explained in a meeting with Aycinena,
"in effect they wanted nothing more than the perfect reestablishment of
public tranquility."[76] The Salvadoran uprising was not a movement for
outright independence but rather an effort by local creoles to take advantage of unstable conditions and improve their political position vis-
à-vis certain unpopular Spanish provincial officials. The creoles wanted
power, but not at the price of unrestrained popular mobilization. With
the captain general and his new creole intendant offering "unalterable
tranquility" in return for obedience, the Salvadoran elite quickly capitu-
lated.[77]

The rapid resolution of this first significant challenge to the Central
American colonial order, however, failed to prevent other provincial tensions and local grievances from erupting into open rebellion. By the
time Aycinena and Peinado arrived in the intendancy, in fact, the towns
of Usulután, Santa Ana, and Metapán had all confronted lower-class disturbances. The succession of revolts during the last two months of 1811
that began in San Salvador and ended in Granada, Nicaragua, no matter
how insignificant they proved to be in the long term, increasingly taxed
the cooperation between creole elites and the peninsular-dominated
colonial government. As colonial stability was disturbed, as military
units were activated to restore order, as prisons filled up with suspected
insurgents, and as the justice system became the scene for widening disputes between the crown and its Guatemalan subjects, Bustamante became convinced of the need for his government to pursue an active
counterinsurgency agenda in the kingdom at the expense of reform.
This perspective was best expressed in a letter to the Guatemala City
ayuntamiento by José María de Hoyos, a regidor in the ayuntamiento
of San Miguel and a commander of the local militia forces that advanced on San Salvador in the days after the uprisings. Describing how
the news of the Salvadoran rebellion had greatly disturbed the countryside, Hoyos declared that "the contagion is moving at an incredible
speed; at each moment we receive information about the excesses that
have been committed in many towns by the Indians and ladinos: in
these sad circumstances, and in light of the limited forces and resources
that we can count on, a massive explosion is greatly feared."[78]

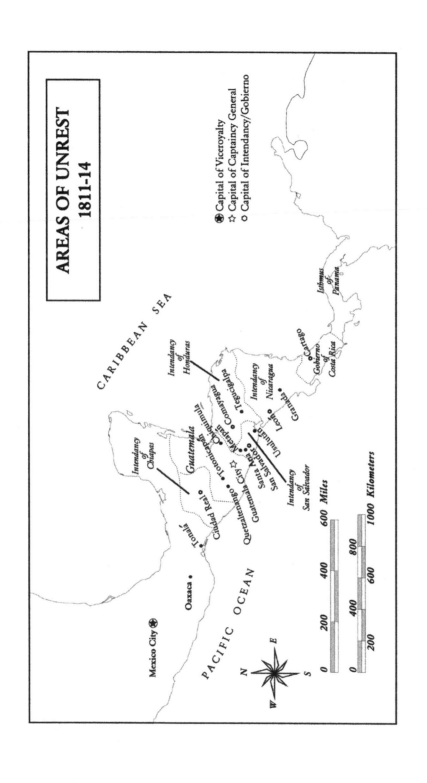

The excesses to which Hoyos referred occurred in the towns of Usulután and Santa Ana on 17 November. At Usulután, with the normal political order overturned by the events in San Salvador and in an atmosphere of rumor and uncertainty, the lower-class, mostly ladino and mulatto neighborhoods of la Pulga and Cerro Colorado rose up and removed from office their *teniente* and *juez real,* Ignacio Domínguez. The mob then proceeded to the town jail, where they released the inmates, who immediately joined the insurrection. With cries of "*mueran los chapetones*" (death to the chapetones) and "*repartamonos sus intereses*" (let's divide up their goods) in the air, the crowd turned its attention to the houses and stores of the elite, ransacking and pillaging whatever could be taken away. By this time most of the peninsular merchants had fled into the hills. As the afternoon progressed the mob began to tire, but only after having left most of the town in "a thousand pieces." By nightfall the last of a series of mob-appointed *tenientes,* José Francisco Perdomo, and two priests, Ignacio Ramírez and Mateo Castilla, were hard at work trying to calm emotions and restore order. In the end, the disturbances led to two minor arrests but were quickly forgotten amidst the good feelings that accompanied the pacification measures of Intendant Aycinena.[79]

In contrast to the revolt at Usulután, the events that took place in Santa Ana were better organized, but they ultimately proved less destructive. According to testimony from the alcaldes ordinarios, Mariano Menéndez and Bartolomé José Telles, a group of rabble-rousers in the lower-class barrio of España attempted to incite the *pardo* population of the town to rise up against the local authorities. In a tumultuous meeting on the evening of the seventeenth, the conspirators declared their intention to do away with the tribute, the royal monopolies on tobacco and *aguardiente,* and the *alcabala* (the royal sales tax). They planned to expel all peninsulars and nonnative creoles from the town and set up a government along the lines of that of San Salvador. Notified of these plans the next day, the local authorities called on all loyal citizens to unite in defense of "Religion, King, Nation, and Patria" and then proceeded to march on the barrio. Most of the suspected insurgents were captured, and on 22 November the ayuntamiento sent them to Guatemala City to be tried for sedition. In the capital, the prisoners were interrogated to see whether they had been encouraged to revolt by anyone above their class. By January 1812, convinced that the rebellion was little more than a mob-inspired movement, Bustamante released all except its suspected leaders, Francisco Reyna and Ramón Salazar.[80]

The political tension reached another boiling point in the town of Metapán. There, as Alcalde José Antonio Martínez described it, a large group of Indians and ladinos assembled in the early evening of 24 November, armed themselves with rocks and other makeshift weapons, and in a "scandalous tumult" marched on the center of town, where they violently deposed the *alcalde segundo*, the Spaniard Jorge Guillén de Ubico. In an unambiguous gesture the mob gave Ubico's *vara* (staff of office) to the creole José Antonio Hernández and then proceeded to the home of Ignacio Faro, who held the monopoly on *aguardiente*. After breaking down the doors, the insurgents took as much alcohol as possible and then poured out the rest of his supplies. They then turned to the administrator of the *alcabala* and ordered him not to collect the tax any more, and this pressure was repeated at the home of the administrator of the tobacco monopoly. Arriving at the town jail, they swarmed inside and released the prisoners. After expending the rest of its energy on some unfortunate bystanders, the mob agreed to disperse, having been promised by the local authorities that any grievances would be heard the next day.[81]

The following morning Martínez, Hernández, the parish priest, leading creoles, and the ayuntamiento met with the insurgents. The creole authorities managed to keep disturbances to a minimum by asking the *sublevados* to put their demands on paper, a process that took most of the rest of the day. On 26 November, despairing of the political vacuum in the town and the collapse of order, the council decided to send two representatives, the *administrador de correos* Juan de Dios Mayorga and Francisco Xavier Menéndez, to Santa Ana, where they hoped to reach Intendant Aycinena. News of this delegation caused the ladino population to reassemble, and Alcalde Martínez armed a small group of creoles to resist them. By nightfall, the Indians had joined the ladinos again, despite desperate efforts by the parish priest to calm the situation. Protesting that the Spaniards were guilty of treason, the mob let loose a hail of rocks. When the authorities responded with gunfire, the crowd quickly melted away and returned to their homes. Later that night, Alcalde Martínez opened communications with the Indians, who told him that they had been pressured into joining the mob. The alcalde assured them that he blamed the ladinos for the uprising and promised that if the Indian barrio helped restore "peace and tranquility" to the town no punishments would be forthcoming. Martínez, however, decided that it would be best to keep an armed guard at hand "until tranquility is truly achieved."[82]

A number of suspected insurgents were in fact taken into custody in the days following the unrest in Metapán. Aycinena directed that a careful investigation of their cases be made, so as to uncover the true leaders of the movement (*los primeros motores*). By 3 December, the vast majority had been pardoned, having confessed their errors, while nine prisoners were sent to Guatemala City for further questioning. There they discovered that the colonial government did not believe that the ladinos and Indians of Metapán had revolted without outside assistance. Asked to name the people who encouraged the uprising (*los sugestores*), one of the accused, José Planas, testified that it was rumored that the creoles Juan de Dios Mayorga, Juan José Escobar, Antonio Hernández, and Pablo Ruíz were involved in one form or another.[83] On 9 June 1812, eight of the nine ladino and mulatto conspirators were released under the terms of a general pardon. By this time, the attention of the authorities had focused almost exclusively on Mayorga as the principal instigator and intellectual author of unrest in the region around Metapán.

According to numerous local witnesses, Mayorga, who had been the subject of an earlier investigation by the *Tribunal de Fidelidad*, was a vocal supporter of creole rights and a fierce advocate for American autonomy. Juan Francisco Menéndez testified that as early as the summer of 1810, Mayorga, whom he considered an *afrancesado*, had declared "that now was the happy time in which the Americas could throw off the yoke that had oppressed them for so long." Others stated that he regularly spoke out in favor of the revolutions occurring in the rest of the empire, saying that he hoped Guatemala could follow the example of Mexico and that the colonies owed nothing to Ferdinand VII. Once the uprisings began in San Salvador, he apparently encouraged the lower classes of Metapán to rise up and help the creoles take power. On the day the mob took over the city, Mayorga met with its leaders and was seen passing out *aguardiente* to the crowd.[84]

The question of Mayorga's role in the Salvadoran uprisings underscores the complexity of the movements and the difficulty in establishing clear motivations for those involved. In his defense, Mayorga, who was originally from Chiquimula, Guatemala, argued that he had been framed by the local oligarchy for his popularity among the lower classes and his rapid acquisition of the offices of *administrador de correo* and *administrador de alcabalas,* positions that he could have developed into alternative bases of power. His political views, which undoubtedly encompassed the idea of independence, made him a provocative and unique figure at the time, and it seems likely based on the evidence that these sentiments contributed to the outbreak of revolts in Metapán.[85] Whether in San Salvador, Santa Ana, Usulután, or Metapán, local political rivalries that were exacerbated by the growing peninsular/creole divisions and new interest in creole autonomy combined with long-standing economic and social concerns among the urban lower classes in an atmosphere of intense political tension at the imperial level to produce the conditions necessary for small-scale rebellions. Over the next five months the Salvadoran unrest sparked similar movements in Nicaragua, Honduras, and Guatemala. At the time, this trend appeared to the colonial government in Guatemala City to presage a massive kingdomwide drive for independence. And, with every new challenge to his authority Bustamante found it increasingly difficult to respond with his policy of *conciliación prudente,* despite the fact that most of Central America remained loyal to Spain. In retrospect, the relative ease with which these threats were diffused confirms their localized character, their general unpopularity, and the fragmented—and often conflicting—goals of the participating groups.

The disturbances in the intendancy of San Salvador had scarcely subsided when, on 13 December, the provincial capital of León, Nicaragua, rose up against its peninsular authorities. Tensions in the city had been high since the tenth and were apparently sparked by popular opposition to the commercial activities of one Mariano Murillo.[86] Reports of a general insurrection caused the long-serving and unpopular intendant, José Salvador, to call for a *cabildo abierto,* which was attended by the ayuntamiento, the bishop, and other leading citizens. In return for a restoration of order, the authorities promised to restrict Murillo to the city and not to prosecute those responsible for the disturbances. However, by the evening of the thirteenth, "thousands" of men, armed with sticks and machetes, had surrounded the house of the intendant, crying out for justice for years of abuses, calling for the end of government monopolies, and making threats against the Spanish merchant community. Despite "pathetic exhortations about peace, quiet, and respect for authorities" from Bishop Nicolás García Jerez, the mob forced its way inside to confront Salvador, who had by then given up his office. Violence against some peninsulars and creoles who opposed the movements followed, and many homes and businesses were sacked.

The following day, to end the popular unrest that was sweeping the town, the Leonese elite, led by the ayuntamiento, organized a provincial governing junta composed of deputies from each barrio and presided over by Bishop García Jerez. It then sent word to Bustamante of its actions, declaring itself completely loyal to the king and the governing authorities in the colony. In its effort to restore order, however, the junta gave itself complete judicial, military, political, and economic authority over the intendancy, a process that scarcely recognized a governing role for Guatemala City or Madrid. As with San Salvador, this development provoked a negative reaction from most of the rest of the province and kingdom.[87]

Once the news about the latest unrest and its consequences spread, the town and *partido* of Nueva Segovia refused to recognize the new junta. This act was seconded by the ayuntamiento of Cartago, Costa Rica, which took the opportunity to renew its pledge of allegiance to the crown. Later, it voted to cut off all communications with León, establish urban militias throughout the province, initiate regular patrols of the countryside, and set up a garrison of troops along the Costa Rican border with Nicaragua.[88] On 29 December, the ayuntamiento of San Salvador met in an extraordinary session to discuss the news and voted to reject the legitimacy of the Leonese junta. The Salvadoran intendant, José de Aycinena, who also attended this meeting, wrote to the Guatemala City council of the "supreme disgust" he felt after being informed of the uprising and declared his wish that he were back in the capital where he could unite his vote to those of the Guatemalan regidores "and show the entire world that if some parts of this kingdom have allowed themselves to be taken by surprise by the deceitful promises of the vile tyrant of Europe there remain other parts that will not allow them access, and Spanish hearts that are still symbols of loyalty and constancy."[89]

Like its counterparts, the ayuntamiento of Guatemala City also came out in opposition to the events in León, despite efforts by the junta to win its approval. Fearing the effects of distance and rumors on the Guatemalan response to its actions, in a 20 December letter to the capital the Leonese emphasized their success in restoring public tranquility and preserving "the reverence towards Religion, the recognition of . . . Ferdinand VII, the observance of our laws, the decorum and respect owed to the installation of the governing authority, and the rescue of some Europeans against whom the resentment of the people resonated."[90] No support was forthcoming, however. Instead, it quickly became apparent that the Leonese could not contain the contagion of unrest in Nicaragua. On 22 December, a mob in the city of Granada overthrew its peninsular officials and, after a week of disturbances, installed a new governing ayuntamiento composed solely of creoles.[91] More ominously, this body refused to submit to the authority of the provincial capital of León, an act of stubborn localism that would lead to five months of self-government before a royalist army restored crown rule in the intendancy by force. The Granadan leaders attempted to justify their actions as a consequence of popular unrest that threatened the "peace and tranquility of this city." At the same time, they asserted their continued loyalty to the crown.[92] Concerned about the precedent, however, Guatemalan leaders, both creole and peninsular, simply refused to recognize the legitimacy of the new council.

Captain General Bustamante sent reports on the "seditious events" in the intendancy of San Salvador to Spain on 22 and 23 December 1811 and summarized the Nicaraguan uprisings in a letter to his superiors one month later. By then he had come to some definite conclusions about the origins of these rebellions that would affect his governing strategies for the rest of his administration. He was convinced that these "partial alterations" were the "natural daughters of the barbarous rebellions in neighboring kingdoms" and that they were produced by small groups of innovators.[93] The insurgents of León, he argued, received encouragement from Mexican and Venezuelan rebels as early as 1810, causing then governor González to authorize Bishop García Jerez in a secret memorandum to assume power if Intendant Salvador were deposed. Similar reports of seditious behavior caused Bustamante to maintain detailed correspondence with Leonese authorities and influential citizens throughout 1811. Despite the fact that all assured the governor of

the tranquility of the province as late as 10 December, the uprisings occurred, leaving Bustamante with much less faith in subsequent assur-
ances of the political stability of the kingdom. In the mind of the governor the leaders of the rebellions were demagogues who exaggerated
the size of their support, the unrest among the lower classes, and the
popularity of the new ideas promoted by the rebels. As a result, he was
much more severe with the instigators than with the masses, whom he
saw as victims of the turbulent times.[94]

Within a year of the arrival of José de Bustamante as the new governor and captain general of the colony, the Kingdom of Guatemala appeared to be as inundated with rebellion as any other part of the empire.
Toleration, appeasement, and cooperation had failed to mitigate the
spread of unrest and anti-Spanish sentiment, leaving the captain general
with few viable options to preserve Spanish authority. As a result, at the
end of 1811 the governor began to consider a military solution to the turmoil. The first step, which he announced in a 3 December decree, was
the creation of new militia units designed to serve in the absence of
Spanish troops. Bustamante expected to use these forces as regular patrols in the prevention of disorder and the punishment of "criminals,
bandits, partisans, and rebels." Considering the gravity of the situation,
Bustamante was even willing to allow the formation of companies of
Indian militiamen. He declared that such actions were now necessary
because Central America's "tranquility, which disgracefully has been altered in some towns, to the scandal and affliction of their loyal inhabitants, demands the adoption of legal measures dictated by experience."[95]

However, the establishment of unreliable, poorly equipped and trained
militia units was not a solution to the problem. As 1812 unfolded with
little improvement in the peninsular situation, rising political activism
on the part of creole leaders, and a more dangerous threat from Mexican
insurgents, Bustamante found his ability to preserve order dependent
upon increasingly coercive measures. Convinced that the continued stability of the Kingdom of Guatemala rested upon the active mobilization
of the population in defense of Spanish rule, the captain general now
had to decide whether to take the offensive and move ahead with the use
of military force and martial law in the face of insurrection.[96]

5

The Counterinsurgency State, 1812

Between 1808 and 1811 the colonial administration in the Kingdom of Guatemala struggled to preserve Spanish rule on the isthmus in the face of the collapse of the Bourbon monarchy, the fear of French intervention and invasion, the questionable legitimacy of the loyalist governments in Spain, the growing sentiment for autonomy among many American subjects, and the start of movements for independence in the rest of the empire. In the two years that followed the outbreak of the first rebellions in Central America, Captain General Bustamante also found his position challenged by the quixotic imperial policy of the Spanish Cortes and its liberal constitution. As this period progressed, the Spanish colonial administration came to the conclusion that its policy of *conciliación prudente* was an inadequate response to the growing unrest in the region. As a consequence, by building on the foundations established by his predecessors and other colonial governments, Bustamante proceeded to fashion a counterinsurgency strategy that helped confirm Spanish sovereignty in the kingdom for the rest of the decade. At the same time, however, this approach to rebellion—and the potential for rebellion—contributed to the erosion of the legitimacy of Spanish rule among important segments of the population of Central America.

The spirit of discord fostered by the Salvadoran and Nicaraguan uprisings reached Honduras at the beginning of January 1812. On the first two days of the year the ladinos and mulattos who comprised the lower class (*pueblo bajo*) of Tegucigalpa began to agitate in opposition to an effort by the town council to seat two unpopular alcaldes ordinarios.[1] Spurred by fears of reprisals from the local elite, the *castas* became more radical in their actions. After imprisoning the local subdelegado, the mob, with the help of a few creole supporters, issued a series of demands for municipal reform that included lower-class representation in city government in the form of an elected *diputado procurador síndico,* the establishment of *alcaldes de barrio,* and the creation of a primary school for the children of castas. At the same time, the leaders of the movement declared that their actions were not intended to be prejudicial to the Church nor to the established authorities but rather were a response to intolerable conditions and desperate circumstances.

As in San Salvador and Nicaragua, the uprisings in Tegucigalpa encompassed two distinct elements: a traditional, lower-class movement against bad government, which professed loyalty to the established order and had limited expectations of change, and a much smaller, more radical, creole-dominated faction, which tried to encourage and direct the *pueblo bajo* to push for more significant reforms. In this particular case, following the initial disturbances the mob quickly turned to two creoles, Julián Romero and José Antonio Rojas, for guidance and leadership. Although the degree to which these men helped precipitate the unrest remains unclear, Intendant José María Piñol y Muñoz reported that Romero and Rojas used the local Convent of San Francisco as a base for their plots and conspiracies, a refuge that allowed them to meet with other "sinister" figures such as Francisco Ariza, the creole son of a Frenchman, before the revolts took place. Piñol was so concerned about the subversive role of the clergy, in fact, that he asked Bustamante to expel the Franciscan order from the province. In any event, in their role as the principal negotiators and propagandists for the castas, Romero and Rojas clearly had their own agenda, one that included a greater degree of social reform than the *pueblo* had proposed at the beginning.[2]

Convinced that most Spaniards remained ignorant of the conditions faced by the lower classes, Romero took it upon himself to guide the people of Tegucigalpa toward a successful resolution of their legitimate complaints. In a representative proclamation addressed to the "Loyal People" (*Leal Pueblo*) of Tegucigalpa, he wrote:

Keep your hands innocent of those great crimes that do not admit ex-
cuses, as you have so far. Do not worry about the reforms you have made.
. . . Do not be slaves; now is the time for you to assume possession of your
rights, and you may now ask for whatever agrees with your well-being,
just like any other citizen of the state. But you do not know everything:
ask for guidance from people of character and integrity, and be sure that
they will give it to you completely.[3]

Aware of the destructive nature of such movements and the probable
response of the Spanish government to this challenge to the established
order, Romero—who assumed the office of subdelegado following the
arrest of the incumbent, Antonio Franquilino de la Rosa—repeatedly
sought to pacify the lower classes during the month of January:

Do you want the ruin of the community, of its art, mines, agriculture,
and commerce, the exile of its most useful and best citizens, or that
the town be made a desert? Well, insurrection, disorder, and civil war
is, has always been, and will now be the most infallible way of achieving
it—there is no real choice between the two, either you calm down or
Tegucigalpa will become a mountain of ashes or a hospital of poverty
and misfortune . . . You already have two judges whose goodness is well
known. You have taken part in their election, and you have conducted
yourselves with laudable moderation and prudence. They have promised
to be your protectors and fathers. What more do you want?[4]

As it turned out, the masses were quickly satisfied. Once the pueblo
achieved its initial goal of removing the alcaldes and the subdelegado,
the unrest ended. In fact, through their proclamations and letters Romero and Rojas made the Tegucigalpa revolt appear more radical than it
was by overemphasizing the degree to which it was motivated by a desire
for social equality and other liberal concepts.

Unfortunately for Romero and his casta supporters, the provincial authorities in Honduras and the colonial government in Guatemala City
found it impossible to ignore even a well-behaved, limited uprising,
especially in the poisoned atmosphere of post–San Salvador Central
America. What might have been smoothed over as a local political dis-

pute only a couple of months earlier was now the latest in a series of challenges to Spanish rule that threatened to become a general conflagration. Therefore, as part of the wider mobilization of the military forces in the kingdom in preparation for a march on Granada, troops under the command of Major Pedro Gutiérrez occupied Tegucigalpa in mid-February and arrested Romero and Rojas on charges of sedition. From the perspective of the Bustamante administration, these men were guilty of serious offenses. By suggesting and promoting the "impolitic and unjust pretensions of the ladinos" to full equality with Spaniards, Romero and Rojas had contributed to the subversion of the social order, leaving open the possibility that the castas would then push for "superiority and the annihilation of Spaniards."[5] While the full weight of the colonial judicial system would fall on these men in the months ahead, the rest of the population of Tegucigalpa did not experience any form of retribution from the government. Although he ordered two hundred troops to occupy the town as a symbol of his authority, Bustamante also decided that it would be prudent to acquiesce to a long-standing desire on the part of the *partido* of Tegucigalpa for the restoration of its status as an alcaldía mayor. The captain general then appointed the local priest, Juan Francisco Márquez, to the post of alcalde mayor and relocated the office of *juez de minas* to the province.[6] Clearly, Bustamante remained hopeful that a surgical excision of the most radical elements of the population in combination with certain conciliatory gestures would preclude future disturbances.

The damage that an individual or a small number of determined conspirators could do to the established order was also highlighted by the arrest of Manuel Antonio Gordón on 22 January. Gordón, a first sergeant in the Guatemalan infantry, was picked up after raising the suspicions of his fellow soldiers with a number of subversive comments. Subsequently, a letter that had reached some of the leading citizens of San Salvador in an attempt to reignite the November uprisings was traced to him. Fearing a wider conspiracy, the government immediately expanded the scope of the investigations and charged Gordón with infidencia.[7] The letter, written on 3 January, demonstrated to Bustamante that a virulent strain of anti-Spanish sentiment existed in the kingdom, though its extent could not yet be determined.

In the correspondence, Gordón expressed his profound dissatisfaction that Aycinena and Peinado had managed to pacify San Salvador and were not thrown into prison instead. According to him, this turn of events had the effect of "disheartening many subjects here who were planning the same thing." He argued that the new intendant and his assistant had no right to govern, "for although they are creoles, they were sent by a *Chapetón* president, and even if [Bustamante] had not sent them why should a man from another *Patria* go and govern a city where so many could be governors?" The author then declared that a new uprising would prove to be more successful, particularly if it could be made to coincide in some manner with the unrest in Nicaragua: "Although troops are being sent over from Zacapa I know for a fact that they will go over to your side, for even the women want the opportunity to go and help kill *chapetones,* and odds are that within fifteen days the entire province of Chiquimula and Zacapa will be in revolt. Even this city will not wait long before doing the same. And with all the provinces of the kingdom up in arms, whom do you think they will send against you?"[8]

The colonial administration could not ignore such statements. In San Salvador, Aycinena opened investigations of Ramón Fornier and Domingo Durán, the recipients of the letter, which seemed to indicate that Gordón had been deeply involved in plotting against the government for the past year. Although no evidence emerged that indicated a general willingness among Salvadorans to repeat their November experience, events in Guatemala in February gave more credence to the belief among Spanish authorities that a broad-based creole conspiracy was in fact emerging to challenge the colonial order.

The "uprising" that occurred in the province of Chiquimula in February 1812 was in many respects the culmination of the climate of fear and suspicion that had dominated the isthmus since the fall of the monarchy in 1808.[9] On the twenty-third of that month, Francisco Cordón, the *juez preventivo* of San Agustín, a small town on the road between Guatemala City and the Caribbean, became concerned about a shipment of two hundred muskets that some men were escorting to the capital. In the opinion of Cordón the shippers lacked the requisite documentation and authorization for such unusual goods. Having received orders from the corregidor, Pedro Arrivillaga, to imprison suspicious characters, Cordón decided to impound the shipment and its guards and march them to nearby Chimalapa. Upon arrival, he discovered that the town was full of rumors about an invasion of the province by French soldiers dressed as priests and that Chimalapa's *juez preventivo*, Isidro Salguero, and the priest of Acasguastlán, Roman Cabrera, had begun to organize a local defense. The officials then concluded that the arms had been collected by spies working out of Zacapa and were destined for the French invasion forces.

Uncertain of what to do next, Cordón, Salguero, and Cordón's brother Patricio, who served as the *juez preventivo* of Usumatlán, decided to write the corregidor and ask for advice. In the meantime, however, tensions increased as people began to express concerns about being surprised by the French. At that point, the three *jueces* agreed to distribute the muskets among the gathered crowd for the purpose of defending "our Religion, Country, and Crown." In their zeal, they latched onto a rumor that Bustamante and Archbishop Ramón Casaus were in league with Napoleon to take over the isthmus and, as a consequence, made an attempt to take the artillery pieces stored in Zacapa. Viewing these actions as a direct challenge to his authority and determined to restore order by force, the corregidor quickly arrived with the priest of Chiquimula at his side and supported by an artillery company. Arrivillaga disabused the local population of the rumors of French subversion and began arresting those who had directed the unrest. Although he initially escaped capture, Cordón was eventually taken into custody and charged with infidencia for disturbing the peace of the province.

The colonial government had little reason to doubt now that the kingdom was full of subversives, and future developments only confirmed this impression. In late March reports began to reach Guatemala City that Juan de Dios Mayorga had attempted to incite another revolt in Metapán. On the basis of witness testimony, the administration had already come to the conclusion that Mayorga was the principal instigator of the November uprisings there. As part of that investigation, which lasted well into 1812, evidence also came out that placed Mayorga in Chiquimula in the days before the unrest in that province. After this episode, he reportedly returned to Metapán and tried to raise support for an assault on the *quartel de armas* of the town. On the basis of Mayorga's long record of confrontations with colonial authorities, the large number of witnesses to his subversive conduct, and the climate of suspicion dominating policy decisions at the time, Bustamante ordered Francisco Castejón, a captain in the militia battalion of Chiquimula, to go to Metapán, arrest Mayorga, and lead an investigation into these latest charges. In particular, Bustamante wanted detailed witness testimony on "the conduct of Mayorga, his propensity to subvert and disturb towns, and any seditious machinations and productions he might have discussed, including times, places, and people." He also asked for a report on the measures taken by the local authorities to prevent the seizure of their arms.[10]

On 19 April, Mayorga arrived in Guatemala City and was detained on suspicion of infidencia. He found himself imprisoned alongside Mateo Antonio Marure, another liberal creole from Guatemala, who had also been charged with infidencia following a series of denunciations of his conduct and revolutionary ideas. Linked to the original Salvadoran uprisings via correspondence with its leaders and a suspicious travel itinerary that placed him in the part of the intendancy that experienced the greatest unrest during the last two months of 1811, Marure and a "club of conspirators" allegedly tried to subvert the pacification measures taken by Aycinena and Peinado during December. Having failed in this endeavor, he was captured after seeking refuge "in León, which was in revolt, and in Mexico where he could let his revolutionary ideas unfold and live freely with the fomenters of insurrection."[11] From the perspective of Bustamante and the colonial administration, Marure, Mayorga, and Gordón were the best evidence to date that a small network of revolutionary creoles was actively subverting Spanish rule in the kingdom.

The hardening attitude of Bustamante and his administration toward this series of minor disturbances and debatable conspiracies at the beginning of 1812 must be seen in light of the fact that Nicaragua remained in a state of open rebellion at the time. On 2 January, Bustamante officially appointed the bishop of León, Nicolás García Jerez, to be the interim intendant of the province in the hope that this highly respected prelate and reluctant president of the Leonese junta would be able to restore order without recourse to force.[12] Attached to this decree was a pardon for those involved in the uprisings. At the end of the month, however, when the captain general wrote to the authorities in Spain about the state of the kingdom, he was compelled to report that

only the town of Nueva Segovia had recognized García Jerez as governor.[13] Operating under the presumption that negotiation and conciliation remained the best ways to end the revolts, Bustamante decided to
open up direct communications with local ayuntamientos and influential citizens in the intendancy in an attempt to gather support for the
bishop. At the same time, he recognized that military force might have
to be applied in case such methods did not succeed. On 12 January,
forces under the command of Major Gutiérrez were ordered to assemble
in Juticalpa and Olancho, Honduras, to prepare for an invasion of Nicaragua.[14]

In a letter to García Jerez dated 3 February, Bustamante decided that
the time had arrived for an ultimatum. He remained incredulous that
the province had not yet come around, considering the fact that the colonial government promised "justice, peace, and tranquility," but he was
reluctant to resort to "extreme measures, those most painful to my paternal heart." Still, he declared that García Jerez had to be recognized as
the new intendant immediately or the pardon would be nullified and the
residencia of former Intendant José Salvador would be suspended. To
underscore the illegitimacy of the Leonese rebellion, Bustamante also
expected the bishop to end all association with the governing junta.[15] In
his private instructions to García Jerez, the captain general expressed the
importance of communicating these orders directly to all town councils,
judges, priests, and influential citizens, while at the same time reassur-
ing them that upon the restoration of order all their complaints would
be addressed. He wanted them to know that his primary goal was the
restoration of "concord and tranquility" and that he hoped to achieve
this state through "benign measures," such as those taken in the case of
San Salvador.[16]

When the bishop wrote back on 20 February, he was able to report
that León had dissolved its junta and recognized his authority.[17] Yet
García Jerez also implored Bustamante to send a military contingent of
some six hundred soldiers, one large enough to allow him to preserve
order. He explained that such a display of force would be enough to restore peace to León without the shedding of blood, but that Granada
and Masaya needed to be confronted with at least fifteen hundred more
troops before they would submit. The bishop-intendant urged Bustamante to appoint a permanent governor as soon as possible and men-

tioned that José María Peinado would be a good choice but that any qualified creole would be welcomed. He also recommended another general pardon be issued to reinforce the impression that the Spanish government was willing to turn its back on the past. In a note the following day that reported the capitulation of the town of Rivas, García Jerez repeated his belief that Granada "is very sick and will not let itself be cured" and pressed Bustamante to send in an army.[18]

Drawing on these reports from Nicaragua and hoping to find the right balance between repression and conciliation, Bustamante issued a major proclamation on 3 March. First, he underscored his willingness to use force to end the standoff with Granada by ordering the following military preparations: Gutiérrez was to march on Granada with the battalion of Olancho as quickly as possible and incorporate units from the surrounding area until his army totaled some twelve hundred troops; the governor of Costa Rica was to arm and supply the forces at his disposal and set out toward an eventual rendezvous with Gutiérrez in Nicaragua; at the same time, troops in San Miguel were directed to León, where they would be placed at the disposal of the bishop-intendant. The captain general then admonished his commanders to show restraint amongst "brothers and neighbors," to defer to civil officials under normal circumstances, and to use force only when it was absolutely necessary to ensure respect for the legitimate authorities.[19]

Unwilling to restrict himself to a military solution to the crisis, Bustamante also made the decision to offer a final "pardon and complete forgiveness for all the illegal acts that have occurred in [Nicaragua] since 10 December." In return, the insurgents had to recognize García Jerez as intendant, allow those who were forced out of office to return to their positions, and welcome back to their homes, businesses, and community those who fled the unrest and who deserved "the fraternal affection" owed to all Spaniards. Using García Jerez's own words, Bustamante declared that if the reconciliation occurred in this manner he would be willing to throw "a thick curtain over the past."[20] Of course, Bustamante did not neglect to state that he would consider his amnesty null and void for those who failed to accept it or who relapsed in their crimes.

Following the publication of these orders, the kingdom's military units began to mobilize for the march on Granada. If Bustamante expected this process to proceed smoothly and without incident, he was quickly disabused. In Honduras, the climate of suspicion and fear that dominated the isthmus at the time became a potentially destabilizing issue as Major Gutiérrez readied his mostly ladino, mulatto, and Carib forces for departure. On 26 March, Vicente Artica, a slave of one of the leading citizens of Tegucigalpa, was placed in custody in Juticalpa for attempting to incite a company of grenadiers of the militia battalion of Olancho to mutiny.[21] When the troops departed for Tegucigalpa, Artica was released; however, he managed to catch up with the battalion and found himself arrested again for the same crime. This time, Gutiérrez ordered all his troops to assemble in the town square, where Artica was tied to a post and given more than 250 lashes. In a report to Guatemala City, the major justified his actions by noting that he had had information at the time that a number of "revolutionary emissaries" were intent on dispersing his troops.[22] However, the only sign of troop unrest discovered in the course of the military investigation against Artica for infidencia occurred on the night of the lashing when an officer of the grenadiers was confronted by a group of soldiers who declared that they would not march to Nicaragua. When asked to explain their reasons, the men replied that their captain had promised that they would be able to keep the new uniforms that had been issued, but the clothes had been taken away, leaving some of them half naked.[23]

Despite a lack of evidence, Gutiérrez was clearly concerned about the potential for the subversion of his troops. At the same time that he made Artica a symbol of the punishment given to rebels, the major replaced the chaplain of the Olancho battalion, Pascual Martínez, because he suspected the priest of being the "author and executor" of all the plans being made to incite the army to revolt. Gutiérrez, who viewed Martínez as another Hidalgo, argued to his superiors that the priest was using his office to promote revolutionary and anti-Christian sentiment among the troops in Juticalpa and Tegucigalpa, intending thereby to collect a sufficient force to "defend the iniquitous plan of insurrection."[24] Considering this atmosphere, he declared that it was a great achievement to leave for Nicaragua on 1 April with his troops in a decent state of subordination and discipline. However, Martínez, who was ordered to remain in Tegucigalpa, followed the army on its path to Granada. In Estelí, Gutiérrez accused him of conspiring with the local priest to incite the troops from Segovia. In the end, after the expedition had completed its operations, Martínez was compelled to return to Comayagua and await the results of an official investigation.[25]

In spite of whatever real or imagined conspiracies existed to disrupt their progress, the royalist forces assembled outside Granada by the third week of April. Once there they found the city, having rejected the 3 March amnesty, armed and fortified against an assault. Bustamante, still hoping to end the conflict without bloodshed, made one more effort to pacify the *Granadinos* with an official pardon. This failed as well, and on 21 April fighting broke out between the two sides. After two days of half-hearted skirmishes, Gutiérrez entered into negotiations with the rebel leaders, proposing to sustain the amnesty in return for an immediate cessation of hostilities and a peaceful occupation of the city by the royalist army. On the basis of this offer, Granada surrendered on 25 April.

By the time the news of the capitulation reached Bustamante, however, he had already been informed that the insurgents had fired on the king's soldiers. This act of hostility infuriated the captain general and, in one of the most controversial decisions of his administration, he disavowed the agreement made by Gutiérrez. Reasoning that the *Granadinos* had lost their chance for a pardon when they refused his second amnesty proposal, Bustamante ordered García Jerez to arrest all those involved in the four-month rebellion. The bishop-intendant nominated Major Alejandro Carrascosa, a peninsular officer known for his strictness and disdain for creoles, to supervise the investigation. Often indiscriminately and with utter impunity, Carrascosa proceeded to imprison leading citizens and sequester their property. To the dismay of the creole community across the isthmus, he kept many of the prisoners in solitary confinement for months without taking their testimony or examining the evidence being compiled against them.[26]

The outcome at Granada had a profound effect on Bustamante and his policy toward insurrection. Until the point when the rebels fired at the royalist army, the captain general was able to argue that the unrest in the kingdom developed from a combination of traditional grievances and unstable times and could be resolved through negotiation and *conciliación prudente*. Granada, however, convinced him that revolutionary sentiment and activity had reached a new level on the isthmus. In order to contain it, the captain general concluded that his government's official response to rebellion would have to be more forceful than it had been over the previous year. Opponents of his administration described this new period of repression, which lasted through the end of his term in office, as *el terror bustamantino*. However, instead of showing an inexplicable and arbitrary "metamorphosis" of Bustamante from constructive, cooperative governor to hard-line, inflexible tyrant, these policy changes paralleled developments in New Spain, where Viceroy Francisco Javier Venegas and Felix María Calleja, the commander of the royalist armies, had already begun to implement new counterinsurgency techniques.[27] Aware of the heavy-handed, often brutal, but quite successful response to rebellion in the neighboring colony, Bustamante made a concerted effort to import some of the same measures into Central America as the situation on the isthmus began to deteriorate.

Mexico's first experiment with counterinsurgency was the *Junta de Seguridad y Buen Orden,* an institution established in September 1809 to coordinate internal security and to protect the colony from French and *afrancesado* subversion. When the Hidalgo revolt broke out a year later, the viceregal government moved further toward the complete militarization of society: authorities immediately assembled a force of some twenty-two thousand militiamen and ten thousand professional soldiers to put down the insurrection and, in a move that Bustamante would later copy, the viceroy also ordered the creation of citizen militias under the title Distinguished Patriotic Battalions of Ferdinand VII.[28]

Confronted by a massive armed challenge to their authority, the colonial officials of New Spain became increasingly dependent on coercion and force when dealing with the local population. In April 1811, Viceroy Venegas uncovered a plot to overthrow the government in Mexico City and responded by imprisoning more than fifty of the suspected conspirators. Another plot hatched in the Augustinian convent in August was more brutally suppressed. Within a month six of the conspirators had been executed, and Venegas used the opportunity to impose martial law on the capital. This included the establishment of strict controls on travel with the use of a system of internal passports and the creation of a new Junta of Police and Public Security charged with uncovering future conspiracies.[29] The *Junta de Seguridad* remained in place as a judicial tribunal, assuming special jurisdiction over cases of subversion and infidencia in an attempt to speed up the conviction process. As such, it became a major part of Venegas's efforts "to take all possible steps and precautions in order to assure myself that the most faithful inhabitants of Mexico are not exposed again to such consternation."[30]

By this time, the "basic blueprint for royalist counterinsurgency" had already been developed.[31] On 8 June, General Felix Calleja published his "Civil Defense Regulations," a fourteen-article plan that provided for a system of decentralized, local defense networks, an emphasis on civil militias, greater use of patriotic clergy and propaganda, and an aggressive, offense-oriented response to insurrection.[32] Calleja had determined after ten months of fighting the insurgents that compromise was not a viable option in the containment of the rebellion. In the blunt words of one of his subordinates, "we must spread terror and death everywhere so that not a single perverted soul remains in the land."[33] Following the final defeat of the first phase of the insurgency in the spring of 1811, Calleja proposed to return its leaders to Mexico City "by way of the middle of the kingdom and the principal cities along the route to demonstrate to everyone the certainty of their capture," an idea that might have been the inspiration for Bustamante's treatment of the Granada prisoners who, in 1813, were made to walk the entire way to Guatemala City.[34] Unlike Bustamante, though, who always followed basic judicial procedure and never actually executed anyone found guilty of a capital offense, the colonial government of New Spain quickly came to the conclusion that its interests were best served through immediate public executions of captured rebels. In fact, in June 1812, when the Morelos rebellion was at its zenith, Viceroy Venegas issued a decree on the treatment of rebels that declared that "anyone could kill insurgents: all the leaders of these movements who were apprehended were to be shot . . . and finally, a tenth of those who only figured as subordinates."[35]

Thus, by the time Bustamante began to question the value of his conciliatory policies in the wake of the Salvadoran and Nicaraguan uprisings, he was able to give serious consideration to the alternative framework for the suppression of unrest already well established and somewhat legitimized in the neighboring kingdom. With the Mexican model to guide him, the captain general proceeded to focus his new counterinsurgency efforts on four areas: expansion of the captaincy general's police and judicial authority over insurgents, improvement in the kingdom's military readiness, development of new instruments of propaganda and civil control, and suppression of the reforms of the constitutional government in Spain. Not surprisingly, these policies found little support among the creole elite. Inconveniently for Bustamante, the development of counterinsurgency strategies by Spanish colonial administrators paralleled the adoption of an unprecedented, liberal constitution in Spain that provided creoles with far greater opportunities for political action within the empire. Thus, the measures that the captain general felt were integral to the preservation of order in a rebellious kingdom and that he believed were reserved to his discretion as the highest colonial official on the isthmus found opposition within a creole community energized by imperial legitimization but of questionable loyalty to the crown.

Bustamante spent the last month of 1811 and the first months of 1812 improving his military readiness by promoting the establishment of companies of "Volunteers of Ferdinand VII" in Guatemala City and local militia units in the provinces of Quetzaltenango, Chiapas, and Costa Rica. Then, initially in response to the Granada crisis and eventually because of the movement into Oaxaca of insurgent armies under the command of General Mariano Matamoros, he began to reorganize the location of his forces. After the Nicaraguan campaign ended, the captain general transferred a number of mulatto troops from the Caribbean port of Omoa to Guatemala City, which caused a protest from the ayuntamiento, and finally to the kingdom's western border, where they served as a barrier to unrest from Mexico.[36] Although these measures were clearly influenced by events in New Spain, demonstrated royalist military strength, and raised the visibility of the armed forces in Central America, they did not result in the transformation of the colony into an armed camp. The Spanish administration in Guatemala did not have the resources, the supplies, or the professional soldiers to project the kind of force that Calleja wielded so successfully in Mexico.

Inspired by a different page of Venegas's counterinsurgency handbook, Bustamante also attempted to implement a superintendency of police in the Kingdom of Guatemala. On 16 January 1812, the captain general sent a draft of a decree ordering the creation of this institution to the audiencia for its approval: "in view of the measures lately adopted in Mexico; it being well known that similar ones exist in almost all the provinces and parts of the monarchy; [I have] reached the conclusion that a system of precautions is absolutely necessary for this kingdom, so as to protect its loyal and honorable inhabitants from attacks, traps, and the secret machinations of the nefarious spirit of rebellion and anarchy."

Bustamante viewed the superintendency as a means of dramatically expanding his authority in the midst of the imperial crisis. Unlike the traditional police, whose functions remained entirely reactive, local, and subject to municipal control, this tribunal, envisioned as an arm of the captaincy general to be directed by the *asesor de la Presidencia* and *auditor de guerra*, Dr. Joaquín Ibáñez, was to have a completely different role: the kingdomwide prevention of sedition and defense of the peace. As such, Bustamante empowered it with the proactive authority to investigate the following threats:

I. Reunions, gatherings, or meetings contrary to law and public order.

II. Foreigners who might enter the kingdom without the proper authorization, those who have already entered, having caused just suspicion, and those who hide and give them shelter.

III. Political libel, seditious and inflammatory writings.

IV. Correspondence with the enemy and rebels, and with countries occupied by them.

V. The spreading of false notices of disasters or national disgraces, and of false triumphs, forces, and plans of our external and internal enemies—a crime which all law experts number among crimes of state in times of war, which is of the greatest concern in the present circumstances, and which is committed with indiscretion and ease, by ignorance more than malice.

VI. In general all acts, affairs, deeds, and sayings that might upset the peace, promote sedition, and cause or disseminate discord in towns and among their inhabitants, in which cases no privilege or exemption has any value, as the royal dispositions declare.[37]

To assist the tribunal in its efforts, the decree ordered all heads of households, overseers, teachers, professionals, and anyone in a position of authority to give sworn statements about their subordinates, reports that were expected to include information about names, origins, position,

duties, work records, conduct, associates, and patriotic sentiment. Bustamante inserted a provision reinforcing previous measures taken against
strangers (*forasteros*) and then imposed a system of passport controls
for travel within the kingdom. Returning to a familiar theme, the captain general also announced that

> finding myself with positive and faithful notices that, in addition to the
> French emissary described in public edicts, very dangerous individuals
> with the most depraved intentions and coming from countries infected
> with the unfortunate vertigo of insurrection have entered or are trying to
> enter the capital; for the just relief of the ordinary judges, and without
> prejudice to their functions, I will name special commissioners, men of
> integrity, who, on my orders, will visit and patrol the neighborhoods,
> homes, and places of suspicion, without offending honorable people and
> with the instructions and competent authority that I will delegate ac-
> cording to the specific case.[38]

Bustamante was keenly aware that his new superintendency and other
counterinsurgency measures threatened to upset the long-standing balance of power among the governing institutions of the kingdom, pre-
empting as they did a number of established jurisdictions, rules, and
regulations. He attempted to explain his actions by appealing to the
unprecedented state of the empire. In the fourth provision of the superintendency decree, the captain general inserted an unattributed maxim
of "political prudence" that he hoped would justify the existence of the
new tribunal and that in effect served as the guiding philosophy of his
administration's response to rebellion: "there are cases in which scrupulous justice would be the most sovereign injustice; where the Magistrate,
servant of the Law, should proceed in one manner, and the Government,
obligated to conserve the public peace, in another much different manner. And that the Prince or his representative should always do what
must be done, so long as he is attending to and considering the welfare
and security of the people."

Unfortunately for Bustamante, the audiencia did not look favorably
on this argument. When they received the decree, the judges expressed
their immediate concern that similar tribunals in other areas had generated a great deal of public hatred and that, considering the present state

of the kingdom, this would not be good policy. They recognized that it developed out of the success of New Spain's increasingly repressive attitude toward insurrection but noted that the situation there was much worse than in Central America. In Guatemala, such measures would be seen as despotic and the police as instruments of tyranny. Since Bustamante had begun his tenure with conciliatory gestures, the audiencia recommended that these be continued and that vigilance be maintained "loosely without being tyrannical; so that the hand of government, like that of Providence, can be felt everywhere without being seen."[39] In a 27 January meeting of the *real acuerdo* Bustamante's proposal for the superintendency of police was rejected. In spite of this setback, however, the perspective that inspired its creation continued to influence the captain general, and the counterinsurgency strategy was simply implemented in a more subtle fashion.

As before, Bustamante continued to rely heavily on the established administrative infrastructure in the kingdom to root out subversion, and many officials within the system proved to be zealous defenders of the interests of Spain. On 18 January 1812, Narciso Mallol, the alcalde mayor of Totonicapán y Huehuetenango, sent the governor a report on Manuel Paz, an Indian from the town of San Martín Cuchumatán, who was suspected of "having declared himself in opposition to the government of Europeans under influence of the events in San Salvador."[40] The case had originated late in the previous month when a Mercedarian priest, Manuel Echeverría, while traveling through the Cuchumatán Mountains, stopped at San Martín. According to Echeverría, Paz, who served as the postmaster of the town (*maestro de postas*), approached him and asked him for news about San Salvador. The priest replied that all was quiet there, at which point Paz apparently insinuated that the Salvadorans had done the right thing in rising up against the Europeans. Echeverría, "in virtue of the present circumstances," went immediately to the nearest magistrate, the *juez preventivo* of Chiantla, Joaquín Mont, to report the incident. Informed of the situation, Mallol gave the order for Paz's arrest and the embargo of his property.[41]

When Mont took Paz's testimony on 17 February, the suspect had a different story to tell. He declared that he remembered talking to a priest on 27 December but insisted that Echeverría had simply asked him, "why haven't they caught the emissary?" Paz replied that no spy had come through the town but that everyone was on the lookout now that Bustamante had publicized his distinguishing characteristics. In response, the priest said that he must have been caught already, for even Hidalgo, with so many supporters, had been captured and killed; then he warned Paz to watch out because the kingdom was full of emissaries. At this the Indian expressed concern that the number of *chapetones* who passed through the region made it hard for him to distinguish the subversives. Echeverría told him to examine their passports and to imprison those without documentation. Paz then said that this was being done in accordance with the governor's orders, and their conversation ended. When the case ended up in front of the audiencia in March, the tribunal ordered Paz released for lack of corroborating evidence to support Echeverría's version of events.[42]

The prosecution of Paz demonstrated the excessive zeal that increasingly characterized the administration's response to subversion and rebellion. At the time, however, such scrupulous attention on the part of provincial officials to conversations and insinuations about sensitive topics was viewed as prudent governance. And the course of regional events only reinforced the government's impression that its policy was the correct one. On 3 February 1812, Bustamante wrote Mallol to beware of a new threat to the western province: the arrival of emissaries and supporters of the Morelos insurgency that had recently begun to threaten Oaxaca. Four days later Mallol passed the warning on to his subordinates. Joaquín Mont replied that though he was sure his security measures had been successful to that point he would redouble his vigilance.[43]

Despite the strenuous efforts of many of these officials, it seemed that one of the greatest obstacles to a successful counterinsurgency campaign was the local population itself. By 26 September, Mallol had come to the conclusion that his warnings about subversion had fallen on deaf ears. In a proclamation to his province he declared his frustration with the "disdain with which the decrees [*bandos*] ordering all the inhabitants of the towns of this jurisdiction to give a punctual account of all those who receive lodging have been viewed . . . with the result that bad people have been hidden."[44] Apparently, the regulations against association with strangers threatened a thriving contraband economy in the western highlands. When confronted with this fact, the inhabitants of

Totonicapán simply ignored their alcalde's orders, and Mallol did not have the power to impose them by force.

Undaunted by the audiencia's rejection of his superintendency of police, still determined to give his government a viable instrument of social control, but sensitive to the fact that the new policy of counterinsurgency would consume significant resources, Captain General Bustamante opened a new phase in his campaign to ensure domestic tranquility with a 10 April decree calling for a kingdomwide donativo patriótico to pay for the raising of troops.[45] Again, the inspiration for this decision came from Mexico. After the fall of the monarchy, New Spain, like the Kingdom of Guatemala, was called upon to help support the loyalists on the peninsula through voluntary contributions and loans. By the end of 1810 the amount collected reached more than six million pesos. With the outbreak of the Hidalgo revolt, the viceroyalty itself became desperate for funds to raise and support the royalist armies. However, unlike the earlier donations, the contributions solicited by Venegas were viewed as compulsory, and forced loans with no expectation of repayment became commonplace in New Spain by 1812.[46]

Bustamante's April donativo was very much in this tradition, although it was couched primarily in terms of a patriotic appeal to support the war in Spain. For the captain general, the peninsular war was a "common, equal, and inseparable" cause that linked all parts of the empire. Because of the heroic efforts of the Spanish troops against Napoleon, Central America enjoyed peace and freedom from the "French phalanxes"; therefore, "it is an obligation of conscience and of justice . . . to sustain the fight in Spain."[47] Bustamante then emphasized "another obligation of equal justice, one much closer and more urgent, which is to attend to our own internal tranquility." Citing the decision of Spain's new government to abolish certain sources of income, such as the Indian tribute, and the impact of the international wars on the kingdom's economy, the governor argued that his administration could not meet its defense obligations. Therefore, he expected the population of Central America to perform its patriotic duty by contributing to the new subscription. He called on the creole elite to serve as an example by contributing as much as possible but hoped that everyone would be involved at some level. To facilitate the collection of funds, Bustamante declared that donations in kind would be acceptable and that lists would be created in each community to record those who had made their contribution. Once made, the offerings would become "obligatory," to be collected on a monthly or annual basis by a commissioned ecclesiastic. The total amount would then be invested "with necessary preference in the military needs of the kingdom, and the surplus sent to Spain."[48]

The audiencia approved the plan one week later, with Regent Astegueta going on record to urge everyone to view the donativo as a way of encouraging the "most vital feelings of loyalty and patriotism." The captain general also received the fervent support of the Guatemala City archbishopric, an essential ally since Bustamante expected the Church to be the primary administrative instrument for the subscription and the pulpit the primary vehicle of propaganda. Archbishop Casaus stepped forward at this time to legitimize the donativo and by extension, Bustamante's leadership in a proclamation that circulated throughout the province. He declared:

> During such sad and dangerous times, the most turbulent passions have been unleashed to plot at every step disturbances, destruction, plunder, and barbaric punishments and assassinations; other countries, once the most tranquil and blessed of America, have been and continue to be not only ravaged by war but soaked in human blood, because they lacked at the start of their insurrections a corresponding force to contain and punish the first perfidious seducers, thieves, and fraternal assassins. . . . With the most vile and base passions over-excited to an incredible degree, with rivalries inflamed, and with hatred and revenge, shrouded under the cape of the public good, provoked, who can live peacefully, even in the bosom of one's own family, and who can feel secure without the vigilance and determination of the governor of the kingdom? We have already seen the happy results of his prompt and vigorous measures in El Salvador, León, and other areas. . . . So long as all those who have been deceived and perverted have not been disillusioned and converted and so long as all the violent demons and hotheads have not been restrained, there is an urgent need for every man to help sustain the defenders of order and public tranquility at every opportunity.[49]

Although creole clerics proved to be the source of much of the anti-Spanish sentiment in the colony, the peninsular-born hierarchy under

Casaus strongly supported Bustamante and played a fundamental role in disseminating official policy, recruiting royalist allies, and rooting out subversives during the 1810s.

By the summer of 1812, the captain general had moved quite far from the policies of moderation and conciliation that had dominated his first year in office. With the support of the colonial bureaucracy, military, and Church, he had managed to secure important elements of a counterinsurgency state in the Kingdom of Guatemala. Now, following the call for the donativo patriótico, Bustamante turned his attention to the judicial system in an effort to consolidate his authority over the prosecution and punishment of subversives. This particular element to his counterinsurgency strategy, however, had unintended consequences. More than any other divisive issue that emerged during these tumultuous times, the debate between the captain general, the audiencia, and the Guatemala City ayuntamiento over the treatment of those suspected of infidencia drove a wedge between the governing elites in Central America and marked the beginning of the period of outright hostility that would last until the end of Bustamante's tenure. Ultimately, this jurisdictional conflict contributed to the conditions that brought independence to Central America in 1821 by eroding the legitimacy of the crown as the supreme and incontrovertible source of justice and institutional stability in the colony.

Infidencia denoted a very broad category of crimes that included thoughts, words, and actions that threatened public security, challenged the authority of the state, and/or questioned the legitimacy of the sovereign (*lesa Majestad*). From 1808 through the end of the colonial period, most individuals suspected of some form of subversive activity were charged with this offense, regardless of the details of their cases. Defining the crime was never a problem, however, for everyone seemed to know it when they saw it. Instead, in 1812 a major conflict erupted over its adjudication. The audiencia, later supported by the ayuntamiento, argued that cases of infidencia had traditionally been placed under civil jurisdiction (*jurisdicción civil* or *ordinaria*) and that, following the abolition of special legal privileges (*fueros*) by the loyalist government in Spain, suspects should continue to be tried by the criminal courts (the *Sala del Crímen*). The oidores and other supporters of civilian rights supported their claim first by referring to a *Real Decreto* of 18 February

1811, which gave imperial audiencias this authority, and second by quoting a *Real Orden* of 25 August 1811, which stated bluntly "that in cases of infidencia, whose jurisdiction pertains to the territorial audiencias, to the exclusion of all privileged *fueros,* those who apprehend suspects and conduct a preliminary investigation, whether they are civil or military magistrates, should complete their reports as quickly as possible and send them, along with the criminal, to the territorial audiencia without delay." [50]

Initially, Bustamante did not appear to have a problem with this arrangement. He dissolved the *Tribunal de Fidelidad,* which threatened to replace the audiencia as a court of infidencia, early in 1811 and accepted the 25 August *Orden* when it arrived in Guatemala in November. He revised his opinion, however, when a new royal decree arrived in Guatemala City on 10 March 1812. By this time, of course, the situation on the isthmus had changed dramatically. The prisons in the capital and the provinces were full of suspected subversives from the various rebellions in the kingdom, the administration was concerned about future challenges to its authority, reports from Mexico indicated that the special *Junta de Seguridad* was now prosecuting cases of infidencia with great success, and Bustamante, in keeping with his personal inclinations, had begun to impose a greater military presence on the colony.

The decree, which was dated 6 October 1811, was an attempt by the Council of Regency to take account of the negative effect a state of war could have on normal judicial functions and procedures by returning to generals and military governors the authority over certain cases of infidencia that had been outlined in the *Ordenanza general del Ejército* (General Ordinances of the Army). Concerned that the loss of the power to investigate and punish "spying or other crimes which directly threaten and challenge defense measures and destroy the armed efforts of armies and fortified sites" would undermine the position of military leaders throughout the empire, the council decided to make an exception for these cases, "in spite of His Majesty's decrees of 18 February and 25 August." [51] This decision endorsed military courts to exercise jurisdiction over civilians or clergy if the alleged crimes of these individuals fell within the bounds of the previously established *fuero militar.*

In his role as captain general Bustamante was a military governor, and he was very sympathetic to the argument that military justice was a better, more efficient way of dealing with subversion. The arrival of this decree gave him the opportunity and the authority to concentrate cases of infidencia under the jurisdiction of the captaincy general, assuming that they could be made to fit within the new legal loopholes. Arguing that the "seditious commotions of some towns in the kingdom" forced him "to take vigorous measures, which included putting various militia companies under arms, so as to maintain tranquility and public order," Bustamante issued a proclamation on 13 April 1812 that, in essence, militarized the prosecution of all crimes of subversion.[52]

Concerned that his decision to expand military jurisdiction might be misunderstood, the captain general inserted into the body of this *proclama* the reauthorized articles from the army ordinances that dealt with infidencia. According to his reading of the pertinent sections, *jurisdicción militar* applied to the following crimes, regardless of the civil status of the accused: contributing to the desertion of the king's troops; setting fire to military quarters, stores, and other buildings; spying; insulting sentinels or guards; *plotting against a military commander, officers, or troops, in whatever form it is attempted or executed* (this item italicized by Bustamante); initiating any form of sedition, conspiracy, or uprising, or inducing others to commit these crimes against those in the royal service and fortified posts; proffering or writing anything that might incline towards sedition or rebellion; communicating with the enemy in times of war, either verbally or in writing; and attempting to steal arms or munitions. The vast majority of these offenses were to be punished by execution.[53]

As these examples indicate, the increasingly militarized environment of Central America and the fundamental nature of rebellion itself made it very difficult for someone charged with the crime of infidencia to escape military jurisdiction. Thus, after the publication of this decree, Bustamante ordered the creation of courts-martial (*consejos de guerra*) to investigate and adjudicate the cases of Manuel Antonio Gordón, Mateo Antonio Marure, Francisco Cordón, Juan de Dios Mayorga, and other less prominent individuals imprisoned for various acts of subversion.[54] The establishment of these military tribunals provoked immediate opposition from the audiencia and members of the creole elite. In response to an audiencia inquiry into the Marure case, which became the most potent symbol of the developing jurisdictional conflict, Bustamante simply pointed to the appropriate section in the *Ordenanza,* which gave the military authority over civilians charged with spying or plotting against the king's forces "in whatever form it is attempted or executed."[55]

This did not satisfy the oidores, however, and in early July the tribunal began to debate the actual meaning of the 6 October decree with respect to infidencia. In a long report on the matter, the oidor fiscal argued that Marure was not subject to military jurisdiction, because the latest regency decree defined military infidencia as a direct assault on defensive measures and an attack on the armed forces. Marure, who was guilty only of "disturbing and perturbing obedience and loyalty," should therefore be tried by the audiencia. Because his case did not include the military component required by the October decree, the 25 August version remained in force. Oidor González noted, in fact, that Bustamante still recognized some civil authority over infidencia by sending the audiencia the cases of a number of prisoners from Metapán and Santa Ana. In light of the dispute, however, he recommended that a report be sent to Spain in the hopes that the crown would clarify the legal boundaries.[56]

Once the audiencia came out against Bustamante's use of military courts in cases of subversion, those charged with infidencia and their families began to ask the tribunal for the protection of the civil jurisdiction.[57] While the judges agreed that all the cases should be adjudicated by the *Sala del Crímen,* their only recourse at the time, since the captain general remained adamant in his belief that his policy was correct and since he held the suspects in military prisons, was to place the matter in the hands of superior authorities in Spain. In the meantime, the debate continued. Judge Advocate Joaquín Ibáñez, Bustamante's principal advisor on this issue, challenged the audiencia's position in late August, stating that the 6 October decree should apply to Marure and the others because their activities put troops at risk by disturbing the peace. A response by the audiencia in September attempted to make the point that Marure's crimes were committed "where there probably wasn't even a bayonet," since the new intendant, José de Aycinena, was not commanding an army in San Salvador. Ibáñez then wrote another detailed report to Bustamante in October, which noted that many of these men were in contact with the enemy during times of war, another military offense, and that the Venegas decree of 12 June appeared to take an even harder line toward this crime.[58]

Ibáñez did not really want to haggle over legalities with the audiencia. In his view, the only thing that this debate, "these troublesome slow steps," achieved was to delay justice and force the prisoners to spend more time in the unhealthy environment of colonial Central American jail cells. His position, and that of Bustamante, was based largely on the belief that military courts were more effective and efficient than civil courts during unstable times. From their perspective the greatest concern with regard to the colonial order was "the slowness that would result in the administration of justice." Nevertheless, because they believed that the audiencia would not give up on its insistence that the civil jurisdiction had authority over these cases of infidencia, they thought it "necessary to report to His Majesty on the state of these cases and to suspend their progress."[59]

On 18 November an account of the conflict was sent to Spain for review, but within two weeks the colonial authorities received a letter from the Council of Regency, dated 2 July, that exacerbated the confusion by appearing to give weight to Bustamante's position:

> [T]he desire that the tranquility and internal peace of your kingdom remain unaltered . . . obligates His Highness to remind you of the need to take all the measures of prudent precaution that are indispensable in the present critical circumstances of those dominions . . . with the goal of keeping suspicious persons from entering or remaining in the provinces under your command, for their depraved goal is to envelop them in the horrors of anarchy and make them part of the plans of subversion which the tyrant of Europe hopes to spread throughout America, where fortunately he is unable to carry his destructive arms. In the view of His Highness nothing contributes as much to this beneficial goal as the vigilance of the superior authorities . . . and their uniform and concerted cooperation in the development and execution of the necessary policies: therefore, His Highness appeals to the accredited zeal of Your Excellency, the Archbishop, and the Royal Audiencia to maintain among yourselves that union and good harmony which has been preserved until now with such

well-known advantages, so that you might form an irresistible force against the evil projects of those who hope to introduce into that kingdom mourning and desolation.[60]

This statement, which in essence directed Bustamante to act as he saw fit in the suppression of rebellion, so long as his policies were taken in concert with the other leading colonial authorities on the isthmus, was followed by a postscript from the council secretary regarding infidencia. Secretary Peruela added that he was instructed by the regency to "recommend in particular to you [the colonial authorities] the greatest exactitude in the pursuit and quick substantiation of cases of infidencia, and in the application of the corresponding punishments for those who are found guilty of such a horrendous crime."[61] Clearly, Spain viewed the expansion of insurrection into the Kingdom of Guatemala, and by extension this crime, as deserving the most vigorous response possible from the colonial administration. This sentiment accorded well with the counterinsurgency state that Bustamante hoped to construct.

Regardless of the efforts by the Council of Regency to encourage a close partnership between the highest elements of the colonial administration in Central America, the debate over infidencia symbolized the increasing inability of civil and military institutions to cooperate effectively during a time when the threat of insurrection was ever present. Despite appearances, this was not an arbitrary and unilateral usurpation of the audiencia's traditional authority over this crime. Bustamante asserted the *jurisdicción militar* in an environment that was highly militarized and in a context where his superiors in Mexico and Spain appeared to sanction such a position. The ramifications of this decision, however, were profound. Already damaged by the conflict over the superintendency of police, the ties between the captaincy general and the audiencia became increasingly perfunctory after 1812, even though the tribunal dropped its claim of jurisdiction over those charged with infidencia within the year.[62]

While the oidores backed away from a confrontation with the captain general, the Guatemala City ayuntamiento decided to take up the cause of civil justice early in 1813. This move, which turned the debate from a jurisdictional squabble between two governing institutions into a question over the treatment of creoles by a peninsular-dominated administration, united the creole elite behind a resonant cause. Basing its position on the need to protect the "personal security of the citizen" from arbitrary authority, the ayuntamiento, an institution that had recently been strengthened by the constitutional reforms emanating from Spain, became the protector of those who were increasingly seen as the creole "victims" of Bustamante's heavy-handed, militarized government.[63]

By the summer of 1812, Bustamante had managed to assemble almost all the major pieces of his counterinsurgency state: his active military forces, which numbered some four thousand troops, had recently quashed the last major rebellion in the kingdom and were available for new campaigns; urban militias throughout the provinces had been set up to guard against future insurrections; his donativo patriótico was in place to fund rising military costs; his alliance with Archbishop Casaus gave him access to the church bureaucracy and resources in his effort to promote patriotic sentiment; and his insistence on military justice in cases of infidencia promised swift and decisive punishment of subversion. After more than a year in office, the captain general could make a convincing argument that his efforts had preserved the peace in the Kingdom of Guatemala despite some serious challenges to the colonial order. As it turned out, the greatest threat to his vision of this order was fast approaching in the form of the Constitution of 1812. This document, marking a revolution in the nature of colonial politics, included no provisions for the type of counterinsurgency state that Bustamante deemed necessary for the defense of Spanish rule. Instead, it transformed the political climate in the colony by appearing to legitimize the efforts of the creole elite and its public instrument, the ayuntamiento, to establish autonomous political power.

During the first half of the year, the ayuntamiento of Guatemala City remained relatively detached from the counterinsurgency efforts, unwilling to assert itself while the colonial government confronted an armed rebellion in Nicaragua and before the arrival of the new constitution. A sign that relations between the captain general and the municipality had already begun to deteriorate, however, came in May when the council decided to celebrate the recent election of José de Aycinena to the Council of State in Spain with a mass and Te Deum. When the notice for the festivities was published in the Gaceta de Guatemala, the regidores discovered that their invitation had been rejected in favor of another that did not give the council credit for originating the idea and that diluted the significance of Aycinena's nomination by adding other reasons for the city to give thanks at that time. When the regidores complained to Bustamante, he responded that it was his own version that made it into print. This perceived slight to the honor of the ayuntamiento disrupted council meetings for the next two weeks until one councilman exclaimed that "the most important thing is to preserve harmony with the superior government . . . and not spend so many meetings dealing with such minor issues."[64]

The excitement generated by Aycinena's appointment to high imperial office, which offered the creole elite direct access to the crown, and the growing sense of anticipation generated by the constitutional debates preoccupied the Guatemalan political community during the summer of 1812 to the exclusion of most other issues. When the ayuntamiento finally received its copy of the Constitution of 1812, on 5 September, the regidores wasted no time in sending a delegation to Bustamante to inquire about plans to hold elections for the offices and institutions mandated by the new imperial system.[65] To the great delight of the creole elite, a series of royal decrees accompanying the charter gave instructions for annual elections to fill two new political organizations: *ayuntamientos constitucionales,* which were designed to replace the old municipal councils in all towns with more than a thousand inhabitants, and *diputaciones provinciales,* which were envisioned as regional assemblies for Guatemala and Nicaragua.[66] At the same time, the imperial reforms resulted in the "demotion" of the captain general to the position of *jefe político superior* (superior political chief) and the audiencia to the status of a supreme court. With much reason, creoles expected to dominate the new governing institutions—and the elections of the delegates to the *Cortes ordinario* in Spain—to the exclusion of the peninsular community and the lower classes and, thereby, to achieve an unprecedented level of political power and autonomy.

At this point the interests and expectations of the Guatemala City ayuntamiento and, by extension, of most of the creole elite, split irrevocably from those of the captain general. In Bustamante's mind, the achievement of creole autonomy via a drastic reorganization of the colonial administrative structure during a period of imperial crisis was tantamount to independence. At the very least, he believed the reforms would be unable to prevent those opposed to the continuation of Spanish rule from destabilizing the colony. As a consequence, in keeping with his counterinsurgency perspective Bustamante treated the Constitution of 1812 as something to be tolerated when possible and obstructed when necessary. Unfortunately for the creole elite, who wanted immediate gratification and complained to Spain about every perceived delay in the process, the captain general jealously guarded his power to set the timetable for the establishment of the new system. Again, Bustamante found ample precedent for this position in the actions of the viceregal government of New Spain.[67]

The confrontation between the captain general and the creole elite over the Constitution of 1812 began immediately and persisted until Ferdinand VII revoked the constitution in the summer of 1814. This result vindicated Bustamante, left the creoles deeply embittered, and, as a consequence, provided the impetus for a series of recriminations and acts of revenge that permanently soured the remaining years of Bustamante's tenure in Central America. In the context of the constitutional experiment, Bustamante's actions have been seen as hypocritical at best and tyrannical at worst. Although many of his policies were obstructionist in nature and patently antithetical to the liberal reforms of the Cádiz government, it must be recognized that the conditions that confronted Bustamante at this time were highly unusual: he had received orders from a government of suspect legitimacy to implement without delay a completely new political system in a very traditional society that faced external and internal subversion. Simple prudence—a word that Bustamante loved to use—dictated that the governing authorities of the colony use restraint during this process. The Guatemala City ayuntamiento, however, was unwilling to accept this position, preferring instead to pressure and threaten the captain general at every opportunity and to assume for itself as much power as it could acquire in the interim.[68]

After the constitution arrived in the capital, the ayuntamiento took upon itself the responsibility to arrange an elaborate public presentation ceremony for the morning of 24 September. As part of the preparations, it decided to build an ornate platform on the Plaza Mayor from which the text of the constitution would be read and five hundred pesos worth of specially minted coins could be distributed to the crowd.[69] Although

Bustamante declined to take part in the deliberations over the details of the service, he approved of the ayuntamiento plan when it was presented to him. Three days later, the council discovered that the captain general was going to issue the public invitation to the ceremony in his name only and thus deprive the regidores of another mark of honor. Following a pointed complaint by the ayuntamiento, Bustamante responded that he had decided in consultation with the audiencia that "as the kingdom's Superior Chief the invitation is my responsibility entirely." Moreover, he declared, "I look with disfavor on all forms of etiquette," a position against pretentiousness that he then recommended the council and its "dignified individuals" assume.[70] Although they promised not to press the matter since the audiencia had been part of the decision, the regidores decided that the issue was important enough to send a formal protest to Spain, especially when they found out that the invitations were distributed by two mounted dragoons.[71]

The Cádiz constitution was presented to the Kingdom of Guatemala on 24 September; however, the official swearing in of the colonial administration did not occur until the next day, when Bustamante and the audiencia assembled in the *Sala de Acuerdo* of the royal palace and swore to protect the constitution *and* be faithful to the king.[72] According to instructions, Bustamante then chose the members of a *Junta Preparatoria* that was charged with organizing the first round of elections under the new system. The committee, which included Bustamante, Casaus, and four members of the ayuntamiento, plus José del Valle as secretary, began meeting on 10 October. By the middle of November Valle had drawn up a list of instructions and regulations for the process, which included details on the election procedure, citizenship and suffrage rights, and the responsibilities of the new *diputados de Cortes,* diputaciones provinciales, and ayuntamientos constitucionales.[73] With this information in hand, Bustamante reported to the ayuntamiento on 20 November that he was prepared to proceed to the elections for the municipal offices of the capital, a process that began two days later with the selection of electors and culminated on the twenty-ninth with the elections for regidores, alcaldes, and síndicos.[74] By the end of the year, then, local elections, which had the important effect of seating the first freely chosen ayuntamientos in the history of the colony, had taken place throughout Central America.

One of the reasons Bustamante did not attempt to delay this first constitutional experiment was that he did not view local political reform as a serious threat to Spanish rule. As described in Valle's instructions, the ayuntamientos constitucionales did not have "such serious responsibilities; but those duties that are left to their care are more important than what they had previously."[75] According to Valle's summary, the powers of the new municipal councils under the constitution included the following: addressing issues of health; assisting the alcaldes in matters of public security and the preservation of public order; administering and investing the funds in the public treasury; providing for the collection of taxes; overseeing primary schools and other educational institutions, hospitals, welfare and charity establishments; directing the construction and repair of roads, bridges, prisons, and other public works projects; and reporting to the Cortes on issues of agricultural, industrial, and commercial development. All other issues were left to the regional assemblies and the colonial authorities in Guatemala City. Thus, Bustamante did not believe that his position would be seriously challenged until the regional assemblies were seated and the Cortes representatives were in Spain. On 27 October, however, the Guatemala City ayuntamiento learned that the crown had agreed to give the council the title of *excelencia*, thereby raising it, in theory, to the ceremonial rank enjoyed by Bustamante. As had been seen on a number of occasions, the regidores were particularly sensitive to issues of rank and ceremony, and they proceeded to take full advantage of their promotion. Until preparations could be made for the elections to the regional and national offices and institutions, the Guatemalan ayuntamiento constitucional assumed for itself the role of chief legislative assembly in Central America.[76]

The new ayuntamiento began its operations on 7 December 1812 with the regidores swearing their allegiance to the constitution and receiving their committee assignments.[77] From the outset, relations between the council and Bustamante were not warm, as both sides seized every opportunity to undermine the other's position and authority. In essence, the ayuntamiento set itself up as the leading advocate for progressive, liberal policies, including press freedom, free trade, open communications with Mexico, and greater power for elected representatives within the imperial bureaucracy. This was, of course, the complete antithesis to what Bustamante considered appropriate considering the circumstances.

The first significant confrontation between the two came within two weeks of the initial constitutional session. Concerned that Guatemala would not be represented in the upcoming *Cortes ordinario,* which was set to meet in Spain on 1 September 1813, the town council formally asked Bustamante to make the necessary preparations for the next round of elections. The request, however, came at another difficult time for the colonial administration. After some months during which debates about the implementation of the constitutional system were the greatest source of political tension in the kingdom, concerns about the kingdom's security now returned to center stage. On 22 December Alcalde Sebastián Melón reported to the ayuntamiento that one of the leading citizens of the colony, Gregorio de Urruela, was planning to take his family to Spain following dire reports about the political situation in New Spain and rumors that the Mexican insurgents were approaching Guatemala. Melón went on to state that others had similar designs and that the entire community "found itself frightened and anxious" over the news. The council then voted to ask Bustamante for the latest reports from Mexico and to inquire about the precautions being taken "to calm public spirits in such critical circumstances."[78]

Later that day the captain general replied that he had nothing new to offer. Although he could confirm that the insurgents had invaded Oaxaca and incited isolated revolts among the Indians of Tehuantepec, he was unable to say whether they had continued beyond that province in the direction of Guatemala. As a result, Bustamante explained that he found no reason for anyone to leave the kingdom; he had given out two passports for travelers heading to Esquipulas but was not going to issue any more. Still, in order to address the concerns of the regidores directly, the captain general decided to make a rare appearance in front of the ayuntamiento. In a closed-door session on the twenty-second, Bustamante repeated his earlier statement to the regidores. Convinced that the captain general was withholding information, Alcalde Melón responded that the fears of the people would not be assuaged without a full disclosure of news from Mexico, details about the state of the kingdom's defense, and measures taken to ensure public security. This caused Bustamante to reply that he had not withheld anything, and he encouraged the regidores to disclose to the public all they had learned in the interest of restoring calm. Before leaving the meeting, he made a point of reminding everyone in the room that the defense of the kingdom was his own responsibility.[79]

Shortly thereafter, the ayuntamiento received a note from the captain general that addressed the question of the Cortes elections. Bustamante stated that the difficult circumstances facing the colony at that moment "threw up all kinds of obstacles in front of the election process" but that as the one responsible for carrying out the crown's orders he would not forget his duties. Unhappy with this answer, the council renewed its petition on the twenty-fourth and then, assuming that Bustamante would not acquiesce to its request, voted to inform the Cortes "of the little power the laws have in these regions, since the public officials have easily conspired to elude your paternal and beneficial oversight with interpretations prohibited by the Constitution."[80]

After a year of fighting to maintain Spanish rule in Central America following the outbreak of the first colonial insurrections of the period, Captain General Bustamante could point to some notable achievements. In a matter of months, his policies, both diplomatic and military, had ended the unrest and conspiracies in the provinces with little damage to the colonial order, and his newly consolidated counterinsurgency measures promised to maintain this state of affairs for the immediate future. As 1812 ended, however, his position was no more secure than it had been in December 1811. The constitutional reforms emanating from Spain threatened his power as governor and captain general and emboldened the creole elites to push for greater autonomy. Although internal unrest appeared to be suppressed by this time, southern Mexico was now largely under the control of the Morelos insurgency, and Bustamante could reasonably assume that Guatemala would be affected either directly or indirectly by this development. As a result, preserving the established order over the next eighteen months proved to be as great a challenge as anything Bustamante had faced before.

6

The Challenge of the Constitution, 1813–1814

Despite the optimism of imperial reformers in Spain and the enthusiasm of the creole elites in Central America, the Kingdom of Guatemala was not a propitious place for political experimentation as the first full year of constitutional order began in January 1813. In concert with viceregal officials in neighboring Mexico, Captain General Bustamante had spent the previous year constructing a counterinsurgency state capable of withstanding internal and external challenges to Spanish rule, and the policies he implemented were not in accordance with the spirit of imperial reform then so popular within the Spanish Cortes, not to mention the Guatemalan oligarchy. From his perspective, however, these precautions were necessary. At the time, the isthmus remained under the shadow of the full-blown Morelos insurgency in New Spain, a threat that was significant enough to cause Bustamante to begin stationing troops in western Guatemala at the end of 1812. Considering the events of the previous year, he also had no reason to assume that the revolts within Central America had been completely suppressed. Even without active unrest against Spanish authorities or clear signs of subversion, denunciations and arrests continued, while destabilizing rumors ran rampant throughout the countryside in the absence of solid news and good communications. In this environment, it would have been out of character for the military-oriented Bustamante to consider, however briefly, the type of power sharing and political reform envisioned by the

Constitution of 1812. Even if the captain general were not ideologically opposed to such a complete deconstruction of the system of enlightened absolutism that governed the empire at the height of the Bourbon period, his experience in colonial administration made him overly cautious about the viability of the liberal experiments during this critical time in the kingdom's history.

In a report to the Council of Regency dated 3 March 1813, Bustamante presented his analysis of the political trends in Central America to that point. According to the captain general, the growing pretension of the creole elite to political power was the greatest challenge to the preservation of the colony, aside from the external threat posed by the Morelos rebellion. After two years in Central America, Bustamante argued that "the spirit of oligarchy is what has dominated these provinces."[1] In his mind, the autonomy that the creoles demanded and that the constitution appeared to offer was actually a cover for independence, a drive to achieve the political hegemony that had been denied them up to then. Therefore, a rapid and complete implementation of the new system, with its constitutional ayuntamientos and regional legislative assemblies, would only speed the process whereby Guatemala would break with Spain.

Bustamante proceeded to make the case that the Spanish authorities on the isthmus faced a concerted and coordinated attack by creoles acting through the institution of the ayuntamiento. He dated the first serious challenge to Spanish rule to 1809, when the municipal council of Ciudad Real overthrew the acting intendant of Chiapas, José Mariano Valero, and installed one of their own in the vacated office, a "sad example which with small variations has been blindly followed in other areas."[2] In his view the reaction from Captain General González had been too conciliatory and had inadvertently contributed to the growing belief on the isthmus that power "should be in the hands of ayuntamientos or juntas comprised of individuals chosen by them."[3] By the end of 1810, the ayuntamiento of Guatemala City had codified this perspective in the *Instrucciones* it prepared for Deputy Larrazábal, a document that, according to Bustamante, urged local (that is, junta) authority over police, taxes, commerce, industry, agriculture, defense, and the treasury, as well as power over nominations to imperial offices and the title of *grande* (*excelencia*) for ayuntamientos. In this version of events, the creole elites, excited by the promise of autonomy and hoping to take advantage of the weakness of the imperial system, attempted to enlist Captain General González in a *golpe de estado* immediately before the arrival of Bustamante. The plot failed, but it was reproduced at the provincial level by the Salvadoran and Nicaraguan uprisings at the end of 1811 and the revolt in Tegucigalpa in January 1812.[4] While he managed to suppress this unrest through his policies of careful vigilance and prudent conciliation, Bustamante argued that he found himself confronted by an increasingly recalcitrant ayuntamiento in the capital that now hoped to achieve its goals by forcing constitutional reform on the isthmus and by blaming the provincial disturbances on his counterinsurgency measures. Offended by the complaints and charges directed to Spain by this council, the captain general asked that his efforts be declared appropriate, that his honor be satisfied, and that he be given "the aid I have requested, sending to me the troops necessary to make the orders of the Government respected and to strengthen even more the general peace and tranquility in the midst of this tempestuous age."[5]

Based on his recent experience with the new constitutional ayuntamiento in Guatemala City, Bustamante had good reason to believe that creole-dominated municipal councils were conspiring against Spanish officials in a thinly disguised quest for power. And, in his role as captain general, the personification of crown authority in Central America, he felt that the majority of those attacks were directed against his own person. In a letter dated 3 January, the ayuntamiento made good on its threat to send a complaint to the Cortes that the colonial administration was not complying with the constitution and, in fact, was actively delaying the elections for *diputado* and the diputaciones provinciales. This action had already been taken when, two days later, Bustamante set the date for the next round of elections, an attempt either to mollify the regidores or to bolster his position in the event of an investigation.[6] In any event, the dispute had moved beyond such a simple resolution by that point.

In their complaint the regidores declared that the elections for ayuntamientos had been a great success and had resulted in a sustained public clamor for the next round. It was essential that the process move quickly so that the provincial representative could reach Spain in time for the opening of the new Cortes and the provincial assemblies could be seated. Nevertheless, "this Government did not try to initiate the elections," a display of intransigence that caused the ayuntamiento to make "respectful" overtures to Bustamante. Although the captain general claimed that the instability of the provinces affected his decision to proceed with the reforms, the council doubted his good faith, because he did not explain himself to the ayuntamiento "in a calm and courteous manner." They then asked the Cortes, "won't it be necessary to make him drop the hardness in his manner and his use of strong language which Spaniards should never hear from their governors?"[7]

Having unburdened themselves of their personal grievances with Bustamante's style of governance and character, the regidores moved on to more substantial issues. In a clear effort to change the balance of power in the colony, the city council argued:

> Even if there were obstacles, inconveniences, difficulties, and delays, who should remove them? Shouldn't it be the Cabildos, those institutions which are the free expression of the will of the People and which are responsible for their happiness and welfare? Shouldn't it be this Ayuntamiento, which has just emerged from the hands of many thousands of citizens and to whom Your Majesty has charged the internal government of the community? It seems that this should be the case, for in no institution or individual will the governor find a greater will to attend to [the people's welfare], nor more skill in promoting it. . . . The governors of America have become accustomed to treating these subjects as if they comprised a colony of slaves, for the distance of the throne and the difficulty of appeal leads to impunity in their rulings. A succession of centuries has instilled in them absolute and despotic power, and it is not easy to reconcile them to the new system, which they will have to be forced into, for so many of their ancient powers and faculties will be lost.[8]

Through this representation, the creole elite in Guatemala City painted Bustamante as an unreconstructed absolutist, a heavy-handed autocrat who sought to preserve his ill-developed authority at the expense of the constitutional reforms mandated by Spain by raising unspecified and mysterious obstacles that only he could address. From this perspective, the political problem in the Americas was a simple one: the empire was governed by officials "who cannot accommodate themselves to a plan of government which limits their authority, for the habit of complete command is not lost overnight, and, therefore, those communities who are far from Your Majesty still have not seen the first sign of the reform for which they have waited so long."[9]

The passionate nature of the ayuntamiento complaint against Bustamante underscores the degree to which the instability and uncertainty of the years following the collapse of the monarchy tended to harden and sharpen partisan perspectives. The captain general was not a tyrant; neither were the regidores advocates of independence. At the time, however, the creole elite of Central America was confronted with its best chance to date to assume significant political power in its undeniable quest for autonomy within the imperial structure. Bustamante, a proud military officer and crown official, believed himself obligated to preserve the complete authority of Ferdinand VII over the Kingdom of Guatemala in the face of serious military threats in and around the isthmus, during the occupation of Spain, and as Cortes politicians sought to limit his power. So long as the king remained in exile and the outcome of the various imperial wars remained in doubt, these interests simply could not be reconciled.

Another controversy erupted in January 1813 that did nothing to diffuse the growing antagonism between the captain general and the ayuntamiento of Guatemala City. After having taken office one month earlier, the *regidores constitucionales* voted to prepare a proclamation that, in light of their new duties as representatives of the people and their expectations for increased authority, stated their firm desire, recently "inflamed by a patriotic fire," to contribute to the public welfare, to enforce the new constitution, and to serve as a conduit for grievances and concerns that might exist among the populace.[10] The completed *proclama* was then sent to the printer, Ignacio Beteta, on 5 January in anticipation of its kingdomwide distribution. After the type had been set, a problem arose, however, for Beteta informed the ayuntamiento that he would be unable to continue the process. The council then took its proclamation to another printer, Manuel Arévalo, who admitted that he would also be unable to do the work for he had orders from Bustamante not to print anything without the explicit permission of the colonial administration.[11]

Furious at this challenge to the press freedoms established both by a November 1810 royal decree and by the Constitution of 1812, the ayuntamiento brought suit against Beteta to force him to print the proclamation.[12] In testimony taken on 18 February before Sebastián Melón, the alcalde segundo, Beteta declared that while editing the text he "found expressions which might sound bad to the government." Not wanting to subject himself to official disapproval, since the 1810 royal decree declared that both "the authors and printers will be responsible respectively for any abuse of this liberty," he offered to print the document only if the offensive statements were removed. Of course, the regidores did not think the printer had the power to make such a decision. Besides, they could find nothing subversive about their *proclama*. On 27 March Alcalde Melón ordered Beteta to print the proclamation within three days, without examination of its contents, or face a fifteen-hundred-peso fine. Beteta appealed this decision to the audiencia, arguing that he would be forced to print something he found "repugnant to my free but regular mode of thinking. . . . I have found the proclamation offensive to the Superior Government under whose protection I live. . . . The liberal ideas which I lack, according to the Asesor, don't affect my necessary discernment regarding the indicated information." This intransigence caused one council member to complain that if the appeal were heard the judicial process would take so long that, regardless of the outcome, the *proclama* would be so out of date that the printer would "win by default." Such was the result. By the time the case ended two years later, with Beteta having to pay court costs, the issue had been overtaken by subsequent events.[13]

Bustamante's restrictions on press freedoms serve as another example of the degree to which liberal idealism clashed with the realities of colonial administration and, once again, were probably influenced by more stringent measures taken in New Spain. When the 1810 decree on censorship arrived in Mexico City, the viceroy made no effort to comply with it and, following months of protests from Mexican delegates to the Cortes, went so far as to ignore a direct order from the Council of Regency to carry out the new laws.[14] Finally, on 5 December 1812, after consulting with the audiencia, Viceroy Venegas actually invalidated Article 371 of the constitution that dealt with the freedom of the press.[15] Such flagrant disregard for the will of the imperial Cortes was justified as a necessary part of the preservation of order in New Spain. According to the Spanish liberals, press freedom was "a means of illuminating the entire Nation, and the only way to uncover the true public opinion."[16] The viceregal authorities, however, operating in the midst of a civil war, believed that an unrestricted press would become a platform for the dissemination of anti-Spanish or insurgent propaganda.

The kind of colonial nullification or obstruction of imperial laws deemed detrimental to regional order, exhibited to such an extreme by Venegas and to a lesser extent by Bustamante, was part of an old imperial tradition known as *obedezco pero no cumplo* (I obey but do not comply). In the early part of 1813, Bustamante could argue quite legitimately that the need for the government to suppress unsubstantiated news, questionable perspectives, and outright misinformation outweighed the potential benefits of a free press.[17] Of course, his escalating rivalry with the ayuntamiento also probably contributed to the hardening of his attitude. As the dispute over the *proclama* indicated, to allow even a loyal institution such as the Guatemalan municipality unrestricted access to kingdomwide public opinion via the printing press was a threat to the captain general's position as undisputed leader of the colony.

The conflict over the implementation of the Cortes decrees on press freedom is not only an example of the intransigence of colonial authorities in the face of imperial reform. It also demonstrates the degree to which these same colonial officials found themselves the victims of vague instructions, differing interpretations, and poor communications when attempting to put the measures in place. In the 1810 decree, for example, the Cortes ordered the creation of a brand-new set of institutions designed to "insure the liberty of the press and at the same time to contain its abuse." In Spain a nine-member Supreme Censorship Board was to assume authority over the new laws for the empire as a whole, while in the Americas five-member censorship boards erected in each colonial capital were expected to administer them at the regional level. According to the decree, the censors, two of whom had to be priests, were responsible for examining publications brought to their attention by administrative and judicial officials and passing judgment on their legality. After allowing for an appeal to the Supreme Censorship Board, the Cortes then laid out the provisions for the seizure of any material found injurious or scandalous, the arrest of the author and printer, and the adjudication of the case by the proper authorities.[18]

For more than two years, however, this basic framework was not followed by any further instructions regarding this important institution. Although the Guatemala City ayuntamiento consistently pressed Bustamante to give the necessary orders to establish the censorship board, the colonial government refused to make the commitment until more information was known about its jurisdiction and operations. On 10 June 1813, after reviewing a number of reports and recommendations on the matter, the Cortes issued a decree that finally provided the critical details. Among the thirty-five additional points that the Spanish government hoped would clarify the role and duties of the censorship boards were the following: the term of office for the censors was set at two years; the boards were made responsible only to the Cortes for their decisions; and material deemed seditious—"any printed matter that conspires directly to incite the population to insurrection"—was added to the list of offenses against the freedom of the press that could be prosecuted by the colonial authorities.[19] Even these clarifications were not enough, however. The following day, the Cortes added thirty-eight more that addressed the responsibilities of all the junta officials, from president down to secretary, established a meeting schedule for the boards, described voting procedures, and defined the relationship between the Supreme Censorship Board and the provincial institutions.[20] As soon as these decrees arrived in Central America, Bustamante allowed the process of installation to begin.[21] While he may have been opposed to this particular reform, his three-year refusal to set up a censorship board was not a clear-cut case of obstructionism. Without the fundamental information provided only in the 1813 decrees, any effort made before that time would probably have withered in the face of intense jurisdictional, legal, and operational conflicts with competing authorities.

Such considerations did not seem to affect the Guatemalan oligarchy too deeply. It continued to expect rapid and substantive implementation of the constitutional reforms and, from its perspective, Bustamante had become an intractable obstacle to the new imperial order. Unfortunately for the Family the only legitimate actions it could take to express its growing opposition to the policies of the captain general were the sharply worded complaints to the Cortes that the ayuntamiento began to send on a regular basis in 1812. The regidores could not assume, however, that the imperial government would respond favorably and decisively to these displays of colonial frustration. In fact, some of their protests actually backfired. On 4 March the ayuntamiento received a reply to its complaint about the events surrounding the publication of the constitution in which Spain simply encouraged the council to work with the captain general in the interest of peace.[22] In September Bustamante forwarded to the ayuntamiento the Cortes response to the detailed charges made on 3 January regarding delays in the elections for *diputados* to the Cortes and the diputaciones provinciales. After reviewing the case, the crown declared that "there is no reason whatsoever to make a complaint against the said captain general," for the colonial authorities "conducted themselves in a manner worthy of praise."[23] Since the term of office of Deputy Larrazábal ended with the closing of the *Cortes extraordinario* and because it appeared unlikely that the kingdom would have its new representatives in Spain in time for the opening sessions of the *Cortes ordinario,* Guatemalan creole interests did not have the influence at the highest levels of imperial government that they needed to undermine Bustamante's monopoly over the administrative agenda in the kingdom.

In January 1813, however, José de Aycinena took his leave of Guatemala City and its leading families in preparation for his departure to Spain, where he was to assume his seat on the Council of State, a position of imperial leadership rarely achieved by an American creole, much less a Guatemalan. At a meeting of the municipal council held in his honor, Aycinena stated that he would exert all his influence on the council and in the imperial government to secure the welfare of the kingdom by providing information on "our situation, our needs, and our resources."[24] The regidores then sent him off with a secret letter to the Cortes that detailed, in a veiled reference to the captain general, "the evils that are afflicting this kingdom."[25] Once in Spain, Aycinena quickly became a powerful advocate for the interests of the creole elite and a determined adversary of Bustamante.[26]

In the meantime, the constitutionally invigorated ayuntamiento continued to challenge the authority and autonomy of the captain general by staking out public positions on sensitive issues and by emphasizing at every ceremonial opportunity its raised status. During the spring of 1813, the regidores took as their cause célèbre the adjudication of infidencia and the treatment of prisoners by the captaincy general. On 5 February the council received a letter from Juan de Dios Mayorga in which the prisoner protested the nature of his imprisonment and the delays in his trial and asked the regidores to enforce constitutional protections for citizens by taking up his case.[27] Such a plea, coming from one of Bustamante's creole victims and promising a strong platform from which to criticize the administration's hard-line judicial policy, proved impossible to ignore. In the middle of March, the council's attorney (síndico), Mariano Beltranena, appropriated Mayorga's arguments and that of the audiencia in a report that declared the public welfare would be greatly damaged if Bustamante were allowed to prosecute cases of infidencia in councils of war.[28] By that time, the trials of Francisco Cordón, Manuel Calderón, and Fulgencio Morales had begun, a situation that helped provoke the ayuntamiento to action. On 16 March it sent Beltranena's report to the captain general, causing Auditor Ibáñez to wonder how the council decided it was qualified to interpret royal decrees on the subject.[29]

Although its foray into the midst of the legal dispute between Bustamante and the audiencia over cases of infidencia did not derail the efforts of the colonial administration to handle subversion in military courts, the ayuntamiento remained committed to the issue and discovered that by asserting its power to conduct unrestricted visits (*visitas*) to the prisons and address conditions in the cells it could continue to act as a constitutional defender of individual rights—and as a thorn in the side of Bustamante. On the same day that Mayorga's letter arrived, the council voted to send Dr. Narciso Esparragosa and Dr. José María Guerra to report on the "comfortableness and healthfulness" of the city's institutions of detention, arguing that the notorious state of the prisons constituted a punishment in its own right and was, therefore, illegal under the Constitution of 1812.[30] The doctors completed their investigation on 22 March and sent their conclusions to the ayuntamiento four days later. They found the living conditions lacking in every respect. Unless augmented by outside means, daily food rations were far too low, consisting of a plate of beans and five small tortillas in the morning and a four-ounce piece of meat with five more tortillas in the evening. The prisons were clean but smelled terrible, for water was scarce and sanitation poor. Air circulation inside the buildings was limited and even the patios felt stagnant, an environment that the doctors felt contributed to the high rate of fever. The individual cells were too small, with tiny windows high overhead providing no ventilation. And, locked up from six in the evening until morning, the prisoners had no way to combat the effects of these conditions through exercise or other means.[31]

On the day after this report came in, the audiencia received a royal decree, dated 9 October 1812, that ordered leading civil, religious, and military officials to make special visits to all prisoners on the two Saturdays before Palm Sunday, Pentecost, 24 September, and Christmas.[32] During these visitas, a priest, two oidores, and two members of the diputación provincial were expected to read the cases of those incarcerated, listen to any complaints, and resolve any problems they might encounter. Since the Guatemalan diputación had not yet formed, the ayuntamiento served as its alternate and immediately made plans to initiate the process for the upcoming Holy Week period.[33] At this point, the pretensions of the upstart council ran up against the weight of three hundred years of administrative tradition and institutional intransigence.

Although the new title of *excelencia* presumably raised the ayuntamiento to the same rank as the audiencia, especially after the constitutional reforms reduced that venerable institution to a simple court of justice, in its dealings with the leading Spanish authorities in the colony the Guatemalan municipal council was never fully accepted as an equal.[34] When the regidores communicated with the tribunal to set up a time for the prison visits, they received an indirect response from one of its secretaries, according to the manner of "the old system."[35] Furious with this apparent slight, the ayuntamiento sent the letter back unopened. The audiencia, however, repeated its action, informing the council through an intermediary that the visitas would take place on 10 April. Similar efforts to contact the archbishop about providing access to ecclesiastical prisoners also proved difficult, though in this case the Church delayed its response to the last minute before informing the regidores that it held no prisoners. Bustamante, himself, refused to set a time for the visits to the military prisoners until 9 April, the day before the prisons were to be opened.[36]

According to Regidores Domingo Antonio de Juarros and Juan Bautista Asturias, the conditions in the *Carcel de Corte* were "horrible" and "necessarily prejudicial to one's health," while the *Carcel de la Ciudad* was almost as bad.[37] In the first they found Mateo Antonio Marure, who was reduced to very poor health after contracting an illness in prison, and in the second a man named Gabriel Ore, who complained that after more than a year he had received no medical attention for his many ailments. Aside from health-related complaints, the commission heard stories of improper judicial proceedings, summary judgments, and excessive punishments. In general the protests came from individuals held by the captaincy general and in particular they came from a group of seventeen Granadan soldiers sentenced by a military court to serve time at Ceuta. In both prisons the regidores found evidence of abuse of the inmates by the guards. Regidores Lorenzo Moreno and Domingo Pavón, however, reported that their visit to the military prisoners resulted in nothing out of the ordinary. Although Archbishop Casaus stated that the Church was not confining anyone, the ayuntamiento had recently received a letter from Pedro Ortíz, a priest who claimed to be imprisoned on orders of the archbishop in the Convent of the Colegio de Cristo.[38] As a result, on the day of the visitas Regidores Valdez and Castillo went to the convent, where they interviewed Ortíz and another priest, Tomás Ruíz, who also stated that he was a prisoner of the archbishop. A visit by Regidores Pedro Batres and Manuel del Castillo to the Convent of La Merced turned up no one else.[39]

From the perspective of the ayuntamiento the information uncovered during the morning visits to the prisons was so significant that it merited immediate attention. That afternoon the regidores assembled and agreed to three responses: first, the council would inform Bustamante of the plight of the prisoners held by the captaincy general; second, a letter would be sent to the archbishop asking him to explain his denial of the existence of ecclesiastic prisoners; and third, the ayuntamiento would begin deliberating ways to improve prison conditions.[40] Convinced that part of the problem was the indifference displayed by the colonial government, the regidores decided on 11 April to send a report of the visita and a list of the inmates' complaints to Spain, along with a specific charge against Bustamante detailing his lack of support and his efforts to force punishment on "those unhappy prisoners."[41]

The captain general's ostensibly cruel treatment of the *reos de infidencia* and his single-minded obsession with punishing subversives was one of the cornerstones of the *terror bustamantino* that emerged in many national histories after Central American independence. He was not likely to give the benefit of the doubt to those suspected of such crimes, and he wanted to see quick and effective justice done to those who ended up being convicted. For the most part, however, the charges relating to Bustamante's handling of prisoners tend to reduce themselves to areas largely beyond the governor's control. Spanish justice was slow, regardless of jurisdiction, and the appeals process made it even slower. Conditions within colonial prisons were invariably bad and often "prejudicial to one's health." Unfortunately, the combination of these endemic factors made both so-called abuses of justice and deaths caused by the insalubrious prison environment commonplace. Bustamante was adamant about detaining suspects until preliminary investigations were concluded, a policy that caused some to languish in prison for months at a time. When these individuals were cleared of the charges brought against them, they were released; when a light punishment was merited, they received it; when a stiff penalty was recommended, it was imposed with no hope for pardon.[42] With little money to make drastic alterations in the kingdom's prisons, little expectation that reform would alleviate suffering, and little conviction to improve the living conditions of those charged with crimes against the crown, the captain general focused his attention on other priorities.[43]

The greatest preoccupation facing Bustamante at this time was a large insurgent army under the command of General Mariano Matamoros, one of Morelos's closest and most gifted lieutenants, which had taken control of the border province of Oaxaca at the end of 1812 and threatened to continue its march into Chiapas.[44] News of these events produced tremendous consternation and anxiety in the colony, for many concluded that even if the kingdom were not invaded, the proximity of the rebels would encourage internal insurrection and indigenous unrest. As a consequence, Captain General Bustamante made the decision early in 1813 to become an active participant in the war in New Spain by going on the offensive against Matamoros's forces. Early in February approximately seven hundred troops from the militia battalions of Quetzaltenango, Ciudad Real, and Tonalá united under the command of Lieutenant Colonel Manuel Dambrini and set out for the isthmus of Tehuantepec, which at the time served as the vague border between New Spain and the Kingdom of Guatemala. Upon crossing into Mexico the royalist troops began a concerted search for insurgents and first came across them in the town of Niltepec on 25 February. In a short engagement the Guatemalans defeated the small group and captured a number of soldiers, including the rebel commander Julián Suárez. Waging war as General Calleja and Viceroy Venegas advised, Dambrini then had Suárez and two dozen others executed on the spot.[45]

Advancing after this victory, the Guatemalan army successfully engaged more insurgents at Niserindami before occupying the town of Tehuantepec early in April.[46] This became Dambrini's base of operations as he proceeded to impose peace on the area. Aside from sequestering rebel property and offering pardons to those who would return to the royalist cause, he used his troops to conduct sweeps of the surrounding countryside in the hopes of rooting out subversives and rebel sympathizers. In the meantime, news of the battle at Niltepec had reached Matamoros in Oaxaca, causing the rebel leader to mobilize his forces for a campaign against the invading Guatemalan royalists. After giving up much ground, Dambrini finally engaged Matamoros outside Tonalá on 19 April and was decisively defeated. The Guatemalan troops retreated deep into the kingdom to await further orders. Matamoros, on the other hand, returned in triumph to Oaxaca after showing no interest in advancing further into Central America.[47]

The first public news of the Oaxaca campaign was recorded at an ayuntamiento meeting on 3 March. With no information about Dambrini's orders or intentions, aside from the fact that he had crossed the border into New Spain, some regidores expressed their intense concern that he would "have the imprudence to provoke the insurgents, which would bring fatal results to this country, for we find ourselves so poorly defended and weak that we might not be able to avoid total ruin."[48] On 18 March more news about the invasion reached Guatemala City, along with the first reports of hostilities, though none of the information came from the captain general. Frustrated at Bustamante's silence and unwillingness to "make himself responsible via this ayuntamiento to the people whom it represents" and anxious about the threat from Mexico, the regidores voted, with one dissension, to bring the matter to the attention of the crown.[49]

Bustamante in fact did not inform the council about the events in Oaxaca until 30 April, when he sent a terse message to the regidores that mentioned the "incident" at Tonalá and the "vigorous" actions needed to defend the kingdom in the wake of that defeat. He stated that in light of the continued insurgent activity along the border he had given orders for a redeployment of troops from the Caribbean to the western provinces. During their transit across Guatemala, these forces would need to spend some time in the capital, and the captain general counted on the ayuntamiento to make the necessary arrangements for housing, food, and supplies. Regarding the preservation of public tranquility in Guatemala City in the midst of the crisis, Bustamante declared that he was satisfied with the vigilance of the council and expected it "to dedicate all its strength toward ensuring that there will be no alteration in that state."[50]

The ayuntamiento met in special session the next day to discuss this report. The regidores expressed shock at the news of the defeat but also appeared anxious to "do their part to preserve the peace and public tranquility." In their official response, they asked Bustamante for more information about the deployment; in particular, they wanted to know how long the troops would be in the capital, the numbers involved, and the type of structures needed for their lodging. Concerned about the impact of large numbers of black troops on the capital, the council asked that significant restrictions be placed on their movements.[51] Perhaps sensing some weakness, the regidores also saw this occasion as an opportunity to confront Bustamante on his governing style and voted to send Alcalde Melón and Regidor Moreno to inform the captain general that

> he has maintained from the beginning of his command a notable aversion to all the inhabitants of this city, particularly with respect to its most esteemed and highly regarded segment, but also to the Indians; that he works only by himself, without consulting any well-informed subjects; that to a certain degree he has tended to inflame the divisions between Europeans and Americans by manifesting a bond to the former which has become obvious to the people; that he does not know the character of the sons of Guatemala, so inclined to gentleness; that the many denunciations and ill-advised imprisonments have exasperated the public, because it realizes that the foundations for these often are just misunderstandings . . . that such rigorous secrecy surrounding news of pub-

lic events is not fitting since everyone wants information and mystery can help no one. Finally, His Excellency disdains advice and separates himself from those subjects who have surrounded him until now, individuals who because of their stature express the opinions and general disaffection of the people and who advise him that among the causes of the disgust that the people have for him not the least is their suspicion and presumption that the mail [which the colonial government had been intercepting] is not worthy of their confidence.[52]

On 4 May Melón and Moreno reported on their meeting with Bustamante. According to their summary of the discussions, the captain general made an attempt to downplay the conflict by expressing his general esteem for the ayuntamiento and its willingness to work for the public welfare. He explained that his inability to attend council meetings was simply a consequence of his many duties and obligations and should not be taken as a snub. The captain general expressed his amazement that anyone would think he had disdain for the local population; on the contrary, "his home is open to everyone, and he, or his wife in his absence, receives all those who request an audience, cordially and with attention." Bustamante referred again to his heavy responsibilities when justifying his limited social activities but noted that he did have a small circle of friends. He argued that those who complained about their exclusion from this group simply did not try very hard to make his acquaintance. Nevertheless, he would welcome with pleasure anyone who made the effort. Bustamante refused to accept any blame for causing divisions between Spaniards and Americans, "for in reality in the area of employment I have tended to give preference to creoles, and in every other category I made no distinction between the groups or esteemed one above the other." He acknowledged that security concerns compelled him to order the opening of letters from areas under revolt, but he believed this was done in accordance with the laws. Finally, he found himself "perplexed" by the ayuntamiento position on the dissemination of news of public interest, arguing a bit disingenuously that he always gave the council whatever news he had at any given point.[53]

Although this exchange cleared the air somewhat between the ayuntamiento and the captain general, it did nothing to reduce the high level of distrust and antagonism that had developed during the first five months of 1813. Disconcerting reports from the ayuntamiento of Ciudad Real about the situation in Chiapas and the early arrival of the Caribbean forces quickly heightened the tension in the capital. Within a week the Guatemalan regidores met to discuss the "present state of things, results which our troops caused through their provocation of the insurgents and which led to the introduction of rebels into Chiapas, the consternation of the people, and above all the consequences that might result from the entrance of troops into the capital and the risk that a popular movement will top off our misfortunes."[54] Of course, many regidores blamed Bustamante for this crisis and made a series of proposals that they hoped would end it. Alejandro Vaca, who believed that the threat from Mexico would disappear on its own, argued that the royalist forces should be recalled from the border and that the Caribbean troops should be denied entry into Guatemala City. Manuel Beltranena, who remained concerned about the security of the colony, declared that the entire kingdom should be armed and that a governing junta comprised of provincial representatives and headed by the captain general should be set up:

> for during these times the many and complicated obligations of government are too much for one person; and once the people are persuaded that these measures are made to secure their welfare and prosperity and to avoid the dangers which are threatening them, they themselves will take precautions and defend with enthusiasm their lives and property, and thus we will do our part to preserve the integrity of the Spanish nation which has found itself so greatly dismembered these days.[55]

Despite the council's clear dissatisfaction with Bustamante's administration of the kingdom, this radical suggestion proved a bit much for it to accept at that point. Instead, it voted to wait and see how things developed before taking further action.

The ayuntamiento continued to expect that significant reform would take place upon full implementation of the constitutional system. With or without Bustamante's obstruction, however, many obstacles remained to be overcome before the Cádiz ideal could be realized in Central America. Between February and May, elections for the Guatemalan diputación provincial were held in the seven districts that made up the new political unit: Sacatepéquez (Guatemala City), Chimaltenango, Quetzaltenango, Sonsonate, Ciudad Real, Comayagua, and San Salvador.[56] Once this process was completed, the ayuntamiento wrote to all the newly elected deputies and asked them to make their way to the capital as quickly as possible so that the assembly could take up its duties by 1 July. However, by the appointed time three had not arrived: the Comayagua deputy, Bruno Medina, was delayed on the road; Sonsonate did not elect its representative, José Cañas, until July; and José María Pérez from Quetzaltenango, a priest, did not want to leave his parish until a replacement could be found who spoke the indigenous language. Concerned about the impact of the delays, the ayuntamiento asked Bustamante on 20 July to allow the assembly to begin work with the four representatives who were in the city plus two alternates. The captain general, however, had no reason to facilitate the establishment of another creole-dominated political institution in the capital. In fact, Bustamante did not believe he could trust the new delegates, much less work with them. Two of the members, José Marías Delgado and José Cañas, had been implicated in the Salvadoran uprising, and of the rest only Bruno Medina met the governor's standard of loyalty. Thus, the Guatemalan diputación provincial did not begin operations until 2 September, and Bustamante, who served as its president in his new role as *jefe político superior,* tried to bypass it as much as possible.[57]

The other major pillars of the constitutional system, the election of provincial representatives to the Spanish Cortes and the establishment of ayuntamientos constitucionales throughout the kingdom, also faced significant impediments. Although the Cortes deputies were selected in March, many were unable to make the voyage to Spain because of a lack of funds. As late as 29 November, José Cleto Montiel, the deputy for Quetzaltenango and Totonicapán, was petitioning the diputación provincial to pay his travel expenses. In this cash-poor and economically depressed colony, however, the assembly had a hard time finding and releasing the money, especially when its jurisdiction over the public treasury was not completely clear.[58] As with the establishment of provincial deputations, it is difficult to ascertain the degree to which Bustamante actively impeded these efforts. Part of the delay in selecting a representative for Guatemala City and Sacatepéquez, for example, was due to the fact that the first choice, José María Peinado, who had been elected on 15 February, declined the honor in favor of remaining in his post as intendant of San Salvador.[59] Thus, when the *Cortes ordinario* opened its doors in October 1813 the Kingdom of Guatemala found itself severely underrepresented.

As soon as the diputación provincial was installed, Bustamante ordered his provincial officials to initiate the establishment of ayuntamientos in towns that did not have municipal representation but whose size of population or regional importance now merited it.[60] Shortly thereafter the captain general began to receive status reports from the alcaldes mayores and corregidores charged with implementing the decree, and these appeared to indicate that the reforms were not going well. On 14 October the alcalde mayor of Verapaz wrote that "in the entire district under his command the only ayuntamiento worthy of the name constitutional that has been established was in the town of Rabinal, although the election was so disgraceful that two professional drunkards, a capital vice among the Indians, were chosen as alcaldes."[61] In a similar vein, Bustamante received a letter from the corregidor of Chimaltenango the following week that bluntly asked for the suspension of the reform because the Indians, who made up the majority of his district, "don't know Christian Doctrine. . . . They are ignorant of Spanish. They don't know paper, ink, or pens, except for what they have seen from a distance."[62] He then argued:

> Ask yourself now if such an Indian could ever set up an ayuntamiento. . . .
> In this situation I can imagine an Indian as *alcalde constitucional* sitting
> on a chair (which he has never used before) with good men at his side,
> and in come litigants, who supposedly only know Spanish, to make their
> case. I see here that there will be no understanding between them, that
> nothing will be reconciled or cleared up, and that the case will remain
> unresolved, especially if the alcalde is drunk, which happens frequently. . . .
> I simply can't believe that if the National Congress were established in
> Chimaltenango it would not suspend the implementation of ayuntamientos until the situation changed.[63]

In many cases such as this, the reformist zeal of the constitutionalists simply ground to a halt in the face of local prejudice, administrative incompetence, and personal ambition. But even when provincial officials made an effort to follow the constitution, problems inevitably surfaced. The establishment of constitutional ayuntamientos, for example, was delayed in the alcaldía mayor of Totonicapán because of the lack of an adequate census of the province.[64] Bustamante had no reason to block the reforms at this level, but neither could he facilitate them. Once the requisite orders were issued from the capital, local and provincial forces determined whether the process remained on track or was derailed.[65] From the perspective of the creole elite and the Guatemala City ayuntamiento, however, as the summer of 1813 came to an end, the Cádiz experiment appeared mired in difficulties that only a change in the office of captain general could rectify.

On 3 August potential deliverance for this group appeared in the form of a Cortes plan to divide the powers of the governor between two officials: one, the *jefe político superior,* would be charged with civil authority, while the other, the captain general, would retain responsibility for military matters. The council immediately voted to petition the crown to name the head of the creole oligarchy, Marquis Vicente de Aycinena, to the office of *jefe político superior,* "for the advantages which his placement will offer the province, where he enjoys a level of esteem and acceptance that makes it extremely likely that he will govern with skill during these very critical times."[66] The news from Spain was not all positive, however. Three days later the regidores learned that their complaint to the Cortes about Bustamante's behavior during the celebration of the constitution in September 1812 had been rejected as unwarranted.[67] One month later, a vindicated Bustamante passed on the Cortes response to the 3 January ayuntamiento protest over electoral delays in the kingdom.[68]

Somewhat on the defensive now, the council reacted strongly and negatively to a rumor that floated around the capital in the month of August that certain provincial ayuntamientos had petitioned the Cortes to confirm Bustamante as governor in perpetuity.[69] Desperate to forestall such an occurrence, the regidores allowed their virulent antagonism toward the captain general to be expressed openly. Declaring that "the character of the *jefe* is not suitable for command at these times and in such critical circumstances, for his inclination to be arbitrary and hard, his opposition to the establishment of the Constitution, and his adhesion to the old system are so well known," the council voted to inform the Cortes again of Bustamante's many infractions of the constitutional system and his "dangerous and risky conduct in office."[70]

The August arrival in the capital of the prisoners taken during the Granada campaign only exacerbated the hostility of the Guatemalan elite toward Bustamante. Many of those arrested were leading citizens in the city, including ayuntamiento members, military officers, and wealthy landowners, and they had much in common with their counterparts in Guatemala City. Acutely aware of these bonds, the Guatemalan oligarchy became forceful advocates for the prisoners' welfare, petitioning the colonial authorities to move the *Granadinos* out of the public prison, where they were forced to mingle with common criminals, and supplying them with food and other necessities during their incarceration.[71] Unmoved by these actions, Bustamante responded somewhat sarcastically that "the prison is comfortable and decent enough, in proportion to the distinguished subjects who find themselves there, and not even corresponding to the enormity of the crime that is attributed to them."[72] Many of the prisoners became ill with diarrhea, dysentery, and other ailments within a month of their arrival. Trying to find a way to balance "humanity" with "indispensable security," the captain general then gave orders for the construction of a special sickroom and made provisions to improve the ventilation within the prison. Complaints of ill treatment continued, however, for as long as the *Granadinos* were imprisoned.[73]

Reinvigorated after a period of illness in the spring and emboldened by the recent decisions of the crown to exonerate him in the constitutional disputes with the ayuntamiento, Bustamante received news from Spain late in November that strengthened his resolve that his policies were in fact the correct ones for the kingdom despite the opposition they engendered on the part of the creole elite. On the twenty-third of that month he passed to the city council the new *Instrucción para el Gobierno Económico-Político de las Provincias,* a document that clearly indicated that the Cortes had decided to step back somewhat from the liberal administrative reforms that predominated in the first year under the constitution.[74]

With this decree Spain again reworked the balance of power between the governor, the provincial deputation, and the ayuntamiento. Municipal councils found their duties limited to issues of local public welfare, including police, sanitation, education, health care, food and water supply, commercial regulation, vital statistics, agricultural and industrial development, and other "general measures of good government which need to be taken to secure and protect the person and property of its citizens." Instead of operating as an autonomous regional legislature, the diputación provincial was now reduced to the level of an advisory council for the provincial governor and charged only with supervising the local ayuntamientos, major public works projects, and the public treasury. Once again, the nonelected governor or *jefe político superior* wielded

> supreme authority within the province in order to preserve public tranquility, peace, security, and the property of its inhabitants, to execute the laws and orders of the government, and in general to take charge of all that pertains to the public order and prosperity of the Province; and since he will be made responsible for any abuse of his power, he should also be punctually respected and obeyed. Not only will he be able to administer the punishments imposed according to the *leyes de policía* and *bandos de buen gobierno*, but he will also be empowered to impose and demand fines against those who disobey him or deny him respect, and against those who disturb the peace and public order.[75]

The Cortes then emphasized that although it still planned to divide the civil and military duties of the governor between two individuals, it recognized that in certain cases "the preservation or reestablishment of public order and tranquility" required the temporary unification of these powers under one command.[76]

This news had a chilling effect on the Guatemalan creole elite, for the *Instrucción* effectively disempowered the governing institutions that the oligarchy hoped to use as a counterweight to the traditionally Spanish-dominated administrative structure. The impact of these changes was immediate: Bustamante found it much easier to justify his limited use of the diputación provincial, and he forcefully asserted his right to call the next annual round of local elections in what became a major dispute with the ayuntamiento at the end of November.[77] However, while the oligarchy found compelling reason to complain about the actions of the obstructionist governor during this period, its own motivations were far from disinterested. Despite its liberal vocabulary, which was suffused with the concepts of political and economic liberties for the individual, the Guatemalan elite was most interested in replacing a peninsular political oligarchy with a creole one. In this environment, the constitutional struggles of 1813 can best be understood as a contest between conflicting interpretations of a new political system that had yet to be clearly defined. With no precedent to guide either side, each tried to stake out the best possible position and secure the strongest allies. But with Spanish politicians engaging in similar fights on the floor of the Cortes and sending conflicting messages to the colonies, few reforms were implemented. Ultimately, this stalemate convinced the most radical among the kingdom's elite that significant change would only come through force of arms.

Between 28 October and 21 December 1813 a group of some two dozen conspirators, including a number of priests, soldiers, and municipal authorities, held a series of meetings at the Convent of Belén in Guatemala City.[78] According to subsequent testimony, these men came together in order to plan and launch a coup against the colonial administration. Through their military contacts, they hoped to cause an uprising within the capital's militia companies on 24 December that would be directed toward the overthrow and imprisonment of the captain general and senior Spanish officials, the release of political prisoners, and the capture of the public treasury. The ultimate goal of the movement appears to have been independence, though much about the intentions of the conspirators remains unclear. In any event, two officers who had been invited to the convent for one of the November meetings, José de la Llana and Macario Sánchez, reported the existence of the conspiracy to the authorities. The Spanish authorities deposed twenty-four more witnesses in order to confirm the meetings. The government then received the unsolicited testimony of Lieutenant Joaquín Yúdice, one of the original members of the plot, who filled in many details and proceeded to name the leaders. On 21 December the conspiracy collapsed following the arrest of most of the named suspects.[79]

While there is no evidence to indicate that the plot against the administration was widespread or that it would have garnered sufficient support had the coup been launched, the fact that ayuntamiento members were implicated confirmed Bustamante's suspicions about the loyalty and trustworthiness of the creole elite. Although one can argue, as historian Mario Rodríguez has, that the Spanish authorities gave the incident "an importance which it really did not have," it is also necessary to recognize that appearances mattered a great deal at that time, considering the climate of insecurity that had affected all parts of the empire since 1808.[80] Upon hearing the news of the arrests, the ayuntamiento debated whether to send a note to the captain general expressing its concern and offering to cooperate in any way to preserve the peace. Since Bustamante had not yet informed the regidores of the situation, the council decided by majority vote not to write the letter.[81]

One month after the exposure of the Belén conspirators, a more serious challenge to the authority of Spain developed in San Salvador. Although it too was suppressed with little difficulty, Bustamante once again had reason to believe that a kingdomwide network of subversion threatened the established order, thereby justifying greater vigilance on the part of the colonial authorities. In a detailed summary of these events to the Council of Regency, Bustamante argued that peace had never truly been restored to the provinces after the unrest of 1811. Instead, the various leaders of the uprisings, who had willingly accepted the royal pardon, continued to meet in secret, promote sedition, and keep their agents active. As a consequence, the captain general stated that he was compelled to watch San Salvador carefully in the two years after its initial pacification to ensure that order was maintained. This responsibility increased as Bustamante began to lose faith in the intendant, José María Peinado, whose close ties to the Guatemalan oligarchy proved hard to ignore.[82]

The governor explained that early in 1813 the Spanish administration had received reports of scandalous graffiti (*pasquines*) in the city. Peinado confirmed this and noted that Fr. Manuel Aguilar, one of the leaders of the 1811 unrest, had begun to give seditious sermons again. Despite these ominous signs, the intendant asked Bustamante not to intervene, saying that he would take care of the problem. By April Peinado reported that the city was completely tranquil. In August, however, investigations undertaken by the intendant of León, Juan Bautista Gual, into seditious statements allegedly made by the Franciscan Juan de Dios Campos turned up connections among Aguilar, his brother Nicolas, and the Nicaraguan priest.[83] The captain general stated he was concerned enough to order Peinado to keep careful watch on Manuel Aguilar, though the intendant downplayed the significance of the links.[84]

On 9 September Bustamante received a message from Peinado describing the unrest San Salvador experienced four days earlier following rumors that the captain general had arrested José Matías Delgado, the Salvadoran representative to the diputación provincial. Once these reports were exposed as false, the city quieted down. Bustamante, however, was not so easily reassured. He wrote to Peinado that he was not convinced the city was truly at peace: "that I feared that the Government was considered weak because of what had been its policy of prudence, that I thought of taking more severe measures to uproot from the bosom of that province those who worked to perturb it, but before deciding on the most opportune [response] I wanted [Peinado], as an eyewitness of the events, to inform me of the most appropriate plan to assure once and for all the public tranquility."[85] According to the captain general, the intendant tried to downplay the recent incident by emphasizing once again the loyalty of the province. Bustamante was temporarily reassured, but in October he received warnings that certain neighborhoods in San Salvador were stockpiling grain and that well-known citizens were behind the *pasquines*. Some of these individuals reportedly had also initiated contact with José María Morelos.[86]

These events set the stage for the uprisings of January 1814. On the last day of December, the latest status report from San Salvador arrived in Guatemala City. In it Peinado complained that he was no longer able to control the population, for "subordination has been lost, [and] the towns seem like cynical academies where the Constitution and Sovereign Decrees, both equally misunderstood, are furiously debated and applied in the support of their vices and with the impunity of the greatest crimes."[87] Bustamante was livid with the "extraordinary and sudden transformation" in Peinado's perspective, and he proceeded to heap a great deal of blame on the intendant for the events that followed.[88] On 9 January Peinado reported the results of the municipal elections and noted that Juan Manuel Rodríguez had won the post of alcalde primero, one of a number of suspicious individuals who managed to obtain local offices. He also mentioned that the newly constituted ayuntamiento had asked him to turn over control of the *sala de armas* to the municipality, a request that caused the intendant to be concerned about the strength of his military forces. The colonial authorities received Peinado's warning in the wake of the Belén arrests. Bustamante believed that this conspiracy was linked to others in the provinces and hoped that its exposure would be enough to discourage future plotters. The captain general told Peinado to use force if necessary to preserve order, and he directed the local military commander, José Rosi, to begin special patrols of the city.

The second uprising of San Salvador began on the evening of 24 January 1814 and continued haphazardly for three days. Directed by some of the leading civil and religious figures in the city, including Rodríguez, Vicente Aguilar, Alcalde segundo Pedro Pablo Castillo, Bernardo José and Manuel José Arce, Miguel Delgado, Domingo Lara, Juan Arauzamendi, Leandro Fagoaga, and Dr. Santiago José Celis, the conspirators hoped to mobilize the population to overthrow the intendant and other members of the colonial administration. Although the crowds that turned out following the ringing of the bells of Aguilar's parish church were large and violent, Peinado refused to capitulate to the demands made by the insurrectionists. For a short time, the city was more or less under the control of the rebels. By the end of the month, however, after two bloody confrontations between the mob and loyalist militia units under the command of Rosi, the royalists managed to restore order. After the disturbances, Delgado, Rodríguez, and Celis were immediately arrested, while Castillo and Vicente Aguilar managed to escape. During a search of Delgado's papers, the authorities found a letter written by the conspirators on 1 May 1813 to Morelos, proving that at least some members of the creole elite were in direct contact with the Mexican insurgents. In addition, local authorities uncovered plans that had been drawn up before the disturbances outlining ideas for a new provincial constitution that gave political sovereignty to an elected junta and a three-member executive.[89]

After imposing martial law on the city and transferring a number of military units to the province, Bustamante ordered a thorough investigation of the uprising with the hope of bringing to justice all those who had some involvement in it.[90] After three years of constant struggle in an effort to preserve the tranquility of the kingdom in the midst of enormous pressures, this latest experience with insurrection completely disillusioned the captain general. In a detailed critique of the events of his administration that captures a profound sense of frustration and alienation toward his subjects, he declared:

> The restless towns do not rise up in response to the pain of any particular wrong that they have been made to suffer. They intrigue, scheme, and agitate to expel from their bosom the European Spaniards, to raise the banner of absolute independence, to cut the ties that form from these provinces and those of the Peninsula one single unit. This is the object of their movements and the spirit that even the most seemingly peaceful towns advertise. I must force myself to say it, because I am obliged to present the truth in its purest form. If they affect the most unalterable adhesion to the Mother Country, if they overpraise the pure loyalty of the people, calling certain provinces most faithful and repeating the donations that certain individuals make, then these same exaggerated statements, which are quite suited to the character of hypocrisy noted here, form part of a great plan—perhaps one meant to surprise the authorities, or to lull the government to sleep, to hide the true object, to open the path of employment to those they want to see placed there. . . . I live in this country, I am an eyewitness to these events and I judge according to the facts. . . . In the year 11 León and Granada had just made the most expressive protestations of loyalty to this government when they were convulsed by more horrible commotions than San Salvador, and [Granada], ignoring the pardon which I offered, went to the extreme of firing on our troops thereby making it necessary to use force. This ayuntamiento of Guatemala, which never ceases to repeat that its most glorious quality is that of fidelity, wanted the authorities to appear before it and swear an oath upon hearing the first news of the renunciations at Bayonne in 810 [sic] and refused to repeat before my predecessor the obedience owed to the royal family; in the same year it published the *Instrucciones* in which it asserted that government and all its branches, including War, should be placed in the hands of a Junta comprised of individuals elected by the ayuntamientos; in a letter which I have reported to you, it wrote to the provincial deputy of Comayagua, Bruno Medina, in the year 13 that circumstances demanded a Government that was the creation of the people; and in a representation directed to the Cortes it let escape a protest manifesting that it would consider invalid any law sanctioned

by the Sovereign Congress without the presence of the deputy of this
province, a protest identical to the one made by New England when the
United States of America prepared itself for its war of independence. . . .
In the towns that agitate to free themselves from a specific complaint,
once the cause of the unrest is removed calm is instantly restored and
all the pleasures of peace are enjoyed. Among those who agitate to declare themselves independent, generous methods, taken to remove the
source of their protests, do not sever the root of the evil, for the dissatis-
fied take advantage of generosity to facilitate their wicked ways. The European who governed San Salvador was removed, an absolute pardon was
granted to the authors of the first movement, a creole from Guatemala
City was named political chief, a constitution more liberal than anyone
could have imagined was established, rights were proclaimed which no-
body knew or desired before. In spite of this, the results have not been
what were hoped. . . . The private sentiment for liberty remains alive in
America and at the same time the right of election conceded to the people
has been abused, to the point where those of the worst reputation, the
suspect, or at least those of the most dubious judgment have been chosen. The authority given to the ayuntamientos has been abused, with
these bodies attempting to extend their influence over departments that
clearly do not pertain to them while assuming a tone of superiority quite
inappropriate to the institution. The generous establishment of the Provincial Deputation has been abused through intrigues that have tried to
fashion them into so many little congresses. The freedom of the press has
been abused through the publication of papers that disseminate poison-
ous seeds, whose vegetation will prove difficult to eradicate some day.[91]

According to Bustamante's analysis of the past three years, most of
America was simply unprepared for the kind of political reform provided by the Constitution. Instead of gradually and carefully applying
the new rights and freedoms, the Cortes had overwhelmed the empire
with a tangled set of modern laws and institutions that the majority of
the population did not have the culture or education to grasp. As a result, the only segment of society able to operate in this environment, the
enlightened, highly educated members of the upper class, tried to take
advantage of the chaotic situation to reinforce creole-dominated oligar-
chies. By manipulating the constitutional reforms and misinterpreting

them to the lower classes, these subversives hoped to alienate the ignorant *pueblo bajo* from Spain and create support for autonomy or independence. After years of experience, the captain general now believed
that those corrupted by these sentiments never changed and, therefore,
must be exiled to preserve the established order.[92]

In Bustamante's opinion, he had in fact been far too accommodating with the creole malcontents. He did not disavow his initial temper-
ance and conciliatory policies; instead, he argued that "the system of
prudent moderation that I adopted was useful, because it will make
the system of justice in which I should operate in the future stand out
even more."[93] The captain general then proceeded to recommend to the
Council of Regency certain measures that he deemed essential for the
continued preservation of Spanish rule in his kingdom and by extension in other parts of the empire. In his view, the greatest challenge
the crown faced was that "the procedures for criminal prosecution, so
time-consuming and complicated, are very dangerous in cases brought
against insurgents," for they allowed suspects to continue to intrigue
and subvert with impunity from prison while the slow machinery of
justice worked its way forward. Justifying his counterinsurgency cru-
sade, he stated:

> Wars of violence [*guerrillas de fuerza*] are not the only ones found in
> these provinces. There are others even more fearful, with more pain-
> ful transcendence and more fatal effects. The malignant war of intrigue
> [*guerrilla de intriga*] is one, this decided protection of prisoners of in-
> fidencia, this deep interest in defending them, recommending them, and
> affecting infractions of the Constitution in order to intimidate the au-
> thorities and cause impunity to triumph; this system of hidden manipu-
> lations whereby popular elections are won by people of suspicion or du-
> bious character instead of Europeans or creoles of proven loyalty; this
> premeditated plan to fill ayuntamientos and diputaciones with specific
> individuals; this secret correspondence of false news . . . this active ef-
> fort to discredit the most zealous employees who are familiar with the
> schemes of unrest and block the path of evil; these arts whereby so much
> loyalty is affected to the distant eyes of the Supreme Government, while
> at the same time plans of independence and emancipation from the Me-
> tropolis are carried out here in different ways, both openly and discretely;

this constant intrigue to discredit at Court and to disdain, persecute, and refuse all consideration in these countries to those who declare themselves addicts of the Government; this hatred and malignant contempt which cannot be hidden from the moment that one decides for the just party of the Nation; this work bent on intriguing so that offices and commissions are not given at Court to those not of the party of the suspicious; these schemes to revoke even those small graces given to those who have merited them for their sincere patriotism and accredited loyalty.[94]

Because he was forced to operate in such unusual conditions, Bustamante asked the crown to reconfirm and reinforce the special powers given to overseas governors by the Laws of the Indies to alter normal judicial procedures during times of crisis. In particular, he wanted license to exile, without warning, individuals, their families, and supporters whose continued presence in certain areas threatened public order. In the same vein, he requested that the adjudication of infidencia be streamlined—that the cases be freed from the formalities that delay regular criminal proceedings. Considering the ease with which he could have unilaterally implemented such extrajudicial measures in the kingdom, as Venegas and Calleja had done in New Spain, it is significant that the captain general felt the need to get authorization for his actions from the crown before proceeding any further.[95]

Bustamante did not expect to be the beneficiary of any change in policy, however. On 18 February 1814 the ayuntamiento received its first communication from José de Aycinena since his arrival in Spain the preceding August. In this letter the regidores learned the shocking news that the crown was going to replace Bustamante with Fernando Millares, the captain general of the province of Maracaibo, Venezuela, and a native of Cuba. The rationale behind this decision is unclear. While the opinions of the new member of the Council of State must have added a great deal of weight to the anti-Bustamante reports received by the crown, Bustamante had been requesting leave to return to Spain for more than a year because of ill health. In any event, the regency gave Bustamante permission to leave the kingdom before the arrival of Millares, in which case the intendant of Honduras, Juan Antonio Tornos, was appointed to serve as interim governor.[96]

Bustamante did not officially notify the ayuntamiento of his recall to Spain until 22 March, although the council had already begun to make preparations for what it expected would be the imminent arrival of Tornos. This did not happen, however. Although both Tornos and Millares accepted their appointments, neither official made it to Guatemala City. It is not known when Bustamante and the ayuntamiento realized that no replacement would be forthcoming. As late as 18 May, the captain general still believed he would be relieved at some point in the near future.[97] The hopes of the council probably continued well into the summer and were not completely dashed until the end of August when the regidores received an enthusiastic letter from Deputy Antonio de Larrazábal, dated 11 March, which stated that the crown had agreed to appoint the Marquis of Aycinena as the kingdom's new political chief. By this point, however, everyone recognized that this appointment was no longer valid. Three days later, in fact, word that the deputy had been imprisoned in Madrid reached Guatemala City. Unfortunately for the creole elite, the issue of Bustamante's transfer fell victim to the enormous political changes that occurred in Spain between March and August 1814.[98]

Reliable notices that King Ferdinand VII had returned to Spain reached Guatemala City in the last days of June and were occasion for tremendous displays of official satisfaction, ranging from military parades to a Te Deum, as well as numerous unofficial celebrations.[99] As far as the oligarchy was concerned, however, this joy turned to consternation on 19 August when Bustamante published the 4 May royal decree that officially abolished the constitution and nullified the acts taken by the *Junta Central* and the Cortes during the absence of the king.[100] Following this pronouncement, the restoration of absolutism throughout the colony proceeded without delay. On 9 September, Bustamante announced that the crown had restored the full powers of the captain general and abolished the office of *jefe político*. One week later he dissolved the diputación provincial. For a couple of months the ayuntamiento operated in a sort of institutional limbo, uncertain of its position or authority. Finally, armed with the royal decree of 30 July the captain general ordered the council on 3 December to reconstitute itself as it existed in 1808. Three days later the constitutional experiment in Central America officially ended. At least in the mind of Ferdinand VII the empire was now going to be administered as if the monarchy had never fallen.[101]

Bustamante, not surprisingly, was an active and enthusiastic participant in the dismantling of the constitutional system. The decision to
reestablish an absolutist government in Spain and the Americas confirmed him in his role as captain general, provided temporary vindication for his hard-line policies of counterinsurgency, and promised at the
very least to discredit his enemies. Now that the imperial crisis had
ended and the king had returned, Bustamante could reflect on his first
three years in power. From his perspective, as a dedicated officer of the
Spanish crown, he had done his duty well: he had survived the calum-
nies and machinations of the creole elite that were designed to drive him
from power, he had diffused Napoleonic efforts to subvert the kingdom,
he had taken the royalist cause into New Spain and confronted the insurgency there, and he had successfully fought the sporadic internal rebellions that threatened to overwhelm the isthmus. As he told the alcalde mayor of Sacatepéquez on 3 July:

> At the present moment there is not one rebellious district in the province
> under my command. Public order has fortunately been reestablished in
> those areas where the malignant spirit of the perverse, who seduced the
> people, arrived to upset it; protected by divine providence the war for jus-
> tice restored to Spain the Monarch whom we loyal Spaniards have so de-
> sired; and, now that a clear day has dawned after the tempestuous ones
> we have suffered, we must believe that the empire of peace and public
> tranquility will consolidate itself.[102]

With overt opposition to Spanish authority effectively ended by 1814, it
appeared that Bustamante had succeeded in preserving the Kingdom of
Guatemala for the crown. Much remained to be done, however, to consolidate this achievement. And this process, on both a personal and political level during the final three years of his administration, would
transform his success into little more than a Pyrrhic victory.

7

The Restoration of Absolutism, 1815–1818

By August 1814, six years after news of the fall of the Spanish monarchy reached Central America and touched off a massive political crisis throughout the empire, the Kingdom of Guatemala found itself at peace again. As if by magic, the *status quo ante bellum* reigned once more as Ferdinand VII proceeded to obliterate all signs of the constitutional experiments undertaken during his absence from Spain. For the first time since taking command of the colony, Captain General Bustamante governed under the system of Bourbon absolutism that had so profoundly shaped his character and his early career as an officer and administrator. Of course, neither the edicts of the king nor the actions of the captain general could erase the fact that the kingdom had experienced significant political and social upheavals during the constitutional period. Certain elite groups within colonial society had benefited greatly from the liberal reforms—or at least recognized the inherent potential of the reforms—while some among the population were permanently radicalized. During the last four years of Bustamante's administration, however, the vast majority of the people of Central America, including the creole elite, expressed no concern that the Constitution of 1812 had been repudiated in favor of the old absolutist order.[1] For all intents and purposes, the kingdom had overcome the spasms of unrest and autonomist sentiment that threatened Spanish rule during the Napoleonic wars and was fully prepared to embrace the restored king and what remained of his empire.

Despite the potential for reconciliation resulting from the successful preservation of the Kingdom of Guatemala for the crown, the last years of Bustamante's tenure as captain general were marked by continued struggles between the governor and the creole oligarchy. Some historians have characterized this period as a Central American "terror" during which Bustamante reimposed the absolutist order with an iron fist and created, in effect, a military dictatorship designed to stifle all signs of colonial dissent. Others, emphasizing the personal nature of the conflict between the captain general and the creoles, have argued that Bustamante's actions at the time were not particularly systematic but, instead, resulted from his obsessive need for revenge against those who challenged his authority in the past. Both interpretations find substantiation for their claims in the series of events that dominated colonial politics in the years between 1815 and 1818: Bustamante's unforgiving attack on the signers of the 1810 *Instrucciones;* the deteriorating relationship between the captain general and the audiencia; two unfortunate deaths that resulted from the administration's continued efforts to combat subversion; the economic persecution of the Houses of Aycinena and Beltranena; and the confusion that surrounded the 1817 decision by the crown to repudiate Bustamante's policies and recall him to Spain.

However, one does not need to resort to well-worn stereotypes of Spanish oppression to understand the motivations and behavior of the captain general at this stage in his administration. While absolutism undoubtedly fit best with Bustamante's style of governance, he did not need to terrorize the population of Central America into accepting a political tradition that most understood better than liberal constitutionalism. Operating with the full backing of the crown for the first time, Bustamante attempted to ensure the future stability of the Kingdom of Guatemala by disempowering the creole oligarchy, which he long considered to be the most dangerous and destabilizing group in the colony. Personal animosity undoubtedly played a role in determining the nature of this campaign, but so did a rational assessment of the leading threat to continued Spanish rule. Unfortunately for Bustamante, the segment of society that he targeted was vocal, well connected, and well represented at court. Once the crown decided that its interests were best served by maintaining a close relationship with the Guatemalan creole oligarchy, the captain general found himself expendable.

Bustamante's negative associations with the creole elite were reinforced at the outset of the restoration period. A few days after publishing the 4 May royal decree, the captain general learned that a letter written by the Guatemalan diputación provincial to the Cortes, charging him with numerous infractions of the constitution, had been published in a March edition of the *Universal de Madrid* and was later picked up by a Cuban newspaper.[2] In keeping with the liberal sentiment still dominant at the time, the editorial commentary surrounding this letter ascribed Bustamante's actions to the general despotism of American governors, implied a link between him and the reviled Godoy, and went so far as to declare the captain general "more criminal than Morelos and his hordes."[3]

The captain general was profoundly insulted by the vehemence of this attack and immediately launched an investigation. In a letter to Archbishop Casaus he argued that the charges were a product of the turbulent constitutional period and the passions and emotions that had run rampant over the established order following the granting of press freedoms. During such a revolutionary time, no one of upstanding character, honor, or loyalty remained immune from what he considered to be libel and calumny. Worst of all in his view was that the deputies, their allies in Spain, and the newspaper editors made vague and unsubstantiated charges for partisan gain without knowing him or making the effort to understand his perspective. Secure in his belief that "my conduct, pure in the opinion of those who know me and speak of me in good faith, does not fear being observed or investigated in any form," Bustamante nevertheless felt that he would be unable to repair the damage to his reputation or honor, since the king had ordered all inquiries into violations of the constitution to cease upon its abrogation.[4] Without this formal avenue of defense open to him, the captain general asked Casaus to interview the former deputies—all were priests—about the evidence and motivations behind their protest. He was most interested in knowing whether the individuals had ever communicated with him before their arrival in the capital, when they sent the dispatch, what documents they had to substantiate their charges, who might have influenced their judgment, and "what are the defects they have noticed in my public and private conduct, addressing each one specifically." In return for their candor, Bustamante promised that he would not use his authority to punish them in any way.[5] Unfortunately, there is no evidence that the archbishop ever succeeded in interviewing the deputies. A similar request for the testimony of Deputy-elect Manuel José Pavón, which was made via Alcalde primero Juan José Aqueche in order to appear less threatening, was also firmly rebuffed.[6]

So long as the constitution remained in force, Bustamante found himself on the defensive in the struggle with the creole oligarchy for political power in the colony. Once it became clear that he would not be replaced as governor but, instead, would preside over the dismantling of the Cádiz reforms in Central America, he saw an opportunity to break the vast political, economic, and social influence this group wielded at the local and regional level. In this respect, Bustamante's war on the Aycinena-led Family, an assault by a professional administrator against an entrenched local monopoly for the purpose of consolidating Spanish rule and expanding economic opportunities, was a quintessential act of a Bourbon reformer.

With this goal in mind, on 18 September 1814 the captain general sent the king an annotated copy of the *Instrucciones para la constitución fundamental de la monarquía española y su gobierno* that had been prepared by the Guatemala City ayuntamiento in 1810 for Deputy Antonio de Larrazábal. Through his footnotes and in a letter that accompanied this material, Bustamante made the case that the *Instrucciones* was a seditious document that showed overt signs of being influenced by acts of the French National Assembly.[7] He then explained that the distribution of this revolutionary sentiment throughout the kingdom fomented discord and sparked the various provincial revolts that occurred during the constitutional period. At the time he was unable to move against those directly involved, but now he believed that the continued stability of Central America required that the signers of the *Instrucciones* be stripped of their offices and barred from any future position of public responsibility in the colony. Bustamante also recommended that all copies of the document be collected and burned.[8]

In the meantime, the captain general worked diligently to restore the political administration of the kingdom to its 1808 framework. During the first few months of 1815, relations between the Spanish authorities and the newly reconstituted ayuntamiento of Guatemala City were relatively circumscribed. The council, in particular, appeared to go out of its way to refocus its attention on local matters and spent the vast majority of its time in February coordinating efforts to protect the city against a severe outbreak of *viruelas* (smallpox).[9] In fact, the institution that had the hardest time accepting the rapid reversal of the political environment in the colony was the audiencia. On 18 November 1814 the *Gaceta del Gobierno de Guatemala* published copies of a number of royal decrees that dealt with the restoration of the old order throughout the empire. Two of these had a direct impact on the status of the audiencia: the *Real Cédula* of 25 June restored to the tribunal all the powers that had been stripped away by the Constitution, and the *Real Decreto* of 8 July reappointed captains general to their traditional position as presidents of this institution.[10]

When Bustamante informed the tribunal on 16 January 1815 that he was going to reassume his presidential duties, however, Oidores Campuzano, Serrano Polo, and Berasuelta urged restraint. Despite the undoubted legitimacy of the material printed in the *Gaceta,* the audiencia argued that the captain general should not rush to act before receiving official copies of the documents and the traditional confirmation from the Council of the Indies. Bustamante, somewhat taken aback, responded that the royal will was clear and that he was simply following the framework laid out in the original 4 May decree that overturned the constitution. In addition, according to the captain general there were even more practical reasons not to wait for more formal authorization. Bustamante had received word early in December that the captain of a schooner carrying official correspondence from Spain had recently dumped seven boxes of letters overboard after being chased by an enemy ship, thereby causing serious delays in mail service throughout the empire.[11] He also made the point that the Council of the Indies had not even re-formed at the time the decrees were prepared; therefore, the necessary supporting documentation might never reach Central America. Although he did not tell the oidores at the time, the captain general had also learned that the viceroy of New Spain had taken possession of the presidency of the audiencia of Mexico after seeing copies of the decrees in the *Gaceta de Madrid*. For Bustamante this was more than enough confirmation of the legitimacy of his position. Accordingly, on 25 January he attended a meeting of the *real acuerdo* and was recognized as president, although the oidores sustained their protest by passing the details of the conflict to the crown.[12]

The desire on the part of Bustamante to reassume the *presidencia* and admit no delay in carrying out the perceived wishes of the king was neither an effort to subjugate a rival institution nor an expression of overwrought zeal. In the midst of the inevitable confusion that paralleled the abolition of the constitutional order and the restoration of absolutism, the captain general was concerned that the administration of justice would suffer if certain orders were obeyed while others awaited confirmation. With the alcaldes ordinarios and other *jueces de primera instancia* taking up their former judicial obligations, the kingdom could not afford to have the oidores sit idle. In a letter to the tribunal written to underscore this point, Bustamante specifically addressed the unprecedented crime wave sweeping Guatemala City at the time, in which upwards of eight hundred people were being injured or killed on an annual basis, and blamed it in part on the reduced role the audiencia was forced to play under the constitution.[13] From his perspective, the old administrative order was simply the most effective form of government for the colony; therefore, it was in his interest to see the tribunal recover its pre-1808 shape and powers as quickly as possible.

Disputes of this sort, however, reflect the degree to which the captain general and the audiencia had become estranged over the course of the constitutional period. Relations were so strained by the beginning of 1815, in fact, that Bustamante had his aide, José del Valle, prepare a report for the crown on the conduct and loyalty of the oidores. One of the primary conclusions reached by Valle was that Regent Joaquín Bernardo de Campuzano and Oidor Juan Gualberto González had become so tainted by their close ties to the creole elite, in particular the Marquis of Aycinena, that they could no longer be trusted to fulfill their duties.[14] In fact, the only member of the tribunal with whom Bustamante had a consistently good relationship over the course of his administration was Antonio Serrano Polo. There was also clearly a partisan advantage to be gained in making this sort of accusation, and Bustamante deftly utilized the fact that oidor aspirants José del Barrio, José Ingenieros Palomo, and Miguel Larreinaga all had links to the Guatemala City oligarchy to block their appointments to the tribunal.[15]

Whether or not these were legitimate charges to make, the fact that the captain general found such fraternization unbecoming an imperial official illustrates some of the personality traits that made Bustamante such a figure of hatred at the highest levels of colonial society. His reputation for aloofness, his upright military bearing, his spartan lifestyle, his guarded nature and reserved manner, his dislike of ostentation, and his scrupulousness in refusing gifts or bribes reflected his strong belief that close associations with local families were unprofessional and a threat to his honor and reputation.[16] Unfortunately, this attitude was often perceived as arrogance and haughtiness and interpreted as contempt or disdain for creole society. In such a close-knit culture where power and influence were highly symbolic and expressed through displays of personal relationships with the governing officials, that the captain general of the kingdom, the epicenter of colonial authority, would not make social calls, attend parties or give them, or cultivate friendships with those who expected such treatment was a significant factor in the consistent opposition to his administration. In part because their tenure in the kingdom was more open-ended, the members of the audiencia were much more willing to forge mutually beneficial alliances with the local elite. During Bustamante's last years in the kingdom the creole oligarchy used this relationship to its advantage in its continuing struggle against the captain general.

Part of the rationale for referring to the years 1815–1818 as the *terror bustamantino* is the presumption that Bustamante had no reason— except for spite and enmity—to continue to subject Central America to counterinsurgency measures. Yet, while the Kingdom of Guatemala showed no signs of unrest following the 1814 San Salvador uprising, to the north and south of the Central American isthmus active independence movements remained a threat to Spanish rule in the Americas. More important, the crown showed no signs of altering its commitment to the use of force as the solution to these challenges, a policy from which Bustamante was not likely to diverge. In the spring of 1815 a large Spanish expeditionary force under the command of General Pablo Morillo, the newly invested captain general of Venezuela, landed in northern South America and proceeded to engage the insurgent forces operating there and in New Granada in a brutal war that lasted until 1820. In New Spain, Viceroy Felix Calleja continued his equally fierce counterinsurgency campaign until his replacement arrived in September 1816, a successful offensive that resulted in the capture and execution of José María Morelos at the end of the previous year.[17]

In this environment, Bustamante considered it to be his primary obligation to remain alert for signs of possible unrest. Having lost the support of the creole elite and the audiencia, however, a number of decisions that he took to further this agenda, none of which approached the level of official repression experienced in Venezuela or New Spain, became extremely controversial. On 27 April the *real acuerdo* met to discuss a series of complaints about the security of the mail that had accumulated over the previous two years. The oidores noted that many inhabitants of the capital had lost confidence in the mail service as a result of unnecessary delays, overt signs that letters had been opened, and a new policy of bringing in the post under the cover of darkness. The lack of faith was so profound that people had resorted increasingly to unofficial means of sending their correspondence, a practice that would have a serious impact on postal revenues if it were allowed to continue. The fact that the colonial administration used its access to the mail to promote its counterinsurgency policies was, of course, an open secret in Guatemala City. In May 1813, Bustamante had admitted to the ayuntamiento that his administration was opening letters sent to and from regions that were considered security risks. Nevertheless, by 1815 the audiencia had come to the conclusion that such a rationale was no longer valid and decided to utilize its newly restored autonomy to launch an official investigation.[18]

That these extralegal security measures were directed primarily against members of the creole elite and their allies ensured that they would not be forgotten, yet the anti-Bustamante forces took advantage of two particularly tragic consequences of the government's antisubversive agenda to underscore the brutality of the *terror bustamantino*. The first case arose out of the Belén conspiracy and Bustamante's futile efforts to capture one of the accused, José Francisco Barrundia, who had been a regidor on the ayuntamiento at the time of the arrests. Convinced that Barrundia had gone into hiding in the Yucatán, the captain general intercepted a letter from another member of the municipal council who was suspected of anti-Spanish sentiment, José Francisco Córdova, that was being sent to José Mariano Argüelles, a young man living in Campeche. Believing that either Argüelles was in fact Barrundia or he was part of a conspiracy to hide the fugitive, Bustamante ordered the authorities in Campeche to send Argüelles to Guatemala City for questioning. En route to the capital, however, the prisoner fell ill at the "unhealthy site of Palenque" and died.[19]

The next controversy to fan the flames between the captain general and his increasingly consolidated group of opponents occurred on 20 July 1815. On that date Bustamante reported to the *real acuerdo* about a case of potential subversion being brought against José Francisco Alfaro, captain of the schooner *Maria*, who had been taken into custody following a voyage from Cuba under suspicion of being a French emissary. The initial evidence against Alfaro was circumstantial at best: he had reported Napoleon's return to France from Elba, he had made comments about the strength of the emperor's forces and the antipathy of the French toward Louis XVIII as the Hundred Days' conflicts reignited European hostilities, and he had passed on comments attributed to General Morillo during the siege of Cartagena. More seriously, his last name had been found on a list of Napoleonic emissaries that had previously been compiled by the Spanish ambassador to the United States. Upon examination of his personal belongings, however, the charges against Alfaro quickly became more legitimate. A letter to the captain of another ship, the *Josef Garcia*, was discovered that had three and a half lines written in code; the cipher key was also found. Armed with this material, Bustamante decided to keep the captain in solitary confinement and received tentative audiencia approval for this act. Unfortunately, the investigation ended abruptly on 20 August when Alfaro committed suicide in his prison cell.[20]

By the end of Bustamante's administration, both of these cases had become symbols for the creole elite of unrestrained and arbitrary prosecutorial zeal on the part of the captain general. Although the counterinsurgency measures devised in 1812 remained in force after the apparent end of local opposition to Spanish rule and clearly played a role in the deaths of these suspects, the fact that Argüelles and Alfaro both died under tragic circumstances does not provide enough evidence to support the myth of a general terror. In all likelihood, based on earlier examples of the investigation of subversion under Bustamante, Alfaro eventually would have been released if the evidence of spying found in his belongings had proven as innocuous as the governor's enemies later declared it was. One month was never enough time for the kind of thorough examination a case of possible infidencia invariably received in the Spanish judicial system. Similarly, if Argüelles had been confused with Barrundia, his arrival in the capital would have disabused all of this belief. If he was wanted for other purposes, Bustamante was well within his rights to request his testimony as part of an ongoing investigation into the Belén matter.

A related development that occurred over the course of 1815 and that might have given the creole elite an exaggerated sense of the repressive nature of the Bustamante administration was the perceived militarization of society that resulted in part from the effort to call up new recruits for the Guatemala City Militia Battalion and Companies of Dragoons. The captain general had reported a serious loss of strength in these units at the end of 1814 and ordered the enlistment of upwards of 250 men to restore them to full strength. At the time, the four companies that made up the *Escuadrón de dragones de milicias disciplinadas* and the eight companies that made up the *Batallón de milicias disciplinadas* in the capital totaled some 540 troops. In September 1815, after the ayuntamiento had completed a survey of the men eligible for the call-up, Bustamante decided that the numbers could sustain an increase of 360 new enlistees. This focus on military readiness at a time of relative peace in the kingdom, along with the fact that the captain general rarely traveled now without his two military aides, Luís Toledano and Francisco Cáscara, worried those aligned against Bustamante.[21]

The event that, more than anything else, caused a de facto declaration of war between the creole elite and Bustamante occurred on 22 August 1815. In one of his rare appearances before the ayuntamiento, the captain general informed the regidores that Ferdinand VII, in a *Real Orden* dated 31 March, had decided to recognize the 1810 *Instrucciones* as "seditious and disruptive of order" and punish those responsible for it. According to the wishes of the king, José Antonio Batres, Lorenzo Moreno, Antonio Palomo, the Marquis of Aycinena, Luís Barrutia, Miguel Asturias, Antonio de Juarros, Francisco Arrivillaga, and José María Peinado were to be stripped of all public offices and prevented from holding any position of public responsibility in the future. Four other regidores, Sebastián Melón, Miguel González, José de Isasi, and Antonio Aqueche, who signed the *Instrucciones* after voting against them and who prepared their own *Apuntes instructivos* for Deputy Larrazábal, were exempt from this decision. In addition, the crown gave permission to the colonial administration to collect and destroy all copies of the offensive document. To add insult to injury, before departing the meeting, Bustamante castigated the council for permitting the portraits of José de Aycinena, Manuel Pavón, and Antonio de Larrazábal to remain on the walls of the chamber —a direct violation of the royal determination to expunge all signs of the constitutional period from the empire.[22]

This news came as a brutal shock to these men of considerable local standing and influence who suddenly found themselves blacklisted from public office and stigmatized by royal condemnation. The punishment, in fact, was one of the harshest that the crown could pass down to such individuals, for the decision meant the loss of privileges, power, position, and titles, all of which served as the primary indicators of status in the colony. The inevitable result was an avalanche of pleas for mercy from those involved to the audiencia. The ex-regidores filled their appeals with protestations of loyalty, character references, royal citations, and other proofs of good citizenship. Some, most notably Intendant Peinado, attempted to use Bustamante's own words against him by citing letters written to them by the captain general that were full of praise and appreciation for past works. A rapid response was essential, for, in the words of the widow of the Marquis of Aycinena, writing on behalf of her recently deceased husband:

> we cannot, Sir, look with indifference upon a disgrace of such magnitude. We have been, we are, and we will forever be the most religious observers of the law, and our conduct has always corresponded to these sentiments. We wish to fly to the base of the throne and provide His Majesty with the most intimate and exuberant expression of our patriotism and love for his royal person ... with the satisfaction of knowing that if we have erred in having signed the cited part of the *Instrucciones,* it was not even remotely with any depraved intention, nor any other provision or object, except the sane and sensible one to which we aspired in good faith.[23]

The ex-regidores were convinced that Bustamante had framed them and believed that with the right allies the evidence in support of their positions would validate their protestations of loyalty. Peinado, in particular, found himself in the depths of despair after learning that his work was considered the cause of the uprisings in Central America and declared that it was his only desire to clear himself of the "weight" of this charge. Referring to the 1811 Salvadoran and Leonese unrest, he asked the audiencia:

> What was the first step taken by both towns during their respective commotions? The election of Juntas and the deposition of their local authorities. And the Instructions taught them this? I defy my accuser to show me the line that states this. Didn't the Peninsula present many examples? If one is looking for the cause of these evils, wouldn't it be better to look at Mexico, Caracas, Cartagena, Santa Fe, Buenos Aires, Quito, Chile, or one of the many other places where this scene was played out?[24]

The ex-intendant turned over to the tribunal three volumes of documents that attested to his faithful work as the king's representative in San Salvador. Then he, like the others, asked the oidores to intercede with the king on the behalf of those in disgrace.

After reviewing the material collected by the deposed regidores, the audiencia decided to advance a petition to the crown for a systematic review of the accusations made by Bustamante. Fiscal Berasuelta spoke for the tribunal as a whole when he stated in his summary of the case that he had never been under the impression that the *Instrucciones* had caused any discontent with Spanish rule in the kingdom. In addition, he believed that the work done by the regidores and the intendant on behalf of their king and country was a model of good citizenship and should mitigate whatever crimes they had committed. As such, he considered it to be the duty of the audiencia to promote reconciliation between the king and his faithful subjects, for "the pious heart of our beloved Sovereign will be filled with pleasure to see those whom he had condemned as guilty now purified at his feet."[25] With Campuzano and Serrano Polo in agreement, the petition was sent to Spain on 18 November. In the face of the effective decapitation of the Guatemala City oligarchy, the budding relationship between the oidores and the creole elite had now be-

come an overt alliance with significant implications for the success of
the Bustamante administration in Central America. With the audiencia
in active opposition, the captain general found it extremely difficult to
advance his agenda, much less establish the kind of dictatorship that his
enemies associated with this period.

As 1815 came to a close, however, Bustamante's efforts to humble
the Family and its allies appeared to be succeeding. On 10 October, the
ayuntamiento received a royal order that stripped it of the title of *excelencia,* a decision that it had feared for months and that the regidores
decided to appeal immediately.[26] In a symbolic celebration of his victory
over the oligarchy, the captain general informed the council on 22 December that the *Instrucciones* were to be burned in a public ceremony
that morning on the Plaza Mayor, and this act was carried out by Bustamante's aide and official *pregonero* (town crier) Francisco Cáscara.[27]
Although the political influence wielded by the Family via the Guatemala City ayuntamiento did not end with the seating of the new council
on 2 January 1816, there were signs that its monopoly over that institution had begun to break. Among the new regidores the names Pavón,
Batres, Aycinena, Asturias, and Vaca continued to be represented, but
other, less familiar names appeared for the first time.[28] Even more indicative of the troubles faced by the traditional elite of Guatemala City
at this time was Bustamante's assault on the economic foundations of
the creole oligarchy. Through this focus, the captain general expected a
number of beneficial results. In his view, if the commercial monopoly
wielded by the Family in Central America could be crippled, more opportunities would open up both for the producers of goods, mainly
artisans and provincial farmers, and for rival merchant houses across
the colony, thereby stimulating general economic growth and providing
economic assistance to those groups more inclined to be royalists.

Confronted by a treasury depleted by years of economic depression,
the cost of colonial defense during the independence wars, and expenses incurred under the Cádiz system, Bustamante first decided to
force those who had been the primary supporters of the constitution—
in effect, the creole oligarchy—to repay the 500,000 pesos the royal government spent to support the Cortes deputies.[29] He then turned his attention to the issue of contraband trade, in particular English goods
entering through Belize, which had become one of the more profitable

enterprises controlled by Guatemala City merchants in the years since Captain General González relaxed restrictions on imports at the beginning of the century. Bustamante had been a longtime opponent of contraband, which threatened the Spanish commercial monopoly, undercut local industries, and deprived the treasury of much-needed customs duties, and he considered the question of free trade, which was a prime desire of the creole elite, in terms of loyalty to the crown. As a consequence, finding himself in a strong position after the restoration of absolution the captain general increased patrols in the Caribbean and brought suit against those suspected of engaging in illegal trade.[30]

The first victim of this more aggressive stance was the House of Aycinena, the leading commercial firm in Central America, whose fortunes had already begun to decline somewhat by the time this new challenge emerged. According to Mariano de Aycinena, problems began in 1811 with the departure of his brother, José de Aycinena, first for San Salvador and then for Spain. This was a serious blow to the financial stability of the House, for it left all commercial operations in the hands of the eldest brother, the marquis, who was simply not equipped to handle the responsibility and died in 1815 "weighed down by public and domestic burdens."[31] By March 1814, José del Valle reported "a scarcity of money in the House of the Marquis," a situation that was exacerbated when the captain general sued the family for over thirty-five thousand pesos in back taxes owed on English imports, blocked it from participating in the commercial affairs of the administration, and forced it to pay a large deposit for the recovery of suspicious goods seized from the schooner *Carmen*.[32]

The other merchant firm to experience extensive persecution from Bustamante was the House of Beltranena, a close ally of the Aycinenas. In 1816, operating under the assumption that vessels from Cuba, which enjoyed much more liberal trading rights than the rest of the empire, were being used to bring English contraband into Central America, the captain general confiscated a shipment of cotton from Havana that had been purchased by this firm and valued at more than forty thousand pesos. Furious at this turn of events, Gregorio Beltranena demanded a passport to plead his case directly to the king. Although the merchant never received permission to travel to Spain, the crown did hear his appeal and in the end ordered the embargoed goods restored.[33]

The anticontraband and anti-Family measures promoted by Bustamante were extremely popular among certain segments of the population and reflected a continued interest in promoting the welfare of the
kingdom according to the Bourbon framework. As a counterweight to
the ayuntamiento/audiencia alliance, the captain general cultivated the
support of the Guatemala City Consulado de Comercio, the bastion of
the Spanish commercial monopoly and traditional economic thought in
the colony. Made up of both peninsulars and creoles, the Consulado
represented a more conservative, royalist, and mercantilist segment of
the merchant elite, men like José and Gregorio de Urruela, who operated outside the orbit of the Family and had long been two of Bustamante's primary backers. For this community, the government's policies
promised increased business, the stimulation of colonial industries, and
greater authority over isthmian development. Other segments of society, such as the more conservative artisan class, which suffered from
the influx of cheap foreign goods, and those provincials who felt con-
strained by the economic hegemony of Guatemala City, also found the
administration's position advantageous, though it is difficult to document the degree of public support for Bustamante at this level. Because
the opposition to the captain general was so vocal, organized, and influential, it has tended to become the de facto position ascribed to the
population as a whole. Clearly, the population of Guatemala City found
itself sharply split over the governor, and this division most likely repli-
cated itself in the provinces as well. While the evidence for a silent majority of Bustamante supporters remains elusive, obscured by the large
numbers of people who were simply pro-Spanish and those who held no
firm political opinions either way, the repression experienced by the
Guatemalan oligarchy was not necessarily shared by the rest of society.

Even if Bustamante had managed to cultivate significant support
among overlooked segments of colonial society, the groups that would
have benefited the most from his policies were in no position to defend
him once his position began to be undermined in Spain. Two years after
the restoration of Ferdinand VII, imperial politics had moderated somewhat, and the counterinsurgency framework still operating within the
Kingdom of Guatemala started to appear counterproductive to senior
crown officials who desired improved relations with local elites.[34] With
rebel forces in retreat all across its American possessions, the imperial

government found itself for the first time in a position to withdraw the proverbial stick and, instead, offer a carrot to those colonies that demonstrated their continued loyalty. During this critical time, the Guatemalan oligarchy had two extremely well-placed advocates on the Council of the Indies, José de Aycinena and Juan Gualberto González Bravo, who knew the political situation in Central America intimately and were able to make a strong case to their less well-informed colleagues that to allow Bustamante to continue as captain general jeopardized the continued peace and tranquility of that kingdom.

The first evidence that the crown's perspective on Central America had begun to evolve away from its previous hard-line stance came in a *fiscal* report to the Council of the Indies on 19 August 1816.[35] This document originated as part of the official response to Bustamante's letter of 18 May 1814 that attempted to explain the course of independence sentiment in the colony and that requested, among other things, that the crown authorize the continuation of the extrajudicial measures that had been imposed to control insurrection. As the council addressed the general question of how to confront unrest, the report became an indictment of the present administration in the Kingdom of Guatemala.

After reviewing four years of Bustamante's letters to Spain and contrasting them with other documentation from the period, the author of the report, the *fiscal del Perú,* came to the conclusion that the captain general was a reckless and inattentive governor who could not be trusted to provide complete and accurate accounts of the state of the colony. Although he agreed with Bustamante that the unrest in Central America developed, more or less, from the same source as the broader independence movements in Spanish America, the *fiscal* was unable to accept at face value the governor's analysis of what precipitated the various rebellions in the kingdom once contradictory testimony to the same events had arrived. In fact, he believed that Bustamante actually exacerbated the problems by refusing to continue the "peaceful measures" that restored order to San Salvador and, instead, promoted hard-line policies that required him to break with time-honored laws and traditions, led to conflict with the audiencia, and caused people to lose "respect for authority."[36] While Bustamante made some "judicious reflections . . . concerning the nature of the commotions of America and the means to suppress them," which might have been useful at the time they were presented, "[t]oday other, less contradictory principles govern. The Council has consulted and adopted the general provisions that it considers proper, following the spirit of the legislation of the Indies; and its first and greatest concern has been the restoration of law and order according to the administration of justice, accompanied by military measures."[37] The result was that the council decided to reject Bustamante's two-year-old application for extraordinary powers and, because "one can put so little faith in [his] recommendations," to revisit the issue of the blacklisted regidores. The report ended by proposing a new governing attitude for the colony:

> What seems appropriate is to cut off at the roots the hatred and the resentment that, apparently, has been building in that kingdom ever since [Bustamante's] arrival in spite of the royal wishes and repeated decrees of His Majesty, to observe the law in the administration of justice and to forget the past, without prejudicing the vigorous measures which the same [laws] anticipate against those who continue to disturb the land after this period, and also without prejudice to the favors which his faithful servants have become worthy of, for after all has been made tranquil again and as soon as there is more information, it will be possible to see who really deserves them.[38]

In general, without a clear view of events across the Atlantic, the Spanish crown often deferred to the judgment of its overseas officials in matters of local governance. During the imperial crisis Bustamante was a frequent beneficiary of this tendency. However, as this case indicates, the quantity of material collected in favor of a particular cause could also influence the crown. By 1816 a wide variety of sources had come together to oppose the Bustamante administration, and their testimony, however subjective it might have been, was difficult to ignore. Unfortunately for the captain general, his administration lost a prime opportunity to reinforce its position in 1815 when three of Bustamante's supporters, Archbishop Casaus, Rafael Trullé, and José del Valle, declined a royal request to write a history of the revolts in the kingdom.[39] Without credible and weighty substantiation for the policies of the governor, whatever advantage Bustamante once held in the fight with the Guatemalan oligarchy to shape the perspective of the crown began to disappear in the avalanche of audiencia appeals and regidor supplications.

Although both sides were unaware of what was taking place in Madrid at the time, the oligarchy continued to devote most of its energy toward reconciling with the crown, while Bustamante remained focused on the preservation of order. To increase the pressure at court, on 1 October 1816 the ayuntamiento made final preparations to send a special present to the king. The council planned to deliver to José de Aycinena a box containing the gold medallions that had been struck in honor of Ferdinand's ascension to the throne in 1808, along with a copy of the memorial written to celebrate that event. The regidores hoped that Aycinena would then present the gift to the king and remind the sovereign of "the feelings of love and loyalty toward his Royal person by which [this body] finds itself possessed."[40] This move paved the way for the council's decision to appeal the loss of the rank of *excelencia,* which Regidor Juan Fermín de Aycinena emphasized would result in having to collect "the many acts which prove the loyalty of the body, along with its patriotic services . . . during the recent events in the metropolis."[41] Somewhat reinvigorated by this drive to confirm its patriotism, the ayuntamiento also appeared more willing to confront Bustamante during the spring of 1817. In an echo of its former disputes with the captain general over protocol, the council vigorously challenged the right of *Fiscal interino* José del Valle and *Contador interino* Tomás Morena to take a seat with the audiencia during official ceremonies and decided to take its case to the crown when both Bustamante and the tribunal rejected the complaint.[42]

Still feeling secure about his position, the captain general repeatedly demonstrated his commitment during this time to the goal of uncovering anti-Spanish sentiment and maintaining the hard-won tranquility of the kingdom. Although incidents of subversion were not as commonplace as they had been during the constitutional period, Bustamante saw no reason to relax his vigilance, for a serious threat could come from anywhere. On 3 December 1816, the captain general received a report that Manuel Castillo, a grenadier in the *Batallón fijo* of the capital, had been approached a week earlier by a priest who tried to entice him and a companion to join what the soldiers thought was a plan for an uprising. While they were having a drink together, the priest, who was later identified as Juan Salvatierra of the Convent of Santo Domingo, reputedly made disparaging comments about a passing European, informed the men that he had taken part in the unrest in San Salvador, made inquiries about the availability of guns and ammunition in the military units, and then asked whether there were any other soldiers who would be interested in meeting with him. Castillo and his friend tried to draw more information out of Salvatierra and then agreed to get together later with the priest. After informing their superiors, the grenadiers went searching for Salvatierra, but he had disappeared. His brother, José Manuel, was immediately arrested as complicit in the plot, and by 21 December Fr. Juan was also in custody.[43]

The brothers Salvatierra denied all of the accusations made against them. Despite the fact that many witnesses corroborated Castillo's story, the government had no hard evidence to link the suspects to any conspiracy. True to form, however, Bustamante was determined to pursue the investigation as far as possible. Late in March he authorized the military prosecutors who were in charge of the case to repeat the questioning of both the accusers and the accused. At the same time, the captain general also permitted the prisoners to acquire defense attorneys in preparation for the more formal phase of the judicial proceedings.[44] The process continued in a deliberate manner until the beginning of July when all criminal prosecutions in the capital stopped precipitously with the arrival of a *Real Cédula* granting a complete pardon to all those suspected or convicted of the crime of insurrection in the Kingdom of Guatemala.[45]

All at once, the counterinsurgency state constructed by Bustamante began to collapse as prisoners across the isthmus applied for release under the pardon. The ongoing case against the Salvatierra brothers was one of the first to be affected by this development. On 5 August, after reading the appeal by the brothers' attorney, José del Valle, the newly appointed *auditor interino de guerra,* accepted their eligibility and recommended their release. This was carried out on 10 September after a further review of the situation by the *Real Sala del Indulto,* the audiencia-led body set up to administer the pardon.[46] The relative ease with which this decision was made indicates that Bustamante was willing to obey the royal will to a certain point. However, the captain general also sought ways to limit his compliance and slow down a process that he feared would destabilize the colony.

While the *cédula* appeared to cover all *reos de infidencia* in Central America, it tried to make an allowance for the truly subversive elements among them by authorizing the administration to send to Spain anyone "whose permanence in those provinces should be considered dangerous."[47] A subsequent clarification of this measure gave jurisdiction over these special cases to the *real acuerdo*.[48] Recognizing an opportunity to intervene in the application of the pardon, Bustamante informed the audiencia that he would attend a special meeting of the *acuerdo* on 1 September to go over the procedures required to carry it out. At this meeting a discussion developed over whether the amnesty covered all prisoners or just those under the *jurisdicción ordinaria*. In a unanimous decision, the *acuerdo* authorized Bustamante to refer the question to the crown. In the meantime, those under military jurisdiction, which included the vast majority of the *reos de infidencia*, remained in custody. More than a year would pass, in fact, before those imprisoned for the Salvadoran and Nicaraguan uprisings and the Belén conspiracy were released. While these delays have been interpreted as another example of Bustamante's arbitrary obstructionism and vindictiveness, the fact that the audiencia had no objection to remitting the pardon to the crown for clarification, knowing that the issue would not be resolved for another year, indicates a broad concern among the oidores that the amnesty might lead to instability. Considering the general state of hostility that existed between the captain general and the tribunal, the audiencia had no other reason to resist a royal order and ratify a unilateral motion designed solely to frustrate the creole elite, particularly when the entire capital was aware by this point that the crown had decided to replace Bustamante.[49]

News that the Kingdom of Guatemala was going to receive a new governor was made public on 19 August after Bustamante sent the ayuntamiento a copy of the 18 March *Real Orden* that named Carlos de Urrutia, then serving as captain general of Santo Domingo, as his successor.[50] Although it is doubtful that anyone was prepared for such a shocking change in the political environment of the colony, the regidores had received word from Aycinena early in July that the king had accepted their offering of the medallions with great pleasure, indicating that "those who have been impenetrable walls against the barrages of seduction during the political convulsions that have agitated those regions" would reap the benefits of his gratitude.[51] By September, therefore, all signs seemed to indicate that the efforts of the creole elite to document its loyalty to Spain and restore its relationship with the crown had succeeded.

After September the political tension in the capital began to increase, for the one issue that had not been resolved concerned the fate of the blacklisted regidores. As a result, during the fall of 1817 this group waited impatiently for word from Spain that they had been restored to favor, while Bustamante was forced to make preparations for his ignominious departure. In October rumors began to circulate that copies of a brand-new *cédula* had arrived in the capital.[52] This new decree, it was said, abrogated the *Real Orden* of 31 March 1815, castigated Bustamante for deceiving the crown, and completely rehabilitated the creoles. On 6 November, the former regidores, led by José María Peinado, presented the audiencia with a sealed document (*pliego*), addressed *Por el Rey al Regente y Oydores de la Audiencia de Guatemala* (From the King to the Regent and Oidores of the Audiencia of Guatemala), that had come into their possession and, according to their agents, contained the desired *cédula*.[53]

Although they have been portrayed as another sad example of Bustamante's obstructionism and arbitrary rule, the events surrounding the opening of this royal pliego are best described as a comedy of errors, a drama that illuminated the byzantine nature of Spanish colonial administration and underscored the high-stakes conflict between the captain general and the creole elite. When the pliego arrived at the audiencia only Oidor Moreno and Fiscal Valdez, the two junior members of the tribunal, had been present. Considering the gravity of the situation and the obvious importance of the document, they decided to wait until all the members of the *real acuerdo* had assembled before opening it. Concerned about leaving it in the box where the *libro de acuerdos* was kept, Moreno took the pliego home with him, locked it in his private strongbox, and entrusted the key to his wife.

On 17 November everyone was in attendance except Serrano Polo, the *oidor decano*. Three days later, Serrano Polo was absent again, this time due to illness. By now, the regidores had presented their third appeal to the tribunal requesting immediate action on the pliego, but they were unable to speed up the process.[54] On 24 November a civic celebration kept the *acuerdo* from meeting according to its normal schedule. Three days later, all the oidores were assembled, but this time Serrano Polo brought a message from Archbishop Casaus asking that the opening be suspended because of concerns about public tranquility and the impact of the proceedings on the ability of the captain general to carry out his duties. Following a meeting with the archbishop, the oidores decided on 2 December to ask Bustamante to be present when the time came to open the document so as to demonstrate to the public that the correct form was being followed and the government was not in the midst of a crisis.[55]

Because of prior commitments, Bustamante did not meet with the *acuerdo* until 5 December. At this time, he warned the tribunal that the city had fallen into turmoil over rumors about the pliego. Even though the decision had been made to suspend its opening until a complete *acuerdo* could be formed, something that the recent illnesses of Serrano Polo and, subsequently, Fiscal Valdez precluded, the presumption on the streets was that the government was deliberately blocking the implementation of the decree. Already humiliated by his fall into royal disfavor and convinced that this case was simply the coup de grâce, the captain general insisted that the pliego be opened with all due consideration to his honor. He was horrified that it did not arrive "in the manner which His Majesty provides for in the *Real Ordenanza de Correos* (Royal Mail Ordinance)" and at the unconventional manner in which this supposedly official document was received. He therefore requested that it be returned to the archives, resealed, and locked up. Moreno, who had left the pliego at home and was forced to send for it, then argued that Bustamante should not have any say in the matter whatsoever.[56]

The *acuerdo* now found itself in a complete state of confusion about how to proceed. The creole elites wanted immediate action and threatened disturbances in the event their demands were not met. The captain general, who had no authority or influence to block the proceedings so long as the audiencia held the pliego, found the potential for unrest serious enough to increase the military presence in the capital during the first two weeks of December.[57] While this decision appeared to some as preparations for a *golpe de estado*, there is no evidence to indicate that Bustamante considered even for a moment such an unprecedented move. Instead, it appeared to be a reaction to rumors, which were intended to incite the populace and which reached their peak on the night of 13 December, that he had fled the city.[58]

In the midst of such a charged environment, the audiencia feared that the decision to open the document would carry as many heavy consequences as the decision to wait. Nevertheless, on 15 December, after two officials of the royal mail testified that the document showed signs of tampering, the pliego was finally opened with great formality in front of Bustamante and the assembled oidores. The officials discovered two letters when the envelope was removed, one sealed and addressed to the "President, Governor, and Captain General of the Kingdom from the King" and the other from the secretary of the Council of the Indies to the regent and oidores of the audiencia. The second document, dated 16 June, ordered the audiencia to place the first in the hands of the "successor of the current President." As a result, the *acuerdo* agreed to redeposit the *cédula* "in the secret archives" of the institution until Bustamante's replacement, Carlos de Urrutia, took office.[59]

At this point, the chronology of the crown's actions against Bustamante merits careful attention, for the issue of what the captain general knew about his impending disgrace, when he knew it, and what he did—or did not do—about it has at times been distorted in the historiography. The 19 August 1816 *fiscal* report to the Council of the Indies was the first serious blow to Bustamante's reputation in Madrid, although José de Aycinena had been working toward that end over the previous two years. Based on this particular analysis of the situation in the colony and lacking an alternative perspective, the crown decided in January 1817 to tear down the counterinsurgency state that Bustamante had erected in Guatemala. The first step was the amnesty issued to the *reos de infidencia*. In March, the king went even further and agreed to replace the controversial captain general. Bustamante learned of this action in August and had eight months to prepare to turn power over to Carlos de Urrutia, who did not reach Guatemala City until March 1818.

In order to validate these decisions, the king and council drew heavily on the 1816 *fiscal* report. In fact, large portions of it found their way into a 12 May *Real Cédula* addressed to Bustamante's successor.[60] This decree ratified the *fiscal*'s conclusions regarding the proper way to admin-

ister the kingdom and ordered the colonial government to suspend a
broad range of Bustamante's policies. While Urrutia officially received
the *cédula* on 8 April 1818 and proceeded to execute it, no evidence has
emerged to indicate when the decree actually arrived in Guatemala City.
If Bustamante had seen it, he would certainly have had confirmation of
the crown's changing policy, but there was nothing in this particular
cédula that would have affected the fate of the opponents of his administration, much less the *reos de infidencia,* had he followed proper
procedure and set it aside for the new administration. In fact, the royal
decree that did the most to damage Bustamante's reputation and transform the balance of power in the colony was the 13 June *Real Cédula* in
favor of the blacklisted regidores. As has been seen via the minutes of
the *real acuerdo,* however, the crown expected Urrutia to implement the
royal will in this matter as well. Even though the entire colony was aware
of what the infamous pliego contained before it was opened, Bustamante simply did not have the authorization to restore the regidores to
their positions before his term in office expired.[61]

For Bustamante, ever a faithful and dutiful servant of the king, the
13 June *cédula* proved to be a stinging personal and professional rebuke.
Because of the series of royal decisions taken since January 1817, the regidores' recovery of their honors, titles, and status was unpleasant but
not unexpected news. What must have shocked the captain general,
however, was the manner in which the king justified the revocation of
the 1815 decree. According to Ferdinand, he had authorized the punishment of the regidores "believing that the expressions of the President
were based on true events and were born from the desire to procure the
peace and tranquility of the provinces which I had given him to command." Instead, the *fiscal* report and the documentation sent by the
audiencia to support the creole cause illuminated serious contradictions
in Bustamante's case and caused the king to focus on "the strange conduct of the President." The alternate version of events presented Bustamante as a liar, a hypocrite, and a partisan by emphasizing his early
conciliatory policies and pro-constitution sentiment and by ascribing
his attack on the regidores as an assault by one political faction against
another. Convinced of the truth of this perspective, the king ordered
that "the conduct shown by don José Bustamante be condemned and
that my Royal Displeasure concerning this be conveyed to him." To en-

sure that the entire kingdom was made aware of this decision, Ferdinand commanded the colonial government to publish the *cédula* in all provincial capitals.[62]

According to the decree, Bustamante had made an effort in November 1815 to convince the crown to ignore the initial appeal from the regidores, which the audiencia had just agreed to handle, because it was based on deceitful testimonials and "false narratives constructed with intrigue and craftiness."[63] To be sure, each side in this struggle was guilty of exaggeration and obfuscation in the quest to burnish its own reputation while doing as much damage as possible to that of its opponent. In the end the crown had to decide which story to believe, but that does not mean the regidores' appeal won on merit. In 1815 it was in the interest of the newly restored king to support Bustamante while the situation in the Americas was still uncertain. In 1817, however, with most insurgencies on the defensive, imperial policy had shifted and the imperial government decided it was more beneficial to cultivate the loyalty of the Guatemalan creole elite rather than bolster an aging captain general who had already served for six tumultuous years and was due for replacement. To charge Bustamante with hypocrisy for entering into his duties in the spring of 1811 with some misplaced optimism about the developing constitutional government in Spain and about a colony that showed no signs of being infected by independence-era unrest and to saddle him with the blame for the highly divisive and partisan political environment that developed in Guatemala City was simply an effort by the crown to rationalize the decision to side with the creoles.

Bustamante's standing in the capital was tremendously affected by the series of repudiations he suffered over the course of 1817, and by the beginning of 1818 his position must have been especially uncomfortable. As the capital began to prepare in earnest for the arrival of a new administration, he found himself relegated to the shadows, still in possession of the title of governor but stripped of much of the moral authority to exercise his powers. Secure in the knowledge that Bustamante was finally going to be replaced, the creole oligarchy began to direct its energy toward ingratiating itself with his successor. In this environment the captain general was forced to suffer in silence the news that José de Aycinena had been awarded the *Gran Cruz de la Orden de Isabel la*

Católica, one of the highest imperial honors, as well as the fact that the king had restored to the ayuntamiento the title of *excelencia.*[64]

On 28 March 1818 Bustamante's seven-year administration of the Kingdom of Guatemala quietly ended. The smooth transfer of power stood in marked contrast to the turmoil of his tenure in office. Urrutia, hoping to use the occasion to promote some reconciliation between Bustamante and the creole elite, urged the ayuntamiento to pay its respects to the ex-governor before his departure. The following day, the regidores went as a group to Bustamante's residence and found themselves the target of a torrent of abuse and recriminations.[65]

Although no details of the meeting exist, in a letter to Urrutia written two days later Bustamante provides some indication of the degree to which the events of the previous year had upset and confused him. Referring to his forty-seven years of unblemished service to the king, the ex-governor stated that the events surrounding the opening of the pliego and the details of the 13 June *cédula* had been the most scandalous and denigrating experience any honorable official could face. Unable to reconcile this disgrace with his lifetime of loyalty and faithfulness to the crown, Bustamante concluded that it was a conspiracy on the part of the Council of the Indies to vilify him and ruin his honor and reputation:

> my enemies within the Council have intended from the beginning to twist the measures I took in the governance of this Kingdom . . . during the critical and dangerous period it has experienced by disfiguring the facts and substituting papers, removing and hiding those favorable to me, in order to insult me as much as possible, take the will of His Majesty by surprise, and cause him to be inclined to agree with the opinion that produced the exaggerated and deafening *cédula.*[66]

He then asked Urrutia to suspend the implementation of the decree until after the king responded to the defense he planned to make back in Spain. Convinced that his counterinsurgency policies had saved the kingdom, Bustamante believed he would be vindicated; therefore, any attempt to carry out the wishes of his enemies meant risking the hard-won tranquility of the colony for the benefit of two dozen disgruntled creoles. In this context, his emotional reaction to the ayuntamiento delegation can be seen as stubborn defiance in the face of those who had misrepresented his policies and stained his reputation. Desperate to escape the poisoned atmosphere of Guatemala City and determined to restore his honor, Bustamante took his leave of the kingdom just four days later.[67]

Bustamante's departure cleared the way for the creole elite to recover all of its former power and influence in the capital and colony. Unlike his predecessor, Urrutia actively sought the support of the local families and brought many members of the oligarchy into his administration. Perhaps in part because of his willingness to consider the issue of free trade, some believed that the new captain general had fallen completely under the influence of the Aycinenas, Pavóns, and Palomos. Despite this turn of events, however, the shadow of the previous governor continued to fall across the isthmus. To a great degree, the political factions that coalesced between 1818 and 1821 separated supporters of Bustamante from his long-time opponents. While these lines had been emerging since 1811, the struggle for power under a more pliable captain general brought these divisions into sharp focus, helping to establish the framework for the political conflicts of independent Central America.[68]

One of the primary reasons behind Bustamante's lingering presence in spirit in the colony was that the official investigation into his tenure in office, the *residencia,* which began in April 1820, delved deep into past controversies, reopened old wounds, and created a highly charged forum for debate about his legacy. In fact, the portrait painted of the former governor and his administration by the lead prosecutor in this inquiry, Francisco de Paula Vilches, served as the foundation for much of the subsequent Bustamante myth. Vilches, who also became *oidor regente* of the audiencia, received his appointment from the crown in October 1818 but did not arrive in Guatemala City until 11 April 1819 and did not initiate his investigation for a full year after that. A long-time imperial official like Bustamante, Vilches had previously served as oidor on the audiencia of Caracas, where he was profoundly affected by the first years of the struggle for independence in that colony. Significantly, he traveled to the colony in the company of former Deputy Antonio de Larrazábal and Antonio Batres, two leading members of the creole elite with strong opinions about the Bustamante years. Once in the capital, Vilches became even more closely linked to the oligarchy as he established himself in the colony. While his investigation of Bustamante was supposed to be objective, the impact of his Caracas appointment and these creole associations on the *residencia* must not be ignored.[69]

The four-month inquiry into the Bustamante administration ended on 16 October 1820. After deposing twenty-five primary witnesses and a number of supporting ones, Vilches presented the crown with forty-seven detailed charges against the former captain general.[70] In his summary of the case, the oidor argued that he had uncovered substantial evidence of crimes by Bustamante and that severe punishment should be given out to "a chief who, according to the indictments, did not observe well the obligations that corresponded to his position, who broke the laws, who denied Justice, who failed to obey royal decrees and was insubordinate to the Council of the Indies, who was arbitrary in command, [and] who caused insult and injury to individuals."[71] Most important in Vilches's opinion, the testimony seemed to indicate that Bustamante had caused the dissension between creoles and peninsulars. Drawing on his own experience in the colonies, the oidor declared that the wars for independence would end only if peninsular officials were just and impartial with Americans. Since acts of reconciliation were never more important than at that moment, Vilches asked the crown to make an example of Bustamante by invalidating him from future command in the Americas, imposing pecuniary fines, and issuing a public declaration of his guilt to the aggrieved ayuntamiento. In his view this was the only way to restore the confidence of the Guatemalans in their government and promote "the consolidation of peace and tranquility."[72]

Despite the weight of a forty-seven-count indictment, the charges laid out against Bustamante represent a wide range of accusations.[73] Some are serious, while others are technical violations of convoluted regulations. Many are crimes of interpretation and can best be described as minor infractions. A few are completely frivolous. Taken as a whole, the prosecution appears more as a persecution and reflects a concerted and partisan effort to blacken Bustamante's legacy and ruin his reputation. The charges are as follows:

1. Leaving his post without naming legal representation.
2. Leaving his office without posting the requisite bond.

3. Failing to pay the *media anata* (a deposit on his salary due to the crown).

4. Taking a six-month advance on his pay for travel expenses.

5. Bringing to the kingdom from a Mexican convent his nephew, Fray Manuel de la Madre de Dios, a Carmelite priest, without the permission of the prelate.

6. Keeping Fray Manuel at his home, away from a convent, during his entire administration and letting the priest participate in governmental affairs.

7. Taking Fray Manuel back to Spain with him without the necessary license.

8. Accepting gifts (food, drink, furniture) from Francisco Pacheco y Beteta to the tune of six thousand pesos upon his arrival in 1811.

9. Appointing Pacheco to various provincial posts (e.g., alcalde mayor of Chimaltenango) as payback despite his lack of qualifications.

10. Using only half a signature in his decrees, orders, judgments, and correspondence.

11. Failing to be gentle and positive with his subjects in violation of the *ley de partida*.

12. Appointing partisans and supporters to his government, showing a lack of faith in the creoles, and promoting division between the two groups in general, thereby making civil war more likely.

13. Displaying arbitrary justice in many cases: e.g., failing to comply with many royal decrees; detaining the goods of Gregorio Beltranena; making the House of Aycinena pay fees for the recovery of property; withholding the salary from shipbuilder Isidro Sánchez; acting against the regidores for the 1810 *Instrucciones*.

14. Receiving but refusing to obey the royal decree of 13 June 1817; attempting to convince Urrutia to suspend it in March 1818; acting against the public tranquility and the interests of the leading citizens of the city.

15. Promoting arbitrary delays in the commercial case against the Marquis of Aycinena.

16. Detaining the goods and ship of José Francisco Alfaro; ordering the arrest that led to his death.

17. Causing the death of José Mariano Argüelles after his extralegal arrest.

18. Displaying arbitrary rule and lack of justice in a case against *Oidor honorario* Luís Pedro Aguirre.

19. Impeding the administration of justice in a quarrel between Benito Cervantes and Pedro Gutiérrez.

20. Proceeding informally and aggressively during the auction and sale of the homes of the oidores according to an order from the Cortes; failing to follow the procedure for selling goods of the royal treasury.

21. Failing to comply with the royal order of 10 October 1816 in assigning commissions proportionately to oidores; showing partiality in giving most to Serrano Polo and least to Moreno.

22. Aggressively assuming the presidency of the audiencia.

23. Arbitrarily removing Manuel Talavera from the *Agencia fiscal.*

24. Showing partisanship in appointing Pedro Arroyave to the *Agencia fiscal criminal* despite his lack of qualifications; having a similar rationale for the appointment of Francisco Javier Rivera as *Relator de la Junta Superior de la Real Hacienda* and Tomás Morida as *Contador interino*, even though José Mariano Batres requested this position.

25. Suspending the salaries of various subalterns of the audiencia.

26. Denying the audiencia the requisite military honors and refusing his carriage to the oidores for public ceremonies.

27. Allowing Fray Manuel to participate in the 1814 ayuntamiento elections.

28. Showing less interest in apprehending and punishing *reos de contrabando* than in seizing goods.

29. Failing to pay sales tax on the goods sold before departure; selling some foreign goods (including clothes, sheets, and silks) despite the prohibition against selling what could be removed; taking advantage of the good prices of the capital.

30. Breaking the laws against opening mail between 1814 and 1818.

31. Failing to undertake a census of the Indian communities; failing to pay either interest or principal on the more than 100,000 pesos removed from the *cajas de comunidades* (community chests).

32. Failing to consult with the audiencia before making plans to establish a superintendency of police and to alter the legal procedures for certain cases.

33. Failing to give adequate care to prisoners or to improve prison conditions.

34. Showing no interest in improving the public roads.

35. Showing no interest in combating disease or smallpox outbreaks.

36. Failing to maintain peace and tranquility with the audiencia; failing to show due respect to it and the ayuntamiento.

37. Showing no interest in keeping the capital city clean and free of vagrants.

38. Failing to promote the conversion or the religious instruction of the Indians with zeal.

39. Failing to stop subaltern judges from conducting commercial business in their jurisdictions.

40. Failing to punish public sins.

41. Failing to take care of the arms of the kingdom.

42. Using a dedication made in his honor by Juan Santos Madrid as proof of his good service; printing and distributing it throughout the colony for his own benefit.

43. Suppressing certain positions and offices without royal approval.

44. Creating the post of *Pagador* (paymaster) for Sonsonate and Trujillo.

45. Paying fifteen pesos per month from the royal treasury to Francisco Saldaña to allow him to enter the *Batallón fijo* as a cadet.

46. Suppressing the posts of *zelador de pólvora* and *fiel de almacenes de tabaco* to the detriment of the royal treasury.

47. Using treasury funds (some 625,000 pesos) for military expenses without authorization.[74]

Viewed dispassionately, these accusations simply do not conjure up images of Bustamante the Ogre or the *terror bustamantino*. Instead, they represent the profound frustrations of two groups, the creole elite and the audiencia, who found their traditional access to offices, status, and influence reduced as a result of the imperial crisis and the counterinsurgency priorities of the captain general. More than anything else, the controversies that so deeply marked Bustamante's tenure in Central America resulted from a struggle for power between rival institutions during a particularly unstable time in the history of the empire. The *residencia* demonstrated that in the Kingdom of Guatemala, at least, Bustamante lost the fight.

Destined for vilification in Central America, Bustamante found vindication much easier to come by in his native land. The final journey to Spain brought him first to Campeche and then to Cuba, where he probably crossed paths with Vilches.[75] There he rested for the remainder of the year before boarding the frigate *Sabina* in February 1819 for the last part of the trip home. In May, despite rumors that the ship had gone down, he was back in Madrid working hard to restore his position at court. These efforts quickly met with success, demonstrating the extent to which his removal from office had been little more than a political gesture designed to placate the creoles. By the end of 1819, in fact, Ferdinand VII had recognized the many years of service of his loyal servant by awarding Bustamante the *Gran Cruz de San Hermenegildo* and the *Gran Cruz de la Orden de Isabel la Católica*. Full restoration to favor occurred in 1821 when the crown refused to consider any of the charges brought against Bustamante during his *residencia*.

In the remaining years of his life, the aging admiral served "with skill, zeal, and activity" in a number of important imperial offices. In February 1820 Bustamante returned to the *Junta de Fortificación y Defensa de Indias*. Three months later he took over as interim director general of the navy, an honor that he received in recognition of his loyalty to the king during the second constitutional period and that he held until August 1822. In failing health and disconsolate over the death of his stepdaughter, Bustamante spent most of 1823 on official leave. However, his experience remained an asset to the crown, and the king appointed him to the new *Junta facultative y consultative para las expediciones de América* in December. In April 1824 he assumed the vice presidency of the *Junta del fomento de la riqueza del reino*. After fifty years of continuous service to Spain and its empire, José de Bustamante died in Madrid on 10 March 1825. By this time, the controversy surrounding his temporary disgrace had completely passed—at least in Spain. Regarding his tenure in the Kingdom of Guatemala, his obituary declared:

he took possession of his office in Guatemala on 14 March 1811, at a time when the rebellions in Mexico, Buenos Aires, and [Venezuela], and the perverse example of Oaxaca and Caracas had already begun to spread to various provinces under his command; but Bustamante with his zeal and vigilance, with his patriotism and activity, managed to expose the ideas and plans of the revolutionaries, dissolve the anarchical junta that had been established in León de Nicaragua, and make them recognize the authority legally deposited in the hands of the bishop. At the same time he discovered and suppressed other partial insurrections in the capital that might have been powerful influences on neighboring provinces. These careful measures did not keep him from attending to the improvement of colonial administration, where he achieved savings in Guatemala of 1,257,359 pesos during the first six years of his government and reestablished the tribute, adopting there prudent and politic measures for such delicate circumstances. By these efforts, followed with consistence and at the cost of great fatigue, all of which contributed to the deterioration of his health, he managed to preserve for the King to great advantage that precious part of his dominions, thus befitting the confidence that he had earned.[76]

Bustamante probably would not have wanted any other kind of tribute.

Conclusion

José de Bustamante and the Preservation of Empire

The Kingdom of Guatemala emerged from a decade of unprecedented local, regional, and imperial turmoil in the spring of 1818 with no significant changes to its political, social, and economic infrastructure. As in April 1808 a well-established, peninsular-dominated bureaucracy administered Central America for an absolutist Spanish king. As in 1808 this government operated more or less in concert with an entrenched creole oligarchy that held most of the economic and social power on the isthmus. As in 1808 the colony still suffered from a severe economic depression caused by the collapse of its traditional export markets during the Napoleonic wars. Yet, as in 1808 the kingdom as a whole showed no signs of wavering in its loyalty to the crown or challenging its colonial status.

Although the traditional order seemed firmly entrenched at the time that Captain General Bustamante gave up power, the first two decades of the nineteenth century did witness social unrest and the first signs of the political divisions that would dominate the region's postindependence history. Yet, while specific examples of frustration and antagonism toward various aspects of the colonial order could be found among all levels of Guatemalan society—grievances that in certain instances led to the outbreak of armed insurrection—no broad consensus emerged either among social groups or between them to press for a break with Spain. In most cases, the demands of those who participated in the uprisings of this period were limited and easily accommodated by the crown. In more complicated situations, such as San Salvador, the movements tended to break down quickly as a result of the conflicting interests and expectations of those involved. Colonial society at this time was remarkably fragmented, and this factor contributed greatly to the preservation of Spanish rule. The crown cultivated its role as mediator between social groups and guarantor of peace, and in the Kingdom of Guatemala, surrounded by bloody and devastating race and class wars occurring in Haiti, New Spain, and Venezuela, this message carried more weight than the call for independence.

Still remarkably cohesive and influential, the Guatemala City creole elite remained at the top of the kingdom's social pyramid, jealously guarding its sources of power and prestige. Anxious for reforms that would consolidate its position and expand its influence, the oligarchy, nevertheless, was primarily a conservative force and a bastion of support for the colonial order—so long as Spain could be counted on to defend its interests. The elite suffered greatly at the hands of Bustamante for advocating autonomy and challenging the authority of the captain general, but it showed no signs of deserting the crown en masse during this tumultuous period. Instead, it worked within the system for the removal of the controversial governor and recovered its privileged status with the arrival of the more moderate, pliable Carlos de Urrutia.

While the Guatemalan oligarchy struggled to maintain its traditional position, the political, social, and economic transformations of the late Bourbon period did have a radicalizing impact on two increasingly differentiated social groups in the upper levels of colonial society: the provincial elite and the professional classes. Through the implementation of intendancies, the Bourbon reforms helped foster a degree of provincial self-awareness that would become a major source of political instability during the 1810s and would not diminish for many decades. To a great extent, the uprisings in San Salvador and Nicaragua can be seen as expressions of this trend, one that appeared as an urge to reduce dependency on Guatemala City more than on Madrid. Undoubtedly, the short-term indigo boom in San Salvador contributed to the growing sense of regional sentiment, as did the constitutional measures that briefly separated Nicaragua from the political oversight of Guatemala in 1813. It is significant, however, that provincial unrest diminished after 1814 and would not reemerge until the restoration of the Cádiz constitution in 1820 and the arrival of the *Plan de Iguala* in 1821. Honduran, Nicaraguan, Salvadoran, and Costa Rican landowners and merchants feared the consequences of social anarchy and lower-class mobilization as much as their Guatemalan cousins. Until Spain demonstrated its inability to defend their interests in Central America and preserve order, the kingdom's elites proved unwilling to gamble on independence.

The group most affected by the revolutionary ideology of the period and the liberal experiments of the Spanish loyalist governments was that of the professionals—doctors, lawyers, intellectuals—who, along with some of the merchants and landowners, constituted a sort of disenfranchised middle class. Restricted from significant political, social, and economic advancement as a consequence of the tight framework of colonial society yet educated enough to understand many of the potential ramifications and benefits of liberal philosophy, certain individuals associated with this fragmented class expressed much of the independence sentiment found in the colony in the 1810s and, as a consequence, found themselves the primary victims of Bustamante's counterinsurgency policies. Men like Juan de Dios Mayorga, Mateo Antonio Marure, Juan Francisco Barrundia, Julián Romero, and the Belén conspirators represent this segment of society well. They played significant roles in the series of uprisings that occurred between 1811 and 1814, they sustained a rather weak sentiment for independence from 1814 to 1821, and they came to dominate the construction of an independent Central America. While concern about their influence kept the colonial government on alert during the Bustamante years, the threat of subversion belied their limited numbers and lack of popular support both from above and below.

The largest segment of colonial society was the urban and rural lower classes, both ladino and indigenous. While their grievances were profound, these groups, who exercised power and accumulated wealth in inverse proportions to their numbers, never channeled such sentiments into the kind of massive challenge to the traditional order that the Viceroyalty of New Spain experienced with the Hidalgo revolt. Conservative in outlook and extremely divided, this class as a whole remained particularly loyal to Spain. The urban artisans and shopkeepers, in particular, found protection in the trade policies of the crown, while the indigenous groups found some degree of solace in the autonomy they had managed to carve out as legal wards of the state. The uprisings in San Salvador, Metapán, Santa Ana, Tegucigalpa, and Chiquimula all had large elements of lower-class participation, but the objectives of the urban masses were invariably limited and local. Absent the encouragement and manipulation of proindependence creoles, these manifestations of lower-class discontent cannot be distinguished from other examples of unrest that occurred before the imperial crisis of 1808.

A dramatic example of the continuing faith in and dependence on the crown among all segments of society in the Kingdom of Guatemala was the indigenous revolt in the alcaldía mayor of Totonicapán in 1820. Significant for its isolation, the uprising led by Atanasio Tzul resulted from efforts by colonial officials to reimpose the tribute on the native populations of Central America, a financial burden that Spain had removed shortly after the fall of the monarchy and that Ferdinand VII restored after recovering his throne. Although Bustamante received credit for reestablishing the tribute in the colony, provincial authorities did not make serious attempts to collect it until after he left office. Opposition to these efforts culminated in the 1820 Totonicapán revolt. Although it had to be put down by force, there is no evidence to indicate that the participants were motivated by anti-Spanish sentiment. Equally important, local and regional elites rallied to the support of the colonial government instead of taking advantage of the threat to assert their own interests.[1] Scarcely a year before independence actually occurred, the Kingdom of Guatemala showed no signs of taking the critical step toward breaking with Spain.

Much of the credit for this achievement—and from the royalist perspective it was a remarkable achievement—must go to José de Bustamante. Despite the enormous challenges facing a colonial governor in the era of the Latin American independence movements, Captain General Bustamante successfully preserved Spanish rule in Central America. By maintaining a firm grip on power, acting in a quick and decisive manner when confronted with signs of unrest, and constructing a viable counterinsurgency system to absorb the inevitable threats to the colonial order, he gave the colony the political stability it needed to weather the collapse of the monarchy and the resulting imperial crisis.

Although his administration was repressive at times, Bustamante made a determined effort to avoid the unilateral extremism of Venegas and

Calleja. Acutely aware of the tenuous nature of his position, he incorporated compromise, negotiation, and alliance building into his administrative agenda as much as possible. However, the rapid and widespread succession of revolts between November 1811 and April 1812 combined with the chaos of the constitutional experiments compelled him to seek more hard-line solutions to what he perceived to be the kingdom's primary sources of instability. The evidence indicates that he entered into this decision in a rational manner, confident that his position was bolstered by viceregal policies in New Spain and supported by the restored absolutist government of Ferdinand VII. His targeting of the creole elite, however, eventually undermined him once the crown found itself interested in American allies during the later stages of the independence wars. Despite the disgrace of his removal from office in 1818, Bustamante spent another five years as an effective and valuable imperial official, a fact that does not accord well with the argument that his tenure in Central America had left him mentally unbalanced.

From this perspective, the Bustamante administration in Central America should not be viewed as an isolated and perverse case of Spanish oppression but rather as an example of a relatively successful, if short-lived, campaign by Spanish authorities to preserve the empire. After the shock of the first independence movements had worn off, colonial officials throughout the empire struggled to rebuild and maintain their positions as the legitimate representatives of the sovereign power. Only Argentina and Paraguay, in fact, actually made a rapid and complete break with Spain during this time. In the rest of the empire, the struggle for independence waxed and waned for more than a decade. Like Bustamante, Viceroys Venegas and Calleja of New Spain, Viceroy Abascal of Peru, and Captain General Morillo of Venezuela managed to withstand independence pressures for a number of years. And Cuba, which resembled Central America in many ways, remained a Spanish colony until 1898. As a colonial official, Bustamante had an obligation to preserve the Kingdom of Guatemala as an integral part of the Spanish crown, and he was one of many who struggled to fulfill this duty.

Why then did Spanish rule in Central America collapse, and what role did Bustamante play in that development? As the Cuban case indicates, such a result was not inevitable, though neither was it unthinkable. The history of the twenty-one years preceding independence shows a colony emerging precipitously and haphazardly from a long period of stagnation and isolation into a time of unprecedented transformations. By 1800 the indigo boom had provided unprecedented wealth and access to power to the creole oligarchy; the Bourbon reforms had stimulated local and regional development, as well as provincial autonomist sentiment; and the Age of Enlightenment had promoted a new-found sense of identity, *criollismo,* among local elites and a broader worldview among other educated Americans. With the Napoleonic invasion of Spain and the collapse of the Bourbon monarchy, the Kingdom of Guatemala had all the elements necessary to produce an independence movement. It did not happen, however, either in 1808 or at any other likely time before 1821. Despite the many potential sources of destabilization during that period, colonial Guatemalan society showed no interest in independence so long as Spain remained a viable power in the region. In the midst of the growing divisions between Guatemala City and provincial elites, between the oligarchy and the professional groups, and between the upper and lower classes in the Kingdom of Guatemala, all segments of society continued to look to Spain to preserve order.

What finally broke the fragile balance between the crown and its Central American supporters was the 1820 Riego revolt in Spain that compelled Ferdinand VII to restore the liberal Cádiz constitution or face civil war. With almost no warning and without the controlling hand of Bustamante to moderate the reforms, this development, which underscored the continuing political instability at the heart of the empire, promised to strip the colonial institutions and authorities in the Kingdom of Guatemala of their remaining base of legitimacy and create a political vacuum. By the end of the year elections to fill local and regional representative assemblies had given provincial autonomy a tremendous boost, thereby providing the first significant institutional challenge to the traditional hegemony of Guatemala City. Similarly, the electoral process gave members of the professional classes a new opportunity to threaten the political monopoly heretofore held by the Family and its allies. It was during this political campaign that Central America witnessed the crystallization of the political factions that, once independence was achieved, evolved into clearly defined parties and shaped the outcome of the early national period.[2] While the faction led by José del Valle found itself defined as the Bustamante party, the captain general served more as a highly charged symbol than the determining factor in the emerging political divisions. The fact that the fiercely anti-Bustamante oligarchy eventually joined Valle to form the Conservative party underscores this point.

From the perspective of the oligarchy, the political chaos in Spain, coupled with the expansion of provincial and lower-class rights under the Cádiz constitution, created the potential for a disastrous breakdown of the traditional social order. A similar sentiment infused the Mexican elite at this time and resulted in the decision by the creole royalist officer Agustín de Iturbide to proclaim the independence of New Spain under the conservative *Plan de Iguala* early in 1821. The publication of this proposal precipitated numerous calls for the Kingdom of Guatemala to break with Spain as well, for continued colonial status was no longer a reasonable option. With New Spain likely to achieve independence, strategic considerations made in Mexico now dictated the fate of Central America regardless of the sentiment of the local population. However, few members of the Guatemalan Family actually believed that the impoverished colony could be viable on its own or, more important, manage to protect the social position of the local elites. To them, unification with Mexico, with its enormous size and potential, not to mention its recently proclaimed commitment to the traditional institutions of Church and monarchy, appeared as a more secure alternative to the uncertainties of complete independence.

As a result, over the summer of 1821 the Guatemalan oligarchy came to the conclusion that separation from Spain was necessary, if only to unite with Mexico. At the same time, to further their own interests other groups began to press for complete sovereignty, both at the provincial and regional levels. On 15 September 1821, with most of the kingdom having already declared in favor of the *Plan de Iguala,* Gabino Gainza, who had recently replaced the ailing Urrutia as captain general, proclaimed Guatemala independent. Within four months, the former colony had become part of Iturbide's new Mexican Empire. This association survived until the spring of 1823 when the abdication of Emperor Agustín I precipitated a second and final proclamation of Central American independence.

On the basis of this history, it is difficult to accept the argument that Bustamante both inhibited the independence of the Kingdom of Guatemala through his counterinsurgency measures and precipitated the break with Spain by establishing a system of repression that drained away local support for the crown. While the captain general quickly became an object of intense hatred on the part of a small number of independence-minded radicals and autonomy-minded elites, he appears to have left the colony as disposed toward Spanish rule in 1818 as it had been in 1808. Had he never been posted to Central America it is likely that another captain general would have implemented similar measures to combat unrest and would have targeted the same individuals. While another governor might not have engendered such an emotional opposition, the fact that the creole elite did not break with Spain during Bustamante's tenure makes it hard to believe that it would have done so had Urrutia, for example, received his appointment some years earlier. Instead, the oligarchy worked with the colonial administration, if not with Bustamante, to preserve order and maintain its privileged position. Only when this was threatened in 1821 did the Family seek pseudo-independence with Mexico as a final remedy. Had New Spain remained loyal to the metropolis at this time there is every reason to believe that the Kingdom of Guatemala would have as well.

Relatively effective at a certain level, Bustamante's counterinsurgency policies nevertheless had limited reach and scope. He was forced to rely upon the discretion and enthusiasm of provincial officials at a number of different stages in order to implement his orders, a process that was rife with delay and obstacles. His numerous jurisdictional conflicts with the audiencia and the Guatemala City ayuntamiento inhibited the smooth functioning of the judicial system. And, even with his military buildup, the forces available to combat unrest were limited, poorly trained, and made up primarily of Americans. As a result, without the tacit support of an inherently loyal population his position and that of the entire Spanish population on the isthmus would have been untenable.

The Bustamante myth that emerged after independence was created and cultivated by a divided society desperate to establish and promote the historical foundations of nationhood. According to this framework, the account of a united struggle against the forces of oppression served to stimulate patriotism in a region that failed to develop an independence hero along the lines of Washington, Bolívar, or Hidalgo. Designed to explain away a condition that was shared by much of the empire but became an anachronism following independence, this interpretation created a villain and a monster out of José de Bustamante, an imperial official who had the unenviable task of governing a colony in the midst of war, revolution, and economic distress. A reserved, austere, and phlegmatic soldier, he was easily stereotyped as a reactionary. Nevertheless, he, his administration, and his times deserve to be seen from a different perspective, one more sensitive to the complexities and uncertainties of the 1810s. So long as the issues and individuals associated with the preservation of empire are downplayed in favor of the struggle for independence in Latin America, the history of this crucial period will be incomplete.

Notes

Introduction

1. See Vincent Uribe, "The Enigma of Latin American Independence: Analyses of the Last Ten Years," *Latin American Research Review* 32, no. 1 (1997):236–55.

2. Alejandro Marure, *Bosquejo histórico de las revoluciones de Centroamérica desde 1811 hasta 1834* (Mexico: Libreria de la Viuda de Ch. Bouret, 1913), 1:1–2.

3. Ibid., 1:3–4.

4. Ibid., 1:4.

5. Ibid., 1:4–5.

6. Miguel García Granados, *Memorias del General Miguel García Granados* (Guatemala: Editorial del Ejército, 1978), 19–20.

7. Agustín Gómez Carrillo, *Estudio histórico sobre la América Central* (San Salvador: Tipografía "La Concordia," 1884), 88.

8. Ibid., 90.

9. See, for example, Ramón A. Salazar, *Manuel José Arce* (Guatemala: Editorial del Ministerio de Educación Pública, 1952), and Carlos Meléndez Chaverri, *Próceres de la independencia centroamericana* (San José: Editorial Universitaria Centroamericana, 1971).

10. Rafael Aguirre Cinta, *Lecciones de historia general de Guatemala* (Guatemala: Impreso en la tipografía nacional, 1899), 71.

11. Ibid.

12. Ibid.

13. Marure, *Bosquejo histórico*, 1:10.

14. Aguirre Cinta, *Lecciones de historia*, 71.

15. Antonio Batres Jáuregui, *La America Central ante la historia* (Guatemala: Tipografía Sánchez & De Guise, 1920), 2:605–7. See also Manuel Coronado Aguilar, *Apuntes*

histórico-Guatemalenses (Guatemala: Editorial "José de Pineda Ibarra," 1975) for a similar perspective.

16. Ramón A. Salazar, *Historia de veintiún años: la independencia de Guatemala*, 2 vols., 2nd ed. (Biblioteca guatemalteca de cultural popular; Guatemala: Editorial del Ministerio de Educación Pública, 1956), 2:163. Echoes of Salazar's argument can be found across Central American historiography: see, for example, Medardo Mejia, *Historia de Honduras* (Tegucigalpa: Editorial Universitaria, 1969), 1:434–35, 452.

17. Salazar, *Historia de veintiún años*, 2:180.

18. José Antonio Villacorta Calderón, *Historia de la Capitanía General de Guatemala* (Guatemala: Tipografía Nacional, 1942), 471.

19. Ibid., 471.

20. Ibid., 480–85.

21. Ibid., 488.

22. Ibid., 489; Salazar, *Historia de veintiún años*, 2:164, 171, 174.

23. Sofonías Salvatierra, *Contribución a la historia de Centroamérica: Monografías documentales* (Managua: Tipografía Progreso, 1939), 2:450.

24. Arturo Valdés Oliva, *Caminos y luchas por la independencia* (Guatemala: Secretaría de Divulgación Cultural, 1956), 53. A similar perspective can be found in José Mata-Gavidia, *Anotaciones de historia patria centroamericana* (Guatemala: Cultural Centroamericana, S.A., 1953).

25. Valdés Oliva, *Caminos*, 53.

26. Ibid., 65–69.

27. Ibid., 90.

28. Rodolfo Barón Castro, *José Matías Delgado y el movimiento insurgente de 1811: Ensayo historico* (San Salvador: Ministerio de la Educación, 1961), 102.

29. Ibid., 103.

30. Hubert H. Bancroft, *History of Central America, 1801–1887* (vol. 3). Vol. 8 of *The Works of Hubert Howe Bancroft* (San Francisco: The History Company, 1887).

31. Louis Bumgartner, *José del Valle of Central America* (Durham, N.C.: Duke University Press, 1963), 41.

32. Ibid., 65–66, 69.

33. Clemente Marroquín Rojas, *Historia de Guatemala* (Guatemala: Tipografía Nacional, 1971), 35.

34. Ibid., 39–40.

35. Ibid., 41, 42, 44–48.

36. Ibid., 59.

37. Julio C. Pinto Soria, *Centroamérica, de la colonia al estado nacional (1800–1840)* (Guatemala: Editorial Universitaria de Guatemala, 1986), 103. See also André Saint-Lu, *Condición colonial y conciencia criolla en Guatemala (1524–1821)* (Guatemala: Editorial Universitaria, 1978).

38. Pinto Soria, *Centroamérica*, 99–100, 108.

39. R. L. Woodward, *Central America: A Nation Divided* (New York: Oxford University Press, 1976), 84–85.

40. Miles Wortman, *Government and Society in Central America, 1680–1840* (New York: Columbia University Press, 1982), 201.

41. Ibid., 203.

42. Mario Rodríguez, *The Cádiz Experiment in Central America, 1808–1826* (Berkeley: University of California Press, 1978), 104.

43. Ibid., 116.

44. Ibid., 116, 121–22. See also Mario Rodríguez, *La conspiración de Belén en nueva perspectiva* (Guatemala: Centro Editorial "José de Pineda Ibarra," 1965), 5, 19–24.

45. Carlos Meléndez Chaverri, *La independencia de Centroamerica* (Madrid: Editorial MAPFRE, 1993), 86–88.

46. Ibid., 84–85.

47. Héctor Pérez Brignoli, *De la ilustración al liberalismo (1750–1870)*, vol. 3 of Edelberto Torres Rivas, ed., *Historia General de Centroamérica* (Madrid: FLASCO, 1993), 78–79.

48. Ibid., 81–82.

49. See, for example, Hugh M. Hamill, "Royalist Counterinsurgency in the Mexican War for Independence: The Lessons of 1811," *Hispanic American Historical Review* (hereinafter cited as *HAHR*) 53(August 1973):471–89; Brian R. Hamnett, "Mexico's Royalist Coalition: The Response to Revolution 1808–1821," *Journal of Latin American Studies* 12(May 1980):55–86; Brian R. Hamnett, *Roots of Insurgency: Mexican Regions, 1750–1824* (Cambridge: Cambridge University Press, 1986; Timothy E. Anna, *The Fall of the Royal Government in Mexico City* (Lincoln: University of Nebraska Press, 1978); Timothy E. Anna, *The Fall of the Royal Government in Peru* (Lincoln: University of Nebraska Press, 1979); Timothy E. Anna, *Spain and the Loss of America* (Lincoln: University of Nebraska Press, 1983); Jorge I. Domínguez, *Insurrection or Loyalty: The Breakdown of the Spanish American Empire* (Cambridge: Cambridge University Press, 1980); and Michael Costeloe, *Response to Revolution: Imperial Spain and the Spanish American Revolutions, 1810–1840* (Cambridge: Cambridge University Press, 1986). Surprising parallels to the Bustamante case are found in Stephen Stoan, *Pablo Morillo and Venezuela, 1815–1820* (Columbus: Ohio State University Press, 1974).

50. See Christon I. Archer, ed., *The Wars of Independence in Spanish America* (Wilmington, Del.: Scholarly Resources, 2000) for some of the latest research on rebellion and counterinsurgency across the empire; for Mexico, see also Christon I. Archer, ed., *The Birth of Modern Mexico, 1780–1824* (Wilmington, Del.: Scholarly Resources, 2003); Eric Van Young, *The Other Rebellion: Popular Violence and Ideology in Mexico, 1810–1821* (Stanford: Stanford University Press, 2001); Virginia Guedea, *La insurgencia en el Departamento del Norte: los Llanos de Apan y la sierra de Puebla, 1810–1816* (Mexico: Universidad Nacional Autonoma de Mexico, 1996); and John Tutino, *From Insurrection to Revolution in Mexico: Social Bases of Agrarian Violence, 1750–1940* (Princeton: Princeton University Press, 1986).

51. See Allan J. Kuethe, *Cuba, 1753–1815: Crown, Military, and Society* (Knoxville: University of Tennessee Press, 1986); Allan J. Kuethe, *Military Reform and Society in New Granada, 1773–1808* (Gainesville: University Presses of Florida, 1978); Leon G. Campbell,

The Military and Society in Colonial Peru, 1750–1810 (Philadelphia: American Philosophical Society, 1978); Christon I. Archer, *The Army in Bourbon Mexico, 1760–1810* (Albuquerque: University of New Mexico Press, 1977); Brian R. Hamnett, "The Counter Revolution of Morillo and the Insurgent Clerics of New Granada, 1815–1820," *The Americas* 32(April 1976):597–617; José Luís Mora Mérida, "Comportamiento político del clero secular de Cartagena de Indias en la preindependencia," *Anuario de Estudios Americanos* 35(1978):211–31; Nancy M. Farriss, *Crown and Clergy in Colonial Mexico, 1759–1821* (London: Athlone Press, 1968).

1. The Creation of a Spanish Colonial Official

1. John Lynch, *Bourbon Spain, 1700–1808* (London: Basil Blackwell, 1989), 226.

2. Genealogical information on the Bustamante family appears in Alberto y Arturo García Carraffa, *Diccionario heráldico y genealógico de apellidos españoles y americanos,* vol. 17 (Madrid: Imprenta de Antonio Marzo, 1925), 168–86. Details of his early life are drawn from the *Archivo biográfico de España, Portugal e Iberoamerica: una compilación de 300 obras biográficas, las más importantes y representativas, editadas entre el siglo XVII y los inicios del siglo XX* (Munich and New York: K. G. Saur, 1986) and the Bustamante obituary found in *Suplemento a la Gaceta de Madrid del martes 5 de julio de 1825* (Otto G. Richter Library, University of Miami).

3. Demographic statistics on the valley of Toranzo can be found in the Archivo Histórico Provincial de Cantabria, Santander, Spain. See the Catastro del Marqués de La Ensenada (1752–1753), legajos 565–66, in particular. Ontaneda was beholden to the Bustamante family for a number of civic endowments and benefits that helped raise the status of the town, including the securing of its *título de villa,* the founding of a renowned *colegio* for children, the establishment of a market, and the construction of the family *palacio.* Between 1788 and 1790 the northern provinces of Spain were hit with severe food shortages, but Santander and the Montaña found their suffering alleviated through the efforts of Bustamante's uncle and brother, both members of the *comercio de Cádiz,* who managed to funnel corn and wheat from Philadelphia to the region. See José Antonio y Alfredo del Río, "Marinos Ilustres de la Provincia de Santander (1881)," in *Archivo biográfico de España,* 363–65.

4. According to Juan González de Riancho, a seventy-six-year-old resident of Ontaneda, Bustamante family members were known to have "exempciones de Nobles" and "escudos de Armas." They were well regarded in the community as "alcaldes, regidores, [and] procuradores" and for being "temorosos de Dios, y observantes de su Santa ley, y preceptos, dando a todos buen exemplo, como es publico." Archivo Histórico Nacional, Madrid, Spain, Ordenes Militares—Santiago, Prueba de Caballeros—José Joaquín Bustamante y Guerra, 1784 Ontaneda, caja 243, exp. 1296.

5. Lynch, *Bourbon Spain,* 248–50. For more on the Bourbon reforms see D. A. Brading, *The First America: The Spanish Monarchy, Creole Patriots, and the Liberal State 1492–1867* (Cambridge: Cambridge University Press, 1991), 467–91; D. A. Brading, *Miners and Merchants in Bourbon Mexico 1763–1810* (Cambridge: Cambridge University Press, 1971);

Mark A. Burkholder and D. S. Chandler, *From Impotence to Authority: The Spanish Crown and the American Audiencias 1687–1808* (Columbia: University of Missouri Press, 1971); Richard Herr, *The Eighteenth-Century Revolution in Spain* (Princeton: Princeton University Press, 1958); and W. N. Hargreaves-Mawdsley, *Eighteenth-Century Spain, 1700–1788: A Political, Diplomatic, and Institutional History* (London: Macmillan, 1979).

6. Lynch, *Bourbon Spain*, 253, 329–33.

7. Ibid., 254.

8. Ibid., 166; José Cervera Pery, *La marina española en la emancipación de Hispanoamérica* (Madrid: Editorial MAPFRE, 1992), 15–17. See also J. P. Merino Navarro, *La Armada española en el siglo XVIII* (Madrid: Fundación Universitaria Española, 1982).

9. The prereform navy was divided between the Armada de Guardia de Indias, the Armada del Mar del Sur, and the Armada de Barlovento. For more on the colonial Spanish navy, see Bibiano Torres Ramírez, *La Armada de Barlovento* (Sevilla: Escuela de Estudios Hispano-Americanos, 1981); Pablo E. Pérez-Mallaína and Bibiano Torres Ramírez, *La Armada del Mar del Sur* (Sevilla: Escuela de Estudios Hispano-Americanos, 1987); Gaspar Pérez Turrado, *Las Armadas españolas de Indias* (Madrid: Editorial MAPFRE, 1992); and Cesáreo Fernández Duro, *Armada española desde la unión de los reinos de Castilla y de Aragón*, vols. 8–9 (Madrid: Museo Naval, 1973).

10. Lynch, *Bourbon Spain*, 176.

11. Quoted in Cervera Pery, *La marina española*, 14.

12. Lynch, *Bourbon Spain*, 315–16. In 1770 naval expenditures reached twenty percent of the total government budget, a level that remained relatively constant for the next twenty years.

13. Cervera Pery, *La marina española*, 16. Also see Otto von Pivka, *Navies of the Napoleonic Era* (David & Charles: London, 1980), 203–4. Bustamante himself contributed to this massive buildup of Spanish naval strength. In 1789 he received permission from the crown to launch a subscription drive in La Montaña toward the construction of the *Montañés*, a seventy-four-cannon ship-of-the-line, which was built out of "un verdadero amor patriótico hacia mi país la Montaña, unida a los deseos de significar mi gratitud al cuerpo de la Armada." See Bustamante to Antonio Váldes, 28 July 1789, Archivo General de la Marina "Álvaro de Bazán" (hereinafter cited as AGM), Viso del Marqués, Spain, Defensa, leg. 20-21.

14. Manuel Lucena Giraldo and Juan Pimentel Igea, *Los "Axiomas políticos sobre la América" de Alejandro Malaspina* (Aranjuez: Doce Calles, 1991), 26–27.

15. Lynch, *Bourbon Spain*, 314.

16. The following summary of Bustamante's naval career is drawn from the documents contained in his service record, located in the AGM, Hoja de Servicio de José de Bustamante y Guerra, leg. 620-181.

17. The records for Bustamante's application to the Order of Santiago are housed in the Archivo Histórico Nacional, Ordenes Militares—Santiago, Prueba de Caballero—José Joaquín Bustamante y Guerra, 1784 Ontaneda, caja 243, exp. 1296.

18. Virginia González Claverín, *La expedición científica de Malaspina en Nueva España (1789–1794)* (Mexico: El Colegio de Mexico, 1988), 23–31. For more on Malaspina's

background, see John Kendrick, *Alejandro Malaspina: Portrait of a Visionary* (Montreal: McGill-Queens Press, 1999).

19. González Claverín, *La expedición*, 21. See also Lucena Giraldo and Pimentel Igea, *Los "Axiomas políticos*,*"* 11–12.

20. Virginia González Claverín, *Malaspina en Acapulco* (Mexico: Turner Libros, 1989), 10.

21. González Claverín, *La expedición*, 34–35.

22. Ibid., 38. Interest in the expedition has produced a number of fine works in recent years. See, in particular, María Dolores Higueras Rodríguez, ed., *Catálogo crítico de los documentos de la expedición Malaspina (1789–1794) del Museo Naval*, 3 vols. (Madrid: Museo Naval, 1985, 1987, 1994); María Dolores Higueras Rodríguez, ed., *La expedición Malaspina 1789–1794*, vol. 9, *Diario general del viaje: Corbeta Atrevida*, by José de Bustamante y Guerra (Madrid: Ministerio de Defensa, Museo Naval y Lunwerg Editores, 1999); Andrew David, Felipe Fernández-Armesto, Carlos Novi, and Glyndwr Williams, eds., *The Malaspina Expedition 1789–1794: Journal of the Voyage by Alejandro Malaspina* (London: The Hakluyt Society, 2001).

23. John Kendrick, ed. and trans., *The Voyage of Sutil and Mexicana 1792: The Last Spanish Exploration of the Northwest Coast of America* (Spokane: Arthur H. Clark Company, 1991), 18.

24. González Claverín, *La expedición*, 442–43.

25. González Claverín, *Malaspina*, 36; Alejandro Malaspina, *En busca del paso del Pacífico* (Madrid: Historia 16, 1990), 150.

26. González Claverín, *La expedición*, 27–31.

27. Cervera Pery, *La marina española*, 17.

28. The report, presented to the Ministry of the Navy in 1796, was entitled "Memoria sobre un plan de defensa para la America meridional y las islas Filipinas para interceptar el gran comercio de los ingleses con la China al primer rompimiento y derrotar desde Chile a las costas de Nueva Holanda, o bahía Botánica, y regreso a las del Peru." It seems likely that this report was a factor in Bustamante's appointment to colonial service. Bustamante referred to the manuscript in a letter to Manuel Godoy, 7 January 1798, Archivo General de Indias, Seville, Spain (hereinafter cited as AGI), Estado 81, no. 19. It is also cited in Fernández Duro, *Armada*, vol. 8.

29. Lynch, *Bourbon Spain*, 394.

30. The following information is drawn from Francisco Bauza, *Historia de la dominación española en el Uruguay*, 3rd ed. (Montevideo: Tall. Graf. "El Democrata," 1929), 355–73.

31. For more information on the duties of governor in the colonial system, see C. H. Haring, *The Spanish Empire in America* (New York: Harcourt Brace Jovanovich, 1975), 128.

32. Bustamante focused his attention on the poor state of the port of Montevideo and the desperate need for the construction of new docks. Governor Bustamante's report is found at the AGI, Estado 81, no. 8.

33. Bauza, *Historia*, 360–62. Bustamante found time for other things during his tenure in Montevideo, as well. Shortly after his arrival he made the acquaintance of María

del Pilar de Azlor y Villavicencio, the young widow of a former president of the audiencia of Cuzco, who was returning to Spain with her four-year-old daughter. By the end of the year the couple were engaged. See Bustamante to Viceroy Antonio Olaguer, Montevideo, 2 January 1798, among other documents collected in his application for a marriage license, AGM, Hoja de Servicio de José de Bustamante y Guerra, leg. 620-181.

34. Bauza, *Historia,* 371.

35. Ibid., 373.

36. Ibid., 360.

37. *Gaceta de Guatemala,* 7 May 1811, vol. 15, no. 216, in Archivo General de Centro América, Guatemala (hereinafter cited as AGCA), A3, leg. 61, exp. 1214.

38. José de Bustamante, *El Presidente Gobernador y Capitán General de Guatemala . . . ,* 13 April 1811, Decree in the Latin American Library, Tulane University, New Orleans, 6.

39. Ibid., 1.

40. By 1800 Bustamante was already fed up with the "terquedad y la ignorancia" of the Consulado de Comercio in his efforts to raise funds and seven hundred soldiers for the defense of the Banda Oriental. This institution and the viceroy also challenged his authority over Montevideo's naval forces and his attempts to crack down on contraband trade. See Bustamante's letters to Tomas Ugarte, 19 November 1800 and 19 January 1803, Museo Naval, Madrid, Ms. 2146.

41. Fernández Duro, *Armada,* 8:264–68. This attack on the frigates, which caused Charles IV to declare war on Britain, was a precipitating event in the collapse of the Peace of Amiens. See the Manifiesto del Rey Carlos IV, 14 December 1804, AGM, Expediciones a Europa, 1804, leg. 84.

42. Fernández Duro, *Armada,* 8:280–83.

43. See Brian R. Hamnett, *La política española en una época revolucionaria, 1790–1820* (Mexico: Fondo de Cultura Económica, 1985).

44. Bustamante, *El Presidente,* 4n.

45. AGCA, B1, leg. 20, exp. 768.

2. The Kingdom of Guatemala on the Eve of Independence

1. Murdo J. MacLeod, *Spanish Central America: A Socioeconomic History, 1520–1720* (Berkeley: University of California Press, 1973).

2. For more on the impact of the Bourbon reforms on Central America see Troy Floyd, "The Guatemalan Merchants, the Government, and the Provincianos, 1750–1800," *HAHR* 41(February 1961):90–110; Troy Floyd, "Bourbon Palliatives and the Central American Mining Industry, 1765–1800," *The Americas* 18(October 1961):103–25; Miles Wortman, "Bourbon Reforms in Central America: 1750–1786," *The Americas* 32(October 1975):222–38; Wortman, *Government and Society;* and Richmond F. Brown, "Profits, Prestige, and Persistence: Juan Fermín de Aycinena and the Spirit of Enterprise in the Kingdom of Guatemala," *HAHR* 75(August 1995):405–40.

3. Miles Wortman, "Government Revenue and Economic Trends in Central America, 1787–1819," *HAHR* 55(May 1975):276.

4. James Lockhart and Stuart B. Schwartz, *Early Latin America: A History of Colonial Spanish America and Brazil* (Cambridge: Cambridge University Press, 1983), 338.

5. Richmond F. Brown, *Juan Fermín de Aycinena: Central American Colonial Entrepreneur, 1729–1796* (Norman: University of Oklahoma Press, 1997), 22–24; and Domingo Juarros, *Compendio de la historia del Reino de Guatemala* (Guatemala: Editorial Piedra Santa, 1981), 13.

6. Domínguez, *Insurrection*, 69.

7. Alfonso García-Gallo, "La Capitanía General como institución de gobierno político en España e Indias en el siglo XVIII," *Memoria del Tercer Congreso Venezolano de Historia,* tomo 1 (Caracas: Academia Nacional de la Historia, 1979), 542–47.

8. Haring, *The Spanish Empire*, 110.

9. Ibid.

10. Carlos Molina Argüello, "Gobernaciones, alcaldias mayores y corregimientos en el Reino de Guatemala," *Anuario de Estudios Americanos* 17(1960):109–10.

11. Oakah L. Jones, *Guatemala in the Spanish Colonial Period* (Norman: University of Oklahoma Press, 1995), 45.

12. Haring, *The Spanish Empire*, 111–12.

13. Ibid., 121.

14. Barbara A. Tenenbaum, ed., *Encyclopedia of Latin American History and Culture* (New York: Charles Scribner's Sons, 1996), vol. 1, "Audiencia," by Mark Burkholder.

15. Haring, *The Spanish Empire*, 122.

16. Jones, *Guatemala*, 45.

17. Bernabé Fernández Hernández, *El Reino de Guatemala durante el Gobierno de Antonio González Saravia 1801–1811* (Guatemala: Comisión Interuniversitaria Guatemalteca de Conmemoración del Quinto Centenario del Descubrimiento de América, 1993), 153–54, 162–63.

18. Haring, *The Spanish Empire*, 112.

19. Fernández Hernández, *El Reino de Guatemala*, 153–54, 162–63.

20. Ibid., 54; Haring, *The Spanish Empire*, 135; see also H. H. Samayoa Guevara, *Implantación del régimen de intendencias en el Reino de Guatemala* (Guatemala: Editorial del Ministerio de Educación Popular "José de Pineda Ibarra," 1960), and the entry on intendants in Tenenbaum, ed., *Encyclopedia of Latin American History and Culture;* for a case study of one of the Central American intendancies see Michael Polushin, "Bureaucratic Conquest, Bureaucratic Culture: Town and Office in Chiapas, 1780–1832" (Ph.D. diss., Tulane University, 1999).

21. Fernández Hernández, *El Reino de Guatemala*, 156–58.

22. Brown, *Juan Fermín de Aycinena*, 27; Haring, *The Spanish Empire*, 131. See also Manuel Rubio Sánchez, *Alcaldes mayores* (San Salvador: Ministerio de Educación, Dirección de Publicaciones, 1979). For a case study, see Jorge González, "History of Los Altos, Guatemala: A Study of Regional Conflict and National Integration, 1750–1794" (Ph.D. diss., Tulane University, 1994).

23. Fernández Hernández, *El Reino de Guatemala*, 156.

24. Haring, *The Spanish Empire*, 151.

25. Juarros, *Compendio*, 234–35.

26. Fernández Hernández, *El Reino de Guatemala*, 165.

27. Haring, *The Spanish Empire*, 156–57; for more on the ayuntamiento of Guatemala City see Ernesto Chinchilla Aguilar, *El Ayuntamiento colonial de la Ciudad de Guatemala* (Guatemala: Editorial Universitaria, 1961), and Christopher Lutz, *Santiago de Guatemala, 1541–1773: City, Caste, and the Colonial Experience* (Norman: University of Oklahoma Press, 1994). See also Jordana Dym, "A Sovereign State of Every Village: City, State and Nation in Independence-Era Central America, ca. 1750–1850" (Ph.D. diss., New York University, 2000).

28. Juarros, *Compendio*, 12–13; see also Adriaan van Oss, *Catholic Colonialism: A Parish History of Guatemala, 1524–1821* (Cambridge: Cambridge University Press, 1986).

29. Wortman, *Government and Society*, 41–42.

30. Brown, *Juan Fermín de Aycinena*, 27–30.

31. Domínguez, *Insurrection*, 74, and Jones, *Guatemala*, 219–30. Research on other colonial militaries includes Campbell, *The Military and Society in Colonial Peru, 1750–1810*; Kuethe, *Military Reform and Society in New Granada, 1773–1808*; Kuethe, *Cuba, 1753–1815*; and Archer, *The Army in Bourbon Mexico, 1760–1810*.

32. Fernández Hernández, *El Reino de Guatemala*, 173–74.

33. Ibid., 174–75.

34. Ibid., 175. According to numbers cited in Domínguez (*Insurrection*, 74–81) for other parts of the empire, the estimated figure of 10,000-plus troops for the defense of the Kingdom of Guatemala seems conservative. For the years 1767–1768, Jones puts the number at 30,000. *Milicias disciplinadas* are specially trained militia forces. Jones, *Guatemala*, 223.

35. Brown, *Juan Fermín de Aycinena*, 16–17.

36. Woodward, *Central America*, 78–79; Fernández Hernández, *El Reino de Guatemala*, 74.

37. Woodward, *Central America*, 74.

38. Pérez Brignoli, *De la ilustración al liberalismo*, 78–79.

39. Brown, *Juan Fermín de Aycinena*, 132–42, 147.

40. Fernández Hernández, *El Reino de Guatemala*, 82; see also Gustavo Palma Murga, "Nucleo de poder local y relaciones familiares en la ciudad de Guatemala a finales del siglo XVIII," *Mesoamérica* 12(December 1986):253–67.

41. Bumgartner, *José del Valle*, 14–22. See also Blake Pattridge, "University and Society in Nineteenth-Century Latin America: The University of San Carlos of Guatemala, 1821–1885" (Ph.D. diss., Tulane University, 1996).

42. Robert Shafer, "Ideas and Works of the Colonial Economic Societies, 1781–1820," *Revista de Historia de America* 44(December 1957):341.

43. Bumgartner, *José del Valle*, 41.

44. Pérez Brignoli, *De la ilustración al liberalismo*, 77; see also Pinto Soria, *Centroamérica*.

45. Woodward, *Central America*, 76.

46. Ibid., 80.

47. See, in particular, David McCreery, *Rural Guatemala 1750–1940* (Athens: University of Georgia Press, 1994).

48. Wortman, *Government and Society,* 138, 157–71.

49. See Wortman, "Government Revenue and Economic Trends," 278–80.

50. See Floyd, "The Guatemalan Merchants," 90–110.

51. R. L. Woodward, *Class Privilege and Economic Development: The Consulado de Comercio of Guatemala, 1793–1871* (Chapel Hill: University of North Carolina Press, 1966), xi–xiv.

52. Ibid., xiii.

53. Ibid., 20.

54. Wortman, *Government and Society,* 185–90.

55. R. L. Woodward, "The Economy of Central America at the Close of the Colonial Period," in *Estudios del Reino de Guatemala,* ed. Duncan Kinkead (Sevilla: Escuela de Estudios Hispano-Americanos, 1985), 125–27.

56. Wortman, *Government and Society,* 153.

57. Wortman, "Government Revenue and Economic Trends," 253.

58. Wortman, *Government and Society,* 152–53, 150 table.

3. The Imperial Crisis and Colonial Defense, 1798–1811

1. José Domás y Valle to Junta Superior, Guatemala, 21 October 1794, AGCA, A3, leg. 2165, exp. 32519.

2. Ibid.

3. Actas Capitulares, Guatemala City, 1808, AGCA, A1, leg. 2188, exp. 15734, fol. 74, 93. (The Actas Capitulares are records or minutes of city council meetings.)

4. The officials then renewed their oaths of fidelity to Ferdinand VII "and to the laws that presently govern us, while observing complete unity and conformity with the magistrates so that our Sacred Religion can be preserved unscathed and public order and tranquility can be preserved, and promising not to admit any foreign authority whatsoever." Actas Capitulares, Guatemala City, 1808, AGCA, A1, leg. 2188, exp. 15734, fol. 93.

5. Actas Capitulares, Guatemala City, 1808, AGCA, A1, leg. 2188, exp. 15734, fol. 108, 116; Salazar, *Historia de veintiún años,* 2:116. According to Simón Beragaño y Villegas there were "200 infantrymen in the militia and 40 dragoons" in Guatemala City in 1808. Bumgartner, *José del Valle,* 58.

6. Bumgartner, *José del Valle,* 58.

7. Demetrio Ramos Pérez, *España en la independencia de América* (Madrid: Editorial MAPFRE, 1986), 113.

8. For an overview see John Lynch, *The Spanish American Revolutions, 1808–1826* (New York: W. W. Norton & Company, 1973) or Jaime E. Rodríguez O., *The Independence of Spanish America* (Cambridge: Cambridge University Press, 1998).

9. *Causa* contra Simón Beragaño y Villegas, 1809, AGCA, B2, leg. 31, exp. 777; Bumgartner, *José del Valle,* 57–59.

10. Fernández Hernández, *El Reino de Guatemala*, 180.

11. Salazar, *Historia de veintiún años*, 1:116–17; also Fernández Hernández, *El Reino de Guatemala*, 179.

12. Bumgartner, *José del Valle*, 57.

13. The first official correspondence between Napoleon and Spanish America after the abdications at Bayonne was prepared on 17 May 1808. Included in the material that the emperor sent to Spanish officials in the Americas to convince them of the legality of the acts was a letter from the minister of foreign affairs, the comte de Champagny, that observed that "the dynasty has changed, but the Monarchy survives." Quoted in Carlos Villanueva, *Napoleón y la independencia de América* (Paris: Garnier Bros., 1912), 175.

14. See the correspondence between Napoleon and his minister of the navy published in Caracciolo Parra-Pérez, ed., *Bayona y la política de Napoleón en America* (Caracas: Tipografía americana, 1939), 61–65.

15. Napoleon's impact on the struggle for independence in the Americas has not been studied intensively for many years. The most important works on this topic, in addition to the Villanueva and Parra-Pérez studies cited above, are Ramos Pérez, *España en la independencia de America*, 215–18, and Enrique de Gandiá, *Napoleon y la independencia de America* (Buenos Aires: Editorial Antonio Zamora, 1955).

16. See Gandiá, *Napoleon y la independencia*, 192–93, 210.

17. Junta Central decree of 14 April 1809, AGCA, A1, leg. 4643, fol. 154.

18. Antonio González to Prudencio de Cózar, Guatemala, 3 August 1809, AGCA, A1, leg. 6111, exp. 56092.

19. Causa de infidencia contra Agustín Vilches, Guatemala City, 1809–1810, AGCA, B2, leg. 31, exp. 773.

20. Vilches, a well-educated, fifty-year-old *pardo* from Nicaragua, was probably an *afrancesado*. As of May 1811 he was still in prison in Guatemala. *Causa* contra Vilches, AGCA, B2, leg. 31, exp. 774–75.

21. Cózar to González, Guatemala, 10 July 1809, AGCA, A1, leg. 6093, exp. 55337.

22. Luís Aguilar contra el Regidor José Antonio Bustos, 1809, AGCA, A1, leg. 6920, exp. 56916.

23. The majority of the case against Valero can be found in *Causa* contra José Mariano Valero, 1808–1809, AGCA, B2, leg. 31, exp. 768–76.

24. Ibid., exp. 776, fol. 43.

25. Ibid.

26. Ibid.

27. See Polushin, "Bureaucratic Conquest, Bureaucratic Culture," for more on early nineteenth-century Chiapas.

28. *Real Orden*, 27 June 1809, AGCA, B1, leg. 5, exp. 136.

29. Ramos Pérez, *España en la independencia*, 219–22.

30. Ibid., 227.

31. Ibid., 228.

32. In late December 1809, the archbishop-viceroy of New Spain wrote to González expressing his concern about the imminent fall of Spain and what should be done in the

event it occurred. He noted the influence of French spies and remarked on the "zeal and prudence" of the captain general. AGCA, B1, leg. 5, exp. 152.

33. R. L. Woodward, "The Guatemalan Merchants and National Defense: 1810," *HAHR* 44(August 1964):453.

34. For more on late colonial creole consciousness see Saint-Lu, *Condición colonial.*

35. Aside from repeated declarations of loyalty and participation in the donativos patrióticos, the ayuntamiento of Guatemala City struck a commemorative medallion in honor of Ferdinand at the end of 1808 and sent exemplars to all the ayuntamientos of the kingdom. AGCA, B20, leg. 571, 575–81.

36. Each ayuntamiento in the colony chose three candidates for the position of deputy and then picked one name out of a hat to send to Guatemala City. The assembled names were reviewed by the *real acuerdo* and three were selected as finalists. The ultimate winner, Manuel José Pavón, was chosen in another blind draw. See Salazar, *Historia de veintiún años,* 1:119–21.

37. As Brian Hamnett states, the incorporation of creoles in the decision-making process, to the obvious detriment of traditional peninsular offices, would become more pronounced in the years to come with the establishment of diputaciones provinciales and ayuntamientos constitucionales. See Hamnett, "Mexico's Royalist Coalition," 65.

38. Quoted in Saint-Lu, *Condición colonial,* 180.

39. AGCA, A, leg. 2189, exp. 15736, fol. 27.

40. At the beginning of 1810 the following individuals sat on the ayuntamiento: José María Peinado and Antonio Palomo, alcaldes ordinarios; Marquis of Aycinena, Manuel José Pavón, José de Isasi, Sebastián Melón, Miguel González, and Juan Antonio de Aqueche, regidores; and Francisco Arrivillaga, síndico. AGCA, A, leg. 2189, exp. 15736, fol. 4. During the year deaths and replacements would add José Antonio Batres, Luís Francisco de Barrutia, Antonio de Juarros, Lorenzo Moreno, and Miguel Ignacio Alvares de Asturias.

41. AGCA, B, leg. 20, exp. 566, 586.

42. AGCA, A, leg. 2189, exp. 15736, fol. 15; see also Woodward's treatment of this debate in "The Guatemalan Merchants," 452–62.

43. AGCA, A, leg. 2189, exp. 15736, fol. 16.

44. Ibid., fol. 31.

45. The following account is drawn from the 1811 Capitanía Indiferente entitled *Sobre que se ponga en estado de defensa este Reyno,* AGCA, B, leg. 32, exp. 783.

46. González spent most of April and the first half of May taking the baths at Antigua in an attempt to alleviate what was described as his "mal de nervios." As a result, he officially delegated his governing authority to Méndez for the duration of his absence from the capital. AGCA, B, leg. 20, exp. 590. The ayuntamiento, however, expressed its concern over this, with Regidor Juarros stating that the public was not happy with the fact that Méndez had married a French woman. AGCA, A, leg. 2189, exp. 15736, fol. 34.

47. The junta determined the peacetime prices for these arms to be the following: one musket, 11 pesos; one pair of pistols, 5 pesos; one sword, 3 pesos. AGCA, B, leg. 32, exp. 783, fol. 9.

48. Ibid., fol. 11.

49. Woodward, "The Guatemalan Merchants," 454. The junta reports published here can also be found in AGCA, B, leg. 32, exp. 783, fols. 15v–26.

50. AGCA, A, leg. 2189, exp. 15736, fol. 34v.

51. AGCA, B, leg. 32, exp. 783, fols. 34, 38, 39; see also AGCA, A, leg. 2189, exp. 15736, fol. 42, and AGCA, B, leg. 20, exp. 586.

52. This extract and the following summary were drawn from the expediente entitled *Medidas de seguridad dictado por el Superior Gobierno contra los emisarios franceses,* AGCA, A, leg. 6112, exp. 56127. It includes the colonial government's ordinances of 22 April and 10 May and official correspondence between the captain general and the alcalde mayor of Totonicapán during the month of May in which the subject of French subversion is discussed, names of emissaries are listed, and provincial *bandos* issued by the alcalde mayor are added.

53. These directives are included in a letter dated 15 May from the captain general to Prudencio de Cózar, alcalde mayor of Totonicapán. AGCA, A, leg. 6112, exp. 56127. The naval commander of Montevideo, José María Salazar, imposed similar restrictions on his colony following reports of espionage activity and French naval squadrons in the vicinity. See José María Salazar to Antonio de Escaño, 8 February 1810, and Salazar to Gabriel de Ciscar, 20 June 1810, AGM, leg. 620-1092.

54. González to Cózar, 17 May 1810, AGCA, A, leg. 6112, exp. 56127.

55. *Providencias de Seguridad contra los Emisarios del intruso Govierno Frances,* AGCA, B, leg. 3, exp. 48. The names of the emissaries in the Americas apparently came from English intelligence and were passed to officials across the empire by Spain's minister to the United States. For the complete list of the agents and a purported letter of instructions, see Villanueva, *Napoleón y la independencia de América,* 237–46.

56. Bando from Prudencio de Cózar to the inhabitants of the alcaldía mayor of Totonicapán, 28 May 1810, AGCA, A, leg. 6112, exp. 56127.

57. AGCA, B, leg. 23, exp. 687, fol. 27. O'Horan spent four years in prison before being exiled in 1814 to his home province of Campeche.

58. AGCA, B, leg. 32, exp. 781.

59. Ibid.

60. AGCA, B, leg. 32, exp. 783.

61. Isidro Sicilia, *Nos el Dr. D. Isidro Sicilia, Dean de esta Santa Iglesia Metropolitana de Guatemala, Provisor, Vicario Capitular, y Gobernador del Arzobispado,* 4 January 1811. Decree in the Papers of Alejandro Marure, Ayer Collection, Newberry Library, Chicago.

62. Isidro Sicilia, *Nos el Doctor Don Isidro Sicilia Arce-Dean de esta Santa Metropolitana Yglesia, Provisor Gobernador y Vicario capitular de este Arzobispado,* 23 May 1810. Decree in the Papers of Alejandro Marure, Ayer Collection, Newberry Library, Chicago.

63. AGCA, A, leg. 2214, exp. 15866. This expediente includes the official decree and the measures taken by the ayuntamiento of Guatemala City to comply with the order.

64. Manifesto issued by the captain general, 22 May 1810, AGCA, B, leg. 1, exp. 29.

65. Salazar, *Historia de veintiún años,* 1:128.

66. Ibid.

67. Notes from the first meeting of the tribunal, 9 June 1810, AGCA, A, leg. 6093, exp. 55344, fol. 53.

68. Hamnett, "Mexico's Royalist Coalition," 63.

69. Anna, *The Fall of the Royal Government in Mexico City*, 60.

70. *Inventorio de los negocios pertenecientes al Tribunal Superior de Fidelidad del Reino de Guatemala*, AGCA, A, leg. 6921, exp. 56919.

71. Salazar, *Historia de veintiún años*, 1:134.

72. Hamnett, "Mexico's Royalist Coalition," 63.

73. In a not untypical case from Santa Ana involving a man named Francisco Cienfuegos and his brothers, both sides in the dispute traded charges of disloyalty and appealed to Ferdinand. AGCA, A, leg. 6921, exp. 56923.

74. AGCA, A, leg. 2189, exp. 15736; AGCA, B, leg. 1, exp. 29.

75. The following information is taken from the Actas Capitulares of 1810, AGCA, A, leg. 2189, exp. 15736, fol. 51v–56v.

76. AGCA, A, leg. 2189, exp. 15736, fol. 61. In a ten-page dissenting opinion, Regidores Peinado, Aycinena, Barrutia, and Juarros argued that the transfer of legitimate authority from the Junta Central to the council was not an act of the entire Spanish nation, as it should have been, but rather an illegal imposition.

77. Ibid., fol. 68.

78. Quoted in Barón Castro, *José Matías Delgado*, 95.

79. Ibid.

80. AGCA, A, leg. 2189, exp. 15736, fol. 74.

81. This quote and the following information are taken from the expediente found in AGCA, B, leg. 3, exp. 44.

82. Mario Rodríguez does the best job analyzing the *Instrucciones* and placing it in the context of the wider political movements of the time in his *The Cádiz Experiment*.

83. *Instrucciones para la constitución fundamental de la monarquía española y su gobierno de que ha de tratarse en las próximas Cortes Generales de la Nación dadas por el M.I. Ayuntamiento de la M.N.Y.L. Ciudad de Guatemala* (Guatemala: Editorial del Ministerio de Educación Pública, 1953). See also Salazar, *Historia de veintiún años*, 1:131; Woodward, "Economic and Social Origins of the Guatemalan Political Parties (1773–1823)," *HAHR* 45(November 1965):557.

84. AGCA, A, leg. 2189, exp. 15736, fols. 87v–89v, 95. The dissenters were Alcalde Moreno and Regidores Isasi, Melón, and Aqueche.

85. D. León Fernández, ed., *Documentos relativos a los movimientos de independencia en el reino de Guatemala* (hereinafter cited as *DRMIRG*) (San Salvador: Ministerio de Instruccion Pública de El Salvador, 1929), 3.

86. Ibid.; AGCA, A, leg. 2189, exp. 15736, fol. 95.

87. AGCA, B, leg. 3, exp. 48.

88. AGCA, A, leg. 2189, exp. 15737, fol. 1v.

89. Quoted in Barón Castro, *José Matías Delgado*, 97.

90. AGCA, A, leg. 2189, exp. 15736, fol. 117.

91. Ibid., fol. 148; AGCA, A, leg. 2189, exp. 15737, fol. 21v.

92. AGCA, A, leg. 2189, exp. 15737, fol. 15.

93. AGCA, B, leg. 20, exp. 613.

94. Bustamante to Ayuntamiento, 16 July 1810, AGCA, B, leg. 20, exp. 582, 583.

95. AGCA, A, leg. 2189, exp. 15737, fol. 35.

96. Ibid., fol. 37.

4. The Preservation of Empire, 1811

1. Actas Capitulares, 1811, AGCA, A, leg. 2189, exp. 15737, fols. 17v, 24, 26, 37–38, 41.

2. Ibid., fols. 30v, 40–41.

3. The regidores returned to the town hall furious after having been preempted in their welcoming duties by Bernardo Martínez of the *cabildo ecclesiástico* when by law they had precedent. For this and details of Bustamante's arrival see AGCA, A, leg. 2189, exp. 15737, fol. 43–43v.

4. *Libro de Títulos*, 1811–1815, AGCA, A, leg. 2651, exp. 22247.

5. Bustamante to Ayuntamiento, 24 March 1811, *Boletín del Archivo General del Gobierno* (hereinafter cited as *BAGG*), vol. 3, no. 4 (July 1938): 491–92.

6. Bustamante to Ayuntamiento, *BAGG*, 3:490.

7. AGCA, A, leg. 2189, exp. 15737, fol. 51.

8. José de Bustamante, *El Presidente Gobernador*, 1–4.

9. Ibid., 5.

10. Ibid., 7.

11. Ibid., 9. On 3 September 1811 Bustamante summarized his views on Central American development in a report to the Council of State. In it he explained that he was using military forces along the coast to enforce his anticontraband policies. See the letter from Jose de Limonta to the Secretary of State, 24 April 1812, AGI, Audiencia de Guatemala, leg. 417.

12. Bustamante, *El Presidente Gobernador*, 10–11.

13. Ibid., 11.

14. Ibid., 12.

15. Ibid., 12–13.

16. Ibid., 13.

17. Oscar R. Benítez Porta, *Secesión pacífica de Guatemala de España: ensayo histórico-político* (Guatemala: Editorial "José de Pineda Ibarra," 1973), 184–85.

18. Quoted in Barón Castro, *José Matías Delgado*, 118, n. 8.

19. Ramón Casaus to Kingdom of Guatemala, 13 May 1811, *BAGG*, 3:492.

20. AGCA, A, leg. 2189, exp. 15737, fol. 60–61, 64v.

21. AGCA, B, leg. 5, exp. 142.

22. AGCA, A, leg. 2189, exp. 15737, fols. 78v, 84.

23. Though appreciative of the tip, Bustamante was confident enough to respond to Venegas that he had already taken steps to prevent the introduction of "personas sospechosas" into the kingdom and had provided clear and precise instructions on the subject to all judges, magistrates, port commanders, and other officials. This led him to state

that "no me parece tan proxima la introduccion de viles emisarios." Bustamante to
Venegas, 18 June 1811, Archivo General de la Nación, Infidencias, vol. 165, exp. 43, 166.

24. AGCA, A, leg. 2189, exp. 15737, fol. 89.

25. AGCA, A, leg. 6113, exp. 56224.

26. Bustamante to Narciso Mallol, 15 June 1811, AGCA, A, leg. 6113, exp. 56162; Bustamante to Mallol, 25 June 1811, AGCA, A, leg. 6113, exp. 56237.

27. Bustamante to Mallol, 18 June 1811, AGCA, A, leg. 6113, exp. 56216.

28. Mallol to Bustamante, 4 July 1811, AGCA, A, leg. 6113, exp. 56212.

29. Ibid.

30. Bustamante to Mallol, 2 August 1811, AGCA, A, leg. 6113, exp. 56239.

31. Bustamante to Mallol, 3 August 1811, AGCA, A, leg. 6113, exp. 56230.

32. Ibid.

33. Bustamante to Mallol, 9 September 1811, AGCA, A, leg. 6113, exp. 56231.

34. Hermenegildo López to Mallol, 21 September 1811, AGCA, A, leg. 6113, exp. 56194.

35. Nasario Argueta to Mallol, 24 September 1811, AGCA, A, leg. 6113, exp. 56193.

36. Marcos Castañeda to Mallol, 9 October 1811, AGCA, A, leg. 6113, exp. 56139.

37. Bustamante to Mallol, 13 September 1811, AGCA, A, leg. 6113, exp. 56183.

38. This description reads: "Es alto de cuerpo, grueso, lleno de cara, bermejo, pelo
cortado al la frente, naríz larga y abultada, ojos grandes azules, dentadura blanca com-
pleta, patilla hta la barba= edad de 30 a 35 a, vestido de lebita o fraqe, de paño celeste de
primera, con gorrita de pico alto, cinturon negro de lustre laboreado de plata=Caballo
tordillo flaco, herrado de los quatro pies, silla brida, anquera de paño azul con fleco
amarillo, estribera de plata." AGCA, A, leg. 6113, exp. 56150.

39. Mallol decree, 11 November 1811, AGCA, A, leg. 6113, exp. 56150.

40. Mallol to Bustamante, 6 December 1811, AGCA, A, leg. 6113, exp. 56209.

41. *Inventario de los negocios pertenecientes al Tribunal Superior de Fidelidad del
Reino de Guatemala*, AGCA, A, leg. 6921, exp. 56919.

42. Contra Manuel Osorio, AGCA, A, leg. 6921, exp. 56920; Contra Tomás Torres,
AGCA, A, leg. 6921, exp. 56925.

43. Contra Encarnación Balladares por ciertas palabras de infidencia, AGCA, A, leg.
6921, exp. 56934.

44. Report of Oidor Fiscal González, 26 July 1811, Contra Pedro Barriere, AGCA, A,
leg. 6921, exp. 56924.

45. Ibid.

46. Actas Capitulares, 1811, AGCA, A, leg. 2189, exp. 15737 fol. 97.

47. AGCA, A, leg. 2189, exp. 15737, fol. 109v.

48. Ibid., fol. 128v.

49. Ibid., fol. 132.

50. See, for example, the correspondence from the ayuntamiento of la Villa de Nica-
ragua to Guatemala City, 4 June and 5 July 1811, AGCA, B, leg. 496, exp. 8449, 8451; San
Salvador to Guatemala City, 28 June 1811, AGCA, B, leg. 496, exp. 8450; San Miguel to
Guatemala City, 27 June 1811, AGCA, B, leg. 20, exp. 608; and Ciudad Real to Guatemala
City, 16 July 1811, AGCA, B, leg. 20, exp. 605.

51. AGCA, A, leg. 2189, exp. 15737, fol. 132v.

52. *Representación del M.N.Y.L. Ayuntamiento de Guatemala al Excelentisimo Señor D. José de Bustamante* . . . , 7 June 1811, in the papers of Rafael Heliodoro Valle, Biblioteca Nacional of Mexico, Mexico City.

53. Ibid.

54. Ibid., 36.

55. Ayuntamiento de Quezaltenango to Ayuntamiento de Guatemala, 8 October 1811, AGCA, B, leg. 496, exp. 8454; AGCA, A, leg. 2189, exp. 15737, fol. 145.

56. Hamnett, "Mexico's Royalist Coalition," 65. For more on these institutions see chapter three of Rodríguez O., *The Independence of Spanish America.*

57. AGCA, A, leg. 2189, exp. 15737, fol. 139, 142v.

58. Bustamante to Ayuntamiento, 15 October 1811, AGCA, A, leg. 2189, exp. 15737, fol. 151.

59. The Family was well represented, with the Marquis of Aycinena leading the list of captains. Other elite names included José María and Manuel Peinado, Luís Barrutia, Juan Bautista de Marticorena, Gregorio and José de Urruela, Mariano and Pedro Beltranena, Antonio Palomo, Miguel and Juan Bautista Asturias, Lorenzo Moreno, Domingo Pavón, Antonio and Francisco Arrivillaga, Francisco Pacheco, Mariano Gálvez, Pedro Batres, and Manuel Montúfar. AGCA, A, leg. 2189, exp. 15737, fol. 152.

60. Bustamante to Ayuntamiento, 8 November 1811, *BAGG,* 3:367.

61. Bustamante to Ayuntamiento, 12 November 1811, *BAGG,* 3:368. In an 8 November pastoral, Archbishop Casaus threatened excommunication to "los que tengan pasquines, o papeles sediciosos y subversivos y no los entreguen; o no denuncien a los autores y propagadores de ellos, y a los que siembran la cizaña de la discordia civil." Francisco Monterrey, *Historia de El Salvador: anotaciones cronológicas, 1810–1842* (San Salvador: Editorial Universitaria, 1977), vol. 1, 19; Salazar, *Manuel José Arce,* 5.

62. AGCA, A, leg. 2189, exp. 15737, fol. 163.

63. Bustamante to Ayuntamiento, 12 November 1811, *BAGG,* 3:368.

64. Agustín Estrada Monroy, "La Iglesia en la independencia de Centroamerica," *Estudios Centroamericanos* 26(October–November 1971):662. For the entire letter see Estrada Monroy, *Datos para la Historia de la Iglesia en Guatemala,* vol. 2 (Guatemala: Sociedad de Geografía e Historia de Guatemala, 1974), 239–41.

65. In an 1813 report to the Council of Regency on the unrest in Central America, Bustamante wrote that he was so concerned about the political climate in San Salvador that he had seven hundred muskets and over one hundred thousand pesos removed from the provincial capital in August 1811, more than two months before the outbreak of insurrection. Bustamante to Council of Regency, 3 March 1813, *Revista de la Academia Hondureña de Geografía e Historia* (hereinafter cited as *RAHGH*), vol. 55 (January–June 1972), 57.

66. See the Proclamation of the Ayuntamiento of San Salvador, 7 November 1811, in Monterrey, *Historia de El Salvador,* vol. 1, 16–18. Also, see the dissertation by Adolfo Bonilla Bonilla, "The Central American Enlightenment 1770–1838: An Interpretation of Political Ideas and Political History" (University of Manchester, England, 1996), 289–92.

See also Barón Castro, *José Matías Delgado*, 139–40; Marure, *Bosquejo histórico*, 1:5–6; Bancroft, *History of Central America*, 3:13–14; and Rodríguez, *The Cádiz Experiment*, 103.

67. Benito Molina to José Antonio Bustos, 10 November 1811, AGCA, B, leg. 22, exp. 670; AGCA, A, leg. 2189, exp. 15737, fol. 161v.

68. Domingo Payes to Audiencia, 23 November 1811, AGCA, B, leg. 22, exp. 680; Antonio Gutiérrez to Audiencia, 18 November 1811, AGCA, B, leg. 22, exp. 681.

69. AGCA, B, leg. 22, exp. 681; Monterrey, *Historia de El Salvador*, vol. 1, 19.

70. AGCA, A, leg. 2189, exp. 15737, fol. 154; the *oficio* is found in fol. 155.

71. Similar declarations of loyalty can be found in responses to the 12 November proclamation from the ayuntamientos of Tegucigalpa, 7 December 1811, AGCA, B, leg. 38, exp. 862, and Nicaragua, 23 November 1811, AGCA, B, leg. 22, exp. 670, not to mention the town councils of San Miguel, San Vicente, and Santa Ana.

72. Ayuntamiento of León to Ayuntamiento of Guatemala City, 29 November 1811, AGCA, B, leg. 38, exp. 837. In a letter very similar in tone to that of the Leonese, the ayuntamiento of San Salvador also expressed its satisfaction with the Guatemalan stand against Napoleonic machinations, that is, the efforts of French emissaries to promote unrest and divisions between creoles and peninsulars. This reply demonstrates clearly that the Central American creole elite was most concerned about challenges to order from below and still saw a place for Spain in colonial government. Ayuntamiento of San Salvador to Ayuntamiento of Guatemala City, 26 November 1811, AGCA, B, leg. 38, exp. 842.

73. AGCA, A, leg. 2189, exp. 15737, fol. 159v.

74. Bustamante to Council of Regency, 3 March 1813, *RAHGH*, 59.

75. See Barón Castro, *José Matías Delgado*, 203–5. Details on the Guatemalan reception in San Salvador can be found in the many dispatches from Aycinena and Peinado to the ayuntamiento of Guatemala City during November and December, AGCA, B, leg. 22, exp. 677–79, and AGCA, B, leg. 38.

76. Aycinena to Ayuntamiento of Guatemala City, 10 December 1811, AGCA, B, leg. 22, exp. 677.

77. The phrases *restablecimiento de la tranquilidad pública* and *restablecimiento de quietud* appear so frequently in the correspondence between Aycinena and the ayuntamientos of San Salvador and Guatemala City at this time that such goals must be considered a clear expression of the creole elite mentality toward insurrection. Both Aycinena and the Salvadorans showered the Guatemalan ayuntamiento—and at times Bustamante—with praise for leading the way to peace and tranquility. See AGCA, B, leg. 38, exp. 838, 840, 841; AGCA, B, leg. 22, exp. 677.

78. José María de Hoyos to Ayuntamiento of Guatemala City, 19 November 1811, AGCA, B, leg. 38, exp. 859.

79. Details of the revolt come from a report to the audiencia by Domingo Payes, who was requesting royal support in the recovery of his property, 23 November 1811, AGCA, B, leg. 22, exp. 680.

80. AGCA, B, leg. 22, exp. 676, 682.

81. *Sobre la Sublevacion de Metapán*, AGCA, B, leg. 26, exp. 715–17.

82. Ibid. Aycinena was thrilled with the way in which order was restored in Metapán. He offered Martínez more substantial assistance in case it proved necessary but hoped that "los medios suaves nacidos de las paternales entrañas del Exmo. Sr. Presidente" would be enough to maintain tranquility. Aycinena to Martínez, 26 November 1811, AGCA, B, leg. 26, exp. 716.

83. Testimony of José Planas, AGCA, B, leg. 26, exp. 716.

84. Witness testimony against Mayorga can be found in *Contra Don Juan De Dios Mayorga, de Metapan, por Sedicioso*, AGCA, B, leg. 26, exp. 717. Persecuted as a subversive during Bustamante's administration, by 1818 Mayorga was the elected mayor of Metapán. He later became an official in the Central American Federation.

85. AGCA, B, leg. 26, exp. 715, 717.

86. In his *Historia de veintiún años*, Ramón Salazar argues that the Leonese revolts were instigated and directed by Benito Miguelena, a Mercedarian friar and native of Guatemala, who also had a role in the Belén conspiracy of 1813. I have seen no direct evidence to confirm this, however. See Salazar, *Historia de veintiún años*, 2:166. The Leonese ayuntamiento argued strongly in a letter to the audiencia that the uprising was a result of long-standing frustrations with the administration of Intendant Salvador. See, Ayuntamiento of León to Audiencia, 30 January 1812, AGCA, A, leg. 6922, exp. 56949.

87. Junta Gubernativa de León to Bustamante, 20 December 1811, in *DRMIRG*, 9–15; Junta Provincial Gubernativa to Bustamante, 15 December 1811, AGCA, B, leg. 24, exp. 688; Chester Zelaya, *Nicaragua en la independencia* (San José: Editorial Universitaria Centroamericana, 1971), 70–71; Bustamante to Council of Regency, 3 March 1813, *RAHGH*, 60; Salazar, *Historia de veintiún años*, 2:166–68.

88. Reports from the ayuntamiento of Cartago, 28 December 1811 and 3 March 1812, in D. León Fernandez, ed., *Colección de documentos para la historia de Costa Rica* (hereinafter cited as *CDHCR*), vol. 10 (Barcelona: Imprenta de Viuda de Luís Tasso, 1907), 344, 366.

89. Aycinena to Ayuntamiento of Guatemala, 29 December 1811, AGCA, B, leg. 24, exp. 689; AGCA, B, leg. 24, exp. 690–91.

90. Junta de León to Ayuntamiento of Guatemala, 20 December 1811, AGCA, B, leg. 24, exp. 692.

91. At the same time, the towns of Rivas, Masaya, and Nicaragua experienced minor disturbances. For the Granada uprising see Salazar, *Historia de veintiún años*, 2:167–68; Bancroft, *History of Central America*, 3:15–16; Zelaya, *Nicaragua en la independencia*, 75.

92. Ayuntamiento of Granada to Ayuntamiento of Guatemala, 25 January 1812, AGCA, B, leg. 24, exp. 693.

93. *Informe del capitan general de Guatemala al secretario de Gracia y Justicia*, 30 January 1812, *DRMIRG*, 17.

94. Ibid., 20.

95. José de Bustamante to the Kingdom of Guatemala regarding the rules for the establishment of the Cuerpos de milicias honradas, 23 December 1811, AGCA, A, leg. 2189, exp. 15737.

96. Ibid.; *Informe del capitan general de Guatemala al secretario de Gracia y Justicia*, 30 January 1812, *DRMIRG*, 23.

5. The Counterinsurgency State, 1812

1. This account of the Tegucigalpa uprisings comes from the *causa* against Julián Romero, AGCA, A, leg. 6922, exp. 56939, 56946.

2. According to Bustamante, the *pueblo* "no tuvo por objeto sacudir el que los inquietos denominan yugo español, ni perseguir a los europeos, ni aspirar a la independencia." Instead, they simply wanted the removal of the hated subdelegado, who happened to be a creole. Bustamante to Council of Regency, 3 March 1813, *DRMIRG*, 61.

3. AGCA, A, leg. 6922, exp. 56946.

4. Ibid.

5. Ibáñez report on the case of Romero and Rojas, 1 July 1812, AGCA, A, leg. 6922, exp. 56946.

6. Bustamante to Council of Regency, 3 March 1813, *DRMIRG*, 62.

7. The case against Gordón is found in AGCA, B, leg. 33, exp. 789, and AGCA, B, leg. 34, exp. 790, 792.

8. Unsigned letter [probably written by Gordón] of 3 January 1812, AGCA, B, leg. 33, exp. 789.

9. The following account is drawn from the *causa* against Francisco Cordón, found in AGCA, B, leg. 28, exp. 723–25, 728, 730, 732–33, 735, 736. When reviewing the sentences of those involved in the uprising, the king cited as a mitigating factor the fact that the *Gaceta de Guatemala* of 13 February 1812 had published reports from the *intruso* court at Madrid regarding plans for French expeditions to the Americas.

10. Bustamante to Castejón, 24 April 1812, AGCA, B, leg. 26, exp. 717, fol. 4.

11. *Sobre se juzgue en Consejo de Guerra al Mtro. Dn Antonio Marure*, AGCA, B, leg. 32, exp. 788.

12. Bustamante to Audiencia, 3 January 1812, AGCA, A, leg. 6922, exp. 56949.

13. In a 13 April 1812 letter to their Guatemalan counterparts, the regidores of Nueva Segovia argued that the 12 November proclamation by the Guatemala City ayuntamiento helped persuade them to remain loyal to the established order, "unico y capaz para mantener el orden, gozar de la paz, y defenderse de la astusia seductora de los Emisarios directos o indirectos del execrable Napoleon," AGCA, B, leg. 24, exp. 696.

14. Bustamante to Secretario de Gracia y Justicia, 30 January and 3 March 1812, *DRMIRG*, 17–23, 25–28.

15. Bustamante ultimatum, 3 February 1812, *DRMIRG*, 29–31.

16. Bustamante to García Jerez, 3 February 1812, *DRMIRG*, 33–35.

17. AGCA, B, leg. 6, exp. 220; García Jerez to Bustamante, 20 February 1812, *DRMIRG*, 37–40.

18. García Jerez to Bustamante, 21 February 1812, *DRMIRG*, 41–44.

19. Bustamante *oficio* of 3 March 1812, *DRMIRG*, 45–48; also AGCA, B, leg. 24, exp. 694. One year later, Bustamante explained that he always felt active-duty military forces

were essential to the success of his policy of *conciliación prudente*, in order to "situarlos en los parajes oportunas para acudir con rapidez a las provincias conmovidas, con el fin de imponer respeto a todas y ocurrir con la fuerza donde fuese necesaria." He stated that by the time of the Granada crisis he was able to mobilize some four thousand troops. Bustamante to Council of Regency, 3 March 1813, *DRMIRG*, 60–61.

20. Bustamante to García Jerez, 3 March 1812, *DRMIRG*, 49–51. The pardon affected the intendancy of San Salvador as well. On 4 March, Bustamante authorized the audiencia to release the Metapán and Santa Ana prisoners under its provisions. AGCA, B, leg. 24, exp. 694.

21. The case against Artica is found in AGCA, A, leg. 6922, exp. 56938.

22. As Artica received his punishment, Gutiérrez reportedly yelled, "Tu infame esclavo pretendiente insurrectarme el Batallón en Olancho y te dejé preso y huyendote de las Carceles, has venido siguiendome hasta esta Villa a insurrectarme el Batallón, y asi por vil esclavo os tengo de asotar." AGCA, A, leg. 6922, exp. 56938.

23. Artica's case was remitted to the captaincy general and judged to be a crime of infidencia, which fell under military jurisdiction. The official investigation began on 15 June 1812 and was not completed until 23 May 1814. In the final ruling, *Auditor de guerra* Joaquín Ibáñez completely exonerated Artica of the charges against him. AGCA, A, leg. 6922, exp. 56938.

24. The case against Martínez is collected in AGCA, B, leg. 82, exp. 2377.

25. Martínez completely denied these accusations and received a great deal of support from the bishop of Comayagua, who described the creole priest as above suspicion. Soldiers from the battalion also testified in his favor. Again, the process took two years to complete, but in the end Bustamante accepted the decision of his *auditor de guerra* to absolve Martínez on 2 April 1814. AGCA, B, leg. 82, exp. 2377.

26. Carrascosa had orders to "averiguar los autos de la convulcion, personas que la fomentaron, y quienes dirigieron la temeraria resistencia que se opuso a las tropas Reales quando entraron en la ciudad." AGCA, B, leg. 81, exp. 2365. For more on the Granada uprising, see Salazar, *Historia de veintiún años*, 2:167–68; Bancroft, *History of Central America*, 3:15–16; Zelaya, *Nicaragua en la independencia*, 75. Evidence for the degree to which the military confrontation affected Bustamante can be found in the case brought against thirteen soldiers of Granada's Fixed Infantry Battalion, who were charged with firing on the royalist army. After a rapid court martial, on 20 November 1812 Bustamante sentenced them to eight years' imprisonment at the Spanish North African fortress of Ceuta, a punishment one called "a little less than capital." After many appeals, however, they were ordered to Omoa, Guatemala, where they were pardoned in 1818. AGCA, A, leg. 72, exp. 1484.

27. Rodríguez, *The Cádiz Experiment*, 104. The nature of the Mexican counterinsurgency model has been the subject of much recent study. In addition to Hamill, Anna, and Hamnett, see Archer, ed., *The Birth of Modern Mexico*; Van Young, *The Other Rebellion*; Guedea, *La insurgencia en el Departamento del Norte*; and Tutino, *From Insurrection to Revolution in Mexico*. See also Juan Ortíz Escamilla, *Guerra y gobierno: Los pueblos y la independencia de México* (Mexico: Instituto de Investigaciones José María Luís Mora,

1997), and Peter Guardino, *Peasants, Politics, and the Formation of Mexico's National State: Guerrero, 1800–1857* (Stanford: Stanford University Press, 1996). Bustamante sympathized with his viceregal counterpart and drew inspiration from many of the unprecedented measures implemented in Mexico to combat insurrection. However, whether through prudence or a heightened sensitivity to the precariousness of his position, he did not unleash in the kingdom of Guatemala the kind of military or political terror that became commonplace in New Spain.

28. Anna, *The Fall of the Royal Government in Mexico City,* 66.

29. Ibid., 77–81. Details on the April plot and Venegas's bando on passports, which was published in February 1811, can be found in J. E. Hernández y Dávalos, *Colección de documentos para la historia de la guerra de independencia de Mexico de 1808 a 1821,* vol. 5 (Mexico: José María Sandoval, Impresor, 1881), 244–46, 867–72; Venegas's proclamations on the August conspiracy are in vol. 3, 332–34.

30. As Hugh Hamill notes, its caseload was five times greater than that of the *Sala del Crímen* between 1810 and 1812. In the four months after Venegas's imposition of martial law, 350 people came before it. Hamill, "Royalist Counterinsurgency," 481–82.

31. Hamill, "Royalist Counterinsurgency," 479.

32. Felix María Calleja, "Civil Defense Regulations of June 8, 1811," in *Problems in Latin American History,* ed. Joseph S. Tulchin (New York: Harper & Row, 1973), 43–46.

33. José de la Cruz to Calleja, 18 April 1811, quoted in Hamill, "Royalist Counterinsurgency," 483.

34. Ibid., 483–84.

35. Venegas's bando of 25 June 1812, AGCA, B, leg. 24, exp. 701, fol. 35.

36. Wortman, *Government and Society,* 205–6; Cartago Ayuntamiento to Bustamante, 3 March 1812, *CDHCR,* 366–68.

37. Decree regarding the establishment of the superintendency of police, AGCA, B, leg. 7, exp. 290.

38. Ibid.

39. Oidor fiscal on superintendency of police, AGCA, B, leg. 7, exp. 290.

40. *Contra el Yndio Manuel Paz,* AGCA, A, leg. 6922, exp. 56945; Bustamante's interest was so piqued that he wrote back and asked the alcalde mayor to keep him informed about the progress of the investigation, Bustamante to Mallol, 30 January 1812, AGCA, A, leg. 6114, exp. 56319.

41. AGCA, A, leg. 6922, exp. 56945, fols. 2–3.

42. Ibid., fol. 4.

43. AGCA, A, leg. 6115, exp. 56349, 56396.

44. Mallol to inhabitants of Totonicapán, 26 September 1812, AGCA, A, leg. 6115, exp. 56383.

45. Bustamante decree on the donativo patriótico, 10 April 1812, AGCA, B, leg. 76, exp. 2249.

46. Anna, *The Fall of the Royal Government in Mexico City,* 151–53.

47. Donativo Patriótico, AGCA, B, leg. 76, exp. 2249.

48. Ibid. Despite the compulsory nature of the donation, it did not appear to go very

far in relieving the kingdom's financial problems. The town of Santa Maria Magdalena de Macholoa, in the province of Comayagua, responded that it was happy to contribute but could only collect thirty-one pesos. A similar response came from Guatemala City. The municipality declared that it would have to see whether its deficient treasury would permit a donation. AGCA, A, leg. 6922, exp. 56940; AGCA, A, leg. 2190, exp. 15738, fol. 32v.

49. *Carta Circular del Illmó. y Revmó. Sr. Dr. y Mtró. D. Fr. Ramón Casaus y Torres . . . ,* 20 April 1812. Decree in the papers of Alejandro Marure, Ayer Collection, Newberry Library, Chicago.

50. *Real Orden,* 25 August 1811, AGCA, B, leg. 5, exp. 190. The 18 February decree is found in AGCA, B, leg. 5, exp. 177. Despite the best intentions, the reality confronting colonial officials during the independence period often inhibited a smooth functioning of the system. With the 25 August order in front of him, the alcalde ordinario of León wrote the audiencia on 10 February 1812 to say that he recognized the tribunal's authority over the imprisoned *reos de infidencia.* However, he explained that he could not send the prisoners to Guatemala City for lack of funds and fear that they would be freed by rebels on the way. AGCA, A, leg. 6922, exp. 56948.

51. Decree of Council of Regency, 6 October 1811, inserted in Proclamation of Bustamante, 13 April 1812, AGCA, A, leg. 6090, exp. 55243. The decree reads in part: "Que el conocimiento del delito de trato de infidencia por espías o de otra forma que ataca y ofende directamente los medios de defensa, e inutiliza los esfuerzos de las armas en los Exercitos y Plazas, sea privativo como lo ha sido hasta aqui de la jurisdiccion militar en el modo y forma prescripta en la ordenanza general del Exercito, para los casos y delitos en que la jurisdiccion militar conoce de reos independientes de ella."

52. Bustamante Proclamation of 13 April 1812, AGCA, A, leg. 6090, exp. 55243.

53. Ibid.

54. Gordón chose as his defender José Francisco Barrundia, who later became a fierce advocate for independence. AGCA, B, leg. 33, exp. 789.

55. *Sobre que se juzgue en Consejo de Guerra don Antonio Marure,* AGCA, B, leg. 32, exp. 788.

56. Report of Oidor Fiscal González to Audiencia, 9 July 1812, AGCA, A, leg. 4567, exp. 39186. In the case of Julián Romero, Bustamante ultimately accepted the audiencia's claim of jurisdiction after asking for its opinion on the matter. Still, it took months of wrangling between the two sides before the issue was settled. AGCA, A, leg. 6922, exp. 56939.

57. Gordón's brother made an appeal on 20 July 1812; María Teresa Escobar, Mayorga's wife, wrote on 19 August; and on 6 October, Margarita Villavicencio, the wife of Marure, issued a plea on behalf of her husband, Gordón, and Fulgencio Morales. See AGCA, A, leg. 6922, exp. 56951 and 56936.

58. The course of this debate can be found in AGCA, B, leg. 32, exp. 788.

59. Bustamante report of 6 October 1812, AGCA, A, leg. 6922, exp. 56936. The delay that this debate caused took its toll on the prisoners, both physically and emotionally. On 5 October, during one of the prescribed visits to the various prisons in the capital, a frustrated Mayorga, who refused to recognize military jurisdiction over his case, confronted

Oidor Serrano Polo. The prisoner asked the oidor whether he was in jail by arrangement of the audiencia. After learning his name, Serrano Polo replied that he was under the authority of the captain general, to whom any complaints should be addressed. Unsatisfied, Mayorga asked the same question to the alcalde primero and then to the alcalde segundo, receiving the same answer each time. Finally, in a rising tone, he exclaimed, "well, if I am not here because of the audiencia or the alcaldes ordinarios, then tell the bailiff to come and set me free!" AGCA, B, leg. 26, exp. 716.

60. *Carta Acordada* from the Council of Regency, 2 July 1812, AGCA, B, leg. 6, exp. 243.

61. Ibid.

62. In the strange case of José Gabriel O'Horan, who was arrested during the Granada campaign and accused of inciting the Indians of Masaya to rebel against their subdelegado, Auditor Ibáñez initially made him subject to military jurisdiction but changed his mind in May 1813 and passed the case to the audiencia. After the report of the *fiscal,* the tribunal tried to return him, arguing that this case was a more convincing example of a military crime than those of Marure, Mayorga, and the others, who had already lost their appeal. But then Ibáñez cited a royal order of 10 November 1800 that stated infidencia against magistrates or governors of a town is subject to *jurisdicción ordinaria,* while infidencia against military commanders, officers, or troops fell under *jurisdicción militar.* Bustamante agreed in July 1814 and O'Horan was left in the hands of the audiencia. AGCA, B, leg. 29, exp. 742.

63. The ayuntamiento first expressed its opposition to military tribunals for cases of infidencia on 14 March 1813, taking the audiencia position that the 6 October 1811 decree was for special cases. AGCA, B, leg. 28, exp. 789; see also Mariano Beltranena's report on the issue in AGCA, B, leg. 4, exp. 121.

64. Actas Capitulares, 1812, AGCA, A, leg. 2190, exp. 15738, fol. 43.

65. Ibid., fol. 135.

66. 1812 Decrees from Spain, AGCA, B, leg. 6, exp. 246–48.

67. Anna, *The Fall of the Royal Government in Mexico City,* 98–99 and the general discussion that follows. Venegas's obstructionism began in 1810 when he refused to implement decrees establishing press freedom and reached such a level of opposition that the viceroy annulled the first constitutional elections for ayuntamientos constitucionales in December 1812 in what Anna argues was a viceregal coup d'etat. With the support of the audiencia, Calleja continued this policy after taking over for Venegas in March 1813, arguing that the constitution damaged crown authority. Until the restoration of Ferdinand VII in 1814 he simply ignored the decisions of the Mexican diputación provincial.

68. Although I disagree with his characterization of Bustamante's behavior as "arbitrary," Mario Rodríguez's analysis of the creole perspective on the constitution and the obstacles to its implementation in *The Cádiz Experiment* is a first-rate account of this period. See especially chapter five.

69. The obverse was marked "Guatemala 24 September 1812" and the reverse "Por la Constitucion Politica de las Españas." Actas Capitulares, 1812, AGCA, A, leg. 2190, exp. 15738, fols. 140v, 148. Six gold coins were minted: one each for the Cortes, the Coun-

cil of Regency, Larrazábal, Bustamante, Casaus, and José de Aycinena. Other details of the celebrations included special lighting for the platform and the city as a whole, a lunch banquet, church services, and cannonades. AGCA, A, leg. 2190, exp. 15738, fol. 144.

70. Actas Capitulares, 1812, AGCA, A, leg. 2190, exp. 15738, fol. 146.

71. Ibid., fols. 147, 152–53.

72. For a description of 24 September see the *Gaceta de Guatemala,* 2 October 1812, vol. 16, no. 280, or Rodríguez, *The Cádiz Experiment,* 101–2. For 25 September, see AGCA, B, leg. 6, exp. 252. The oath reads: "¿Jurais por Dios, y por los Santos Evangelios guardar, y hacer guardar la Constitucion Politica de la Monarquía Española, Sancionada por las Cortes Generales y extraordinarias, y ser fieles al Rey?"

73. *Instruccion formada de orden de la Junta Preparatoria para facilitar las Elecciones de Diputados y Oficios Consejiles,* Actas Capitulares, 1812, AGCA, A, leg. 2190, exp. 15738, fol. 112.

74. Bustamante to Ayuntamiento, 20 November 1812, Actas Capitulares, 1812, AGCA, A, leg. 2190, exp. 15738, fol. 101.

75. *Instruccion formada de orden de la Junta Preparatoria para facilitar las Elecciones de Diputados y Oficios Consejiles,* Actas Capitulares, 1812, AGCA, A, leg. 2190, exp. 15738, fol. 121v.

76. Actas Capitulares, 1812, AGCA, A, leg. 2190, exp. 15738, fols. 96–97. Bustamante simply refused to recognize the promotion whenever possible.

77. The constitutional council included Sebastián Melón, alcalde primero; Francisco Salmón, alcalde segundo; Domingo Antonio de Juarros, *decano;* Lorenzo Moreno; Domingo Pavón; Juan Bautista Asturias; Pedro Batres; José Francisco Valdez; José Francisco Barrundia; José García Granados; Felix Paggio; Manuel del Castillo; José de Urruela; Eusebio Castillo; Alejandro Vaca, síndico; Manuel Beltranena, síndico; Francisco Córdova, *escribano.* Actas Capitulares, 1812–1813, AGCA, A, leg. 2190, exp. 15739, fol. 1.

78. Ibid., fol. 12.

79. Ibid., fol. 12–12v.

80. Ibid., fol. 14v.

6. The Challenge of the Constitution, 1813–1814

1. Bustamante to Council of Regency, 3 March 1813, *RAHGH,* 56.

2. Ibid.

3. Ibid., 57.

4. Ibid., 58–59.

5. Ibid., 63.

6. Actas Capitulares, 1812–1813, AGCA, A, leg. 2190, exp. 15739, fols. 17–18v. The elections for *compromisarios* at the parish level were to begin on 10 January with the process completed by the beginning of March. The regidores stated that they got the news at the moment they were signing the letter and could not call a new meeting to debate the issue. In addition, Bustamante gave the order without addressing their complaints, an action that exemplified "his hard and dominant character." See Actas Capitulares, 1812–

1813, AGCA, A, leg. 2190, exp. 15739, fol. 20. Bustamante's order is found in AGCA, B, leg. 4, exp. 114, immediately following a copy of Síndico Beltranena's report on the delays, dated 24 November 1812, which stressed the point that elections were the best solution to internal unrest for they offered aggrieved citizens the opportunity to elect representatives.

7. Ayuntamiento complaint to the Cortes, 3 January 1813, Actas Capitulares, 1812–1813, AGCA, A, leg. 2190, exp. 15739, fols. 19–21.

8. Ibid.

9. Ibid.

10. Ayuntamiento *Proclama,* 5 January 1813, AGCA, A, leg. 6923, exp. 56982.

11. *Certificación extendida por el Secretario Córdoba relativa a cierta proclama que el Ayuntamiento de Guatemala había redactado, BAGG,* 3:518–19.

12. The 1810 decree stated in part that "all bodies, and private persons of whatever status or condition, have liberty to write, print, and publish their political ideas, without the necessity of a license, revision, or approval." Quoted in Anna, *The Fall of the Royal Government in Mexico City,* 103; see also the complete text in AGCA, B, leg. 7, exp. 297.

13. The case is found in *El Exmo. Ayuntamiento de esta Capital contra Dn. Ygnacio Beteta sobre escusarle a imprimir cierta Proclama,* Audiencia Indiferente, 1813, AGCA, A, leg. 6923, exp. 56982.

14. The order was sent on 6 February 1812; Anna, *The Fall of the Royal Government in Mexico City,* 103–5.

15. Ibid., 113. In an echo of the Bustamante/ayuntamiento confrontation, the ayuntamiento of Mexico City became the most vocal supporter of press freedoms and the constitution once Venegas began to display his overt opposition to reform in 1812. The Mexican regidores also sent repeated complaints to the Cortes about their despotic governor. Anna, *The Fall of the Royal Government in Mexico City,* 105.

16. 10 November 1810 royal decree, AGCA, B, leg. 7, exp. 297.

17. The Cortes seemed to agree, establishing in section 4 of the 1810 decree that "los libelos infamatorios, los escritos calumniosos, los subversivos de las leyes fundamentales de la monarquía, los licenciosos y contrarios a la decencia pública y buenas costumbres serán castigados con la pena de la ley, y las que aqui se señalarán." AGCA, B, leg. 7, exp. 297.

18. Ibid. See also Anna, *The Fall of the Royal Government in Mexico City,* 103.

19. Royal decree of 10 June 1813, AGCA, B, leg. 7, exp. 297.

20. Royal decree of 11 June 1813, AGCA, B, leg. 7, exp. 297.

21. The Guatemalan *Junta de Censura* began operations on 23 November 1813, and its Nicaraguan counterpart announced its first meeting on 17 April 1814. AGCA, B, leg. 39, exp. 896–97.

22. Secretary of State to Ayuntamiento of Guatemala City, 4 March 1813, AGCA, B, leg. 496, exp. 8476.

23. Secretary of State to Bustamante, 30 June 1813, AGCA, B, leg. 7, exp. 316.

24. Actas Capitulares, 1812–1813, AGCA, A, leg. 2190, exp. 15739, fol. 28.

25. Ibid., fol. 30v.

26. Aycinena arrived in Cádiz on 21 August after a voyage that cost the life of his six-year-old daughter. He was sworn in on the twenty-eighth and began work on the first of September 1813. Aycinena to Ayuntamiento of Guatemala City, 14 September 1813, AGCA, B, leg. 496, exp. 8478.

27. Actas Capitulares, 1812–1813, AGCA, A, leg. 2190, exp. 15739, fol. 46.

28. Beltranena report on infidencia and subsequent debate, AGCA, B, leg. 28, exp. 729; also AGCA, B, leg. 4, exp. 121; *BAGG*, 3:519–21.

29. Ibáñez to Bustamante, 31 March 1813, AGCA, B, leg. 28, exp. 729.

30. In the words of the regidores, "the prison is not a punishment, but should serve only to detain the prisoners." Actas Capitulares, 1812–1813, AGCA, A, leg. 2190, exp. 15739, fol. 46.

31. Esparragosa and Guerra report on prison conditions, 22 March 1813, AGCA, B, leg. 8, exp. 332.

32. Royal decree on visitas, 9 October 1812, AGCA, B, leg. 7, exp. 273.

33. On its surface, this decree gave the council access to *all* prisoners, from those held in the three main prisons, the *Cárcel de Corte,* the *Cárcel de Cadenas,* and the *Cárcel de la Ciudad,* to those confined in other places by the army and the Church. Actas Capitulares, 1812–1813, AGCA, A, leg. 2190, exp. 15739, fol. 97.

34. In a representative ceremonial dispute that developed out of the shifting power arrangement and that enflamed institutional rivalries to destructive levels, the ayuntamiento argued early in 1813 that it should receive the same treatment during religious functions as the captain general and the audiencia. The problem revolved around the question of seating (on *sillas* or *bancas,* in front or behind) and who would receive the *pax,* with the council maintaining that it should be included in everything now, despite the ceremonial tradition that had previously reduced it to a secondary role. Of course, the audiencia refused to give up its remaining vestiges of rank, the Church backed the traditional roles, and Bustamante simply hoped that the council would be flexible in the interests of "*buena armonía*" and bend to the wishes of the oidores. Instead, after the Holy Week celebrations, the ayuntamiento sent a protest to Spain asking the crown to pass a decree on ceremonies and the new roles of the audiencias and ayuntamientos. Actas Capitulares, 1812–1813, AGCA, A, leg. 2190, exp. 15739, fols. 52–53, 97–98, 103–9.

35. Actas Capitulares, 1812–1813, AGCA, A, leg. 2190, exp. 15739, fol. 95v.

36. Casaus finally reported back on 5 April. Actas Capitulares, 1812–1813, AGCA, A, leg. 2190, exp. 15739, fols. 97–98, 103v.

37. Ibid., fol. 103v.

38. Ibid., fols. 98, 103v. The letter was covertly passed to Secretary Córdova during a religious ceremony at the church of Santo Domingo. Ortíz gave a detailed description of his sufferings, a seven-month imprisonment in stifling surroundings without any charges being brought against him, and asked to be remembered during the visitas the next day.

39. In a scathing response to the ayuntamiento visits to the convents, Archbishop Casaus bemoaned what he viewed as a direct assault on ecclesiastical immunity, an "in-

sult to my authority," and a usurpation of undeserved powers by the council. He argued that Ruíz was confined because of his history of trouble making, religious convents were not prisons, and their prelates were not guards. Actas Capitulares, 1812–1813, AGCA, A, leg. 2190, exp. 15739, fol. 154.

40. Ibid., fol. 103v.; a *Comision de Carceles* immediately set to work devising a "plan de la reforma que deba hacerse en las bartolinas a fin de hacer de ellas unas piezas utiles y saludables." On 10 May Pavón and Batres went to the *Carcel de Cadenas* to inquire about the cost of installing eleven more windows, building two more cells, and cleaning the building. As part of this process, Esparragosa returned to the prisons in August to make more specific recommendations about ways to make them more hospitable. AGCA, B, leg. 8, exp. 332.

41. Actas Capitulares, 1812–1813, AGCA, A, leg. 2190, exp. 15739, fol. 109.

42. For example, a case of infidencia was brought against Juan Modesto Hernández in November 1812 after he was linked to the Gordón and Marure cases. Ibáñez found no evidence of his involvement and recommended his release. Bustamante agreed and freed Hernández on 10 March 1813. AGCA, B, leg. 32, exp. 786. Another case was brought against Miguel Juarez "por palabras sediciosas" by the Comayagua intendant, Juan Antonio Tornos, in the spring of 1813. Here, Bustamante found nothing of interest and passed the case on to the audiencia, which freed Juarez five months after his arrest following a full investigation. AGCA, A, leg. 6923, exp. 56969. Other examples of Bustamante's discretion when investigating subversion can be found in the 1813–1814 cases against Marcos Gongora, José Contreras, José Méndez, José Romero, Miguel *El Cochero*, José and Vicente Luna, and Yldefonso Santa Ana, collected in AGCA, B, leg. 35.

43. In a not-so-subtle challenge to the ayuntamiento's priorities, Bustamante sent Major Ignacio Larrazábal to the council on 27 April with a letter stating that the guards at the *Carcel de la Ciudad* were lacking a number of things necessary for their continued service and comfort. Since the public treasury financed their needs, Bustamante asked the regidores to release the necessary funds. The message was clear: do you support the guards or the prisoners? Actas Capitulares, 1812–1813, AGCA, A, leg. 2190, exp. 15739, fol. 114.

44. In a particular blow to the Spanish authorities in Guatemala, former Captain General Antonio González, who had become a senior royalist officer in New Spain after his transfer in 1811, was captured and executed by Matamoros during this campaign. See Lucas Alamán, *Historia de Mexico*, vol. 3 (Mexico: Instituto Cultural Helénico, Fondo de Cultura Económica, 1985), 344.

45. Ibid.

46. Dambrini's decree to the inhabitants of Tehuantepec, 6 April 1813, AGCA, B, leg. 40, exp. 907.

47. Alamán, *Historia de Mexico*, 344. After spending the summer in Quetzaltenango, Dambrini returned to the border in October 1813 with reinforcements from mulatto companies stationed in the Petén, Omoa, and Trujillo. After the royalist recapture of Oaxaca early in 1814, Dambrini tried to integrate his forces into the Mexican Seventh Division of Southern Tehuantepec but was snubbed. He spent the next three years patrolling the frontier with New Spain, capturing suspected insurgents, and running up a

large deficit. He died in 1818, some months after the Guatemalan forces were finally recalled. See AGCA, A, leg. 6934, exp. 57442, 57445–48, 57450–68; A, leg. 131, exp. 2358–78; A,
leg. 6116, exp. 56468–72; B, leg. 40, exp. 907–12.

48. The report was made by Beltranena, Actas Capitulares, 1812–1813, AGCA, A,
leg. 2190, exp. 15739, fol. 73.

49. In his dissenting vote, José de Urruela argued that the ayuntamiento should not
involve itself in military matters, for the constitution gave the captain general sole responsibility for the kingdom's defense. Actas Capitulares, 1812–1813, AGCA, A, leg. 2190,
exp. 15739, fol. 86v.

50. Bustamante to Ayuntamiento, 30 April 1813, Actas Capitulares, 1812–1813, AGCA,
A, leg. 2190, exp. 15739, fol. 117.

51. Ayuntamiento to Bustamante, 1 May 1813, Actas Capitulares, 1812–1813, AGCA, A,
leg. 2190, exp. 15739, fol. 118.

52. Ibid., fol. 116v.

53. Actas Capitulares, 1812–1813, AGCA, A, leg. 2190, exp. 15739, fol. 120.

54. Ibid., fol. 129v.

55. Ibid.

56. Respectively, the new deputies were Manuel José Pavón, Mariano García Reyes,
José María Pérez, José Simeón Cañas, Eulogio Correa, Bruno Medina, and José Matías
Delgado. The Nicaraguan assembly comprised the five districts of León, Granada, Se-
govia, Villa de Nicaragua, and Nicoya in Nicaragua and two from Costa Rica. See Bonilla
Bonilla, "The Central American Enlightenment," 298; for a more complete account of
the activities of the diputación, see Rodríguez, The Cádiz Experiment, 108–23.

57. The Nicaraguan diputación was not seated until 22 November. Actas Capitulares,
1812–1813, AGCA, A, leg. 2190, exp. 15739, fols. 144v, 155, 177v; AGCA, B, leg. 9, exp. 357, 365.
Probably in anticipation of the time when he would have to defend his actions, Bustamante had a report drafted that emphasized the anti-Spanish sentiment of the diputados. See Bumgartner, José del Valle, 67, n. 43. In a letter to the Council of Regency he
had already argued that Guatemala could not support twelve deputies due to its depressed economic state. See Rodríguez, The Cádiz Experiment, 121.

58. According to the alcalde mayor of Sonsonate, Bustamante agreed with the decision of the provincial deputation to fund the voyages of four of the deputies, but when
the captain general asked him to contribute to the cost, he explained that his treasury
was empty. Mariano Bujano to Bustamante, 8 December 1813, AGCA, A, leg. 6923, exp.
56966; see also AGCA, A, leg. 6923, exp. 56963, 56964, 56967.

59. See Actas Capitulares, 1812–1813, AGCA, A, leg. 2190, exp. 15739, fol. 62. The ayuntamiento, in fact, was asked by the regidores of Santa Ana to help keep Peinado in the
intendancy, "pues interesa la tranquilidad de aquel pais en hallarse dirigido por dicho
Sr." See Actas Capitulares, 1812–1813, AGCA, A, leg. 2190, exp. 15739, fol. 80.

60. Until the constitutional reforms, only fifteen towns on the isthmus had functioning councils. Bustamante decree, 2 October 1813, AGCA, B, leg. 16, exp. 476.

61. Alcalde Mayor of Verapaz to Bustamante, 14 October 1813, AGCA, A, leg. 6923,
exp. 56968.

62. José del Barrio to Bustamante, 20 October 1813, AGCA, A, leg. 222, exp. 5230.

63. Ibid.

64. AGCA, B, leg. 9, exp. 367.

65. As late as 22 June 1814 the diputación provincial reported that "aun no se han establecido Ayuntamientos a pretesto de dudas, embarazos y dificultades" and agreed that Bustamante should demand compliance with the constitution from the provincial and local authorities. AGCA, A, leg. 6923, exp. 56993.

66. Actas Capitulares, 1812–1813, AGCA, A, leg. 2190, exp. 15739, fol. 185v.

67. Ibid., fol. 187v; the 4 March decree is found in AGCA, B, leg. 496, exp. 8476.

68. Regency decree, 30 June 1813, AGCA, B, leg. 7, exp. 316. Although it accepted the verdict, the council immediately wrote to Larrazábal of the surprise it felt upon receiving this news. Within ten days it received the deputy's explanation: "pues la distancia no permite que alla se forme una idea exacta del estado de las cosas en Ultramar y que aun se duda de las exposiciones de los SS. Diputados de America." Actas Capitulares, 1812–1813, AGCA, A, leg. 2190, exp. 15739, fol. 220v. Mario Rodríguez notes that Larrazábal might have contributed to the belief within the ayuntamiento that some of Bustamante's relatives had put pressure on the crown to come to this conclusion. There is no direct evidence of this, however. See Rodríguez, *The Cádiz Experiment*, 121.

69. The regidores blamed Bustamante's intimate associate José del Valle as the instigator of the petition. Actas Capitulares, 1812–1813, AGCA, A, leg. 2190, exp. 15739, fol. 198v; Bumgartner, *José del Valle*, 67–68.

70. Actas Capitulares, 1812–1813, AGCA, A, leg. 2190, exp. 15739, fol. 198v. The council also took the opportunity to complain about the audiencia's position on press freedoms. See letter of 17 August, AGCA, B, leg. 4, exp. 105.

71. Actas Capitulares, 1812–1813, AGCA, A, leg. 2190, exp. 15739, fol. 197; Bumgartner, *José del Valle*, 65–66. Valle, apparently, found the charity of the oligarchy hypocritical, for it was never directed toward anyone except the *Granadinos*.

72. Actas Capitulares, 1812–1813, AGCA, A, leg. 2190, exp. 15739, fol. 209.

73. The captaincy general also came under fire for confiscating much of the property of the prisoners, an action that it justified in order to help defray some of the costs of the trial and incarceration. *Colección de Escritos particulares presentados por los Reos presos en esta Capital, remitidos por la Comisión de Granada*, 1813, AGCA, B, leg. 25, exp. 707; Actas Capitulares, 1812–1813, AGCA, A, leg. 2190, exp. 15739, fol. 258v. Sixteen of the *Granadinos* were condemned to death for their role in the revolt, three to life in prison, and 133 to lesser terms. None were executed, however. Some ended up in overseas fortresses, and others were confined in Omoa and Trujillo. Inevitably, conditions and climate took their toll on the prisoners, with some dying in exile before pardons were issued in 1818–1819. Monterrey, *Historia de El Salvador*, vol. 1, 47.

74. *Instrucción para el Gobierno Economico-Politico de las Provincias*, 23 June 1813, Actas Capitulares, 1812–1813, AGCA, A, leg. 2190, exp. 15739, fol. 263.

75. Ibid.

76. Ibid.

77. Both corporations vehemently complained about Bustamante's entrenched policies to the Cortes. As shall be seen, the protest of the Guatemalan diputación caused quite a stir after it was published in the Madrid newspaper *El Universal*. Actas Capitu-

lares, 1812–1813, AGCA, A, leg. 2190, exp. 15739, fols. 273–77; Rodríguez, *The Cádiz Experiment*, 122.

78. The following summary of the Belén conspiracy comes primarily from judicial records found in AGCA, B, leg. 29, exp. 742–59; documents on the case published in the *Anales de la Sociedad de Geografía e Historia de Guatemala*, 11, no. 1 (1934): 13–27; and the most thorough interpretation of the incident, Mario Rodríguez's, *La conspiración de Belén en nueva perspectiva*.

79. Yúdice named Fray Juan de la Concepción (prior of the convent), Dr. Tomás Ruíz, Cayetano Bedoya, Fray Victor Castrillo, Manuel Ibarra, José Francisco Barrundia (*escribano de la ayuntamiento*), Andrés Dardón, Manuel Tot, Juan Hernández, and Fray Manuel de San José. Others implicated included León Díaz, Síndico Venancio Lopez, Fray Benito Miguelena, Juan José Alvarado, Felipe Castro, Francisco Montiel Cartujo, Mariano Cárdenas, and José Ruíz. Barrundia, Ibarra, and Cárdenas escaped capture by fleeing the kingdom. The others were imprisoned, tried, and convicted by a council of war on charges of infidencia. Years of appeals and pleas for pardons kept the majority in the *Carcel de Corte* until 1818 when the crown ordered their release. See *Anales de la Sociedad de Geografía e Historia de Guatemala*, 11, no. 1 (1934): 15; AGCA, B, leg. 29, exp. 746–59.

80. Rodríguez, *La conspiración de Belén en nueva perspectiva*, 5.

81. Actas Capitulares, 1812–1813, AGCA, A, leg. 2190, exp. 15739, fol. 300. In an April 1814 appeal to Spain for a pardon of those imprisoned in Guatemala, Síndico Nájera argued that the kingdom was at peace, but "si en uno u otro [pueblo] ha habido pequeños movimientos, estos han sido acaso resultados de la conducta de sus funcionarios, efectos de exasperacion y deseos de mudar de mandatarios, pero nunca un designio de sustraerse de la justa dominacion española." AGCA, B, leg. 4, exp. 134.

82. Bustamante to Council of Regency, 18 May 1814, *CDHCR*, 467–91.

83. Fr. Juan de Dios Campos had been under investigation by the colonial government since 1810. He was imprisoned in León on 22 July 1813 after getting involved in a conversation about the defeat of Dambrini's forces, and among his belongings were found a number of seditious papers and pieces of correspondence. Considered a "highly dangerous person" by Bustamante, he was exiled to a convent in Panama in 1815. His case presents one of the best examples of the conflict between military, civil, and religious jurisdictions during these years. See AGCA, A, leg. 6921, exp. 55921; AGCA, B, leg. 24, exp. 701; and AGCA, B, leg. 25, exp. 710.

84. Bustamante to Council of Regency, 18 May 1814, *CDHCR*, 468–69.

85. Ibid., 470.

86. Ibid., 471.

87. Ibid. The quotation is from Bustamante's summary of Peinado's report.

88. Peinado, of course, defended his actions in a subsequent investigation of the uprising, arguing that Bustamante had expressed his pleasure with the way the intendancy was run up until January, when he needed a scapegoat. Either way, the correspondence indicates the high degree of autonomy that Peinado enjoyed during his administration. See AGCA, B, leg. 11, exp. 420.

89. Ibid., 474–75. The letter to Morelos can be found in the case against Miguel Del-

gado, AGCA, B, leg. 30, exp. 760. It is also quoted in Salvatierra, *Contribución a la historia*, 2:440.

90. Bustamante appointed Colonel José Méndez to assume military command over San Salvador and the *teniente letrado* of the intendancy, Juan Miguel de Bustamante (no apparent relation to the captain general), to direct the prosecution of suspects (he was replaced by Isidro Marín in 1815). Over a period of months, most of the leaders of the insurrection were captured, including the Aguilar brothers, Castillo, and Manuel José Arce, and convicted of *infidencia* in proceedings that saw little influence from Guatemala City. Except for Manuel Aguilar, the prisoners remained in the intendancy for the duration of their terms. See the records of the trials in AGCA, B, leg. 30, exp. 760–66, and AGCA, A, leg. 6924, exp. 57003–6.

91. Bustamante to Council of Regency, 18 May 1814, *CDHCR*, 482–84.

92. Ibid., 484–85. Bustamante included in this category the prisoners from Granada, whose continual complaints and requests for support from the local elite he considered to be destabilizing.

93. Ibid., 486.

94. Ibid., 487–88.

95. Bustamante specifically requested the reauthorization of the following Laws of the Indies: *ley* 61, *título* 3, *libro* 3; *ley* 18, *título* 8, *libro* 7; and *ley* 7, *título* 4, *libro* 3. Bustamante to Council of Regency, 18 May 1814, *CDHCR*, 489–90.

96. Aycinena's letter of 14 September 1813 is found in AGCA, B, leg. 496, exp. 8478; the notice of transfer of 14 September 1813 is located in AGCA, B, leg. 496, exp. 8489; the ayuntamiento received Aycinena's letter on 18 February but did not get the official notice from Bustamante for another month: Actas Capitulares, 1814, AGCA, A, leg. 2191, exp. 15740, fol. 29v, 50. Bustamante's service record is littered with requests for time off for reasons of health. Repeatedly wounded in battle and the victim of a serious accident on board the *Atrevida*, he was granted leaves of absence from the navy in 1795, 1808, and 1823. While he might have had ulterior motives for requesting an end to his service in Guatemala, one cannot discount the fragile state of his health in 1813—and in 1817—as a major motivation. See Bustamante to Juan de Langara y Huarte, 1 March 1796, AGM, leg. 620-181.

97. The council received word that Tornos had begun his journey to the capital on 1 March but learned three weeks later that he had been delayed "a causa de una indisposicion." In what was probably devised as a way to encourage the intendant, the regidores decided to send Tornos an official congratulations for his appointment. See Actas Capitulares, 1814, AGCA, A, leg. 2191, exp. 15740, fol. 48. Tornos wrote to the ayuntamiento on 6 April thanking it for its kind words but said nothing about his travel plans: AGCA, B, leg. 496, exp. 8491; Millares wrote to the ayuntamiento on 1 February in order to introduce himself, but the letter did not arrive until 7 June. It is found in AGCA, B, leg. 496, exp. 8488. Bustamante mentioned his imminent replacement in his 18 May letter to Spain as proof that he was not interested in augmenting his own authority: Bustamante to Council of Regency, 18 May 1814, *CDHCR*, 486.

98. Actas Capitulares, 1814, AGCA, A, leg. 2191, exp. 15740, fols. 135v, 140v. It is possible

that the crown decision to shift the appointment to the Marquis of Aycinena on 25 January 1814 upset the plans to send Millares to Central America.

99. The news was also occasion for another ayuntamiento complaint to Spain, for Bustamante had invited the archbishop to a military review on 25 June without passing the invitation to the regidores as well. Actas Capitulares, 1814, AGCA, A, leg. 2191, exp. 15740, fols. 101v, 105v.

100. The captain general made sure to send the ayuntamiento copies of the *Gaceta Extraordinaria del Gobierno de Guatemala* of 20 and 24 August, which included the royal proclamations and other news from Spain reported during the month of May. Actas Capitulares, 1814, AGCA, A, leg. 2191, exp. 15740, fols. 133v, 141v. The 4 May royal decree and other documents pertinent to the restoration of absolutism can be found in *BAGG*, vol. 4, no. 1 (October 1938): 13–24.

101. Actas Capitulares, 1814, AGCA, A, leg. 2191, exp. 15741, fols. 155, 168, 182, 185v, 187v, 188v.

102. AGCA, B, leg. 8, exp. 335.

7. The Restoration of Absolutism, 1815–1818

1. On 17 February 1815, José de Aycinena sent a letter to the ayuntamiento in which he noted that he had passed to the king all the council's recent messages and, in addition, "le hize presente que esta virtud en ese fidelisimo Reino ha sido a toda prueba constante en las diversas vicisitudes de los goviernos pasados, sirviendo de motivo e admiracion a la Europa, y de exemplo e imitacion a la America." Actas Capitulares, 1815, AGCA, A, leg. 2191, exp. 15741, fol. 81v.

2. The protest had been sent on 7 September 1813 and was distributed by Deputy Larrazábal once it arrived in Spain. It charged Bustamante, among other things, with frivolously delaying the installation of the assembly, obstructing the election and departure of Cortes deputies (to keep witnesses to his conduct from reaching Spain), refusing to permit a Te Deum in honor of the completion of the election process, and blocking the publication of the results. Documents relating to the complaint are found in AGCA, B, leg. 11, exp. 410. Secretary Ramón Andrade's summary of the case, dated 27 August 1814, and a letter from Bustamante to Casaus, 25 August 1814, are published in *BAGG*, 3:521–24.

3. Andrade summary, 27 August 1814, AGCA, B, leg. 11, exp. 410.

4. Bustamante to Casaus, 25 August 1814, *BAGG*, 3:522. According to Bustamante, the *diputados* were entitled to complain about infractions of the constitution, but not in a way that would accuse specific individuals of crimes without clear and convincing proof. It was the responsibility of the crown to investigate the charges and assign blame where it was required. He was frustrated, in particular, about the charge that he did not want the elected Cortes deputies to travel to Spain, a complaint that he felt could not be proved or disproved, regardless of his true sentiments.

5. Ibid., 522–23.

6. AGCA, B, leg. 11, exp. 410.

7. This was not the first time, of course, that Bustamante made this accusation.

Writing to the crown on 27 October 1813, he blamed the *Instrucciones* for inciting rebellion and called them "a literal copy of the Declaration of the Rights of Man drawn up by the National Assembly of France during the epoch of her horrible revolution." Quoted in Bumgartner, *José del Valle*, 74. Bustamante's annotated copy of the *Instrucciones,* which was one of only a couple to survive, was published in 1953. See *Instrucciones para la constitución fundamental de la monarquía española y su gobierno.*

8. Royal Order of 31 March 1815, AGCA, B, leg. 12, exp. 427; Real Cédula of 13 June 1817, *BAGG,* 4:37–39. This, at least, was the position the crown took in 1817 when it reconsidered its earlier decision to support the captain general. Without Bustamante's original letter, it is impossible to say exactly what he recommended as punishment.

9. Actas Capitulares, 1815, AGCA, A, leg. 2191, exp. 15741, fols. 18–20.

10. The *cédula* of 25 June also outlawed all acts of constitutional ayuntamientos, restored local *jueces de primera instancia* and *jueces de partido,* revived the offices of alcaldes mayores and corregidores, abolished newly formed municipal councils and provincial deputations, and ordered that the papers of the *juntas de censura* be sent to Spain. The other decrees published at this time included the 2 July *decreto* restoring the Council of the Indies and appointing José de Aycinena to the second *Sala de Gobierno* and the 30 July *cédula* that confirmed the restoration of ayuntamientos to their condition as of 18 March 1808. The 18 November edition of the *Gaceta* is included in an *oficio* from Bustamante to the audiencia, 4 November 1814, AGCA, B, leg. 76, exp. 2264.

11. He mentioned this to the oidores in a letter dated 5 December 1814, AGCA, B, leg. 76, exp. 2264. On 14 April Bustamante informed the audiencia that the schooner, the *Galatea,* had been taken by an insurgent ship from Cartagena off Matanzas and was carrying the 8 July *Real Orden.* AGCA, B, leg. 12, exp. 426.

12. The oidores based their complaint on *leyes* 39 and 40, *título* 15, *libro* 2 of the *Recopilación de Indias,* which states that "no se dé cumplimiento a las Cedulas, y Pragmaticas publicadas en Castilla no teniendo el indispensable pase del Consejo de Indias." Audiencia to Bustamante, 24 January 1815, AGCA, B, leg. 12, exp. 426. This debate can also be followed in the Libro de Acuerdos, 1811–1818, AGCA, A, leg. 4663, exp. 39952.

13. Bustamante to Audiencia, 16 March 1815, AGCA, B, leg. 12, exp. 426.

14. Bumgartner, *José del Valle,* 75–76.

15. Ibid., 118.

16. This list of personality traits was drawn from the witness testimony taken in Bustamante's 1820 *residencia.* See AGCA, A, leg. 1740, exp. 11582.

17. The careers of Morillo and Bustamante are remarkably similar in many ways, particularly with respect to the legacies that both men left in the colonies under their command. See Stoan, *Pablo Morillo and Venezuela.* Calleja was replaced by the former captain general of Cuba, Juan Ruíz de Apodaca. The former viceroy wrote on the eve of his departure for Spain that victory over the rebels was assured "if the methods that have served me so well are continued." Apodaca, however, preferred a policy of moderation and amnesty rather than terror. Quoted in Anna, *The Fall of the Royal Government in Mexico City,* 181.

18. Acuerdo Ordinario, 27 April 1815, Libro de Acuerdos, 1811–1818, AGCA, A, leg. 4663, exp. 39952, fol. 76.

19. Many questions remain unanswered about this particular case. According to Salazar, Bustamante ignored the fact that his description of Barrundia did not match that given by those in Campeche who knew the suspect and still requested that Argüelles be sent to Guatemala City. Rodríguez states that the captain general failed to include essential facts in his description of Barrundia—particularly his red hair—that would have alerted those in Campeche that the captain general was in error. The *residencia* charge dealing with this case declares Bustamante at fault both for ignoring the *comandante juez* of Campeche, who vouched for Argüelles's identity, and for leaving out vital information about Barrundia that might have prevented the tragedy. Unless one wishes to believe this to be an example of Bustamante's obsessive mind in action, the most logical explanation is that the captain general was aware that Argüelles was not Barrundia but had reason to question him about the whereabouts of the fugitive. See *Residencia*, charge #17, AGCA, A, leg. 1739, exp. 11581. Also see Salazar, *Historia de veintiún años*, 2:197; Rodríguez, *The Cádiz Experiment*, 127–28.

20. Details on the Alfaro case can be found in the Libro de Acuerdos, 1811–1818, AGCA, A, leg. 4663, exp. 39952, fol. 83; also *Residencia*, charge #16, AGCA, A, leg. 1739, exp. 11581. Also see *Autos para determinar la causa del fallecimiento de Alfaro*, 1816, AGCA, A, leg. 144, exp. 2786.

21. Actas Capitulares, 1815, AGCA, A, leg. 2191, exp. 15741, fols. 148, 151. *Listas del Escuadrón de Dragones de Milicias de la Capital de Guatemala 1815*, AGCA, A, leg. 225, exp. 4767. Bustamante drew the ire of the ayuntamiento in 1815–1816 by refusing to let these troops participate in municipal activities that had long been part of militia service, such as guarding the prisoners who were used to clean the streets of the capital, "por la escasez de la que sirve en esta ciudad." Actas Capitulares, 1816, AGCA, A, leg. 2192, exp. 15742, fols. 29v, 68, 70v.

22. Actas Capitulares, 1815, AGCA, A, leg. 2191, exp. 15741, fol. 138; *Real Orden* of 31 March 1815, AGCA, B, leg. 12, exp. 427. Alcalde Isasi, in particular, was so upset by the refusal of the ayuntamiento to remove the offending portraits that he did not attend any council meetings until this particular one. After Bustamante left, the ayuntamiento voted to keep the paintings where they were but erase from them any inscription that referred to the constitutional period.

23. La Sra. Marquesa de Aycinena et al. to Audiencia, 12 September 1815, AGCA, B, leg. 12, exp. 423. See also the appeals from Lorenzo Moreno, Luís Barrutia, J. M. Peinado, and the others in AGCA, B, leg. 12, exp. 415, 419, 420.

24. Peinado to Audiencia, 6 November 1815, AGCA, B, leg. 12, exp. 420.

25. Fiscal report on deposition of Peinado, 10 November 1815, AGCA, B, leg. 12, exp. 420.

26. On 6 June the council agreed to petition the crown for a confirmation of its title, believing that the pressure to return things to the way they were in 1808 would sweep away this honor. It noted that some ayuntamientos had already begun to leave off the

honorific in correspondence. Actas Capitulares, 1815, AGCA, A, leg. 2191, exp. 15741, fols. 92v, 171, 177.

27. Ibid., fol. 198v; AGCA, B, leg. 76, exp. 2267.

28. The 1816 council included Domingo José Pavón and Juan Antonio Araujo, alcaldes; Juan Asturias, José de Urruela, Francisco Batres, Juan José Echeverria, Rafael Trullé, José Francisco Valdes, Juan Fermín de Aycinena, Felix Antonio Poggio, Benito Español, and Alejandro Vaca, regidores; and José Francisco Arran, síndico (chosen after Francisco Barrutia declined the office). Actas Capitulares, 1816, AGCA, A, leg. 2192, exp. 15742, fol. 1.

29. Wortman, *Government and Society,* 207.

30. Ibid., 207–8.

31. Quoted in a letter dated 20 February 1823 in Ramón Salazar, *Mariano de Aycinena* (Guatemala: Editorial del Ministerio de Educación Pública, 1952), 58.

32. Bumgartner, *José del Valle,* 75, n. 65; Wortman, *Government and Society,* 208; *Residencia,* charge #13, AGCA, A, leg. 1739, exp. 11581. The suit was eventually dismissed.

33. Beltranena to Bustamante, 2 December 1816, AGCA, A, leg. 2641, exp. 22021; *Residencia,* testimony of Juan Nepomuceno de Asturias, AGCA, A, leg. 1740, exp. 11582. Bustamante's attack on the House of Beltranena was used consistently by the witnesses in his *residencia* as an example of his arbitrary rule and poor justice.

34. For more on Spanish politics during the wars of independence, see Hamnett, *La política española en una época revolucionaria;* Anna, *Spain and the Loss of America;* and Domínguez, *Insurrection.*

35. The report is found in *DRMIRG,* 97–121.

36. Ibid., 113–15, 118. The *fiscal* was particularly upset by the fact that it appeared Bustamante had deliberately neglected to mention the influence the persecution and imprisonment of the Aguilar brothers by Archbishop Casaus and the colonial government had on the outbreak of the first disturbances in San Salvador. This kind of selective reporting of events made crown officials wonder what the captain general had suppressed when he launched his attack on the ayuntamiento and its *Instrucciones.*

37. Ibid., 119.

38. Ibid., 120–21.

39. As Bustamante described it, in order to "saber el verdadero origen de las sediciones que se han experimentado . . . los fines, agentes y medios con que se sostuvieron y generalizaron" the king wanted "unas memorias en estilo sensillo y correcto en que se describan con imparcialidad y verdad quantos sucesos de aquella especie hayan sobrevivido en estos paises del distrito de mi mando desde la ausencia y cautividad de S.M." The captain general then chose subjects "de conocida ilustracion, sagacidad, madurez y criterio" to write these histories. While all three were convinced that "con sus providencias nos ha salvado [Bustamante] en crisis tan delicada," they were also concerned that a truthful and objective account would not be worth the risk, for they would have to mention "el nombre y caracter de los que hayan sugerido ocultamente los alborotos y motines: desenvolver todo el plan de sus maquinaciones." As José del Valle argued, "esto, Señor, no es posible hacerlo con pureza en los mismos payses donde existen las familias,

enlazes y relaciones de los autores ocultos y agentes manifiestos de todo el mal." For the full documentation of this incident, see Louis Bumgartner, ed., "Documentos de la independencia de Guatemala," *Antropología e Historia de Guatemala* 13 (July 1961): 55–61.

40. Actas Capitulares, 1816, AGCA, A, leg. 2192, exp. 15742, fol. 134.

41. Actas Capitulares, 1817, AGCA, A, leg. 2192, exp. 15743, fol. 9. The council was so sensitive about the loss of this title that when Juan de Dios Mayorga, who was now the alcalde primero of Metapán, addressed a letter to the ayuntamiento and appeared to draw attention to the honorific of its new, lower rank by underlining *MN* (*Muy Noble*) and twice underlining the *L* in *ML* (*Muy Leal*), the regidores viewed it as "una injuria que se infiere al Cuerpo, cuya lealtad ha sido asendrada en todos tiempos y especialmente en las epocas mas peligrosas." Actas Capitulares, 1817, AGCA, A, leg. 2192, exp. 15743, fol. 74.

42. Ibid., fols. 38v, 39v, 52v.

43. *Contra el Religioso Fr. Juan Salvatierra y José Manuel Salvatierra por Sediciosos,* 1816–1817, AGCA, B, leg. 36, exp. 811.

44. Bustamante has been charged repeatedly with pursuing arbitrary and informal justice in his prosecutions of *reos de infidencia.* While he bemoaned the tedious and twisted paths cases tended to take upon entering the judicial realm, his military upbringing also instilled in him a respect for form that affected his perspective on legal proceedings. Summing up the case against Juan Isidoro Hoyo during the prosecutions of those who participated in the 1814 Salvadoran uprising, Intendant Marín of San Salvador wrote to Bustamante: "No percibo, a la verdad, que más formalidad pudiera observarse que la que se ha observado en las Causas de unos reos, que emplearon toda su astucia, y malignidad en maquinar contra el Govierno mas benefico, y benigno." Despite the fact that "un sabio Autor Español apoyado en razones muy convincentes, es de sentir, que en este genero de causas, el mejor orden de derecho que debe observarse es no observarlo; pero nada de todo esto me ha detenido para darle su entero cumplimiento a la citada Superior providencia de VA." Marín to Bustamante, 30 September 1816, AGCA, A, leg. 6926, exp. 57028.

45. The pardon was apparently formulated on 21 January but the Council of the Indies did not send it to Central America until sometime in February. It was officially received on 4 July. AGCA, A, leg. 29, exp. 859.

46. AGCA, B, leg. 36, exp. 811.

47. AGCA, A, leg. 29, exp. 859.

48. *Real Orden,* 1 April 1817, AGCA, A, leg. 6927, exp. 57053. Bustamante received it late in August.

49. Details on the meeting of 1 September come from the Libro de Acuerdos, 1811–1818, AGCA, A, leg. 4663, exp. 39952, fol. 124.

50. Actas Capitulares, 1817, AGCA, A, leg. 2192, exp. 15743, fol. 90.

51. Ibid., fol. 75v. In a subsequent letter describing the interview with the king, Aycinena declared that the kingdom would "coger los optimos frutos de su constante obediencia, y heroismo." Aycinena to Ayuntamiento, 5 August 1817, AGCA, B, leg. 496, exp. 8504.

52. José de Isasi et al. to Audiencia, 13 November 1817, AGCA, A, leg. 2639, exp. 22002, fol. 6.

53. Regidores to Audiencia, 6 November 1817, AGCA, A, leg. 2639, exp. 22002, fol. 1. Interestingly, the Marquis of Aycinena, who signed this initial petition to the audiencia on behalf of his father, had second thoughts about being associated with something that might injure the honor and reputation of another person (i.e., Bustamante) and asked that his signature be erased. Regidores to Audiencia, 6 November 1817, AGCA, A, leg. 2639, exp. 22002, fol. 3.

54. The various appeals are found in AGCA, A, leg. 2639, exp. 22002. Although they were frustrated with the audiencia, the oligarchy blamed Bustamante and Casaus for the delays. See Regidores to Audiencia, 6 November 1817, AGCA, A, leg. 2639, exp. 22002, fols. 15–19.

55. Libro de Acuerdos, 1811–1818, AGCA, A, leg. 4663, exp. 39952, fols. 130–33v.

56. Ibid., fol. 134. Moreno also argued that Bustamante should not even be present during the opening of the pliego, because it was not addressed to him. The captain general noted that he was unaware of any law that kept him, as president of the audiencia, from attending *acuerdo* meetings and witnessing the opening of royal decrees. Libro de Acuerdos, 1811–1818, AGCA, A, leg. 4663, exp. 39952, fol. 142.

57. Laying the groundwork for some form of public protest while at the same time reiterating its loyalty to the crown, the ayuntamiento stated on 28 November "que las medidas tomadas en el dia por el Superior Gobierno y auxiliadas por algunos Religiosos y particulares, para que no se abra un pliego presentado al Supremo Tribunal de la Real Audiencia, rotulado por el Rey en que segun se sabe contiene la Real Cedula expedida a favor de los Regidores inabilitados, la deposicion del Gefe y algunas otras cosas, tocan en la Raya escandalosas, y suversivas a la obediencia ciega que todo fiel vasallo debe prestar a su Monarca lexitimo, y Soberanas disposiciones; que dichas medidas pueden causar alguna inquietud a la tranquilidad de Guatemala, por los motivos que saltan a primera vista a los ojos del menos politico. . . . Se acordó que los señores Aycinena y Vaca formen la representacion sobre los puntos indicados, expresandose en ella los sugetos y personas que han auxiliado las ideas del Superior gobierno, y manifestando a SM que Guatemala ha sido y será fiel a su Real persona: que estan dispuestos sus habitantes a derramar la ultima gota de sangre por sostener los sagrados derechos de su soberania, y la obediencia ciega a sus leyes." Actas Capitulares, 1817, AGCA, A, leg. 2192, exp. 15743, fol. 124.

58. Libro de Acuerdos, 1811–1818, AGCA, A, leg. 4663, exp. 39952, fol. 142v. He stationed soldiers and artillery in the Plaza Mayor to deal with the anticipated unrest. *BAGG*, 4:39.

59. Libro de Acuerdos, 1811–1818, AGCA, A, leg. 4663, exp. 39952, fol. 144. Bustamante brought in the two postal officials because of concerns that the pliego had been opened and might in fact be a forgery. Although many suspicions were raised about its authenticity, the tribunal proceeded with the ceremony anyway. Real Acuerdo de Guatemala, 15 December 1817, AGCA, A, leg. 2639, exp. 22002, fol. 23. The duplicate copy, which arrived in January 1818, also came via an unofficial route and with signs of tampering. AGCA, A, leg. 2639, exp. 22002, fols. 29–30.

60. Real Cédula, 12 May 1817, AGCA, A, leg. 6928, exp. 57078; also AGCA, B, leg. 36, exp. 817. It stated, among other things, that "no se podia adoptar por injusto e impolitico el pensamiento de enviar Eclesiasticos de España . . . que no se debia aprobar la providencia que tomó [Bustamante] de repartir tierras a los mulatos y franqueandoles capitales para su cultivo del fondo de Communidades . . . que pues las leyes prescriben sabiamente el modo de substanciar los procesos en todas las clases de delitos no habia necesidad de hacer prevencion alguna relativa a los de notoria infidencia . . . que suspendiendose por ahora los premios y las demostraciones de gratitud que propone Bustamante en favor de algunos cuerpos y personas particulares, se os encargase que cuando tengais la instruccion necesario informeis sobre el merito de todos los que se hayan distinguido por su conducta fiel y patriotica."

61. Questions about the *reos de infidencia* were taken up in the 1 September *acuerdo* meeting and referred to Spain for adjudication. While he may not have liked what was happening, the fact that the 18 May and 13 June decrees were not implemented until his successor took office cannot be ascribed to obstructionism on the part of Bustamante, despite the inference of some historians. The *reos* and regidores, perhaps, could have made a case against the byzantine nature of Spanish colonial bureaucracy for the delays but not against the captain general. See, for example, Rodríguez, *The Cádiz Experiment*, 129; Bonilla Bonilla, "The Central American Enlightenment," 309–10. Urrutia implemented the 13 June decree in April 1818. See AGCA, A, leg. 2639, exp. 22002, fol. 41.

62. Real Cédula of 13 June 1817, *BAGG*, 4:37–39.

63. Ibid., 38.

64. Actas Capitulares, 1818, AGCA, A, leg. 2193, exp. 15744, fols. 11, 28v.

65. Ibid., fol. 29.

66. Bustamante to Urrutia, 31 March 1818, AGCA, A, leg. 2639, exp. 22002, fol. 53.

67. Ibid. Bustamante also tried to awaken Urrutia's suspicions about the legitimacy of the 13 June decree. He noted that during the Napoleonic campaigns in the peninsula, false decrees ordering the capture and execution of the captains general Elio Villavicencio and the conde del Abiscal were sent—without success—to Valencia, Seville, and Cádiz. He reiterated that this particular one did not arrive by the official route, that it showed signs of tampering, and that an unusual amount of time had elapsed before it arrived in the colony. Urrutia, apparently, was not convinced.

68. Bumgartner, *José del Valle*, 96–99. The pro-Bustamante group was led by Valle and drew much of its support from urban artisan classes and other more traditional groups. Because of its feud with Bustamante, the Family found itself allied for a time with more liberal segments of society before assuming control of the conservative side of the political debate after 1821.

69. Vilches's commission is found in AGCA, A, leg. 32, exp. 923; Bumgartner, *José del Valle*, 97.

70. The primary witnesses represented a small segment of the capital's political and commercial elite. Most had served on either the ayuntamiento or the Consulado or on both. Most were creoles, though a sizable number of peninsulars were included. They included Juan Bautista de Marticorena (Pen.), Francisco Batres (Cr.), Miguel Jacinto

de Marticorena (Pen.), Manuel Sanchez de Perales (Cr.), Juan Ignacio Yrigoyen (Pen.), Mateo Ibarra (Pen.), José García Granados (Pen.), Antonio Vijil (Pen.), Ramón Bengoechea (Pen.), José Domingo Dieguez (Cr.), Miguel Batres (Cr.), Alejandro Díaz Cabeza de Vaca (Cr.), Eusebio de Jesus Castillo (Cr.), Juan Nepomuceno de Asturias (Cr.), Antonio Batres Asturias (Cr.), Juan Bautista Asturias (Cr.), Julián Yela (Pen.), Valerio Coronado (Cr.), Mariano Herrarte (Cr.), José Ramón Zelaya (Cr.), Santiago Moreno (Pen.), José Mariano Gálvez (Cr.), Francisco Javier Barrutia (Cr.), Juan Sebastián Milches (Cr.), and Antonio Arrivillaga (Cr.). *Residencia* of Bustamante, AGCA, A, leg. 1740, exp. 11582. According to form, they "han de ser sugetos de provided, vecinos de la capital, y sus inmediaciones, que no tengan relacion con el Sr. Residenciado." Vilches asked each one a set of fifty-two questions. Some of these were for general information and clarification, while others were clearly designed to be leading. *Residencia*, AGCA, A, leg. 1739, exp. 11581.

71. Vilches to Crown, 16 October 1820, AGCA, A, leg. 1739, exp. 11581.

72. Ibid.

73. One of the reasons for this comes from the way in which Vilches conducted his investigation. Since he relied heavily upon individual testimony, supported by one or two corroborative witnesses, his charges tend to reflect either a very detailed, personal perspective—e.g., Juan Fermín de Aycinena testifying to the strong sense of injury felt by his House—or a broad, collective presumption of guilt. In this context, rumor and innuendo ran rampant through the pages of the inquiry with many of the witnesses reporting that they "heard it said" (*oyó decir*), "it was said" (*se dijo*), or "it was public and notorious" (*era publico y notorio*) when they had no direct knowledge of a particular event. It must be emphasized that Vilches was acting not as a judge but rather as a prosecutor. He ignored many positive comments made about Bustamante in this testimony and focused instead on trying to prove that crimes had been committed. While there were many people willing to help him do this, only the crown had the authority to pass judgment on the case once Vilches completed his work. It is true, as Mario Rodríguez has noted, that "the judges [on the audiencia] virtually threw the book at him [Bustamante]," but it is misleading to state that they found "him guilty of practically every charge that was brought up." In fact, when the case was reviewed in Spain, Bustamante was completely exonerated. See Rodríguez, *The Cádiz Experiment*, 129.

74. *Residencia* of Bustamante, AGCA, A, leg. 1739, exp. 11581.

75. In a letter from Havana to Gregorio de Urruela, dated 12 February 1819, Bustamante is quoted as saying: "La demora de mi viaje y la benéfica residencia de tres meses fuera de esta ciudad han restablecido mi salud y fuerzos en términos que se admiran todos, y mucho más los que creyeron tristemente de mi existencia." See Bumgartner, *José del Valle*, 94, n. 48.

76. Bumgartner, *José del Valle*, 94–96; Wortman, *Government and Society*, 211. The quote and other information about Bustamante's post-Guatemala period come from his *hoja de servicio*, AGM, leg. 620-181, and his obituary in the *Suplemento a la Gaceta de Madrid*.

CONCLUSION

1. See Victoria R. Bricker, *The Indian Christ, the Indian King: The Historical Substrate of Maya Myth and Ritual* (Austin: University of Texas Press, 1981), 77–84; J. Daniel Contreras R., *Una rebelión indígena en el partido de Totonicapán en 1820: el indio y la independencia* (Guatemala: Imprenta universitaria, 1951).

2. See Woodward, "Economic and Social Origins," 561–62; Bumgartner, *José del Valle*, 105–20.

Bibliography

Primary Sources

Archives and Libraries

Archivo General de Centro América (AGCA), Guatemala City, Guatemala. Government Records, 1790–1821.

Archivo General de Indias (AGI), Seville, Spain. Estado.

Archivo General de la Marina "Álvaro de Bazán" (AGM), Viso del Marqués, Spain. Hojas de servicio; Defensa.

Archivo General de la Nación, Mexico City, Mexico. Infidencias.

Archivo Histórico Nacional, Madrid, Spain. Ordenes Militares.

Archivo Histórico Provincial de Cantabria, Santander, Spain. Catastro del Marques de la Ensenada.

Biblioteca Nacional, Mexico City, Mexico. Papers of Rafael Heliodoro Valle.

Hispanic American Collection, Louisiana State University, Baton Rouge. Francisco de Planas Correspondence, 1812–1821.

Latin American Library, Tulane University, New Orleans. Contemporary Publications, 1809–1821.

Museo Naval, Madrid, Spain. Manuscripts.

Newberry Library, Chicago. Ayer Collection, Papers of Alejandro Marure.

Newspapers

El Editor Constitucional. Guatemala, 1820–1821.

Gaceta de Guatemala. Guatemala, 1809–1815.

Gaceta de Madrid. Spain, 1820–1825.

Contemporary Publications and Published Documents

Anales de la Sociedad de Geografía e Historia de Guatemala. Guatemala. Vol. 11, no. 1 (September 1934), pp. 13–26; Vol. 12, no. 3 (April 1936); Vol. 14, no. 1 (October 1938).

Boletín del Archivo General del Gobierno (BAGG). Guatemala. Vol. 3, no. 4 (July 1938), pp. 366–524; Vol. 4, no. 1 (October 1938), pp. 13–39.

Bumgartner, Louis, ed. "Documentos de la independencia de Guatemala." *Antropología e Historia de Guatemala* 13(July 1961):55–61.

Bustamante y Guerra, José de. *El Presidente Gobernador y Capitán General de Guatemala D. José de Bustamante y Guerra, a todas las autoridades y habitantes del reyno de su mando*. Guatemala, 13 April 1811.

Calleja, Felix María. "Civil Defense Regulations of June 8, 1811." Translated by Hugh M. Hamill. In *Problems in Latin American History*, Joseph S. Tulchin, ed., pp. 43–46. New York: Harper & Row, 1973.

Casaus y Torres, Ramón. *Carta Circular del Illmó. y Revmó., Sr. Dr. y Mtró. D. Fr. Ramón Casaus y Torres . . . a todos los PP. Vicarios de Provincia, Curas y Coadjutores, y a los demas Fieles de esta Diocesi*. Guatemala, 20 April 1812.

Fernández, León, ed. *Colección de documentos para la historia de Costa Rica (CDHCR)*. Vol. 10. Barcelona: Imprenta Viuda de Luís Tasso, 1907.

García, G., ed. *La cooperación de México en la independencia de Centro América*. 2 vols. In *Documentos inéditos o muy raros para la historia de México*, vols. 35 and 36. Mexico, 1911.

Hernández y Dávalos, J. E., ed. *Colección de documentos para la historia de la guerra de independencia de Mexico de 1808 a 1821*. Mexico: José María Sandoval, Impresor, 1881.

Instrucciones para la constitución fundamental de la monarquía española y su gobierno. Guatemala: Editorial del Ministerio de Educación Pública, 1953.

———. *Documentos relativos a los movimientos de independencia en el reino de Guatemala (DRMIRG)*. San Salvador: Ministerio de Instruccion Pública de El Salvador, 1929.

Malaspina, Alejandro. *En busca del paso del Pacífico*. Madrid: Historia 16, 1990.

Ordenanzas generales de la armada naval. Parte primera. Sobre la gobernación militar y marinera de la armada en general, y uso de sus fuerzas en la mar. . . . 2 vols. Madrid: Impr. de la Viuda de Don J. Ibarra, 1793.

Revista de la Academia Hondureña de Geografía e Historia (RAHGH). Vol. 55 (January–June 1972).

Salvatierra, Sofonías. *Contribución a la historia de Centroamérica: Monografías documentales*. Vol. 2. Managua: Tipografía Progreso, 1939.

Sicilia y Montoya, Isidro. *Guatemala por Fernando Septimo el día 12 de diciembre de 1808*. Guatemala, 1809.

———. *Nos el Doctor Don Isidro Sicilia Arce-Dean de esta Santa Metropolitana Yglesia, Provisor Gobernador y Vicario capitular de este Arzobispado*. Guatemala, 23 May 1810.

———. *Nos el Dr. D. Isidro Sicilia, Dean de esta Santa Iglesia Metropolitana de Guate-*

mala, Provisor, Vicario Capitular, y Gobernador del Arzobispado. Guatemala, 4 January 1811.

Secondary Sources

Aguirre Cinta, Rafael. *Lecciones de historia general de Guatemala, desde los tiempos primitivos hasta nuestros dias, arregladas para uso de las escuelas primarias y secondarias de esta republica.* Guatemala: Impreso en la tipografía nacional, 1899.

Alamán, Lucas. *Historia de Mexico desde los primeros movimientos que prepararon su independencia en el año 1808 hasta la época presente.* Vol. 3. Mexico: Instituto Cultural Helénico, Fondo de Cultura Económica, 1985.

Anna, Timothy E. *The Fall of the Royal Government in Mexico City.* Lincoln: University of Nebraska Press, 1978.

———. *The Fall of the Royal Government in Peru.* Lincoln: University of Nebraska Press, 1979.

———. "Provincialism and the Invention of Mexico, 1786–1824." Paper presented at the Annual Meeting of the Rocky Mountain Colloquium of Latin American Studies, Vancouver, B.C., April 1993.

———. "Spain and the Breakdown of Imperial Ethos: The Problem of Equality." *Hispanic American Historical Review* 62(May 1982):254–72.

———. *Spain and the Loss of America.* Lincoln: University of Nebraska Press, 1983.

Archer, Christon I. *The Army in Bourbon Mexico 1760–1810.* Albuquerque: University of New Mexico Press, 1977.

———, ed. *The Birth of Modern Mexico, 1780–1824.* Wilmington, Del.: Scholarly Resources, 2003.

———, ed. *The Wars of Independence in Spanish America.* Wilmington, Del.: Scholarly Resources, 2000.

Archivo biográfico de España, Portugal e Iberoamerica: una compilación de 300 obras biográficas, las más importantes y representativas, editadas entre el siglo XVII y los inicios del siglo XX. Munich and New York: K. G. Saur, 1986.

Bancroft, Hubert H. *History of Central America, 1801–1887,* vol. 3. Vol. 8 of *The Works of Hubert Howe Bancroft.* San Francisco: The History Company, 1887.

Barón Castro, Rodolfo. *Españolismo y antiespañolismo en la America hispana. La población hispanoamericana a partir de la independencia.* Madrid: Ediciones Atlas, 1945.

———. *José Matías Delgado y el movimiento insurgente de 1811: Ensayo histórico.* San Salvador: Ministerio de la Educación, 1961.

Batres Jáuregui, Antonio. *La America Central ante la historia.* Vol. 2. Guatemala: Tipografía Sánchez & De Guise, 1920.

Bauza, Francisco. *Historia de la dominación española en el Uruguay.* 3rd ed. Montevideo: Tall. Graf. "El Democrata," 1929.

Benítez Porta, Oscar R. *Secesión pacífica de Guatemala de España, ensayo histórico-político.* Guatemala: Editorial "José de Pineda Ibarra," 1973.

Bethell, Leslie, ed. *The Independence of Latin America*. Cambridge: Cambridge University Press, 1991.

Bonilla Bonilla, Adolfo. "The Central American Enlightenment 1770–1838: An Interpretation of Political Ideas and Political History." Ph.D. diss., University of Manchester, 1996.

Brading, D. A. *The First America: The Spanish Monarchy, Creole Patriots, and the Liberal State 1492–1867*. Cambridge: Cambridge University Press, 1991.

———. "Government and Elite in Late Colonial Mexico." *Hispanic American Historical Review* 53(August 1973):389–414.

———. *Miners and Merchants in Bourbon Mexico 1763–1810*. Cambridge: Cambridge University Press, 1971.

Bricker, Victoria R. *The Indian Christ, the Indian King: The Historical Substrate of Maya Myth and Ritual*. Austin: University of Texas Press, 1981.

Brown, Richmond F. *Juan Fermín de Aycinena: Central American Colonial Entrepreneur, 1729–1796*. Norman: University of Oklahoma Press, 1997.

———. "Profits, Prestige, and Persistence: Juan Fermín de Aycinena and the Spirit of Enterprise in the Kingdom of Guatemala." *Hispanic American Historical Review* 75(August 1995):405–40.

Bumgartner, Louis. *José del Valle of Central America*. Durham, N.C.: Duke University Press, 1963.

Burkholder, Mark A., and D. S. Chandler. *From Impotence to Authority: The Spanish Crown and the American Audiencias 1687–1808*. Columbia: University of Missouri Press, 1971.

Bustamante, Carlos María de. *Cuadro histórico de la Revolución Mexicana*. Vol. 2. Mexico: Instituto Cultural Helénico, 1985.

Campbell, Leon G. *The Military and Society in Colonial Peru, 1750–1810*. Philadelphia: American Philosophical Society, 1978.

Cervera Pery, José. *La marina española en la emancipación de Hispanoamérica*. Madrid: Editorial MAPFRE, 1992.

Chandler, Dewitt S. "Jacobo de Villaurrutia and the Audiencia of Guatemala, 1794–1804." *The Americas* 32(January 1976):402–17.

Chinchilla Aguilar, Ernesto. *El Ayuntamiento colonial de la Ciudad de Guatemala*. Guatemala: Editorial Universitaria, 1961.

Contreras R., J. Daniel. *Una rebelión indígena en el partido de Totonicapán en 1820: el indio y la independencia*. Guatemala: Imprenta universitaria, 1951.

Coronado Aguilar, Manuel. *Apuntes histórico-Guatemalenses*. Guatemala: Editorial "José de Pineda Ibarra," 1975.

Costeloe, Michael. *Response to Revolution: Imperial Spain and the Spanish American Revolutions, 1810–1840*. Cambridge: Cambridge University Press, 1986.

David, Andrew, Felipe Fernández-Armesto, Carlos Novi, and Glyndwr Williams, eds. *The Malaspina Expedition 1789–1794: Journal of the Voyage by Alejandro Malaspina*. London: The Hakluyt Society, 2001.

Domínguez, Jorge I. *Insurrection or Loyalty: The Breakdown of the Spanish American Empire*. Cambridge: Harvard University Press, 1980.

Dym, Jordana. "A Sovereign State of Every Village: City, State and Nation in Independence-Era Central America, ca. 1750–1850." Ph.D. diss., New York University, 2000.

Estrada Monroy, Agustín. "La Iglesia en la independencia de Centroamerica." *Estudios Centroamericanos* 26(October–November 1971):653–77.

Farriss, Nancy M. *Crown and Clergy in Colonial Mexico, 1759–1821.* London: Athlone Press, 1986.

Fernández Duro, Cesáreo. *Armada española desde la unión de los reinos de Castilla y de Aragón.* 9 vols. Madrid: Museo Naval, 1972–1973.

Fernández Guardia, Ricardo. *La independencia: historia de Costa Rica.* 3rd ed. San José: Comisión Nacional del Sesquicentenario de la Independencia de Centro America, 1971.

Fernández Hernández, Bernabé. *El reino de Guatemala durante el Gobierno de Antonio González Saravia 1801–1811.* Guatemala: Comisíon Interuniversitaria Guatemalteca de Conmemoración del Quinto Centenario del Descubrimiento de América, 1993.

Fidías Jiménez, T. "El ambiente indígena en los movimientos emancipadores de El Salvador." *Anales del Museo Nacional David J. Gúzman* 10(1961–1962):33–47.

Fisher, J. R. *Government and Society in Colonial Peru. The Intendant System 1784–1814.* London: Athlone Press, 1970.

———. "Royalism, Regionalism, and Rebellion in Colonial Peru, 1808–1815." *Hispanic American Historical Review* 59(May 1979):232–57.

Floyd, Troy S. "Bourbon Palliatives and the Central American Mining Industry, 1765–1800." *The Americas* 18(October 1961):103–25.

———. "The Guatemalan Merchants, the Government, and the Provincianos, 1750–1800." *Hispanic American Historical Review* 41(February 1961):90–110.

Gandiá, Enrique de. *Napoleon y la independencia de America.* Buenos Aires: Editorial Antonio Zamora, 1955.

García, Miguel Angel. *Procesos por infidencia contra los próceres salvadoreños de la independencia de centroamérica desde 1811 hasta 1818.* Vol. 1, *Diccionario histórico enciclopédico de la Republica de El Salvador.* San Salvador: Imprenta Nacional, 1940.

García Carraffa, Alberto, and Arturo García Carraffa. *Diccionario heráldico y genealógico de apellidos españoles y americanos.* Vol. 17. Madrid: Imprenta de Antonio Marzo, 1925.

García-Gallo, Alfonso. "La Capitanía General como institución de gobierno político en España e Indias en el siglo XVIII." *Memoria del Tercer Congreso Venezolano de Historia.* Vol. 1. Caracas: Academia Nacional de la Historia, 1979.

García Granados, Miguel. *Memorias del General Miguel García Granados.* Guatemala: Editorial del Ejercito, 1978.

García Laguardia, J. M. "Estado de la opinion sobre convocatoria a cortes constituyentes en 1810: Actitud del Ayuntamiento de Guatemala." *Estudios* (Guatemala) 3(1969): 23–39.

García Peláez, Francisco de Paula. *Memorias para la historia del Antiguo Reyno de Guatemala.* 3 vols. Guatemala: L. Luna, 1851–1852.

Gómez Carrillo, Agustín. *Compendio de historia de la América Central.* 4th ed. Barcelona: Sobs. de López Robert y Ca., impresores, 1916.

———. *Elementos de la historia de Centro-America*. 5th ed. Guatemala: Encuadernación y Tip. Musícal, 1895.

———. *Estudio histórico sobre la América Central*. San Salvador: Tipografía "La Concordia," 1884.

González, Jorge. "History of Los Altos, Guatemala: A Study of Regional Conflict and National Integration, 1750–1794." Ph.D. diss., Tulane University, 1994.

González Claverín, Virginia. *La expedición científica de Malaspina en Nueva España (1789–1794)*. Mexico: El Colegio de Mexico, 1988.

———. *Malaspina en Acapulco*. Mexico: Turner Libros, 1989.

Guardino, Peter. *Peasants, Politics, and the Formation of Mexico's National State: Guerrero, 1800–1857*. Stanford: Stanford University Press, 1996.

Guedea, Virginia. *La insurgencia en el Departamento del Norte: los Llanos de Apan y la sierra de Puebla, 1810–1816*. Mexico: Universidad Nacional Autonoma de Mexico, 1996.

Hamill, Hugh M. *The Hidalgo Revolt: Prelude to Mexican Independence*. Gainesville: University of Florida Press, 1966.

———. "Royalist Counterinsurgency in the Mexican War for Independence: The Lessons of 1811." *Hispanic American Historical Review* 53(August 1973):470–89.

Hamnett, Brian R. "The Counter Revolution of Morillo and the Insurgent Clerics of New Granada, 1815–1820." *The Americas* 32(April 1976):597–617.

———. "Mexico's Royalist Coalition: The Response to Revolution 1808–1821." *Journal of Latin American Studies* 12(May 1980):55–86.

———. *La política española en una época revolucionaria, 1790–1820*. Mexico: Fondo de Cultura Económica, 1985.

———. *Politics and Trade in Southern Mexico 1750–1821*. Cambridge: Cambridge University Press, 1971.

———. *Revolución y contrarevolución en México y el Perú: liberalismo, realeza y separatismo (1800–1824)*. Mexico: Fondo de Cultura Económica, 1978.

———. *Roots of Insurgency: Mexican Regions, 1750–1824*. Cambridge: Cambridge University Press, 1986.

———. "Royalist Counterinsurgency and the Continuity of Rebellion: Guanajuato and Michoacán, 1813–20." *Hispanic American Historical Review* 62(February 1982):19–48.

Hargreaves-Mawdsley, W. N. *Eighteenth-Century Spain, 1700–1788: A Political, Diplomatic, and Institutional History*. London: Macmillan, 1979.

Haring, C. H. *The Spanish Empire in America*. 2nd ed. New York: Harcourt Brace Jovanovich, 1975.

Hawkins, Timothy P. "José de Bustamante and the Preservation of Empire in Central America, 1811–1818." *Colonial Latin American Historical Review* 4(Fall 1995):439–63.

Herr, Richard. *The Eighteenth-Century Revolution in Spain*. Princeton: Princeton University Press, 1958.

Higueras Rodríguez, María Dolores, ed. *Catálogo crítico de los documentos de la expedición Malaspina (1789–1794) del Museo Naval*. 3 vols. Madrid: Museo Naval, 1985, 1987, 1994.

———. *La expedición Malaspina 1789–1794*. Vol. 9, *Diario general del viaje: Corbeta*

Atrevida, by José de Bustamante y Guerra. Madrid: Ministerio de Defensa, Museo Naval y Lunwerg Editores, 1999.

Holleran, Mary P. *Church and State in Guatemala*. New York: Columbia University Press, 1949.

Izquierdo Hernández, Manuel. *Antecedentes y comienzos del reinado de Fernando VII*. Madrid: Ediciones Cultura Hispanica, 1963.

Jones, Oakah L. *Guatemala in the Spanish Colonial Period*. Norman: University of Oklahoma Press, 1995.

Juarros, Domingo. *Compendio de la historia del Reino de Guatemala*. Guatemala: Editorial Piedra Santa, 1981.

Kendrick, John. *Alejandro Malaspina: Portrait of a Visionary*. Montreal: McGill-Queens Press, 1999.

——, ed. and trans. *The Voyage of Sutil and Mexicana 1792: The Last Spanish Exploration of the Northwest Coast of America*. Spokane: Arthur H. Clark Company, 1991.

Kenyon, Gordon. "Mexican Influences in Central America, 1821–1823." *Hispanic American Historical Review* 41(February 1961):175–205.

Kuethe, Allan J. *Cuba, 1753–1815: Crown, Military, and Society*. Knoxville: University of Tennessee Press, 1986.

——. *Military Reform and Society in New Granada, 1773–1808*. Gainesville: University Presses of Florida, 1978.

——, ed. *Reform and Insurrection in Bourbon New Granada and Peru*. Baton Rouge: Louisiana State University Press, 1990.

Ladd, Doris M. *The Mexican Nobility at Independence, 1780–1826*. Austin: University of Texas Press, 1976.

Leyton Rodríguez, Ruben. *Doctor Pedro Molina o Centro America y su prócer*. Guatemala: Editorial Iberia, 1958.

Lockhart, James, and Stuart B. Schwartz. *Early Latin America: A History of Colonial Spanish America and Brazil*. Cambridge: Cambridge University Press, 1983.

Lovell, W. George, and Christopher Lutz. *Demography and Empire: A Guide to the Population History of Spanish Central America, 1500–1821*. Boulder: Westview Press, 1995.

Lucena Giraldo, Manuel, and Juan Pimentel Igea. *Los "Axiomas políticos sobre la América" de Alejandro Malaspina*. Aranjuez: Doce Calles, 1991.

Luján Muñoz, J. "Aportaciones al estudio de la independencia de Centroamerica." *Humanitas* 14(1973):650–77.

Luna, David. "Influencia y paralelísmo de los acontecimientos independentistas de Mexico en Centroamérica." *Historiografía y Bibliografía Americanistas* 15(December 1971):477–94.

Lutz, Christopher. *Santiago de Guatemala, 1541–1773: City, Caste, and the Colonial Experience*. Norman: University of Oklahoma Press, 1994.

Lynch, John. *Bourbon Spain, 1700–1808*. New York: Basil Blackwell, 1989.

——. *Latin American Revolutions, 1808–1826: Old and New World Origins*. Norman: University of Oklahoma Press, 1994.

―――. *The Spanish American Revolutions, 1808–1826*. New York: W. W. Norton & Company, 1973.

McCreery, David. *Rural Guatemala, 1750–1940*. Athens: University of Georgia Press, 1994.

MacLachlan, Colin M. *Spain's Empire in the New World: The Role of Ideas in Institutional and Social Change*. Berkeley: University of California Press, 1988.

MacLeod, Murdo J. *Spanish Central America: A Socioeconomic History, 1520–1720*. Berkeley: University of California Press, 1973.

Marroquín Rojas, Clemente. *Historia de Guatemala*. Guatemala: Tipografía Nacional, 1971.

Martínez Pelaez, Severo. *La patria del criollo; ensayo de interpretación de la realidad colonial guatemalteca*. Guatemala: Editorial Universitaria, 1970.

Marure, Alejandro. *Bosquejo histórico de las revoluciones de Centroamérica desde 1811 hasta 1834*. 2 vols. Mexico: Libreria de la Viuda de Ch. Bouret, 1913.

Mata-Gavidia, José. *Anotaciones de historia patria centroamericana*. Guatemala: Cultural Centroamcricana, S.A., 1953.

―――. *Lo auténtico y lo circunstanciado en la independencia de Centro America*. Guatemala: Imprenta Universitaria, 1953.

―――. *La influencia de España en la formación de la nacionalidad centroamericana (ensayo histórico crítico)*. Guatemala: Editorial "José de Pineda Ibarra," 1981.

Mayes, Guillermo. *Honduras en la independencia de Centroamérica y anexión a Mexico*. Tegucigalpa: Tip. Nacional, 1956.

Mejia, Medardo. *Historia de Honduras*. Tegucigalpa: Editorial Universitaria, 1969.

Meléndez Chaverri, Carlos. *La independencia de Centroamerica*. Madrid: Editorial MAPFRE, 1993.

―――. *Próceres de la independencia centroamericana*. San José: Editorial Universitaria Centroamericana, 1971.

―――, ed. *Centro America en las vísperas de la independencia*. Costa Rica: Imprenta Trejas Hnos., 1971.

Meneray, Wilbur. "The Kingdom of Guatemala under Charles III." Ph.D. diss., University of North Carolina, 1975.

Merino Navarro, J. P. *La Armada española en el siglo XVIII*. Madrid: Fundación Universitaria Española, 1982.

Milla y Vidaurre, José. *Historia de la América Central desde el descubrimiento del país por los españoles (1505) hasta su independencia de España (1821)*. Guatemala: Piedra Santa, 1976.

Molina Argüello, Carlos. "Gobernaciones, alcaldias mayores y corregimientos en el Reino de Guatemala." *Anuario de Estudios Americanos* 17(1960):105–32.

Monterrey, Francisco. *Historia de El Salvador: anotaciones cronológicas, 1810–1842*. San Salvador: Editorial Universitaria, 1977.

Montúfar, Lorenzo. *Reseña histórica de Centro-América*. 5 vols. Guatemala: Tipografía de "El Progreso," 1878–1879.

Montúfar y Coronado, Manuel. "Recuerdos y anecdotas." In *Memorias para la historia de la revolución de Centro America por un guatemalteco*. Jalapa, Mexico: Aburto y Blanco, 1832 and 1837.

Mora Mérida, José Luís. "Comportamiento político del clero secular de Cartagena de Indias en la preindependencia." *Anuario de Estudios Americanos* 35(1978):211–31.

Ortíz Escamilla, Juan. *Guerra y gobierno: Los pueblos y la independencia de México.* Mexico: Instituto de Investigaciones José María Luís Mora, 1997.

Oss, Adriaan van. *Catholic Colonialism: A Parish History of Guatemala, 1524–1821.* Cambridge: Cambridge University Press, 1986.

Palma Murga, Gustavo. "Nucleo de poder local y relaciones familiares en la ciudad de Guatemala a finales del siglo XVIII." *Mesoamérica* 12(December 1986):253–67.

Parra-Pérez, Caracciolo, ed. *Bayona y la política de Napoleón en America.* Caracas: Tipografía americana, 1939.

Pattridge, Blake. "University and Society in Nineteenth-Century Latin America: The University of San Carlos of Guatemala, 1821–1885." Ph.D. diss., Tulane University, 1996.

Peccorini Letona, Francisco. *La voluntad del pueblo en la emancipación de El Salvador.* San Salvador: Ministerio de Educación, 1972.

Pérez Brignoli, Héctor. *De la ilustración al liberalismo (1750–1870).* Vol. 3 of *Historia General de Centroamérica,* Edelberto Torres Rivas, ed. Madrid: FLASCO, 1993.

Pérez-Mallaína, Pablo E., and Bibiano Torres Ramírez. *La Armada del Mar del Sur.* Sevilla: Escuela de Estudios Hispano-Americanos, 1987.

Pérez Turrado, Gaspar. *Las Armadas españolas de Indias.* Madrid: Editorial MAPFRE, 1992.

Pérez Valenzuela, Pedro. *El Ayuntamiento, 1777–1790 (Nueva Guatemala de la Asunción).* Guatemala: Comite de Festejos del Bicentenario de la Ciudad de Guatemala, 1976.

Pinto Soria, Julio C. *Centroamérica, de la colonia al estado nacional (1800–1840).* Guatemala: Editorial Universitaria de Guatemala, 1986.

Pintos Vieites, María del Carmen. *La política de Fernando VII entre 1814 y 1820.* Pamplona: Studium-Generale, 1958.

Polushin, Michael. "Bureaucratic Conquest, Bureaucratic Culture: Town and Office in Chiapas, 1780–1832." Ph.D. diss., Tulane University, 1999.

Ramos Pérez, Demetrio. *España en la independencia de America.* Madrid: Editorial MAPFRE, 1986.

Rodríguez, Mario. *The Cádiz Experiment in Central America, 1808–1826.* Berkeley: University of California Press, 1978.

———. *La conspiración de Belén en nueva perspectiva.* Guatemala: Centro Editorial "José de Pineda Ibarra," 1965.

Rodríguez Beteta, Virgilio. *La mentalidad colonial: ideologías de la independencia.* Paris: Editorial Paris-America, 1926.

Rodríguez O., Jaime E. *The Independence of Spanish America.* Cambridge: Cambridge University Press, 1998.

Rubio Sánchez, Manuel. *Alcaldes mayores.* San Salvador: Ministerio de Educación, Dirección de Publicaciones, 1979.

Saint-Lu, André. *Condición colonial y conciencia criolla en Guatemala, 1524–1821.* Guatemala: Editorial Universitaria, 1978.

Salazar, Ramón A. *Historia de veintiún años: la independencia de Guatemala.* 2 vols., 2nd ed. Biblioteca guatemalteca de cultural popular. Guatemala: Editorial del Ministerio de Educación Pública, 1956.

———. *Manuel José Arce.* Guatemala: Editorial del Ministerio de Educación Pública, 1952.

———. *Mariano de Aycinena.* Guatemala: Editorial del Ministerio de Educación Pública, 1952.

Samayoa Guevara, H. H. *Ensayos sobre la independencia de Centroamérica.* Guatemala: Editorial J. de Pineda Ibarra, 1972.

———. *Los gremios de artesanos en la ciudad de Guatemala (1524–1821).* Guatemala: Biblioteca centroamericana de las Ciencias Sociales, 1978.

———. *Implantación del régimen de intendencias en el Reino de Guatemala.* Guatemala: Editorial del Ministerio de Educación Popular "José de Pineda Ibarra," 1960.

Shafer, Robert. "Ideas and Works of the Colonial Economic Societies, 1781–1820." *Revista de Historia de America* 44(December 1957):331–68.

Stoan, Stephen. *Pablo Morillo and Venezuela, 1815–1820.* Columbus: Ohio State University Press, 1974.

Tenenbaum, Barbara A., ed. *Encyclopedia of Latin American History and Culture.* New York: Charles Scribner's Sons, 1996.

Torres Ramírez, Bibiano. *La Armada de Barlovento.* Sevilla: Escuela de Estudios Hispano-Americanos, 1981.

Tutino, John. *From Insurrection to Revolution in Mexico: Social Bases of Agrarian Violence, 1750–1940.* Princeton: Princeton University Press, 1986.

Uribe, Vincent. "The Enigma of Latin American Independence: Analyses of the Last Ten Years." *Latin American Research Review* 32(1997):236–55.

Valdés Oliva, Arturo. *Caminos y luchas por la independencia.* Guatemala: Secretaría de Divulgación Cultural, 1956.

Van Young, Eric. *The Other Rebellion: Popular Violence and Ideology in Mexico, 1810–1821.* Stanford: Stanford University Press, 2001.

Villacorta Calderón, José Antonio. *Elementos de historia patria ajustados al programa vigente para los alumnos de las escuelas elementales de la republica.* 3rd ed. Guatemala: Tipografía Sánchez & De Guise, 1922.

———. *Historia de la Capitanía General de Guatemala.* Guatemala: Tipografía Nacional, 1942.

Villanueva, Carlos. *Napoleón y la independencia de América.* Paris: Garnier Bros., 1912.

Voutes Bou, Pedro. *Fernando VII: vida y reinado.* Barcelona: Editorial Juventud, 1985.

Woodward, Ralph Lee. *Central America: A Nation Divided.* New York: Oxford University Press, 1976.

———. *Class Privilege and Economic Development: The Consulado de Comercio of Guatemala, 1793–1871.* Chapel Hill: University of North Carolina Press, 1966.

———. "Economic and Social Origins of the Guatemalan Political Parties (1773–1823)." *Hispanic American Historical Review* 45(November 1965):544–66.

———. "The Economy of Central America at the Close of the Colonial Period." In

Estudios del Reino de Guatemala, Duncan Kinkead, ed. Sevilla: Escuela de Estudios Hispano-Americanos, 1985.

———. "The Guatemalan Merchants and National Defense: 1810." *Hispanic American Historical Review* 44(August 1964):452–62.

Wortman, Miles. "Bourbon Reforms in Central America: 1750–1786." *The Americas* 32(October 1975):222–38.

———. "Government Revenue and Economic Trends in Central America, 1787–1819." *Hispanic American Historical Review* 55(1975):251–86.

———. *Government and Society in Central America, 1680–1840.* New York: Columbia University Press, 1982.

———. "Legitimidad política y regionalismo. El Imperio Mexicano y Centroamérica." *Historia Mexicana* 26(1976):238–62.

Zelaya, Chester. *Nicaragua en la independencia.* San José: Editorial Universitaria Centro-americana, 1971.

Index